THE IMPORTANCE OF
BEING EDWARD

Also by Stanley Weintraub

Private Shaw and Public Shaw

Aubrey Beardsley: Imp of the Perverse

Whistler: A Biography

Four Rossettis: A Victorian Biography

The London Yankees

A Stillness Heard Round the World: The End of the Great War

Victoria

Disraeli: A Biography

Albert: Uncrowned King

THE IMPORTANCE OF BEING EDWARD

King in Waiting
1841–1901

Stanley Weintraub

JOHN MURRAY
Albemarle Street, London

First published in 2000
by John Murray (Publishers) Ltd.,
50 Albemarle Street, London W1X 4BD

A catalogue record for this book is available from the British Library

ISBN 0-7195-5767 4

Typeset in 11.75/13.5 Adobe Garamond by Servis Filmsetting Ltd, Manchester
Printed and bound in Great Britain by the University Press Cambridge

For Richard E. Winslow III
whose hand is in many of my books
including this one

Contents

Contents

Illustrations

The author and publishers gratefully acknowledge the following for permission to reproduce illustrations: Plates 1, 3, 9, 13, 14, 24, 29, The Royal Collection, © Her Majesty Queen Elizabeth II; 4, National Portrait Gallery, London; 11, 12, Frederick N. Frank Collection; 18, © the Estate of Max Beerbohm, reprinted by permission of London Management; 27, © The British Library. Plate 17 is from the collection of the author.

Preface

We grovel before fat Edward – E[dward] the Caresser,
as he is privately named ... But I mourn the safe
and motherly old middle-class queen ...
Henry James to Oliver Wendell Holmes, Jr
(January 1901)

'THE PRINT SHOPS are full of *scurrilous caricatures* and infamous things relative to the Prince's conduct,' Jane Austen wrote to a friend about the future George IV, who succeeded to the throne at fifty-seven. Her remark would as aptly have described the next Prince of Wales. Few sovereigns had to wait as long to come into their inheritance as Prince Albert Edward. Born in 1841, he became Edward VII in 1901. His mother, Queen Victoria, niece of the unsavoury George IV, had reigned for nearly sixty-four years after succeeding to the throne, at eighteen, in 1837.

Reigning may require some on-the-job preparation, and the Prince of Wales had ample time for it, but his royal mother would give him nothing to do. She did not trust him. Not measuring up to his high-pressured educational regimen, he had been a slow learner as a boy, and a rapid learner of all the wrong things as a young man. She even blamed him for his sainted father's early death, although Albert, the Prince Consort and a true worthy, had died of an affliction far more grave than anguish over his son's unseemly sexual initiation.

The less that Bertie had to do, the greater the challenge to fill the time on his hands. He attended both Oxford and Cambridge and took no degrees. He did nothing whatever and was given a doctorate in Law. He underwent military training to no effect, and was incapable of leading a platoon, yet he became a field marshal. He was easily bored. He read few books and rarely wrote letters. He governed nothing. The news he made was seldom fit to print. He was guest of honour at uneventful receptions and his presence guaranteed attendance at tedious public dinners.

The Prince gourmandized voraciously, often consuming five meals a day. He hunted foxes and stalked deer, and shot partridges and grouse by the thousand. He travelled abroad, sometimes frenetically and usually with huge entourages. He accepted domestic hospitality for long week-ends, his lavish requirements sometimes bankrupting his hosts. When the whim suited him, he was a volunteer London fireman and let the social barriers down, as he also did when overseeing unlawful prize-fighting matches. He raced thoroughbreds, often purchased with borrowed money he never repaid. He acquired and raced yachts he could not afford. He played cards obsessively, sometimes illegal games like bac-carat, for high stakes. The focus of fashion, he sometimes created his own styles. He drank whisky, brandy and champagne in large quantities. He smoked large cigars, alternating them with strong cigarettes. He patron-ized the opera and the ballet, seldom arriving before the performances began, as well as frequenting houses of much less discreet entertainment. He soaked off his many culinary sins and fleshly dissipations in steamy, sulphurous spas.

As a teenager touring Canada and the United States the Prince of Wales became an immense celebrity, the first ever in the New World. He proved equal to it. Within a few years he was the First Gentleman in the Kingdom, and validated his title. By the time he was thirty, his reputa-tion, even across the Atlantic, was so discredited that when he rallied from a grave illness, a newspaper in Indiana commented acerbically that 'his pig-headed obstinacy in refusing to die when the doctors gave him up' had caused it to postpone publication of his obituary. Reform, however, even for someone seemingly recalled to life, was out of the ques-tion. His insatiable appetite for women sometimes led to his siring children he then stood for as godfather, his only recognition of the rela-tionship. A husband's social success was, on occasion, predicated upon the covert pandering of his pretty wife to the Prince of Wales. Inevitably, he was summoned to testify in seamy divorce and gambling scandals, and pressured to pay blackmail. Being the unemployed heir to the throne of the greatest empire in the world was an arduous occupation.

Was anything that the Prince of Wales did during his extended education worth the doing? Did travel broaden anything but his prodigious bulk? Did he come to the throne prepared for whatever duties remained to the sovereign after democracy had left little to the throne but the throne? This biography attempts to confront these questions. Albert Edward's is a compelling story. From the start, little was expected of him, and often that becomes a self-fulfilling prophecy. That he confounded the critics and the doomsayers may have been as much a surprise to him as to them.

The familiar photographic image of the Prince of Wales shows a rakish and already world-weary playboy, looking older than his early thirties. Beneath the tilt of his tall, silk hat loom hooded eyes which appear already to have witnessed the darker side of sophistication, and a bearded face from which juts the inevitable cigar or cigarette. While the Queen went on and on, his beard would grey, his back would become more stooped with the years, and his coats would require miracles of tailoring to conceal his avoirdupois. His occupation was to wait. Filling in the time in his own fashion, he waited.

Uncle to Europe in an age of monarchies because his prolific mother had been grandmother to Europe, he had links to thrones from St Petersburg and Copenhagen to Berlin and Lisbon. He did not live to see two world wars dispose of most of them. An anachronism in many ways, in others he was a modernist. In his own lifestyle, he shunned the stifling morality that made sexual indulgence a hidden hypocrisy, and the stubborn social prejudices that barred Jews and even Catholics from Establishment offices and drawing rooms. (At one of the Prince's dinner tables, a guest observed with incredulity, sat a Cardinal and a Rothschild.) His contemporaneity revealed itself by his utter lack of religious belief – except where its show was publicly useful – and his trust in the new science, about which he understood little. That he was an early bicyclist and automobilist identified him less as a backer of modern technology than a beneficiary of it.

The problem of what to do with the heir to the throne while its occupant will relinquish none of its emoluments is, in Britain, a recurring one, whenever the succession comes early to a sovereign, as it did with George III and Victoria, and again when Elizabeth II became Queen as a young woman in 1952. It has no successful alleviating precedents. No monarch wants to encourage a rival Court. When the heir was as shrewd, as spendthrift, as conspiratorial and as troublesome as George III's eldest son, the dilemma was agonizingly acute. Inevitably, some impatient critics would compare the ageing sovereign unfavourably with the inexperienced heir, as did W. E. Gladstone when, sorely tried as Victoria's Prime Minister, he said of the Prince of Wales, at the time little more than thirty, 'He would make an excellent sovereign. He is far more fitted for that high place than her present Majesty now is.' But the Prince remained unemployed for the best part of three further decades.

The dynamism of the brief Edwardian age was already stirring in the Victorian 1880s and 1890s. Looking forward to the new kingly era, which came almost symbolically with the dawn of the new century, even ordinary people saw the possibilities of real change for the better in a new reign. A contemporary music-hall lyric caught this mood of optimism:

> Father's going to change his socks and Auntie have a bath,
> On the day King Edward gets his crown on.

While much material new to biographies of Prince Albert Edward appears in the following pages, the basic contours of his life, if not its inner complexity, remain unaltered. As heir apparent he was a walking argument for the defects of primogeniture. Although the Queen's self-imposed purdah threatened the values inherent in monarchy, her son's accession was anticipated by the Establishment with alarm from the moment of his majority, as if he were a time-bomb ticking under the throne. Those apprehensions, it will be seen, were more than justified; yet the monarchy survived, and weathered further familial embarrassments and crises throughout the century.

Since I am probably the first American to research a life of the delinquent heir whom Benjamin Disraeli called Prince Hal (after the gross Sir John Falstaff's errant young friend), I have mined many hitherto unexplored American sources, which have shed further light on how a nineteenth-century Prince Hal turned, in some ways, into a Falstaff. Many Americans, newly affluent and footloose in the later decades of the nineteenth century, aspired to be Victorian Yankees at Queen Victoria's Court, and, in his own interest and their own, the Prince of Wales was a ready intermediary, especially if pretty ladies were involved. Pragmatically, some Americans were less interested in the old Queen than in the future king, the likely fountain of perquisites and privilege in the new century. Their letters, diaries, notebooks, memoirs and reportage provide a relatively unexploited lens through which to observe Edward VII when he was only Albert Edward. Americans, except when currying favour with the Prince, were a notoriously irreverent lot, whose perspective inevitably reflects this.

No one, however, did a greater disservice to the future king than he himself. Like a child engaged in something forbidden, yet perversely satisfying, the Prince savoured his wrongdoings, weighed each of them lightly, and hoped for the best. Eventually, he assumed, his accession would expunge all memory of princely misbehaviour and he would be remembered warmly as king. History has almost validated that, for biographies of Edward VII generally devote as many pages, or more, to his nine years on the throne as to his fifty-nine years' waiting for it. In these pages, however, he is the exasperating Prince of Wales living through his mis-education and misdemeanours, and emerging in dubious and unexpected dignity as king. Shakespeare's Hal – Henry V – having succeeded to the title he coveted, warns Falstaff:

> Presume not that I am the thing I was,
> For God doth know, so shall the world perceive,
> That I have turned away my former self.

Not so Victoria's Prince of Wales. Time, rather than title, had turned opprobrium away. This life examines Edward VII's former self.

S.W.

I

The Future King

1841–1852

THE YOUNG HEIR to the throne of the greatest empire on earth stood at a tall window, gazing vacantly at the gardens and battlements of Windsor Castle. The panes in his schoolroom reached from floor to ceiling, accentuating his littleness. He had a lesson from his tutor, Mr Gibbs, to learn by heart. Instead, nowhere near his desk and blackboard, he was drumming his fingers on the glass. Realizing that he was again daydreaming, Miss Hildyard, his governess, an earnest and pious clergyman's daughter whom the royal children called Tilla, watched with exasperation. Patient and tolerant, she asked the Prince kindly to think about returning to his lesson. His previous tutor had complained before resigning the royal appointment that Albert Edward had a short attention span and was unable to attempt anything 'new or difficult, without losing his temper'. He would, on occasion, display either insolence or mental collapse, but Mr Birch diplomatically conceded, after complaining to the boy's parents or punishing his charge himself, that the Prince of Wales 'always evinced a most forgiving disposition'.

Prince Albert Edward stood at the tall window with his back to Miss Hildyard, obstinately maintaining, 'I don't want to.' Studying was splendid for his accomplished sister Vicky, who, although only eleven months his senior, was years ahead in learning. He hated reading and, when he was much smaller, he would crawl under his desk to tip it over and tumble the detested books to the floor.

'Then', said the governess, stubbornly loyal to her instructions, 'I must put you in the corner.'

'I won't learn,' His Royal Highness – 'Bertie' to his family – declared resolutely, 'and I won't stand in the corner, for I am the Prince of Wales.' As he reminded her of his rank, he kicked out one of the venerable window panes.

Miss Hildyard rose from her seat and walked toward him. 'Sir,' she said, 'you must learn, or I will put you in the corner.'

'I won't,' he insisted, and in emphasis he kicked out a second pane. Miss Hildyard pulled at a bell-cord. A servant quickly entered. She requested him to appeal to the Prince Consort that his presence was required immediately on a pressing matter concerning the young Royal Highness.

Prince Albert came at once, and she described her impasse, after which he turned to his son and, pointing to a footstool, said, 'Sit down there, and wait till I return.' Albert came back shortly with a birch rod and a Bible. 'Listen, now,' he said to the Prince of Wales, 'to what the holy Apostle Paul says to you and other children in your position.' Opening the Bible he read from Chapter IV of the Epistle to the Galatians: 'Now I say, that the heir, as long as he is a child, differeth nothing from a servant, though he be lord of all; but is under tutors and governors until the time appointed of the father.' He might have gone on to quote further from the chapter, that children 'were in bondage under the elements of the world', but putting down the book, he observed, 'It is true that you are the Prince of Wales, and if you conduct yourself properly you may become a man of high station, and even after the death of your mother you may become King of England. But now you are a little boy who must obey your tutors and governors. Besides, I must impress upon you a saying of the wise King Solomon.'

Reopening the Bible to Proverbs XIII, and passing by the opening verse, 'A wise son heareth his father's instruction,' Prince Albert read, 'He that spareth the rod hateth his son; but he that loveth him chasteneth him betimes' – and he reached for his stick and gave the heir to the throne, now pushed prone to the footstool, a sharp switching that would have made the Headmaster of neighbouring Eton proud. Then Albert took the Prince to a corner, warning, 'You will stand here and study your lesson till Miss Hildyard gives you leave to come out. And never forget again that you are now under tutors and governors, and that hereafter you will be under a law given by God.'

Privately the science-minded Albert thought little of the theology in the volume he had drawn upon, but like his wife, the Queen, he approved of its emphasis upon ethics. It was also an opportune admonition to the boy who would some day be crowned as Defender of the Faith. The Prince of Wales on that morning early in 1853 was eleven years old.

Years later his second son, who became George V, was reputed to have said, 'My father was frightened of his mother. I was frightened of my father, and I'm damned well going to see that my children are frightened of me.' Whether or not Albert Edward was intimidated by his mother, who became more overbearing as both grew older, as a child he was terrified of his demanding father, who was determined to turn Bertie into the intellectual monarch-to-be for which the young Prince had neither attributes nor appetite.

Bertie took neither to reading nor writing. In days before such learning disabilities were understood and identified, he was possibly a dyslexic (*dys*, difficult; *lexis*, word). He had a stammer until he was four. He read poorly and struggled to write. Bertie may also have been handicapped by Attention Deficit Disorder. Many of the diagnostic criteria fit his condition, from his lack of persistence at tasks to his restlessness, from his difficulties at reading and writing (and frustration at both) to his inattention and distractability. Although Churchills and Einsteins outgrew such symptoms without parental intervention, the Prince of Wales, born to his calling, endured expectant watchfulness from his first breath. Baron Christian Stockmar, the Coburg physician who had advised Queen Victoria and helped to educate Prince Albert, had prepared strict Germanic memoranda for the upbringing of their heir within weeks of his christening. 'A man's education', Stockmar wrote, 'begins the first day of his life.'

Resuming her diary on 2 December 1841, the Queen recalled that on the morning of 9 November her labour had been 'very severe, and I don't know what I would have done but for the great comfort and support my beloved Albert was to me during the whole time. At last, at 12 m[inutes] to 11, I gave birth to a fine large Boy.... It was taken to the Ministers for them to see.' Almost immediately a Court aide set out for Claremont, the royal estate near Esher (once the residence of Prince Leopold, now King of the Belgians), to escort Mrs Brough, wife of an underservant there and formerly a royal housemaid, to take on her duties as wet-nurse to the infant. She would be one of the highest-paid employees of the Queen, earning £500 while her own child fed – somehow – elsewhere.

As was customary, Court officials confirmed that a live birth of a male heir to the throne had occurred; the news was communicated to crowds that had gathered outside Buckingham Palace; and church bells began to ring across the city, then into the countryside and beyond. A double royal salute of forty-two guns was fired at the parade ground in St James's Park, rattling palace windows. In London theatres the rejoicing disrupted performances. Many playgoers arrived already too full of liquid cheer to sit passively, and demanded repeated choruses of 'God Save the Queen'. A new illustrated weekly, *Punch*, began a 'Paean to the Prince' with

> Huzzah! we've a little prince at last,
> A roaring royal boy;
> And all day long the booming bells
> Had rung their peals of joy.

Referring to the heir's likely education fitting his future, it predicted that he would be taught 'by men of lore' in the way 'Kings have been taught before'. Yet no earlier king's training had been planned in the obsessive detail worked out by Baron Stockmar, who wrote peevishly (yet satisfyingly) that 'the nursery gives me more trouble than the government of a kingdom'.

Much was expected of the future sovereign. Preaching at St Paul's on 14 November, the Sunday after the birth, Canon Sydney Smith prayed with the example obviously in mind of Victoria's corpulent uncle, the wicked previous Prince of Wales, afterwards George IV. Smith entreated the Almighty 'so [to] mould the Prince's heart and fashion his spirit that he may be a blessing and not an evil to the land of his birth…. As he will be the first man in these realms, so may he be the best; disdaining to hide bad actions by high station, and endeavouring always by example of a strict and moral life to repay those gifts which a loyal people are so willing to spare from their own necessities to a good King.'

The child, Victoria wrote to her uncle Leopold, 'is to be called *Albert* and Edward is to be his second name'. Guardedly, Viscount Melbourne hinted that perhaps the names should be reversed, for *Edward* (her father's name) 'is a good English appellation'. Albert, he ventured, might be 'an old Anglo-Saxon name', perhaps derived from Ethelred – 'but it has not been so common nor so much in use since the Conquest'. The Queen was unmoved.

On 4 December 1841, even before his christening, Albert Edward was declared Prince of Wales in a ceremony during which the royal infant, only four weeks old, had an oversized ring put on a tiny finger, a coronet in the form of a cap set on his head, and a gold staff placed in his hand. Further, he was also declared Duke of Cornwall, and eligible to receive the revenues of the dukedom, which in actuality would go to the Queen until his marriage. (He was also created Duke of Rothesay, Earl of Chester, Earl of Carrick and Baron Renfrew.) The glow of popular affection that surrounded the Prince's young parents would diminish when the expenses of the grand christening at St George's Chapel, Windsor, on 25 January 1842 became known to the press.

At first, ignoring the example of George IV, the weekly *John Bull* found cause for celebration in the very title 'Prince of Wales', with which 'some of the best and proudest of our national feelings are associated'. The *Morning Herald* linked 'British greatness' with the 'golden chain of sovereignty' the new Prince represented. A *Punch* collection of nursery rhymes to mark the occasion was dedicated to 'Le Prince de Baleines' – French for 'whales'. Presiding was the Archbishop of Canterbury, William Howley. The chapel organ thundered Handel's 'Hallelujah Chorus' and the Duke of Wellington carried the Sword of State. But the infant's godparents, Frederick William IV of Prussia and his Queen, were as German as the Prince's mother and father, and the English public was sated with German Royals. A satirical publication in 1840 at the time of the marriage of Victoria to Albert had imagined a Teutonic ceremony including 'The Sausage of State', to be borne in procession by the Prime Minister. The German example of authoritarian despotism, though hardly Albertine, was as repellent in England to monarchists as it was to the burgeoning numbers of Chartists and Republicans.

With morality more than democracy in mind, the Archbishop turned toward the designated godfather and asked whether the Prince would 'renounce the devil and all his works, the vain pomp and glory of the world, with all the covetous desires of the same, and the carnal desires of the flesh, so that thou will not follow or be led by the same?' Surrogate for the royal infant, the King of Prussia replied, 'I renounce them all.' With that, Albert Edward was baptized, and his first ceremony of state concluded. While the guests banqueted that evening in St George's Gallery, the Prince of Wales dined upon Mrs Brough and disappeared from events, though not from press speculation.

Determined to move the royal infant out of the smuts and slime of

London, Victoria and Albert had held the christening at Windsor Castle. Escorted by the 72nd Highlanders, the Royal Horse Guards and a battery of Field Artillery, they had departed Buckingham Palace in slush and snow. Windsor would remain the Prince's nursery as well as that of his elder sister and the seven sisters and brothers who were to follow over fifteen more years. Collectively they ensured the succession, as well as complaints about its cost in all but the most monarchist papers. In 1843, *John Bull* published a 'Connubial Vision for 1850' showing Albert buried under increasingly importuning children, and a Court functionary collecting coins in a sack. In 1846, in a cartoon labelled 'A Case of Real Distress', *Punch* depicted Albert, hat in hand, with Victoria surrounded by a brood of children outnumbering reality. In a period of persistent economic plight the burgeoning family seemed less a moral virtue or political necessity than a failure of restraint. The young Queen and her spouse flourished in the marital bed and left the expenses of their progeny to Parliament.

Public interest in the upbringing of the Prince of Wales grew with him. When he was only two, an anonymous pamphlet, *Who Should Educate the Prince of Wales?*, was published in London. The conduct of George IV, the writer warned, 'point[ed] out the necessity for the most watchful attention to the education of him who is to reign'. Anxiety had arisen that, whatever the exemplary nature of the child's parents, there was the danger that his profligate Hanoverian heredity might overwhelm his character. Whiggish and Evangelical in its views, the pamphlet representing the democratizing direction of English constitutional monarchy ratified in the Reform Bill of 1832. 'The Prince must be made sensible', the writer exhorted, 'that our king is a magistrate, honoured greatly, paid most amply; let him therefore be taught that every portion of the wealth he enjoys is the product of the sweat of the brow of his subjects, for the preservation of general order, freedom and security, and is not confided to him as the means of procuring sensual pleasures.'

When the Queen and Prince Albert had consulted Stockmar about Albert Edward's upbringing, he had urged that it was their 'sacred duty' to secure responsible advice. The strait-laced Bishop of Oxford, Samuel Wilberforce, offered the impossible suggestion that 'the great object in view is to make [the Prince of Wales] the most perfect man'. Far more pragmatically, the worldly-wise Prime Minister, Viscount Melbourne, wrote to the Queen, 'Be not over solicitous about education. It may be able to do much, but it does not do as much as is expected from it. It may mould and direct the character, but it rarely alters it.'

In memoranda which Stockmar produced for the royal parents in Albert Edward's early years, he proposed that the Prince of Wales should not be taught by a clergyman but by someone like his father, with scientific leanings befitting 'the spirit of the age'. He should not become a pedant; but, rather, 'a man of calm, profound, comprehensive understanding, with a deep conviction of the indispensable necessity of practical morality to the welfare of the Sovereign and People'. Stockmar's prescriptions drew on the middle-class values of Dr Thomas Arnold, Headmaster of Rugby, which eschewed pleasure as indulgence, while also promoting the industriousness and eagerness for learning that had apparently worked in the education of Prince Albert. Stockmar should have recalled, with some concern, that such a regime had been less than successful in the upbringing of the previous Prince of Wales. For the future George IV, Dr Richard Hurd, Bishop of Lichfield and Coventry, had drawn up his ambitious *Plans for Study for the Princes*, which included religion, morals, law, mathematics, history, natural philosophy (what there was of science) and the literary classics. The exacting Hurd had also decreed lessons on the cello and in boxing, instruction in drawing, agriculture, and even in the baking of bread.

In the nursery at Windsor, precocious Vicky, the slower but good-natured Bertie, and, soon, Alice and Alfred, were instructed by Victoria and Albert themselves, and by three mistresses who taught English, French and German and supervised play under the direction of the widowed governess, Sarah, Lady Lyttelton – 'Laddle' to the youngest children. Laddle made sure that in addition to the lead soldiers, dolls and tea-sets in the children's nursery at Windsor (and soon at Osborne), there were books of children's tales and songs, including stories about Reynard the Fox, Beauty and the Beast, and Robin Hood. As early as November 1844 Victoria secured from Bishop Wilberforce a booklet, *Scripture Reading Lessons for Little Children*, his simplified adaptation of Bible readings, in 42 pages, to be read to the royal children. 'These pages', Wilberforce explained in a Preface, 'are intended to teach Children about Jesus Christ. To do this it was necessary to give a short account of man's creation in innocence, and of his fall into sin.' Although it was important in the Evangelical atmosphere of the time to be seen as heeding advice from the likes of the limited Wilberforce, who

THE FIRST TOOTH.

*Every family celebration of the heir's development was
important news* (Punch, *11 February 1843*)

professed almost no idea with which Albert agreed, she made one
emendation to his text on p. 21, changing 'no one can love God and
Money at the same time' to the more reasonable 'no one can love God
who loves Money more'.

As heir apparent, Prince Albert Edward provided immediate and
continuing copy for the press. He was hardly a year old when *Punch*
published a cartoon, 'The First Tooth', showing an infant in the fussy
feminine garb typical of all very young males, being distracted from
aching gums by servants with silly toys. Later, he was shown on the deck
of the royal yacht offering – as he did in 1846 – a drink to a surprised
crewman, and yet later he was pictured on a rocking horse, his first riding
experience.

In their private apartments at Windsor – and, as of 1846, at the Italianate Osborne House on the Isle of Wight, off Southampton, which Victoria and Albert had built as a family residence for further privacy – the children spoke German with their parents as much as (or more than) they did English. As a result, Bertie always pronounced the letter 'r' with a Germanic roll. (Bernard Shaw later described the Prince's mature speech as *basso cantante*.) He also learned French from his mistresses; a French tutor, Monsieur Brasseur, was called in to assist in enunciation, and Bertie's spoken French, used much in later life, would become impeccable.

The Field, a sporting paper, published an idealized version, 'on reliable authority', of the childhood regimen. They rose early, it reported, breakfasted at eight, and had lunch at two. Their education, Saturdays not excepted, was scheduled 'with almost military exactness', on the hour or half-hour. They studied classical as well as modern languages, the latter 'familiarized and perfected by conversation'. Bertie and his younger brother Affie were also trained in military exercises which taught 'dignity and bearing'. They learned 'the lighter accomplishments' of music, drawing, dancing and dramatics. They had their own riding school, at which Vicky was once thrown off her horse, and Bertie, according to Lady Lyttelton, 'was run away with at the fleetest gallop his pony could go ... , all around the lawns'. Since he was strapped into his saddle, 'had the pony gone against a tree ... we should now be thinking of him in happiness [in the hereafter] such as I trust in mercy he may live to inherit some more distant day. He did not cry, showed no signs of fear after one loud cry for help at first.'

Albert taught them sea-bathing, Bertie learning about sea water first by exposure to it in a tub, substituted later by a cumbersome, offshore floating bath, including a deck and a privacy screen. 'Papa' designed it for swimming lessons (at a cost of £525 14s. 6d. and had it moored to two former battleship masts. The young princes also 'busily engage[d] themselves in a carpenter's shop, fitted up expressly for them, with tools essential to a perfect knowledge of their craft', to become 'not only theoretically but practically acquainted with the useful arts of life'. Also, 'a small laboratory is occasionally brought into requisition, at the instance of the father'. Then the princes 'throw down their saws and axes, unbuckle their philosophy, and shoulder their miniature percussion guns – which they handle with the dexterity of practical sportsmen – for a

EVERY INCH A SAILOR.

The press relished the revelation that the boy Prince,
not quite five, had offered a libation to a sailor
*on the royal yacht (*Punch*, 26 September 1846)*

shooting stroll through the royal gardens'. Finally, 'The evening meal, the preparation for the morning's lessons, and brief religious instruction, close the day.'

Although the schedule was crowded, it did not seem like a martyrdom to future duty, and might have impressed Plato, or even Stockmar. But there was never any question of sending the young princes to school, where they would have learned less, albeit with boys of their own ages. Mingling with the scions of an aristocracy which Victoria and Albert found sleazy, or the sons of nouveau riche commercial and industrial adventurers of suspect bloodlines, was not what the dour and distrustful

Stockmar would have described as 'the great path of civilization'. Albert found the aristocratic products of the élite schools to be frequently useless and ignorant, except when it came to riding, hunting and gambling; Victoria thought such schools bred intolerance and triviality, which to her were the defining traits of English gentlemen.

Since the schedule to which he was subjected at Court was initially without pressure, Bertie suffered only from unfavourable comparison with Vicky, who was intellectually far more her father's child. 'We talked of Vicky and Bertie,' the Queen wrote in her diary on 12 December 1847, when Bertie was six, 'Albert saying the latter ought to be accustomed early to work with and for us, to have great confidence shewn him, that he should early be initiated into the affairs of State. How true this is! So wise and right; and the more confidence we shew him the better it will be for himself, for us, and for the country.' Too premature to be anything but wishful thinking, the hope nevertheless mirrored their continuing expectations of their heir.

At home all was well. Albert carried the younger children on his back, crawled with them on the floor, played games with them, and at Christmas supervised the placing of Germanic table-top trees for every member of the growing family, gifts for each on or under them. The Queen and Prince took the children ice skating, Albert once falling in and having to be rescued by Victoria; and each family birthday – and there were now many – was a happy holiday from schooling.

Even on the Isle of Wight Prince Albert worried about his children's safety. The most important key to the nursery area, Lady Lyttelton wrote to her daughter, 'is never out of Prince Albert's own keeping; and the very thought must be enough to cloud his brow with anxiety. Threatening letters of the most horrid kind (probably written by mad people) aimed directly at the children, are frequently received. I would rather no one but our own family knew about this.' To the royal children, Albert's presence seemed all-encompassing, even overwhelming.

When in London, Vicky and Bertie met, if briefly, distinguished foreign visitors at Buckingham Palace, and even undistinguished but more interesting ones like the famous American midget, 'General' Tom Thumb. The first royal audience for Phineas T. Barnum and his principal exhibit had occurred after the children had gone to bed, and was intended for the Court, but Tom had asked about the Prince of Wales and wanted to meet him. Victoria invited them back, and Barnum's advertisements at

Egyptian Hall in Piccadilly claimed that his performer's appearances were 'Under the patronage of Her Majesty the Queen'. Albert Edward, then two-and-a-half, greeted Tom shyly, but the 'General' boasted, 'The Prince is taller than I am, but I *feel* as big as anybody.' The weekly magazine *The Satirist* quipped 'that the American dwarf, General Tom Thumb, is to become a member of the Royal Household, in the character of *aide-de-camp* to his Royal Highness the Prince of Wales'.

The royal children also saw George Catlin's travelling 'Ioway' Indians, some of them spurious, and Victoria even took Vicky and Bertie to see the wax exhibits at Madame Tussaud's gallery in Baker Street. The family travelled by train and yacht to Osborne, and by train overnight to Scotland, where Victoria and Albert would build a second private home, Balmoral, on the Tweed. In visits to Scotland, first made by sea, Albert Edward wore a miniature sailor suit which, sketched in the illustrated papers, set the standard for little boys' attire for decades to come. Fortunately unsketched was his unprincely behaviour. On a visit in 1847, when Bertie was five, the royal yacht docked at Aberdeen and citizens gathered to pay homage, clustered on seats erected on scaffolding, tier upon tier. Emerging to acknowledge the cheers, Victoria had the Prince of Wales at her side. On deck, a spectator recalled, was 'a splendid sofa ornamented with tassels, and the Prince ... began to pull at some of them in a manner that threatened to detach them'. The Queen ordered Bertie to desist, 'but as soon as her back was turned, [he] seized a tassel again and gave it another jerk'. She anticipated that, and grasped 'the luckless heir apparent ... by the scruff of the neck, elevated one of her feet upon the sofa, hoisted the youngster over her knee ... and gave him a sound spanking.... The illustrious heir kicked and bellowed quite as lustily as children of lower birth are wont to do.' Utter silence settled on the crowd, broken just as suddenly by roars of laughter, 'which could not be repressed by any thought of decorum, respect for the Queen, or sympathy for the victim'. The hilarity at the dock 'recalled the royal mother to a sense of her position, and having turned towards the crowd for a moment, her face suffused with crimson, she hastily descended into the cabin, and was seen no more'.

The wilful Prince would be no stranger to spankings, and L. M. Montgomery, author of the Canadian young person's classic *Anne of Green Gables*, would include a chapter, 'The Woman Who Spanked the King', in her *Emily Climbs* (1925), in which a Scotswoman on the staff at

Balmoral, Mistress McIntyre, loses patience with the Prince, and – improbably – turns him over her knee. 'Prince Bertie', she recalls, 'would not be disobeying me again.' Despite the occasional resort to the rod or the palm, and threats against the family from cranks that worried Albert, life remained uncomplicated and seemingly secure. That would change with the forebodings of Chartist revolution and the real upheavals on the Continent, both in 1848. As Royals and other rulers from across the Channel came scurrying to England for safety, King Louis Philippe incongruously in woman's disguise, the children at Windsor acquired an inkling of the threatening world outside. Victoria had already survived assassination attempts; she was likely to have more children, and death in labour was not uncommon. Her own ascent to the throne was due to the death, in childbirth, of Princess Charlotte, heiress to the future George IV, in 1817. Bertie had to be prepared for kingship. The search for a suitable tutor for him was accelerated.

After lengthy research, Henry Birch, thirty, was selected to serve as principal tutor to the seven-and-a-half-year-old Prince of Wales. Birch's salary, enormous then for an academic, was to be £800 a year. Aside from an excess of Anglican piety he seemed a paragon: as a student at Eton he had been captain of the school, returning there after Cambridge as a master; at King's College he had taken four university prizes. He would need all his skills to cope with Bertie, who, in the year of Albert's scrutiny of candidates, had been slipping further and further behind in his studies. The Queen and Prince Albert had wanted Bertie to learn in tandem with his clever elder sister. Instead, he responded with disobedience and tantrums. Lady Lyttelton reported that he was now doing lessons out of the same book as his younger sister, Alice, which could only have lowered his self-esteem further. Her most important charge, she reported to the Queen, was 'uncommonly averse to learning and requires much patience, from wilful inattention and constant interruptions, getting under the table, upsetting the books and sundry other anti-studious practices'. The expectations of his parents were a burden he could not bear.

With relief Albert wrote on 10 April 1849 to his stepmother in Coburg: 'Bertie will be given over in a few weeks into the hands of a tutor whom we have found. He is a Mr. Henry Birch, a young, good-looking, amiable man, who was a tutor at Eton.... It is an important step.' Prudently, Birch came prepared to escape to a munificent High Church living already promised to him by the Earl of Wilton, on the proviso that he took Holy Orders to become eligible. Lady Lyttelton was delighted to have the education of 'Princey' removed from her charge – 'a real mercy to myself'. When Birch accepted, she hoped he would 'stay on.… He does seem so perfect for his place.'

Surveying the situation, Birch's first move was to combine Bertie's lessons with those of Prince Alfred, although he was a year younger than Alice. Had they been at school, it would have been an embarrassing setback for Bertie; in practice, however, it meant he had a learning companion and less of a challenge. For six days a week, Birch taught them arithmetic, English and geography, supervised language lessons, and scheduled in visiting masters recruited by Albert to teach religion, hand-writing, drawing and music. Because of his Puseyite leanings, religion was considered out of Birch's jurisdiction, and he would not teach any-thing smacking of frivolity. To the Queen, who even danced with kilted servants on festive occasions in Scotland, Birch's glum religiosity seemed absurd. When he announced that he would indeed take Holy Orders, Victoria agreed that he could do so without jeopardizing his appoint-ment if he were not theologically 'aggressive' with the boys, would accompany them to Crathie Church near Balmoral for Presbyterian ser-vices when in residence there, and not absent himself from 'innocent amusements'. But Bertie, the Queen insisted, 'will not go to [any] Church until he has passed his eighth birthday' and was to keep Sunday 'as a day of recreation and amusement'. Birch complained via Stockmar that he knew of no English family that permitted cricket or games on a Sunday, and Victoria promptly told Birch that she did not believe in 'the extreme severity of the Sunday in this country when carried to excess'.

Birch soon discovered that he had acquired fame of a sort. The *Court Circular* for 21 August announced: 'His Royal Highness, the Prince of Wales, attended by Mr Birch, rode out on horseback.' Soon he was reported out angling with the Prince, having determined not to spare *that* kind of rod, yet he shrank from amusements. He accompanied the chil-dren to their father's birthday festivities on 26 August, where the entertainment consisted of demonstrations of mesmerism, then a fash-ionable pseudo-science, and guests permitted themselves to be put into trances and submit to what would have been indignities if awake. Albert would have called it science; the elder children were probably fascinated; Birch was very likely appalled.

Wherever Bertie's schoolroom happened to be, Birch found his charge exasperating within it but charming outside. He wrote to Prince Albert that 'the conduct of the Prince of Wales begins to frighten me. I begin to search myself and see if my ingenuity can devise any other mode of dealing with him but I seem to have tried every expedient.' Trying further to understand Bertie, he wrote later to Albert (whom he considered too rigid), 'I thought it better, notwithstanding his sensitiveness, to laugh at him ... and to treat him as I know that boys would have treated him at an English public school.' The Prince of Wales remained 'extremely disobedient, impertinent to his masters and unwilling to submit to discipline'. He was unable to 'play at any game for five minutes, or attempt anything new or difficult, without losing his temper'. On occasion, 'severe punishment' became necessary because he had little capacity for concentration and became insolent and defiant when forced back to his books. Yet Birch defended his charge (and regimen) by insisting that there were 'few English boys who know so much French and German... . I do not despair of the writing and spelling.' No adult spent more time with Bertie, who was apparently able to separate the man from the mentor. 'I seem to have found the key to his heart,' Birch told Stockmar with some puzzlement.

That key may have been the innovation, feared by the Queen and Prince, of permitting Bertie to encounter at least a sampling of his school-boy peers. It was Birch's opinion, he wrote, that many of the Prince of Wales's 'peculiarities' resulted from 'want of contact with boys his own age, and from being continually in the society of older persons, and his finding himself the centre round which everything seems to move.... He has no standard by which to measure his own powers.' It was no substitute to offer him Affie as playmate or schoolmate, for Prince Alfred 'is much too young and yielding, and nothing that a tutor can say, or even a parent, has such influence as intercourse with sensible boys of the same age, or a little older, unconsciously teaching by example. I always found that boys' characters at Eton were formed as much by contact with others as by the precepts of their tutors.' That experiment had not worked before Birch, and would not work again, but Bertie craved companion-ship. A few boys from neighbouring Eton, including young William Gladstone, son of the future prime minister, had been invited to tea under Albert's supervision, but the formidable adult presence made the situation seem like a visit to a felon in prison, and the strain was compounded by their need to call the churlish child – but future king – 'Sir'.

Uncomfortably, the boys would make their bows when they could, and leave. According to the Queen, if Bertie were ever left alone with boys his age he abused them, and the Headmaster at Eton complained to Albert that the Prince of Wales seemed to show 'pleasure in giving pain to others'.

An example reported several years after the fact by the *Birmingham Journal* had occurred at Osborne when the Prince, walking alone at the seaside, encountered a boy gathering shells. Presuming that high position gave him licence, Bertie upset the basket and shells. 'You do that again', said the boy, 'and I'll lick you.'

'Put the shells into the basket, and see if I don't,' warned the Prince.

'Now touch 'em again if you dare!' the boy challenged as he swept the shells back into his basket. After Bertie upset the shells once more the boy pitched into him. The Prince returned unhappily to Osborne House with a bloodied lip and bruised nose, neither of which could be concealed. When his mother demanded the reason, Bertie confessed, and the Queen had the local lad brought to her.

Timidly, the boy explained, and Victoria, turning to her son, reportedly said, 'You have been rightly served, Sir. Had you not been punished severely already, *I* should have punished you severely. When you commit a like offence, I trust you will always receive a similar punishment.' Then she commanded that the boy bring his parents to Osborne House the next morning. They came with some alarm, only to be told that she wanted to make arrangements for educating their son, and hoped that they 'would make good use of the advantages which should be placed within his reach'.

One Eton boy proved a success. Charles Wynne-Carrington was to become, in due course, 'my dear Charlie', one of the few friends over a lifetime not addressed by surname. A photograph taken in the sunny gardens by Ernst Becker shows nine boys from aristocratic families who 'came to play with us' (as Bertie wrote), none of them showing any evidence of arduous play. Writing to his friend Lord Canning, then Governor-General of India, Lord Granville described his conversation with Prince Albert about the Prince of Wales, and confided that he felt that 'the visits of Eton boys to the Castle for a couple of hours can be of no use.... I believe that a journey will be organised for him, and several boys his own age invited to accompany him. It is intended to send him for a short time to Oxford and Cambridge, and then on a voyage to all the principal British possessions. You will possibly have to receive him in India.'

In the interim, Birch felt trapped 'morning, noon and night in the company of a child', and on rare holidays, when visiting tutors and resident governesses replaced him, he was 'like a colt let out of a dark stable into a green field'. When he determined to resign his charge he claimed religious practice as the reason. Disraeli had already gossiped to Lady Londonderry, 'It seems, that Albert ... holds that all Churches (reformed) are alike ... & that ecclesiastical formulares of all kinds ought to be discouraged, [and he] signified to Birch, the other day, that he did not approve of the Prince of Wales being taught the Church catechism, his R.H. not approving of creeds, & all that. Conceive the astonishment & horror of Birch, a very orthodox, if not very high, Churchman, at this virtual abnegation of all priestly authority! He at once informed H.R.H. that he must resign his post. This could not on the instant be agreed to, as the Queen was devoted to Birch, & Albert, himself, had hitherto greatly approved of him. After this, there were scenes for a week, some very violent.' Disraeli loved a drama, and may have inflated the histrionics, but the episode did result in the Prince of Wales's being taught the catechism, Disraeli claiming that 'the whole esclandre', if made public, would have undermined Albert's reputation, which was – as a result of the wondrous Great Exhibition at the Crystal Palace in London – on an upward trajectory. Birch hung on, but the arrangement was increasingly unhappy.

Late in 1851 he announced his forthcoming release to the rectory of Prestwich-with-Oldham in Lancashire, as promised to him earlier by Lord Wilton. He would have a living worth £3,000 a year plus the assistance of four poorly paid curates – an astounding emolument that would place him immediately within the ranks of the well-to-do and offer no excuse that he was in retreat from his impossible responsibilities. 'Who can blame him?' commented Prince Albert, with evident relief.

The news shocked Bertie into realizing his loss, and Birch was retrospectively elevated to the station of guardian angel who had protected the Prince from his parents. Lady Canning, one of the Queen's ladies-in-waiting, observed, 'It has been a trouble and sorrow to the Prince of Wales, who has done no end of touching things since he heard that he was to lose [his tutor]. He is such an affectionate dear little fellow; his notes and presents [to Birch] were really too moving.'

Albert moved quickly to find a successor. Bertie was ten, and needed more learning, not less. As an activist Chancellor of Cambridge University, Prince Albert consulted Sir James Stephen, Professor of Modern History (better known later as the father of Leslie Stephen and the grandfather of Virginia Woolf). Sir James recommended Frederick Waymouth Gibbs, a Fellow of Trinity College and a barrister. No Puseyite, he adhered to a dissenting sect and was remote from popery. Stephen had raised Gibbs from childhood and saw him as exactly what Albert needed, describing him as 'exceedingly free from all anxious forebodings'; if he had any fault in character it was 'a strength of will which occasionally degenerates into obstinacy'. That seemed no infirmity in dealing with the Prince of Wales. Gibbs was offered £1,000 if he would forgo all other sources of income, and he accepted.

On 15 January 1852 Gibbs arrived to spend a week (excluding Sunday) with Birch and learn the Windsor system. Both Bertie and Affie were miserable at Birch's going, and made no secret of it. The seven-year-old Prince Alfred saw as substitute only an intruding stranger with moustache and sideburns, dapperly attired in morning coat, checked trousers and top hat. More articulate now at ten, Bertie apologized for his sorrow after Birch had left – 'quite overcome at parting', according the Queen. 'You can't wonder if we are rather dull today,' the Prince of Wales explained to Gibbs; 'We are very sorry Mr Birch is gone. It is very natural, is it not? He has been with us so long.'

Gibbs exacerbated the pangs of loss by scheduling seven hours of lessons rather than Birch's five, including riding, exercise and drill. Affie continued to take lessons with Bertie, and a few days later, when Mr Leitch the drawing master came, the Prince of Wales (according to Gibbs's diary) pulled his brother's hair and threatened him with a paper knife. Gibbs cancelled the lesson and confiscated the weapon, leaving Bertie 'very angry'. Two days later a lesson with another tutor, Mr Anderson, 'was stopped because of the P. of W.'s rudeness'. Two days after that, Mr Wellesley, the domestic chaplain who provided religious instruction (and was later to become Dean of Windsor), noted to Gibbs the Prince's 'extreme difficulty in keeping his attention to anything'. Even the amiable Affie was becoming disobedient about reading, and when Gibbs mentioned the problem to the Queen, Victoria maintained that 'his obstinacy had come on since his being with the P. of W. and added that the arrangement had not done him good'.

Gibbs took his troubles to the choleric Baron Stockmar, again on a lengthy visit from Coburg. It would be 'a long task' to make the Prince measure up to the aspirations his parents had for him, Gibbs admitted, but he hoped that Bertie 'would turn out a good man'. Stockmar pondered the 'difficulty' and then explained, apparently alluding to the Prince's troublesome Hanoverian inheritance, 'He is an exaggerated Copy of his Mother'. Ironically, before Albert Edward was two, Victoria had written to her Uncle Leopold, saying how impressed Stockmar was 'with Albert Junior's likeness to his dearest papa, which everybody is struck with'. It was the diplomatic thing to tell the Queen, but she had soon realized it was far from accurate. By three, according to Lady Lyttelton, Bertie was 'not articulate like his sister, but rather babyish in accent. He understands a little French and says a few words, but is altogether backward in language, very intelligent and generous and good-tempered with a few passions and stampings occasionally'. He was also 'very small in every way', a characteristic that was to persist into his teens.

Before Gibbs had been in charge a full month he was called in by the Queen and Albert to ask whether the Prince of Wales was 'unwell' – his anti-social behaviour was often ascribed to colds and other childhood ailments. 'He had behaved rudely to his [elder] sister in their presence.' Gibbs confirmed that Bertie had also been rude to him: 'thrown dirt and swung a large stick at me, and had struck me with a stick in a passion. The Prince told me not to allow this – that if [Bertie] did so, I must box his ears, or take the same stick and rap his knuckles "sharply". The rest of that day was not good, but in the evening I spoke strongly to the P. of W. and shut him up in my room. His Father also spoke to him, and it had a good effect.'

Somehow Gibbs managed to remain with Bertie for eight years, during which few days can have been easy. Even as a boy the Prince was addicted to walking sticks, which he apparently took as the badge of a gentleman yet used as a weapon to work out his frustrations. Gibbs often had to take them away, or use them on the child. At one arithmetic lesson Bertie 'became passionate, the pencil was flung to the end of the room, the stool was kicked away, and he was hardly able to apply [himself] at all'. At Latin lessons, 'He flings things about – made grimaces – called me names, and would not do anything for a long time.' On the strand at Osborne he was 'like a person half silly' – Gibbs using the word in its older sense of seeming irrational – and threw stones at

Gibbs's head. 'He made faces, and spat.' After German lessons, too, Dr Becker (Ernst Becker was Albert's German Librarian and Secretary) complained of the Prince of Wales's 'great naughtiness. There was a great deal of bad words.'

Well after the episode with Miss Hildyard, he 'gave me the idea', Gibbs wrote in his litany of Bertie's misdemeanours 'of a person who has had too strong a tonic', and 'incapable of constant and continued application'. Gibbs advised Prince Albert that he might be able to work off Bertie's excess of misapplied energy in such outdoors pursuits as deer-stalking, and he set aside times for further visits by boys of Bertie's age, such as the two sons of the Belgian Minister to London, Van der Weyer, and some courageous boys from Eton. Albert did not consider it proper to appoint a companion to Bertie, given his future role, but did select one for Affie, Lord Carrington, who was nearer Bertie's age. As Marquess of Lincolnshire, long afterwards, Carrington wrote that Gibbs 'seemed kindly enough' but that Prince Albert appeared to be 'a proud, shy, stand-offish man.... I was frightened to death of him.'

Despite his well-intentioned desire to enhance a monarchy tarnished by Victoria's uncles, George IV and William IV, and even now being diminished by legislative reforms, Albert could not create in the Prince of Wales a future Platonic philosopher-king, or even a Germanic princeling. The boy would never be a mathematician, a military strat-egist, a speechmaker, nor a magistrate. He would seldom, if ever, read a book all the way through. In a long document which Dr Becker wrote to Prince Albert, he attributed Bertie's destructive rages to the strain on mind and body for a child like Bertie. The pressure on him was too great, and in response, 'he takes everything that is at hand and throws it with the greatest violence against the wall or window, without thinking the least of the consequences of what he is doing; or he stands in the corner stamping with his legs and screaming in the most dreadful manner'. Mr Wellesley advised that 'the great object is to instruct him without over-working him.' Dr Voisin, the French tutor, warned Gibbs that Albert's stern system could not transform into a paragon a small boy with no strong intellectual gifts: 'You will wear him out early.... Make him climb trees! Run! Leap! Row! Ride! ... In many things savages are better edu-cated than we are.'

Bertie was indeed coerced into physical activity, especially in spacious Osborne and Balmoral, but when in the London area he was supposed to soak up culture. Victoria and Albert often had command performances of plays and parts of operas at Buckingham Palace and Windsor, and visiting instrumentalists played. All but the very youngest children participated in plays staged for their parents and guests, Bertie at eleven once clad in white, and fitted with a long white beard and flowing locks to match, as 'winter' in a tableau of 'The Seasons'. The elder children were also taken to the theatre, novelist Elizabeth Gaskell crowing to her sister in June 1854 that she had seen the Royals at 'a little play called La joie fait peur.... It is a very small theatre and we saw the Queen & Prince Albert and the Prince of Wales, and Prince Alfred very well. The two boys have coarse features, but look healthy and rosy. The Prince of Wales has a long-tailed coat on, which makes him look very funny [as] he is so young.'

At eleven the Prince was told by Gibbs, perhaps as motivation, that he would one day be king. The idea came as a surprise. He knew that his mother reigned, rather than his father, and that he had an older sister. 'Walked out with Bertie,' the Queen wrote in her journal on 12 February 1852. 'He generally lets out to me, when he walks with me, something or other that is occupying his mind. This time it was how *I* came to the throne.... He said that he had always believed that Vicky would succeed, but now he knew that in default of *him*, Affie, Arthur & "another brother, if perhaps we have one", would come before Vicky. I explained to him the different successions.... He took it all in, very naturally.'

Albert left almost nothing in the future king's upbringing to chance, consulting the Court physician, Sir James Clark, who was no more ignorant than most practitioners, and Dr George Combe, the fashionable phrenologist, who read the contours of Bertie's skull as indicators of character. He reported, much like a fortune-teller who had already found out pertinent facts to make the 'reading' appear prescient, that the Prince's 'intellectual organs' were 'only moderately well developed', which could lead to 'strong self-will, at times obstinacy'. The obsessive Combe, author of the influential *Elements of Phrenology* (1824), took bumps very seriously, advising Albert absurdly that Bertie needed 'exposure to the open air', but that flat places were to be avoided, and also 'moist or absolutely wet' soil, as well as exposure to the sun. Bertie was also to bathe in cold water and have light, plain nourishment. Soft pillows and soft beds were also anathema to Dr Combe.

Fortunately for the Prince of Wales, if not for Europe, the Crimean

War intervened to distract Victoria, and more especially Albert, from the failing experiment of moulding their heir into their ideal of a future monarch. It also provided unexpected opportunities for Bertie to learn about the world beyond Windsor Castle, and how he might fit into it.

II

The World Outside

1852–1860

WITH THE ENTRANCE of Britain into the Crimean War, small alterations in the education of the two elder princes occurred, to Bertie's advantage. According to Frederick Gibbs, the princes were receiving daily instruction 'in Arithmetic and in the first principles of Algebra and Geometry', though not on a level commensurate with school courses. Since they would be in a ruling caste where certain applications might be more useful than others, algebra and geometry were to be studied with reference to 'their applications to Gunnery, Fortifications and the Mechanical Arts'. In a report prepared by Gibbs early in 1856, he noted that the Prince of Wales had become a graceful dancer, but 'dancing being thought rather effeminate, and insufficient to develop a manly frame', he was also going through 'a regular course of military exercises under the instruction of a Sergeant'.

Bertie's royal father dominated his childhood. Since the Queen was often pregnant or in postpartum convalescence – eight times in her thirteen years of marriage, and one further occasion to come – Prince Albert often substituted ceremonially for her, taking with him the elder princes and princesses. On grand occasions, such as the opening of the Great Exhibition in Hyde Park (the first World Fair) in 1851, the entire royal family appeared, as they did again in 1852 at the elaborate funeral procession for the Duke of Wellington.

The beginning of the war in the Black Sea and the Balkans set France and Britain on the side of the crumbling Ottoman Empire, to prop it up against the Mediterranean ambitions of Tsarist Russia; it also

*Albert Edward at his father's right hand at the grand opening of the
1851 Exhibition at the Crystal Palace (*Punch, *May 1851)*

provided new opportunities for Bertie to become acquainted with the
world outside Balmoral, Windsor and Osborne. He went with his father,
sometimes with the Queen as well, to inspections of unprepared and
badly equipped troops as they boarded ships for the Crimea, to naval
reviews of virtually obsolete ships commanded by obsolescent admirals
who had fought with Nelson, and to the first awards of the Victoria
Cross by the Queen for bravery in battle, at which Bertie sat on a pony
next to his mother in the boiling sun in Hyde Park. He also accompanied his parents to the dedications of new military hospitals, and visited
the sick and wounded. According to the diary his father insisted the boy
maintain (but which Bertie kept badly), he saw early photographs of the

war by James Robertson and Roger Fenton and even purchased one of Fenton's pictures, of a tent site looking down into a broad Crimean valley. Bertie was taken to the 'Diorama of the Seat of War' in June 1854, the 'Picture Model of the Town and Forts of Sebastopol' in June 1855, and 'the battle of the Alma' at Burford's Panorama. The children 'drew some things for the Patriotic Fund' at Albert's request, to be exhibited and sold for war relief. The charity, which Albert initiated and chaired, raised a million pounds which a tight-fisted Parliament would not authorize from taxes.

In April 1855, Bertie met the Emperor and Empress of France on their state visit to England, and wrote in his diary, 'The Emperor is a short person. He has very long moustachios but short hair.... The Empress is very pretty.' Popular at the time were 'confession albums', in which visitors were to write something personal, and Bertie presented his to Napoleon III, who proceeded to pen, in German, lines he remembered that were written for him when he was a schoolboy in Augsburg, warning innocent youth not to be swayed by a crowd's praise, or their calumnies, and reminding, in Albertine fashion, that *'Zwischen Klüften geht die Pflicht'* – in the path of duty lay pitfalls. Disraeli carped to a friend that Eugénie was 'too natural for a sovereign' and lacked 'reserve and dignity. ... She was always playing with the royal children, who doted on her.' Bertie was enchanted. Albert, meanwhile, was attempting to charm the Emperor into calling off his planned ego trip to command the bungled war in the Crimea, by citing his importance at home. On his return Napoleon gave in, permitting Sebastopol to fall without him, since the Russians were even more ineffective than the combined British and French. By then the Royals were at Balmoral, where a celebratory cairn had earlier been erected on Albert's orders, when a false report of the surrender had arrived on the still-new telegraph. This time the young princes were awakened to watch the blaze which flared as the Queen's piper played and ghillies toasted the victory in tumblers of whisky. When troops began to return, Bertie confided in his diary that he saw 'a Russian dog that was taken at Sebastopol', and 'had a long talk with Gen. [C. A.] Windham, who told me that he had been in all the battles & all the assaults that had taken place in the Crimea'. The Prince's imagination was fired by the war. He wanted to enlist at the lowest rank the Army offered, and to rise on his merits to general.

A year earlier, Gibbs had sent a memorandum to the Queen urging that the Prince of Wales be offered opportunities for foreign travel 'to remedy in some degree the disadvantages he labours under from a want of companions. He is behind his contemporaries ... in the self-reliance resulting from being thrown on one's resources.' Gibbs also suggested an ancillary tutor expert in natural science, who could 'forward the great object to be kept constantly in view – leading [the Prince of Wales] by every kind of means to use his mind'. Bertie's parents considered the proposal hopeless, but his foreign travel was initiated when he accompanied Victoria, Albert and Vicky on a return state visit to France in August 1856, after the Crimean War had ended. Long privy to adult conversation, he was learning more than he was supposed to know, much of it not from Gibbs's books. Since no one had taught Bertie the virtues of discretion, he was often more proud than prudent about what he overheard. During the war his father had steamed across the Channel for military exchanges with the Emperor. Just prior to the strategy talks, Disraeli told Lady Londonderry, 'At [the] Duchess of Gloucester's infantile assembly ... the Prince of Wales said, Papa is going to France. Upon which there was a hush, and Rev. Gibbs put his finger to his lip, and somebody else her hand on his R.H.'s mouth; but the murder was out.'

What Bertie knew about other unmentionable subjects can only be inferred from gossip, as his talk was largely unrecorded, his writings virtually non-existent, and his deeds, usually mischievous, were only the subject of Court prattle. According to one story he peered through an open bedroom door in a corner of the Castle where he had no business to be, and saw the bridal gown of a maid laid out for her wedding. Filching some paint or ink from his art lessons, he smeared the white dress with red blotches. Caught out, he earned a birching from his father, who perhaps saw only mischief when some early sexual awareness may have been involved.

Some further arousal may have occurred when Vicky and Bertie, then nearly fifteen, accompanied their parents to Paris on a state visit in August 1855. Always dignified but often dowdy, Victoria could not stand up to comparison, even with a new wardrobe, with the beautiful (and younger) Empress Eugénie. Having met her at Windsor, the Prince of Wales was already an admirer of the warm, elegant Empress. She fed his starved self-esteem as much as did the Emperor, who desperately wanted a male heir, and treated Bertie as a surrogate son. (Eugénie had just learned that she was again pregnant, after several miscarriages.) Word had clearly gone out that the French court was to be on its best behaviour, since the nephew of the first Napoleon needed an amenable England on one of its flanks in order to reconstitute the legendary splendours of the First Empire. The Emperor's cousin, the buxom, dark-eyed Princess Mathilde, who lived scandalously outside her marriage with a fashionable painter, was especially kind to Bertie. Eugénie's ladies-in-waiting, perfumed and in deep *décolletage*, made Bertie aware of other French charms he would never forget, and, with a sense of drama that overcame the misgivings of Victoria and Albert, the Emperor staged every event on the royal calendar as theatre. The Prince of Wales was enraptured.

At Les Invalides, the visitors, children included, were escorted by Napoleon and Mathilde, while a storm gathered, to a chapel housing the coffin of the earlier Napoleon until a deep crypt nearby was completed. Around the coffin, covered with a velvet pall, veterans of the hero – once England's mortal foe – stood in homage with flaming torches. In the solemn atmosphere the Queen turned to Bertie, put a hand on his shoulder, and, according to Marshal Canrobert, said, 'Kneel down before the tomb of the great Napoleon.' The Prince of Wales knelt just as the storm erupted with bolts of thunder and lightning. Nothing more wonderful had ever happened to him.

Taking time out from entertaining the Queen and Albert, who visited the Exposition Universelle, the Emperor (who had seemed unprepossessing to the boy when in England, and – indeed – was nearly as short as Victoria) took Bertie on a carriage drive through the newly imposing avenues of Paris, redesigned and rebuilt by Baron Georges Haussmann. Napoleon drove the two-wheeled curricle himself, and servants – very likely security men – sat behind them, attempting to be inconspicuous. Afterward the Sovereign and the Prince strolled together on the terraces of the Tuileries, Napoleon ostentatiously demonstrating his relaxed, imperial style while puffing on cigar after cigar. (Victoria detested tobacco and Albert did not smoke.) Bertie had never experienced anything but tension at home. 'You have a nice country,' he confided to the Emperor. 'I would like to be your son.'

There were balls, plays, concerts and banquets. Bertie, on occasion attired in a kilt, and Vicky, in a grown-up gown, stayed up very late, spoke French everywhere, and did not want the week to end. On Monday 27 August, as the royal family was preparing to leave, Bertie and Vicky arranged to see the Empress and begged her to intercede with their parents to let them remain longer. The Queen and Prince, said Eugénie diplomatically, could not do without them. 'Not do without us!' exploded the Prince of Wales. 'Don't fancy that! They don't want us, and there are six more of us at home!'

The Emperor commissioned the court artist to paint the stag hunt that was the main event of the sixth day of the visit. Hippolyte Bellangé had made his reputation with a canvas, *Napoleon's Return from the Island of Elba*, after which he became a favourite of the next Bonaparte, and produced a series of heroic Crimean War scenes. In his *Imperial Hunt in the Forest of St Germain*, set before a chateau of bright yellow, baying staghounds gather about huntsmen in tricorne hats and brown coats who wear knee-high black boots. Each man has, slung about his torso, a curved brass hunting horn to sound a fanfare to signal the start of the hunt. Officers of the Imperial Guard, on horseback, mingle with the colourful guests, mostly ladies in silks, carrying parasols. The English Royals stand with Napoleon at the foot of the chateau's steps. Next to Albert, who wears a black frock coat and tall silk hat like the Emperor, is the Prince of Wales, a small figure in Highland cap looking on with awe at the scene. It was not great art, but it caught the mood.

Watching the English party depart from the Gare de Strasbourg on 27 August the comtesse d'Armaille observed in her diary that Albert looked 'very bald for his age … and very tired', but 'his boy, on the contrary, kept looking all about him, as though anxious to lose nothing of those last moments in Paris'. The Emperor travelled with them in the imperial railway carriage as far as Boulogne, from which the visitors sailed for home, the children in tears. Albert Edward had passed his first, if informal, diplomatic test. He had been a success. Though his mother perceived him as an ungainly adolescent, he had been handsome, almost exotic, in his kilt; attractive ladies had made a fuss over him; and he had learned that he could turn on a charm he had not known he had. But Bertie had yet to realize that the tinsel gaiety of the Paris of Napoleon and Eugénie was not the real world.

For Bertie, the aftermath of Paris was a stay at Osborne without the family but with all his tutors, to catch up on missed studies, after which his delayed reward for enduring such concentrated schooling was to be a walking tour in Dorset that autumn. His claim to Eugénie that he would not be missed had been at least half true. A few weeks later Victoria would write from Balmoral to the Queen of Prussia, 'Even here, when Albert is often away all day long, I find no especial pleasure or compensation in the company of the elder children … and only occasionally do I find the rather intimate intercourse with them either easy or agreeable. You will not understanding this.' And she went on to explain that she had never grown up in close companionship with young people, and could not even find any rapport with her own nearly adult children. Albert had bonded emotionally with Vicky, who seemed to him a younger and more pleasing version of himself, but neither parent found any bond with Bertie, however much he remained their heir. On returning from France neither had said a word to the Prince of Wales about how well he had carried off his part in Paris. But for the promised escape to Dorset, his regimen resumed.

Walking holidays were a fashion that faded with the advent of the automobile, although even in the nineteenth century well-to-do walkers often travelled, as if on safari, with bearers lingering discreetly behind with provisions and camping gear, sometimes even with carriages. Bertie's tour included only Gibbs and a companion for Gibbs. Even so, the trek, attempted incognito, had to be abandoned at Honiton, west of Axminster. The Prince's identity had leaked out, and loyal demonstrations erupted at every village. It was a poor introduction to public exposure, as the Queen wanted none of that heady visibility for the unprepared Bertie. Yet the experiment was to be repeated. In May 1857 Gibbs requested the Headmaster of Eton to furnish three tutors and four companions of Bertie's age for a walking tour of the Lake District. If the adventure succeeded, all would accompany the Prince of Wales abroad soon after. The chosen boys were William Gladstone, George Cadogan (the future 5th Earl), Frederick Stanley (the future 16th Earl of Derby), and Charles Wood (later 2nd Viscount Halifax). Albert added the Revd Charles Tarver, Bertie's Latin tutor and personal chaplain, to the party, and instructed Bertie to write an essay for Tarver on 'Friends and Flatterers', as the Prince Consort was obsessed by concern that, however distinguished his son's companions, they would use their proximity to exploit him. It was hardly an auspicious start to a holiday, but Bertie shrewdly satisfied parental expectation, describing a friend (in theory) as someone who would 'tell you of your faults', while a flatterer would 'lead you into any imaginable vice'. Tarver reported to Albert that the essay was 'not fully worked up' but 'right-minded'.

If anyone on the expedition led others astray it was Albert Edward, who talked the boys into driving a flock of sheep into Lake Windermere. Perhaps Albert never discovered it, for on 26 July 1857 the Prince of Wales and the same Eton companions left for Königswinter, across the Rhine from the Prince Consort's beloved Bonn. Bertie was to study there for four months and use the location for educational trips into nearby regions of France, into Switzerland, and the German states. Education came early. On their first evening at Königswinter the Prince of Wales, his inhibitions released by the good Rhenish wine at dinner, kissed a pretty girl, and was admonished by his father's Private Secretary, General Charles Grey, and Albert's equerry, Colonel Henry Ponsonby, the senior adult mentors. To their credit the boy's governors omitted to report the incident to Windsor. Young William Gladstone, however, wrote to his mother excitedly about the Prince's lapse, and, from Liverpool, Catherine Gladstone broke the news to her husband, then Chancellor of the Exchequer, in London. On 4 August the elder Gladstone moralized priggishly to Catherine about 'this squalid little debauch', which, although 'a paltry affair', convinced him 'that the Prince of Wales has not been educated up to his position. This sort of unworthy little indulgence is the compensation. Kept in childhood beyond his time, he is allowed to make that childhood what it should never be in a Prince, or anyone else, namely wanton.'

Victoria and Albert never learned of it, but would have ascribed such behaviour to the bad influences of schools and what schoolboys learned from each other. Only the year before Thomas Hughes had published *Tom Brown at Oxford*, which had offended some reviewers because its hero had cradled in his arms a girl who had broken her ankle. One critic protested stuffily, 'If this be muscular Christianity, the less we hear of it the better.'

Albert had heard little from his son, and nearly a month after the royal party had arrived on the Rhine he wrote to Bertie asking him, 'in the absence of lessons', to 'write to us a little more at length and give us your impressions of things, and not the mere bare facts'. It was Albert's intention to inspect all the written work Bertie had accomplished on tour when they returned, and he duly examined a notebook, 'Wits and Whoppers', that recorded instances of schoolboy humour, much of it in the form of rather lame puns. Bertie did report visiting Albert's brother, Duke Ernest, in Coburg, and their reception at a dinner given by the eighty-four-year-old Prince Metternich, at his castle of Johannisberg, at

Niederwald. What the boy remembered from the retired statesman's reminscences is unrecorded; in his diary Bertie, obtuse to recent history, recalled nothing of Metternich's memories of the great, and described the old kingmaker as 'a very nice old gentleman and very like the late Duke of Wellington'. Metternich thought the boy likeable but that he seemed unhappy and ill at ease. Living in the shadow of reproof, he seemed possessed by anxiety.

In Switzerland the party did the expected walking tours along the foothills of Mont Blanc and over the Grosse Scheidegg, returning to Dover on 27 October 1857. Once more the Queen had not missed him. Her ninth and last child, Princess Beatrice, had been born on 14 April, the same accoucheur who had brought Bertie and the other royal children into the world officiating. (The British public referred to Dr Charles Locock as 'deliverer of the nation'.) Beatrice – forever after 'Baby' to the Queen – was to be Victoria's favourite and, despite her dislike of infants, she did not tire of her smallest daughter. Other changes were imminent. Despite his youth, Affie had been permitted to go off to Portsmouth for naval training, which traditionally began early in one's teens, although his first day as a cadet began untraditionally with the yard-arms of his ship, the *Euryalus*, manned in his honour, a salute fired, and luncheon laid out for him in the captain's state cabin. Vicky, her marriage long arranged to the future Crown Prince of Prussia, was to leave the household for what increasingly seemed like exile to Berlin the following January.

In the days before her fiancé Prince Frederick arrived for his wedding, London was in celebratory mood, with hundreds invited each evening to festivities at Buckingham Palace. One observer, on 21 January, was Benjamin Moran, Secretary of the American Legation, who – despite his acerbically Republican sentiments – happily exploited the royal invitations his master, the Minister George Mifflin Dallas, did not use. 'There were', he wrote in his diary, 'not more than 1100 persons present.... The Queen led off in a quadrille, the German Princes & the Court participating. Here, for the first time, I saw the young Prince of Wales.... I looked at this puny and listless boy with more curiosity than I ever before bestowed on a mortal. He was dressed in Highland costume & made a pleasing toy-like appearance, nothing more.... His head is small, his nose rather long and like his mother's; his profile is not good and lacks decision.' Obviously a believer in Dr Combe's phrenological theories, Moran perceived 'good development of the perceptive organs, and this fact will probably save him from imbecility [but] ... the shape of his head indicates a suspicious disposition'. Despite his staunchly Yankee scepticism towards a system that made the Prince, 'brainless or not', the heir to a throne, Moran conceded that Albert Edward 'danced very well, stept with confidence and grace', and 'conducted himself with propriety and never assumed a state beyond his years'. During one polka with his young aunt, the Duchess of Coburg, 'a charming little woman', a lieutenant bumped into the pair and bowed an apology. The Prince 'gracefully shook the officer by the hand, and bowing, returned to his place with a grace and ease rarely equalled. The act bespoke good breeding and displayed a politic and conciliatory spirit.'

Bertie was evidencing a maturity that his parents had despaired of his ever achieving, without their even noticing. He may have also recognized in the officer in Highland dress the soldier he aspired to be. Eager to eschew books, Bertie craved an Army career, and his father at first suggested sympathetically that he might train with the Guards, but the Queen foresaw no way that the heir to the throne could see active duty. She conceded, however (7 January 1858), that while as heir he could not serve professionally, 'he might learn it'. But first came other hurdles. There was his confirmation by the Archbishop of Canterbury, John Sumner, arranged for 1 April in St George's Chapel, Windsor. The Revd Gerald Wellesley had put Bertie through his theological paces and, like many dyslexics, he memorized well. His promised independence in a house of his own, White Lodge, Richmond, and even his Guards training, depended upon his very public performance in a ritual which neither Victoria nor Albert privately took very seriously. It was an open demonstration of fidelity to the official faith – in England, if not in Scotland. 'Love' for the God of Anglican sermons, Albert told Victoria, who later (7 February 1862) confided his sentiments to Vicky, was 'most preposterous'. For Albert, 'the love of God was quite of a different kind – it was the trust and confidence in and adoration of a great, incomprehensible spirit'. That was too subtle, however, to explain to Bertie, for whom it would be enough to go through the appropriate motions without stumbling. And Bertie did, which earned him a fortnight's holiday with his governor in Ireland. 'Bertie answered extremely well,' Victoria wrote to his great-uncle Leopold, King of the Belgians, 'and his whole manner and *Gemüthsstimmung* [frame of mind] yesterday, and again today, at the Sacrament to which we took him, was gentle, good, and proper.' Leopold, a Lutheran who had married first an Anglican, then a Roman Catholic (in each case a dynastic political choice), understood proper form.

At sixteen Bertie was fast approaching legal adulthood. Although he had carried off his confirmation without public embarrassment, his parents felt that future failure remained inevitable. The marginally competent Dr Clark was called in, and recommended that a spartan diet might help both Bertie's alarming temper and his sluggish intellect. The Queen herself had observed that the Prince had indulged in eating and drinking to the point of 'imprudence'. Even so, he had been awarded his own establishment, together with an allowance for such expenditures as clothes – an unprincely hundred pounds. Yet this modest allocation, like the residence for him and his governors, was far from his own, as the Queen had hedged it about with warnings that he was not to wear anything '*extravagant or slang*', as that would demonstrate 'an indifference to what is morally wrong'. Despite her language, there was nothing puritanical about her admonition. She was, as always, considering public perception of the monarchy. As she reproved someone who cautiously criticized the strict upbringing of the heir, 'Remember, there is only my life between his and the lives of his Wicked Uncles.'

In April 1858, the Prince established himself at White Lodge, newly refitted for him and his household. Having married off Vicky a few months earlier, the Queen was now physically free of her eldest children. Bertie, so Albert informed Stockmar (2 April), was to have some Army training and to sample university life in some as yet unspecified form, as well as undergoing an intensive programme of social and mental maturing. To this end, Albert had appointed 'three very distinguished young men of from twenty-three to twenty-six years of age who are to occupy, in monthly rotation, a kind of equerry's place about him'. The junior officers were 'distinguished', 'moral' and 'accomplished'; two had earned the Victoria Cross in the Crimea. They would instruct Bertie, who would not be seventeen until November, in 'Appearance, Deportment and Dress', as well as 'Manner and Conduct towards Others'. He was also to be instructed in 'The Power to Acquit Himself Creditably in Conversation, or whatever May Be the Occupation of Society'. (Evidently Albert had turned his attention from impossible academic goals to purely pragmatic ones.) Bertie was to eschew gossip, cards and billiards, and devote some of his leisure time to music and the fine arts. In dress he was to avoid 'the frivolity and foolish vanity of dandyism'; in manners his young governors were to encourage 'the absence of selfishness'. Furthermore, Bertie was to be 'scrupulously courteous, attentive, punctual'. If high-minded rules and clockwork organization could transform the Prince of Wales into what a king should be, the result would indeed have pleased the shade of Plato. Albert was clearly acting not only on his own, but at the urging of the Queen, who was already hoping that she could outlive the heir she considered unfit to be king. 'He is so idle and weak,' she complained to Vicky. 'God grant that he may take things more to heart and be more serious for the future.... The heart is good, warm and affectionate.'

Albert's disappointment in his eldest son lay in the boy's disinclination towards intellectual pursuits and his lack of motivation to do, or be, anything of which his father approved. Bertie would have preferred the military career his tall, austere (and much older) brother-in-law in Prussia had managed, even though Fritz was destined to be sovereign. That the two cultures were dramatically different was never explained to Bertie, although his father appreciated the distinction, writing to his brother Ernest in Coburg (22 April 1858), that it was 'to be regretted' that Prince Frederick had 'taken up the game of soldiering', yet it was 'not astonishing in a member of his family and a subject of his country'. In militaristic Prussia, Fritz had sought 'a manly occupation, duty, and self-sacrifice, in the service of the state'. If he had not, Albert conceded, he would have had 'absolutely nothing to do and as affairs are at present, I do not know what [else] he should do'.

Fritz, however, was as mature as the combat-tested officers seconded to Bertie, ambitious young men whose military careers had been interrupted, by Albert's order, to furnish role models for his son. Bertie was still little more than a child; lessons and lectures, concerts and exhibitions bored him as much as they did his escorts. Since his sister was married when hardly past seventeen he looked forward to his own seventeenth birthday in November, when he anticipated some further concession of independence, and a promised visit to Vicky in Berlin. While Marlborough House in London, once the vast residence of William IV's queen, Adelaide, was being refurbished to become his London home, at White Lodge the Prince of Wales was obliged to host dinners for politicians and professors who meant nothing to him, and

THE ROYAL RISING GENERATION.

When nearly eighteen, the Prince was granted Marlborough House as
*his London domicile (*Punch, *10 August 1859)*

make an effort to read books for which he had no enthusiasm, including long novels by Sir Walter Scott about a region of more interest to the Prince's parents. Even his mail was scrutinized for inappropriateness, and letters he described in his diary as 'jolly' from Lady Churchill, one of the Queen's favourite members of the Household, were stopped. Lady Churchill, happily married and no threat, had only been attempting to break through the Prince's loneliness and seclusion, but Bertie was to be limited – before an arranged marriage – to masculine society.

At White Lodge on 9 November the Prince received a long birthday letter from his parents, written by Albert, which ostensibly emancipated him from their authority. He was initially to have an annual income of £500 beyond the household expenses managed by his governors. The Queen and Prince Consort explained that, however rigorous he may have considered his education to have been, its only object had been his growth into a worthy heir apparent. Although the transition had already been effectively accomplished, the letter formally relieved Frederick Gibbs of his pedagogic duties and instead appointed Colonel – soon General – Robert Bruce to be his new governor. Bertie's military aspirations were to be satisfied by gazetting him a lieutenant-colonel (unattached) without duties, and entitling him to wear appropriate uniform on ceremonial occasions. Knowing himself to be unfit, Bertie was embarrassed by the premature and unearned rank. The 'freedom document' nevertheless enjoined the Prince to liberate himself 'from the thraldom of abject dependence' – even upon servants. He was to learn to follow Christ's precept 'that you should love your neighbour as yourself, and do unto men as you would they should do unto you'. He was to aspire to become 'a good man and a thorough gentleman'. In character-istic Albertine style it concluded, 'Life is composed of duties, and in the due, punctual and cheerful performance of them, the true Christian, true soldier and true gentleman is recognized.' Bertie took the cold, if well-meaning, letter to Dean Wellesley, thrust it at him, and burst into tears.

On 17 November, three days before Bertie was to leave on his promised trip to Prussia with Colonel Bruce and Major Christopher Teesdale, Albert wrote to Vicky, 'Do not miss any opportunity of urging him to hard work.... Unfortunately, he takes no interest in anything but clothes, and again clothes. Even when out shooting he is more occupied with his trousers than with the game! I am particularly anxious that he should have some mental occupation in Berlin. Perhaps you could let him share in some of yours, [like] lectures, etc.' On the day of his departure the Queen made the Prince of Wales a Knight of the Garter, which gave him another unearned ribbon to wear.

Vicky was to write loyally that she found her brother 'so much improved' – amiable and, despite later political differences, able to make a lasting friend of his brother-in-law Fritz. Bertie returned home three weeks later, recalling no lectures (Vicky was pregnant and preoccupied), but only a round of parties and balls, an atmosphere in which he had thrived. Since German was spoken at home through his childhood (and his spoken English would always betray a light German accent), Bertie used the language easily. He was already a first-class dancing partner and proved to be an amusing dinner companion, returning happy at having accomplished something successfully. 'Bertie has a remarkable social talent,' Prince Albert conceded to his daughter. 'He is lively, quick and sharp when his mind is set on anything, which is seldom.... But usually his intellect is of no more use than a pistol packed in the bottom of a trunk if one were attacked in the robber-infested Apennines.'

School was still on the agenda, and Bertie returned to two-and-a-half hours of re-examination on ancient and modern history. For Gibbs, the Prince had barely managed six desperate and ungrammatical lines on ancient history, beginning: 'The war of Tarentum, it was between Hannibal the Carthaginian General and the Romans, Hannibal was engaged in a war with it, for some time.' On English history Bertie was unable to remember the year of Wellington's death, although he had watched the elaborate funeral procession with his parents in 1852. After months of renewed preparation, Gibbs had, as almost his last effort, invited his own mentor Sir James Stephen to examine the inarticulate Prince, who did little better and was advised 'scrupulously' to consult a dictionary. His command of Latin (although hardly essential to his future monarchical role) was so lame that when his father took him to see a play in Latin acted by the boys of Westminster School, the Queen noted scornfully in her journal (22 December 1858) that although it was 'very improper' and should have stirred Bertie's interest, he 'understood not a word of it'. To Vicky, who had praised her brother's social skills, Victoria appealed, 'Poor Bertie! He vexes us much. There is not a particle of reflection, or even attention to anything but dress! Not the slightest desire to learn, on the contrary, *il bouche les oreilles* [he shuts his ears] the moment anything of interest is being talked of! I only hope he will meet with some severe lesson to shame him out of his ignorance and dullness.' The Queen unreasonably blamed the departing Mr Gibbs, and hoped that Colonel Bruce, Gibbs's successor, could do better.

The Apennines had been on the Prince Consort's mind in his letter to Vicky, perhaps because he intended next to dispatch Bertie to Italy to study art, archaeology and the affairs of troubled southern Europe. He was again to keep a journal for Albert's perusal, and it was predictable that both his parents would find it uninspired and error-ridden. On his return, he was promised, he would study in Edinburgh and then sample the universities of Oxford and Cambridge, and also be afforded opportunity for both military training and foreign travel during the long vacations. With that to motivate him, he left for Rome on 10 January, 1859, accompanied by Colonel and Mrs Bruce, an equerry, a chaplain, a doctor and tutor – his Latinist, Charles Tarver, who could also cope with Italian.

Since even a paragon of a prince should not, at seventeen, travel in state, Lord Malmesbury, the Tory Foreign Minister, wrote to the Queen that he 'entirely agrees with your Majesty that it is desirable that His Royal Highness the Prince of Wales should visit and remain at Rome incognito. It is also indispensable that when there His Royal Highness should receive no foreigner or stranger *alone*, so that no reports of pretended conversations with such persons could be circulated without immediate refutation.' Malmesbury also wrote to the resident British diplomat in Rome, Odo Russell, to inform the Vatican of the visit. As a transparent device to avoid diplomatic ceremonial Bertie would travel as Baron Renfew, the lowest of his string of titles.

Since to reach Rome the Prince's party would have to travel through Piedmont, where Turin was the capital of the Kingdom of Sardinia, Victor Emmanuel II invited the son of his Crimean War ally, whatever his title, to be a royal guest. When polite excuses came from Windsor Castle, as the King was far from being a role model for Bertie, his Prime Minister, Count Cavour, sent assurances to his envoy in London: 'It appears that the Queen hesitates to consent to let him come to Turin, fearing that he might run some danger of losing his innocence.... If they speak to you about it, you may reassure the Court on the score of this precious quality of the Heir to the Throne. If it arrives with him as far as Turin, it is not here that he will lose it.'

En route to Italy, the Prince of Wales's party stopped in Brussels to visit King Leopold, who was to brief him about the European situation, and Bertie wrote the required letter to his father. It appalled Albert: a ball 'went off very well' and was 'very pretty' – possibly a covert reference to dancing companions. The King 'spoke a great deal about the affairs in Italy, & the probability of a war, [&] he was very alarmed about it'. The journey afterward to Cologne was 'prosperous'. Realizing that, despite Leopold's efforts, his son had no conception of what was going on in the part of Europe toward which he was travelling, Albert responded with a painstaking analysis of Italian instability. Bertie replied from Rome, where he received it, with little evidence of comprehension. 'It is very kind of you', he wrote, 'to explain to me the politics of the different nations, which certainly seem very complicated.'

Travelling in leisurely fashion to take in cultural landmarks approved by Albert (who had consulted John Ruskin and the President of the Royal Academy Charles Eastlake), the party reached Rome on 3 February, putting up at the Hotel d'Angleterre. Colonel Bruce reported regularly to Windsor Castle that the Prince of Wales was being kept fully occupied: 'He learns [lessons] by heart in the morning before breakfast, and prepares for his Italian master who comes from 10 to 11 a.m. He reads with Mr. Tarver from 11 to 12, and translates French from 5 to 6 p.m. and has the next hour in the evening for private reading or for music. He has a piano in his room. The afternoon is devoted to the inspection, under expert guidance, of ancient monuments and ancient and modern works of art.' The Prince found 'mouldering stones' lacking in interest.

Bertie's party had hardly unpacked when a major domo representing Pope Pius IX arrived to invite the Prince, whatever his subterfuge of a title, to the Vatican. Within a week of Baron Renfrew's arrival he had an affable audience with His Holiness, both speaking French and raising no substantive issues. (Colonel Bruce coughed lightly when he thought the conversation was in danger of shifting from prearranged niceties.) Nevertheless the meeting caused consternation among the Anglican clergy at home. It afforded recognition of a sort to the enemy, and stories would circulate in England that Bertie came bearing expensive gifts, and that he was exposed to such influences 'as to aggravate the fears of judicious Protestants'. In reality, Bruce reported to Albert rumours that the Pope intended to make 'some handsome present' to the Prince of Wales, and asked, 'What return can be made?' The Prince Consort replied firmly, recognizing the political consequences: 'No present can be made to the Pope in return for the one expected to come from him.' The Pope, Victoria wrote with relief to Leopold (15 February 1859), 'was extremely kind and gracious, and Colonel Bruce was present; it would never have done to let Bertie go alone, as they might hereafter have pretended, God knows! what Bertie had said.'

Despite the care which Prince Albert had taken to furnish no ammunition to Protestant extremists, the fact of a Papal audience was sufficient to raise rumours of an expensive royal gift. In a series of rabble-rousing public letters to the Prince Consort in *The British Standard*, intended to rouse 'slumbering Protestants' against popery, the Revd John Campbell

declared without citing any evidence, 'that the Prince of Wales had transmitted to the "Holy Father" a present, value £50,000'. He was 'quite at a
loss to comprehend the reasons'. He also saw the hand of the Vatican in
the plans to send the Prince of Wales to Oxford, where the 'Romish
system' was ascendant, and alleged that the young Prince had been
reported by Cardinal Wiseman as expressing himself 'in favour of the
Church of Rome'. The Queen and Prince Albert could only privately
deplore the demagoguery.

Now that the Prince had a residence of his own, he felt the need to
bring back from his travels some artifacts by which to recall them. In the
studio of Harriet Goodhue Hosmer, an expatriate American sculptress,
he found a small statue, 33 inches high, of a winged cherub sitting on a
toadstool. Since his father had warned that he could buy nothing expensive from funds allocated for his educational tour, Bertie bought *Puck*
with his own pocket money. Visiting the studio of English painter
Frederic Leighton, whose reputation had been established when Victoria
purchased one of his pictures from a Royal Academy show in 1855, the
Prince saw a picture of a lovely woman apparently reclining in a harem.
It intrigued him enough to earn a laconic line in his journal: 'I admired
three beautiful portraits of a Roman woman each representing the same
person in a different attitude.' She was Nanna Risi, the model and mistress of a German painter, Anselm Feuerbach, who also sat to Leighton.
The canvas was already sold, but Leighton talked George de Monbrison
into letting the Prince buy it, the artist agreeing to make Monbrison a
copy. Bertie was on his way to becoming a connoisseur of pretty women.
And the black-bearded young Leighton, who looked like a pirate but in
riper years would become President of the Royal Academy of Arts, was
to become a lifelong friend.

Since the English colony was expecting the Prince, there were rounds
of dinners, operas and theatre parties, all with boring older folk of no
interest to him. But he enjoyed Bellini and Verdi, and went to the opera
twice a week. In Carnival Week he rode up and down the Corso in a rain
of flowers and confetti. He met the fastidious Robert Browning, who
called him 'a gentle refined boy', and the eccentric Edward Lear, who had
instructed Victoria and Albert in drawing, and described Bertie as 'one
of the nicest lads you could ever see'. He also met the American historian
and diplomat John Lothrop Motley, who found Bertie's smile 'very ready
and genuine'. On a social level he got on splendidly, but Colonel Bruce

suggested in reports home that there was some rebellion at the academic pressure. 'Bertie', the Queen wrote to Vicky, who, now married and abroad, had become her closest confidante, '... is my caricature, that is the misfortune, and in a man – this is so much worse.'

Wherever he went, the Prince, who was slight in build and looked younger than his years, remained formally Baron Renfrew. The Queen did not want him to have an inflated sense of his role as heir. Confiding to Vicky that Bertie was 'such an anxiety', she continued, 'I tremble at the thought of only three years and a half being before us – when he will be[come] of age and we can't hold him except by moral power! I try to shut my eyes to that terrible moment! He is improving very decidedly – but oh! It is the improvement of such a poor or still more idle intellect. Oh! Dear, what would happen if I were to die next winter! One shudders to think of it: it is too awful a contemplation. His journal is worse a great deal than Affie's letters. And all from laziness! Still we must hope for improvement in essentials. But the greatest improvement I fear, will never make him fit for his position.' In her disappointment in her son she had misremembered her own history. He would reach his majority at eighteen that November, and be legally of age to reign then, if necessary, without a regent. Parental control of Bertie until he was twenty-one continued only if he were prince, not king. Victoria had herself evaded a regency under her mother by her accession a mere month after her eighteenth birthday.

What the Queen did not realize was that one motive which was driving her husband to transform Bertie with unrealistic urgency into a model monarch was Albert's own intimations of mortality. He was certain that he had little time remaining to him, but confessed that to no one. Old Stockmar, once a physician, seemed to understand. Not yet forty, Albert looked like a man of sixty. His hair had receded and his side-whiskers had grown heavier. He was paunchy and pale, and always cold, a condition exacerbated by Victoria's policing of fireplaces in every room she entered to make sure they were out. Very likely hyperthyroid, which would account for her bulging eyes and her emotional outbursts, she was intolerant to heat. Wracked by worry and by insomnia, Albert suffered chronically from 'violent cramp[s] at the pit of the stomach', confiding that to Stockmar, and adding, 'I have eaten nothing all the day, to rob my stomach of the shadow of a pretext for behaving ill.' He realized that what was afflicting him was inoperable, and that his ambitions for the

future of the monarchy in a democratizing England rested uneasily on a
boy in whom he had small hopes.

In Rome, Bertie doggedly went through his imposed routine. From
England the future Cardinal Newman wrote to a friend that 'the din of
arms' and 'the rebel shout' might force the faithful to evacuate the Eternal
City. Newman suggested sardonically that the presence in Rome of 'the
little Prince of Wales was the [Pope's] guarantee that no harm just now is
likely to befall him'. The country was going through the throes of
unification. War had begun that April when Victor Emmanuel (who
ruled Piedmont from Turin but was titular King of Sardinia), emboldened by a treaty with the French emperor promising him aid, had drawn
young Emperor Franz Josef of Austria into a conflict that was certain to
cost the latter territory. Austria controlled much of north Italy, and
Napoleon III intended to help himself to the territorial spoils. The Prince
of Wales was ordered home. The Pope hurried gifts to the Hotel
d'Angleterre on 30 April – two inlaid mosaic tables, for the Prince and
for his mother. These were quietly packed with Bertie's baggage. At a farewell audience the next day, 1 May, the Pope confided to Bertie that he
worried about revolution in Rome, and the Prince's safety, but a warship,
the *Scourge*, had already been dispatched to extricate the royal party. On
2 May it weighed anchor for Gibraltar.

The hasty change in plans proved to Bertie's advantage. He noted
indiscreetly but vaguely in his journal that he enjoyed 'plenty of larking'
while in Gibraltar and in excursions inland from such ports as Malaga, as
the *Scourge* made calls on the way to Lisbon. In Portugal he had an
amiable young cousin, King Pedro V, whose father, a Coburger, had
married the late queen of Portugal. On board ship, the press reported, the
Prince acquired a passion for cigars. The merry interlude ended only
when the *Scourge* docked in England late in June. Bertie was just in time
to begin the new educational regimen his parents had planned for him.
While his family holidayed at Balmoral and Albert stalked deer, the
Prince of Wales was to remain in Edinburgh to be crammed for Oxford.
His journal of his adventures in Italy and beyond had been duly scrutinized by Victoria and Albert in segments throughout the tour, and had
already been found largely bare of detail or thought, earning Bertie the
expected admonishment. 'I am very sorry that you were not pleased with
my journal,' he apologized dutifully to his father, 'as I took great pains
with it, but I see the justice of your remarks and will try to profit by them.'

Although Bertie's intentions were always good ones, his writing betrayed a backwardness that had not dissipated as he approached his eighteenth year. On 25 August 1859 he wrote to his 'Papa' with an innocent poignancy,

> I hope you will accept my best wishes for many happy returns on your birthday. May you live to see me grow up a good son, and very grateful for all your kindness. I will try to be a better boy, and not to give Mama and you so much trouble. Very many happy returns of the day.
> I am, my dear Papa,
> Your most affectionate son,
>   Albert

In advance of the Prince, Herbert Fisher, his intended tutor in law and history at Oxford, arrived at dreary Holyrood House, the royal residence in Edinburgh, to prepare for a conference of mentors on 30 August. The Prince Consort had been planning the regimen for at least a month. 'They mean to make him work very hard at Holyrood,' the Queen reported to Vicky. With her usual want of generosity towards her heir, she added: 'He is a little grown ... but his nose and mouth are much grown also; the nose is becoming the true Coburg nose and begins to hang a little, but there remains unfortunately the want of chin which with that large nose and very large lips is not so well in profile.'* Albert was more hopeful, having decided that pure academic work in science in a country being transformed by industrial enterprises was of no use to the future king. Rather, he needed some applied knowledge relevant to the England over which he would reign. 'Dr Lyon Playfair', Albert explained to the absent Stockmar, 'is giving him lectures on chemistry in relation to manufactures, and at the close of each special course he visits the appropriate manufactory with him, so as to explain its practical application. Dr Schmitz (the Rector of the High School in Edinburgh, a German) gives him lectures on Roman History. Italian, German and French are advanced at the same time; and three or four days a week the Prince of Wales exercises with the 16th Hussars, who are stationed in the City.' But he was not permitted to accept invitations to shoot in the

---

* Nothing seemed to change about Princes of Wales and their mothers in succeeding generations. When Elizabeth II visited her infant grandson, William, the day after his birth, she commented, 'Thank goodness he hasn't got ears like his father.'

countryside, and had to endure dinners for uneasy local worthies for which he – at seventeen – was the nominal and awkward host. Aside from his personal entourage, none of whom he had chosen, he was alone. He was confined, yet highly visible, like a goldfish in a bowl. In 'A Prince at High Pressure', *Punch* (20 September 1859) commiserated, with some strained word-order and doubtful rhymes:

> Thou dear little Wales, sure the saddest of tales
> Is the tale of the studies with which they are cramming thee....
> In those poor little brains, sick of learned palaver.
> ... In Edinburgh next, thy poor noddle perplext,
> The gauntlet must [be] run of each science and study.
> Where next the boy may go to swell the farrago,
> We haven't yet heard....

Punch had learned that Oxford would follow Edinburgh to add to the 'cargo of cram', and warned against 'indulging the passion for this high-pressure fashion of Prince-training'. Yet even as the Prince of Wales was submitting to what may have seemed like three months' hard labour in solitary confinement, Albert was negotiating the terms of Bertie's high-pressure residence amid the dreaming spires. Not for the Prince, if Windsor Castle had its way, rooms with congenial undergraduates or affiliation with a venerable college. Frewin Hall, off Cornmarket, was leased for Bertie's large establishment, and £1,155 paid to the London firm of Holland & Sons for furnishing the Prince's rooms. Bruce was pro-moted to major-general and continued as the Prince's governor, and Major Teesdale remained as equerry. Yet Oxford retained mysterious powers beyond those of mere monarchs, and Albert was informed that while the Prince of Wales might live apart from other undergraduates, to be admitted to study required admission to a college. Bertie duly had Christ Church chosen for him, and began residence at Frewin Hall on 17 October, *Punch* marking the occasion on 29 October with an irreverent full-page engraving, 'The Royal Road to Learning', showing the callow young Bertie in new academic gown flanked by rows of bowing, head-bared dons.

No longer quite alone, he listened to his special course of lectures in the company of six hand-picked Christ Church undergraduates. Aside from travel, for the first time in his life he had companions of his own age, although they stood when he entered – just as undergraduates

The Royal Road to Learning: the Prince at Oxford (Punch, *October 1859*)

beyond Frewin Hall rose when the Prince of Wales (who wore a gown and the gold-tufted cap of all student noblemen in that rigidly stratified era) walked into any room, even in the Union. Albert could not have forgotten that his own happiest years, before he had been plucked from obscurity to be the Queen's consort, had been as a scholar at the University of Bonn, where, though he and his elder brother lived in rented quarters with a governor, they went to regular classes with ordinary students. Bertie's situation, however, seemed very different. Prince Ernest would only succeed his father in a tiny Saxon dukedom, and Albert, a second son, had been utterly without prospects. The Prince of Wales would be king of a mighty realm and had to remain free from undue influences while acquiring knowledge unique to his future station. Victoria could not have forgotten – she reminded Vicky of it constantly in her letters – that she was brought up with almost no interchange with children of her age, and suffered for it, yet both she and Albert continued to be anxious that the future king was insufficiently set apart. Albert reminded General Bruce on 27 October that Oxford, for the Prince, was to be, in the national interest, primarily a place of study. His life was '*a public matter*, not unconnected with the present and prospective welfare of the nation and the State.... His position and life *must* be different from that of the other undergraduates; ... his belonging to a particular college ... , which could not be avoided, has another significance from what it bears in other men's lives. He belongs to the whole University and not to Christ Church in particular, as the Prince of Wales will always belong to the whole nation.'

Bertie was duly preached at and lectured at, as planned, and he dined well, having arrived with his own chef, although he was soon warned by his father that there were many dishes 'which an experienced and prudent liver will avoid'. Again, as in Italy, he endured the dinner parties he was expected to host, this time for eminent dons and deans and visiting scholars, sometimes with no other undergraduate present. Often the only way he could be with privileged young people whose favourite reading was the *Racing Calendar* was to make an appearance at debates at the Union, which was acceptable to his mentors, then slip away with agreeable friends of the sort that Victoria and Albert would have deplored. Misunderstanding, Elizabeth Gaskell reported to an American friend, Charles Eliot Norton, that 'one of the most striking of the debates at the Union was against Church-rates, & strongly against the 39 articles. The little quiet Prince of Wales is in the thick of all these discussions, which will, one w[oul]d think, prevent his turning out a second class 1st.' He was known there, she explained, as 'Wales of Christ Church'.

Since Albert Edward was permitted the gentlemanly sport of shooting, he had another avenue of escape from his governors, and would also go out fox-hunting with the lords and gentlemen of the South Oxfordshire Hounds. Although his parents had urged him to confine his athletics to 'tennis and racquets', more gentlemanly sport could not be denied the Prince once he was there, as upper-class thinking was that the curriculum of English universities remained superior to German higher education, which forced new studies like the sciences on young gentlemen who would never need such intellectual equipment, and ignored what really counted. 'The absence of manly exercise', declared *The Times*, 'is one of the defects of the German universities, and, in spite of the erudition of his professors, the German student is, in all that regards bodily training, a far inferior animal to the Oxonian or the Cantab. Our national systems of instruction call loudly for reform,' – an unveiled reference to Albert's efforts as Chancellor of Cambridge – 'but no true patriot could wish to see the boating, the cricketing, the riding of Oxford and Cambridge banished from the precincts of learning.'

On one occasion in March 1860, finding the chase unrewarding, a fox-hunting party that included the Prince returned toward Oxford by a short-cut that brought them across the property of burly Farmer Hedges, who brooked no trespassers. Shutting his gates and brandishing a 'dung fork', he refused to let the horsemen loose until they had paid him a sovereign. One aristocratic huntsman appealed that Hedges (referred to behind his back as 'Lord Chief Justice') was detaining, among them, the future king of England. 'Prince or no Prince,' he growled, rather than begging their pardon, 'I'll have my money.' The students yielded, and the embarrassment got into the newspapers. Albert determined to have Bertie better governed.

The Prince Consort's outlook reflected his continuing struggle not only to mould his son into a role-model monarch but also to maintain a popular role for monarchy amid democratizing institutions and eroding class distinctions. Albert could not have appreciated the insight in *The Times* on Bertie's eighteenth birthday that 'He may be great without the possession of extraordinary talents, and famous without dazzling exploits.' The royal solution, while the Prince of Wales got on at Oxford despite his restrictions (and, indeed, by evading some of them), was to create a grand world stage for the future king that could be, at the same time, his open university. During Oxford's Long Vacation, Bertie was to represent the Queen in the New World.

III

The New World: Canada

1860

Victoria's refusal to venture any further from her realm than Albert's beloved Coburg, and her problem of what to do with the Prince of Wales during the Long Vacation, resulted in the major opportunity of his troubled youth. Her Canadian dominions had invited the Queen to open the new railway bridge, named after her, over the St Lawrence River at Montreal, and to lay the foundation stone of the Parliament Building at Ottawa. Symbolically, she would be presiding over the uneasy and informal union of the erstwhile French and the traditionally English provinces. (Most would finally become part of a federation in 1867.) Hostile to giving her heir anything significant to do, Victoria at first opposed Albert's suggestion to send Bertie instead. Policy, however, prevailed. Her husband's strategy to create meaningful roles for the monarchy in a democratizing era that threatened to make royalty obsolete proved persuasive. Further, the Windsor Castle system of insulating Bertie would keep him safely cloistered: he would travel with his company of governors, and do only what they instructed on the advice of his parents. Prince Alfred, now a naval cadet, would fulfil a similar function, though more briefly, when with his ship in South Africa.

The Prince of Wales, Albert explained to his brother, 'is to represent England' as well as to respond to 'the Canadian wish to show the Americans how happy, free and yet monarchical it is possible to be'. To Baron Stockmar, Albert elaborated upon his concept for modern kingship on 27 April 1860, describing initiatives that went well beyond opening charity bazaars and gracing public functions. 'Almost in the same week in which the elder brother is to open the great bridge … in Canada, the younger will lay the foundation stone for the breakwater for the harbour of Cape Town, at the other end of the world.' The events would demonstrate not only British technological superiority, but 'the useful co-operation of the Royal Family in the civilisation which England has developed and advanced'. He expected that in 'both young colonies' the royal children would be embraced with 'conscious national pride'. Elaborating on his motives at a public dinner in London in May, Albert boasted of the 'present greatness, past history', and 'future hopes' that his princely sons embodied, and 'how important and beneficent is the part given to the Royal Family of England to act in the development of these distant and rising countries, who recognise in the British Crown, and their allegiance to it, their supreme bond of union with the mother country and with each other'. Accordingly, *Punch* predicted,

> They who never saw a Prince before,
> Oh, won't they feast him and caress him!
> Waylay him, and address him. . . .

News of the forthcoming royal voyage led quickly to an invitation from President James Buchanan, former envoy to London, for the great-grandson of George III, the last American king, to visit the United States. Victoria and Albert saw in the extension of the Prince's visit a useful gesture toward better Anglo-American relations. The nations had long bickered over border disputes with Canada and over foreign trade issues, while the United States was deplored in the English press as a land of prosperous barbarians related to the sophisticated mother country only by a common language. The Queen's response, encouraged by the British Minister in Washington, Lord Lyons, was positive, but she set conditions that the Prince be received with less pomp than in Canada. Not yet nineteen, he might find his head turned by the loyal responses of the Queen's own colonists. In the US he would arrive without royal state under his subordinate title of Baron Renfrew, and he would have to lodge in hotels rather than in private residences – although an exception would later be made for the White House. The *Royal Gazette* of Newfoundland declared that the visit foreshadowed closer Canadian ties with the mother country. The colonies thereafter would be 'integral portions of the British Empire'.

On both sides of the Atlantic elaborate plans were initiated to accommodate each day of the journey. The stately, red-bearded Duke of Newcastle, Minister for the Colonies, though plagued by poor health, was placed in charge of the Prince's party. The Earl of St Germans, Steward of the Queen's Household, would be second-in-command, and the Prince's personal entourage, headed by General Bruce, would accompany them. N. A. Woods represented *The Times* and G. H. Andrews, an artist from the *Illustrated London News*, was also aboard, as was Kinahan Cornwallis, reporting for the *New York Herald*. Ordered to convey the Prince and his party, and then bring them home, was the black-funnelled battleship *Hero*, 2,800 tons and carrying ninety-one guns, to be escorted by the two-funnelled *Ariadne* and the *Flying Fish*, with its two 'leaning', cream-coloured funnels. They would leave from Plymouth on 10 July, 1860, with Bertie boarding from the royal yacht after making the first of many short speeches written for him by his father or, later, by the Duke. The Admiralty prepared to remove the guns from the cabin which the Prince was to use, and to redecorate it, but the Queen insisted that 'whatever little addition required to be made for his personal accommodation should be of the plainest kind'.

The first essay at princely speechmaking was a trial run, responding to the welcoming addresses of the Mayor and the Corporation of the Borough of Devonport. Newcastle had files of memoranda prepared by Albert on what the Prince was to say on particular occasions, with the theme of Empire to be stressed in Canada and amity in the United States. At seven the next morning the *Hero* weighed anchor, and from the paddle box of the royal yacht Albert waved goodbye to Albert Edward from his taff-rail. Fourteen miles beyond, south-west of the Eddystone Light, the waiting Channel Fleet, sails trimmed, divided into two lines to permit the *Ariadne*, *Flying Fish* and *Hero* to pass between and, in full sail, out to sea. (Steam-powered vessels prudently carried, and utilized, spreads of canvas.) It would have been difficult not to have one's head turned by the elaborate ceremony. However, despite offering his megaphoned compliments to the red-coated captain of the *Ariadne*, who bowed as it passed close, the Prince was already seasick.

Two days at sea, Albert Edward was ready to begin orientation lessons about Canada with Newcastle and Bruce, who spread out sheaves of maps and pages of historical data on the colonies, including cautionary words on the hostility between French and English colonists, and between the militantly Protestant Orangemen and everyone else. After thirteen days' sailing against strong west and north winds, the party was eager for dry land, but found little that was dry. Rain came down in torrents as they arrived in St John's, Newfoundland, at the broad mouth of the Gulf of St Lawrence, on the evening of 23 July. 'Queen's weather' had long referred to the fine days that usually graced Victoria's public occasions, but the Prince of Wales was to see little of it in Canada and became known as the 'Raining Prince'.

Landing was put off until noon the next day, when the Prince disembarked in his Army uniform and was driven to a reception at Government House, where, despite the small population of the remote fishing station, fourteen welcoming speeches awaited him. Albert Edward responded with well-rehearsed assurances of his mother's 'deep concern' with 'this interesting portion of her dominions', a distinction acknowledging Newfoundland as separate from Canada, which it did not join until 1949. To his parents he wrote, as charged to do, and clearly in part from his briefing material, 'The Governor, who is a rather odd man and about 75, received me very kindly.... St John's is a very picturesque seaport town, and its cod fisheries are its staple produce.' In the same mail packet to the Queen was a letter from Newcastle approving of the Prince's conduct thus far, while Bruce wrote, with mixed feelings, 'H.R.H. acquitted himself admirably, and seems pleased with himself.' A possible reason was that the Prince, without asking his governors, had given a local photographer leave to take pictures. According to the *Art Journal*, 'So soon as the man had got his tools in working order, somebody would run between the lines and the platform, and thus spoil the picture. The special constables were frantic in their efforts to prevent this, and spoilt more [pictures] than anyone else. Women crushed in the crowd were continually making their escape,' and the chaos was 'irritating everybody except His Royal Highness'.

Apart from the large black Newfoundland dog which Bertie received as a gift in St John's (he named it 'Cabot' after the discoverer of the island), the pattern for each visit was much the same whatever the venue in Canada. A reception at which local worthies were introduced would be followed by a carriage ride round the area, then by a private dinner. (Instructions from Windsor Castle, not always practicable, were that the Prince was not to attend formal dinners, perhaps to prevent excesses in eating and drinking.) In the evenings he would be guest at a ball, the first of them at spacious Colonial House in St John's, where, in colonel's uniform, he danced with local ladies – after the leading dowager – regardless of rank (even the wives and daughters of fishermen), until half-past two. Newfoundland was too isolated to trot out a population experienced in the ways of the world, the *New York Herald*'s reporter telegraphed. 'The Prince very affably and good-naturedly corrected some of the blundering dancers, and every now and then called out the different figures of the dance.... He whirled through waltzes, polkas, and quadrilles. While he danced he was repeatedly cheered, and he very properly took a new partner whenever he stood up to dance.' In contrast, the correspondent for the *Illustrated London News* saw only snobbery in the Prince's entourage, for 'the noblemen who attended His Royal Highness did not mingle in the festivities or the dance'. Unlike the adaptable Bertie, they had much to get used to. Newcastle, in his scarlet uniform with the silver facings of a lord-lieutenant, looked too elegant for his raw surroundings.

The wife of the Archdeacon of St John's wrote admiringly of Bertie to relatives in England, 'God bless his pretty face and send him a good wife!' And in the words of a gushing lady – imagined for the occasion – who realized the Prince would go on in time to the United States, *Punch* commented 'If it really *is* the law that he mustn't form a marriage with a nice good *English* girl, I don't know, but I'd like him to bring home a born Yankee rather than be forced for some ridiculous *State* reasons, to give his Royal hand to one of those *Small Germans*, who are doubtless looking out for it.'

That dynastic concern had been public since mid-1858, when it emerged that King Leopold of the Belgians, uncle to both the Queen and Albert, had written to Victoria (although Bertie was then only sixteen) that he had drawn up a list of seven Protestant, and thus eligible, princesses for the Prince of Wales, of whom six were German and the other – only thirteen and much too young to marry – was Alexandra of Schleswig-Holstein-Sonderburg-Glucksburg, whose mother was a first cousin of the childless Frederick VII of Denmark. Her mother's marriage to the Danish Prince Christian had established Alexandra's father as heir to the throne of Denmark.

The royal party intended to visit the Maritime Provinces from the *Hero*, then steam up the broad St Lawrence to Quebec City. There, since the river narrowed, they were to take a chartered steamer to Montreal, then a smaller one up the arc of the Ottawa River to the city of Ottawa, then down again to Kingston, at the eastern end of Lake Ontario. Sailing westward along the lakeshore, they would stop at the larger towns *en route* to Toronto, using carriages and rail to go inland. From Toronto they would round the lower peninsula of Ontario by rail, reaching Sarnia and Windsor in the extreme south-west of the province. Since from that point westwards the rest of Canada was virtually uninhabited, they would then leave British America for Detroit and the United States. It would be an exhausting itinerary, even for a youth of eighteen.

On 30 July, the Prince arrived at Halifax, Nova Scotia, after a stop en route at Prince Edward Island, named after the Queen's father. In Halifax, an integral part of Canada, the Wales mania began in earnest. Tradesmen began deluging him with gifts, including an ebony cane for use at funerals (Victorian society loved the panoply of elaborate obsequies), hoping to identify their products with the Prince. Everywhere he visited, boots, coats, umbrellas, souvenir plates and cups were embellished with his name or face. One could not, a journalist contended, sit down to a meal in a restaurant without having His Royal Highness's portrait loom from beneath the gravy. The *Herald*'s reporter, with an expenses-be-damned budget, transmitted long extracts from Revelations and the Gospels by telegraph in order to monopolize the wire while writing his daily report on the royal doings.

Loyal addresses and cheers followed everywhere, the Prince accepting each in his formulaic responses, as he did the sermon at the Anglican cathedral, 'with much gratification'. And everywhere he travelled, the streets and squares were bridged by arches festooned with garlands and bunting, evergreen branches, Prince of Wales plumes and royal images, while at night illuminations and fireworks lit the sky, though they were sometimes overwhelmed by deluges of rain. From every hamlet, correspondents telegraphed details of the tour: natural wonders seen, salutes given, addresses delivered and acknowledged, pious yet patriotic sermons preached, commemorative verses declaimed, 'God Save the Queen' sung (often with supplementary verses referring to the Prince), hunting and fishing camps visited, regional industries inspected, exhibitions sampled, balls attended and the Prince's fortunate partners identified, always beginning with the spouse of the leading gentleman – a mayoress or the local equivalent. Whatever the welcome, the Prince would respond affably in what *Punch* would deplore as bureaucratic 'slipslop', that it was 'with no ordinary feelings of gratification and interest' that he found himself wherever the efficient Duke of Newcastle had penned in the location.

The dramatic cliffs of Quebec were reached by the *Hero* on Saturday 18 August. Newcastle had anticipated problems in the French – and Catholic – city, and at the suggestion of the Queen and Albert the Duke hoped to alleviate some friction by having the Prince of Wales confer knighthoods on the Speakers of the Houses of Parliament of both Lower and Upper Canada. Henry Smith, Jr, had been the bearer of the invitation to the Queen the year before to open the bridge at Montreal to be named after her, and he had made himself unpopular at home by courting a knighthood for his pains. Since none had materialized, both honours were delicious surprises, with Newcastle intimating His Highness's pleasure and asking the recipients, in turn, to kneel, after which the Prince unsheathed his ceremonial sword and announced, touching both shoulders of each, 'Rise, Sir Narcisse Belleau', and then 'Rise, Sir Henry Smith'. They were the first knighthoods conferred in Canada.

For Bertie it was equally a moment to savour. Permitted to do nothing at home, he was playing sovereign abroad. And to the subjects of the

The Hero *landing the Prince of Wales at Quebec. Sketch by G. H. Andrews for the* Illustrated London News, *1860*

sovereign it was no mere game: he was the embodiment of their fealty to the source of their civilization, their living link to the mother country. Although only eighteen, he was to receive, as surrogate for the Queen, an honorary degree from the Catholic, and French-speaking, Laval University, and address local bishops. In exploring regional sensitivities, the Duke had learned that their desire was to be addressed as 'My Lords', but since that would have provoked resentment in Protestant Upper Canada, Newcastle had instructed the Prince to refer to them as 'Gentlemen'. Resentment came instead from the bishops, already peeved by Newcastle's insistence, as the party arrived in Quebec, that the French tricolor – which had no lawful business there – be removed from the towers of the cathedral. Despite efforts to placate all religious factions, harmony proved impossible. Protestant extremists spread canards that the Prince had participated in Catholic ceremonies (had he not also visited the Pope twice, in Rome?), and that the Host had been unlawfully carried before him. Further, the Ursuline nuns, a teaching order, had greeted him warmly, the younger ladies curtseying together and one, accompanying herself on the harp, singing a song of welcome to the 'Royal Guest' and 'rising star'.

At the usual ball, this time with unlimited champagne, the Prince had danced in twenty-two of the twenty-four dances, from galop to polka to valse, beginning with thirty-one-year-old Hortense Cartier, wife of the much older Premier. Bertie even survived a collision during one dance that sent him to the floor, 'his beautiful partner rolling over him. He quickly picked himself up and continued ...,' remaining happily until half-past four. The champagne may have got to Dr Henry Wentworth Acland, Professor of Medicine at Oxford and the physician for the entourage. At the ball a splendidly attired gentleman whom he should have recognized drew him into conversation about the Prince, and Acland offered some impolitic remarks. Several days later the Prince came down to breakfast flourishing a copy of the *Herald*. 'Acland,' he said, with a smile, 'I see that you think I am very amiable, but I have not the brains of my brother.'

A chartered steamer took the party further up the St Lawrence to Montreal on 24 August, where, the next day, miserable fog and drizzle having given way to sun, Bertie dedicated the Victoria Tubular Bridge, nearly two miles in length, by spreading mortar on the last slab with a silver trowel, then tapping at the last rivet with a wooden mallet. It was a ceremony he had seen his father preside over many times before. Indoors, at an exhibition building modelled on the much larger Crystal Palace, the Fine Arts Association offered him a Canadian picture from its collection, and he selected *The Prince's Squadron at Anchor at Gaspé Basin*. His choice evidenced authentic diplomacy: its artist, Charles Jones Way, was President of the Montreal Art Association. (For the rest of his life the Prince would acquire pictures recalling his travels.)

For Bertie the most significant event in Montreal was his acquisition of a companion nearly his own age. Lord Edward Hinchinbrooke, twenty and heir to the 7th Earl of Sandwich, had been one of the Eton boys sent to Windsor as playmate. Happening to be in Montreal, he attached himself to the Prince's party, General Bruce writing to the Queen cautiously that he was 'a very good companion' for Bertie. (Victoria would agree that he was not 'slang'.) Soon another young acquaintance of the Prince was to join the entourage, Charles George Cornwallis Eliot, a son of the Earl of St Germans. Hinchinbrooke went along with the Prince to see the brilliant illuminations in the city, which remained crowded with celebrants until two on Sunday morning. To protect walkers, the streets were free – by mayoral proclamation – of vehicles. Not realizing that, Bertie set off in his carriage, incognito, and was driven down Notre Dame Street until his horses were halted by constables and turned back. When the coachman protested vainly that he had the Prince of Wales inside, people milling about in the streets tried to detach the carriage and draw it themselves. The coachman whipped his horses away.

Later in the morning, at the Anglican cathedral, another crowd began cheering the Prince as he exited, but his handlers, concerned about Sabbatarian sensitivities to anything resembling joy, let it be known that His Royal Highness was not in favour of such demonstrations on a Sunday. Some of the more rigid Irish Protestants, however, felt aggrieved at his slight of their Temperance Society demonstration, an augury of Orange Lodges extremism that was soon to create further exasperation and have the royal party eager to cross the border into the United States. Exhausted from the pace of his progresses, Bertie needed his quiet Sundays to recover. The following Tuesday he fell asleep over his dinner.

The next stage in the itinerary, after Iroquois and Algonquin demonstrations of lacrosse and war dances on a cricket pitch in incessant rain, was a journey by a white-painted steamer, the *Kingston*, up the

Ottawa River, past villages bedecked with welcoming arches and flags and cheering crowds, to the city of Ottawa – only unprepossessing Bytown until 1854. Adorned with triumphal arches betokening its ambitions to be the capital of a united Canada, it greeted the young man who was to lay the cornerstone for the future Parliament. The welcoming address and reply were hurried through in the relentless rain, which ceased the next morning, 1 September, happily just prior to the placement of the coffin-like white marble block, which had been suspended from a pulley and lowered to have mortar spread with another silver trowel. 'Your Royal Highness,' the Governer-General declared, 'the stone is now laid.'

After an elaborate luncheon, the royal party proceeded to the Chaudière Falls to view the slides over which logs passed en route to the Ottawa River. Enclosed for safety by a box-like embankment was a timber barge constructed by the Clerk of Works for the occasion. The top-hatted and frock-coated young companions of the Prince, lords and mere honourables, climbed aboard with him for a merry ride down the rapids that, had Victoria and Albert known, would have been forbidden as too risky for a future king. The young men hurtled down, losing not a hat, while the assiduous G. H. Andrews drew the scene for an issue of the *Illustrated London News* which arrived at Windsor too late to matter.

Leaving Ottawa, the Duke of Newcastle braced himself for Protestant extremist trouble. The portents had already appeared in 'Orange' sectors of Montreal. Militant Orangemen (named after William III of Orange) had formed a secret society in 1795 to defend Protestantism in Ireland, and enthusiasts had crossed the Atlantic, their vigorous indulgence in banners, bombast and marching still a staple of the movement. When approaching Kingston by steamer on 4 September, the Duke wrote later to the militant Mayor of the town, the royal entourage 'found an arch covered with Orange decorations, and an organized body of many hundreds, wearing the insignia of their Order, with numerous flags; a band and every accompaniment which characterized such processions'. The marchers, numbering about two thousand, brazenly shook sectarian banners and shouted provocative slogans. Newcastle went ashore alone to confer with the Mayor, warning that the Prince could not debark in a partisan atmosphere that would affront Roman Catholics, and requested the Orangemen 'to reconsider their resolve', which, after drinking steadily through the night hours, had become more rigid. Belligerently,

The Prince of Wales on a timber-slide near Ottawa on his Canadian tour
(Illustrated London News)

the town band blared 'Boyne Water', and then, to suggest royal pro-French (and Roman Catholic) bias, '*La Marseillaise*'.

'What is the sacrifice I asked the Orangemen to make?' Newcastle scolded the Mayor, O. S. Strange, 'Merely to abstain from displaying, in the presence of a young Prince of 19 years of age, – the heir to a sceptre which rules over millions of every form of Christianity, – symbols of [a] religious and political organization which are notoriously offensive to the members of another creed.'

To jeers and catcalls from the dock, the royal party remained on board, and the next day bypassed Kingston for Belleville, where church bells rang out gaily; however from the shore nine combative arches zealously decorated with Orange symbols and slogans were clearly visible. Firebrands from Kingston had hurried 200 bandsmen and marchers by train to Belleville after an 'indignation meeting' alleged royal slights to Protestants in Quebec. Discovering that the disturbances had spread, the Duke told the Mayor, who had boarded, that the Prince greatly regretted that he would not be visiting Belleville, and ordered the steamer on to the lakefront town of Cobourg. Trying to force an encounter with the

Prince somewhere, the determined Orangemen hurriedly returned to the railway line, but company officials, now alerted, delayed the train at intermediate stations. By the time the irate militants arrived in Cobourg the royal party had come and gone.

Cobourg showed no signs of Orange activity. The Prince's party went ashore, and by eleven a ball was under way. His Royal Highness danced first with the daughter of the Mayor, then with fourteen other ladies, the music not stopping until a quarter-to four. By steamer and railway the Prince's progress continued west while the royal party seized naps at intervals between stops.

At Port Hope the party passed under a rough log arch – arches were omnipresent in Canada – on which red-shirted lumberjacks stood. An enthusiast running alongside the Prince's carriage stuck his arm into the open window to grasp Bertie's hand, and dozens also seeking handshakes swarmed around the carriages and the labouring horses. Women threw flowers. At Rice Lake the Mississauga tribe of Indians, led by their Chief, who claimed to be one hundred years old, welcomed the eighteen-year-old son of the 'Great Mother'. Later, at Sarnia, on the Canadian side of the St Clair River opposite Port Huron in Michigan, the Prince would be greeted by two hundred Ojibwa (Chippewa) Indians from the Manitoulla Islands, 'real red savages ... adorned with hawks' feathers and squirrels' tails', one of whom, Kanwagashi, or Great Bear of the North, announced, according to his interpreter, 'My heart is glad that the Queen sent her eldest son to see her Indian subjects'. He welcomed their 'Great Brother'. The Prince replied that he would never forget his red brethren, and gave each a medal with a bas-relief of his mother.

In Toronto, then much less populous than Montreal, the Prince on 7 September received the usual addresses 'with lively satisfaction' and saw there (in Newcastle's remarks prepared for him) 'the promise of greatness ... in a youthful country'. An Orange confrontation was averted when an arch which extremists refused to dismantle was permitted if shorn of all sectarian adornments. An equestrian image alleged to be that of the Prince of Wales remained, although Newcastle scoffed, 'Why, they've King William there!' Reluctantly, the party proceeded, taking an evasive route. When Newcastle returned with St Germans to ensure that Orange Billy was also removed, the pair were jostled in the street by die-hards. The Mayor and Corporation of Toronto offered an apology. The Prime Minister and the Queen would endorse Newcastle's hard line. It was fortunate, Viscount Palmerston would write, that the Prince 'had with him a good Head like yours'.

The weekend was wet. Five thousand damp Toronto schoolchildren would sing only two verses of the National Anthem, with added lines about 'Victoria's son and heir' who had no title 'More proud, more dear', before scurrying to shelter. After the usual levées, tours and a ball, the ceremonial planting of a maple tree in the new Botanical Gardens in 'disagreeable' weather which earned Bertie 'a handsome silver spade', and required listening to the most lugubrious sermon thus far, the Prince attended the Royal Canadian Yacht Club's regatta. Taking a cab afterward, the Prince drove to an indoor racket court, threw off his coat, and attempted to play, but when curious youths who climbed on the glass roof to see him broke through and showered His Royal Highness with debris, he left in disgust. The price of celebrity was high.

Although the rain continued to fall in torrents, on 11 September he laid the foundation stone for a statue of his royal mother, collecting yet another silver trowel. According to press accounts the opening of Queen's Park afterward 'was received by the half-drowned people with shouts of enthusiasm'. And the ball in Toronto's reduced version of the Crystal Palace, at which the Prince did not arrive until a quarter-to eleven, was less than a success because the hastily erected building was uncomfortably cold and draughty for ladies in low-cut gowns and literally blue noses.

The Prince's party proceeded by rail to Guelph and then London, where, when he returned to his carriage after responding to an address, a 'rude brute' (according to a press description) lifted off Bertie's hat and said, 'Let's have a look at you.' His Royal Highness retook his hat. Canada seemed the raw edge of civilization.

Returning across the Ontario peninsula to Fort Erie, Niagara Falls and points east, the weary travellers (Newcastle was ill and St Germans regularly went ahead to make advance arrangements) finally encountered good weather. At Niagara Falls a torchlight procession greeted the Prince at the station, and a few hours later he saw the 1,800-foot span of the Canadian Falls illuminated by two hundred bright blue Bengal lights, an intense firework. On 15 September, from the suspension bridge below the cataract, Bertie watched Charles Blondin, an intrepid acrobat of thirty-six from Lyons, cross on a tightrope above the falls. Blondin had hurried there from New York City, where – for a fee

– he had just exhibited his prowess at a monster outdoor political meeting. Defying gravity and a strong wind, perched on a rope 2,000 feet long and 200 feet high, he made awestruck onlookers temporarily forget the forthcoming presidential election in which the country walked a perilous tightrope between accommodation with slavery, and civil war.

As the Prince was to be above politics when he crossed into the United States, his managers eschewed such discussion, but Albert Edward could not help overhearing it. The year before, Blondin had crossed over the Falls for the first time, and was now pondering heart-stopping variations – using a wheelbarrow, carrying a companion, going blindfolded, frying an egg on a portable stove.

There to see him attempt the Falls again was young Salomon de Rothschild, of the Paris branch of the banking dynasty. The third son of the shrewd baron James, who directed the French operations of the brothers, he had been, at twenty-five, seconded to August Belmont in New York, the firm's American representative. 'In spite of the repeated objection of the Prince,' Rothschild wrote to his family, 'Blondin carried his agent [Harry Colcord] on his back the entire length of the rope. He then made the dangerous [return] crossing on stilts, to the great horror of the young man, who was made sick by it. Nevertheless, several pure-blooded Yankees were dissatisfied and wanted their money back because some practical joker had spread the rumour through the crowd that Blondin would carry the Prince of Wales. The naïve spectators felt they had been cheated.'

The Prince, in black morning coat and tan top hat, had been asked only in jest – after Blondin had put on his usual high-wire performance, pretending to stumble, and turning somersaults. When Bertie firmly rejected the acrobat's teasing offer, Blondin had turned to stilts (anchored by hooks) for his return, leaving the throng breathless. Reports that the Prince had accepted, but was prevented from crossing the Falls by his timid entourage, were an invention, but with General Bruce he did go to Blondin's enclosure with a purse of gold coins estimated by the press at £100. Then he donned a hooded oilskin coat to sail to the base of the Falls in the *Maid of the Mist* – still the name for its many tourist-bearing successors.

Summing up the progress through the Canadas, the *New York Herald*'s reporter wrote with unusual frankness, 'Never has the Prince seemed more manly or in better spirits.' At the ball 'he whispered soft nothings to the ladies as he passed them in the dance, directed them how to go right, & shook his finger at those who mixed [up] the figures.... In short [he] was the life of the party. During the evening ... he and the Duke of Newcastle enquired for a pretty American lady, Miss B. of Natchez, whom they met at Niagara Falls and with whom the Prince wished to dance. His Royal Highness looks as if he might have a very susceptible nature, and has already yielded to several twinges in the region of his midriff.' Fortunately for Bertie, Victoria and Albert did not read the *New York Herald*.

On 20 September, after seven demanding weeks in Canada, the party prepared to leave British soil. Having recrossed Lower Ontario courtesy, once more, of the Great Western Railway, their final Canadian social event was a Citizens' Ball in Hamilton, in a hastily constructed hall. More like a bar-room than a ballroom, its walls were blotched with workmen's tobacco juice, and a sickening odour allegedly emanating from the gaslights was soon traced to a sewer under the floorboards. The Prince arrived at eleven, and persevered in the stench until a quarter-to three, when the 600 guests stubbornly still present loudly cheered his departure – perhaps so that they, too, could escape.

Bertie was more than ready to leave Canada. In many ways his journey had been the occasion for affirmation of pride in the links to the mother country, but the people seemed to him backward, and riven by sectarian differences. They were more colonials than Canadians. His exit point, ironically, was a town named Windsor, from which he was to cross to a former colony, and masquerade transparently as just another tourist from England.

IV

Celebrity: the Prince in the United States

1860

THE FIRST ROYAL to visit the United States disembarked in the early evening of 20 September from the Detroit and Milwaukee ferry *Windsor*. Accompanying him from Canada were such Yankee dignitaries as the Governor of Michigan and the Mayor of Detroit. A crowd of thirty thousand was at the dock, some of the curious surging aboard the steamer and spilling members of the official welcoming party into the river. Spectators unwilling to let the Prince recede into memory also crossed loyally from Canada, and a boy from Port Huron, Thomas Alva Edison, recalled scrapping with young invaders from Sarnia, across the water. The London *Saturday Review* warned of over-valuing American response to the Prince, as the United States was 'England without its upper classes, and hence there is nothing to moderate the enthusiasm of an American mob, or to prevent it from defeating its own object by exaggeration and extravagance'. Possibly proving the point, at Detroit a mile-long crowd of boats, festooned with bright lanterns, and fireworks in the harbour, greeted Baron Renfrew – as he was now described. Parading fire and military companies could not get close to the dock because of the thronging crowds. Crushed bonnets and flattened crinolines were the penalty of a close look. Somehow the Prince's carriages traversed the brightly illuminated streets to his hotel, Russell House. An observer quoted in the local press remarked that enthusiasm could not have been greater had George Washington returned to life.

The next morning, 21 September, Baron Renfrew was to tour in an open barouche drawn by four white horses en route to the railway station for his train to Chicago, but the crowds made progress almost impossible. As Albert Edward stood in his carriage with Mayor Bull and bowed his thanks at intervals, the milling Detroit crowds cheered, but let him see little of their city. A special train furnished by the Michigan Central Railroad (the Prince's entourage paid five cents per mile per person throughout the American tour) took them to Chicago, where at 7.30 that evening they arrived to even larger throngs. Bertie's entourage managed to push their way through to Richmond House, their hotel, on the muddy and unpaved streets typical of burgeoning Chicago. The city's mushrooming to more than 100,000 citizens (from 5,000 in 1836) had not erased its raw, frontier ambience.

Officially greeting him was Mayor 'Long John' Wentworth, who dwarfed the slight Prince, five-feet four and nearly fully grown. 'It is believed', a local newsman joked, 'the Prince shook some of [the Mayor's] hand and addressed a few complimentary remarks to his lower waistcoat button.' While Newcastle and Lyons insisted on the Prince's transparent incognito, local worthies cheerfully addressed him as 'Prince'. Happy crowds, possibly inspired by the easy access to drink, sang beneath his hotel windows for much of the night, and Bertie complained in the morning of headache and exhaustion. Newcastle, nevertheless, wrote to the Queen that he was pleased by the enthusiastic reception, as it would 'very much regulate the proceedings in other cities'.

On Saturday the Prince paid his brief public respects to the bustling city, visiting a factory and a grain elevator and public buildings that were to be obliterated in a great fire a decade later. Then he was spirited off by rail to Dwight, a village of 295 souls south of Joliet, for a respite from celebrity status. There he was to stay in the farmhouse of a well-to-do landowner, James Clinton Spencer, for several days of shooting quail, plover and prairie hens on his largely unspoiled 960 acres. (Two other houses on Spencer's property accommodated overflow members of the entourage.) Although it was sunset when they arrived, Bertie, eager to fire at something that moved, called for a gun, and brought down a screech-owl.

A Sunday intervened, and at the tiny Presbyterian church in Dwight the royal party was preached at by Pastor Philander D. Young. On returning they found that a special locomotive had arrived from Chicago with dispatches from the Queen and from the Colonial Office. While a prairie gale blew under a brilliant sun, they got through the remainder of a

The Prince (left) and his party dining outdoors near James Spencer's house in Dwight, Illinois, 1860. Sketch in the Illinois State Historical Library

Presbyterian Sunday by reading and answering mail, and by retiring early for a 5.30 start for shooting the next morning.

Pushing through the undulating acres of tall Indian corn on the Monday, Bertie in one of the hunting parties bagged eleven prairie hens – which, except for their larger size, resembled English grouse. The next day they left at six for Stuart's Grove, thirty miles away and even more expansive. Despite a thunderstorm followed by a spectacular orange prairie fire, Bertie claimed some rabbits, quail and plover, and in the evening at Spencer's lodge both Newcastle and the Prince selected game to be stuffed and sent home as mementos of the West. Over coffee they examined a cartoon in the newly arrived *Harpers' Weekly* in which Albert Edward, returned to Windsor, presents a pretty Yankee bride to the Queen. 'I'll send it to my mother!' said the Prince.

On Wednesday 26 September the party left Dwight for St Louis with real regret, despite the dreary country evenings. The Duke of Newcastle, however, was relieved to move on. Under a blazing sun on the second day of shooting the group had stopped at a farmhouse to seek refreshment, and as they made their way up the path the farmer emerged to welcome them in. 'But not you, Newcastle,' he shouted, recognizing the large, red-bearded Duke. 'I have been a tenant of yours, and have sworn that you shall never set foot on my land!' Embarrassed and confused, the entire entourage hurried off.

At Alton, Illinois, where they arrived by train from Dwight Station, the party boarded a steamer southward on the Mississippi for St Louis, disembarking at six in the evening on 26 September and taking carriages to Barnum's Hotel. The Missouri State Agricultural Fair was in progress, and the next morning Mayor Filley escorted Baron Renfrew's suite to the fair amid what the *New York Herald* reporter described as the 'turbulent irregularity of a mob'. After being escorted around the arena in their open carriages, with the Prince acknowledging the cheers and the waving newspapers and handkerchiefs by raising his tall hat, he was taken about the city, where businesses, banks and the post office were all shuttered for the holiday. But one entrepreneur, the *Herald* observed, was all business. The Prince 'was followed all along the route by a smart Yankee in an advertising waggon, covered with bills eulogising his clothing store'.

Once-popular American novelist Winston Churchill described the St Louis scene in his *The Crisis* (1901), including an account of what the press called the 'forty thousand dollar ball'. Everywhere the Prince went, presidential election turmoil – focused upon whether the nation could survive half-slave, half-free – overshadowed everything but his visit. St Louis was his first venture into slave territory, where, according to the Missouri perspective of *The Crisis*, there was 'the dread possibility of the negro-worshipper Lincoln being elected the very next month'. In the novel Bertie stops at a fair booth presided over by the pretty Miss Virginia Carvel, and he is smitten, remaining longer than his anxious governors would like, his thumbs thrust into his yellow afternoon waistcoat, exchanging light retorts with the young lady. After repeated signals from his handlers to continue on, Lord Renfrew apologizes to Virginia 'that he had already remained too long, thus depriving the booth of the custom it otherwise should have had'. And he is escorted to a buffet luncheon of 'slices of beef, mutton, and buffalo tongue, … great jugs of lager beer, rolls of bread, and plates of a sort of cabbage cut into thin shreds, raw and mixed with vinegar – American coleslaw – where everyone eats with gusto 'by the aid of nature's forks'.

At the expensive and exclusive ball, Miss Carvel dances with the Prince 'by Special Appointment', wearing a Paris gown rare in that city which, not long before, was only a Mississippi dock for river barges; and her jealous local admirer is 'sure that his Royal Highness made that particular dance longer than the others'. But the steamer *City of Alton* which brought him to St Louis returns the next day, and by river and rail in both fiction and fact, on 29 September he proceeded toward Cincinnati, arriving belatedly at two in the morning on the 30th. A freight train had broken down at Vincennes, Indiana, delaying all rail traffic, but crowds at stations along the line had waited unremittingly into the night.

The next day the Prince's retinue had luncheon at the ornate Cincinnati mansion of the proprietor of the rail line. Another ball was scheduled in Cincinnati, at Pike's Opera House, where, as the Sabbath intervened, the Prince danced only until midnight and the crowd left disappointed. Whether or not Sabbatarians had any influence in Ohio, they did in England, and Newcastle was cautious. (All that Kinahan Cornwallis would concede was, 'The less I say about it the better it will please those concerned.') But 'Baron Renfrew' heaved two bouquets toward excited young ladies on departing, and materialized dutifully in the morning with his party at St John's Church to hear Bishop McIlvain preach the sermon.

The next day, 1 October, in a splendid new carriage furnished by the Pennsylvania Railroad, they continued on to Pittsburgh, 'a long and fatiguing railway journey', he wrote to Windsor Castle, 'devoid of any interest'. The area was choked with black industrial smoke. Also, boredom was setting it. One could be sated even with being lionized.

Arrangements, too, were breaking down, as disorganization seemed endemic to democracy. The Prince was yet again to be driven around the local sights in a carriage, but the Mayor had ordered the militia and bands preceding the Prince to keep to a slow march, which enabled thousands of the curious to overwhelm the open carriage, peering intrusively and attempting to shake his hand. The morning after, the entourage steamed out of Pittsburgh while a band played what had become his signature song in Canada, 'Never will I forget you' ('*Jamais je ne t'oublierai*'), heard now at almost every arrival and departure. His Royal Highness bowed courteously but with evident relief.

As the train climbed the Alleghenies, amid forests now brilliant in autumnal red and yellow and orange, a glowing sun was sinking. At the village of Gallitzin, high in the Pennsylvania hills, the train stopped and the Prince and several of his suite climbed daringly upon the locomotive and secured themselves against the handrails and catwalks. A bright moon had risen. The train continued more slowly now, down the valley of the

Juniata, which glistened like molten silver, while the trees in the moonlight and shadow stood out sharply. Belching fire and smoke, the locomotive continued eastward into Altoona, round the sweeping Horseshoe Curve. At the station the young men clambered down and, to Newcastle's relief, returned to their carriage. At Harrisburg, where the party remained overnight, Bertie was received by the Governor. At their hotel, *Herald* reporter Cornwallis awoke to find a large, noisy crowd clustered below the window of his room. He drew the curtain and looked out. 'There he is!' people exclaimed deliriously. The Prince was in the *next* room, asleep.

At twenty-past nine a thousand people crowded the platform to watch the authentic Albert Edward transfer southward on the Northern Central Railroad en route to Baltimore and Washington. Arriving in Baltimore, the *New York Times* reported, 'the August Prince ... seemed fagged out, and heartily tired of everything but sleep'. That alternative was not available. 'Nearly the entire populace' of Baltimore, a local newspaper reported, 'cheered the Prince frantically'. A band played 'God Save the Queen' as he was greeted by the Mayor and City Council and then escorted to the Camden Depot of the Baltimore and Ohio Railroad for the Washington train. At the capital he was welcomed by the Secretary of State, Lewis Cass. By special dispensation from his mother he was again, briefly, His Royal Highness, and was even permitted by Victoria to stay at the White House as guest of the President.*

Washington's streets were crowded as the Prince was escorted in President Buchanan's carriages to 1600 Pennsylvania Avenue, where Bertie was given the second-best bedroom suite, that of the bachelor President's White House hostess, his attractive niece Harriet Lane. She had been with Buchanan in the same capacity when he was in London as American Minister, and remembered the Prince as a boy of twelve or thirteen. To his mother, Bertie wrote, innocently, 'I thought Miss Lane a particularly nice person, and very pretty.' The cautious Buchanan asked Harriet to remove her portrait from her bedroom and put it temporarily in the White House library. (In John Updike's 1974 play *Buchanan Dying*, the President lewdly warns Harriet, 'Take your portrait from the Prince's bedroom, lest it drive his left hand to frenzy.')

* In January 1870, nearly ten years later, the Prince's twenty-year-old brother Arthur visited Washington, and President Ulysses S. Grant was invited to meet him at the Navy Yard. As a matter of protocol he refused to go to meet the Prince; rather, he invited Arthur to the White House for dinner.

Miss Lane, thirty and still unmarried (she was to wed after her White House years), was rumoured in Washington circles to be a potential bride for Bertie, but such patriotic speculation was unrealistic. She was a decade his senior, and did not feature in the matchmaking stratagems of the Queen. Armed with gifts, the Prince presented her uncle with portraits of the Queen and Prince Consort by Franz Xavier Winterhalter, painter to the courts of Europe, and was shown about the White House grounds while a hundred of the élite of Washington society milled about them, and gawkers crowded at the gate railings. The next morning the royal entourage visited the unfinished Capitol, burned by the British during the war of 1812 and its dome still incomplete. (Later he saw the Washington Monument, also unfinished, which was not capped until 1885.) He was escorted through such public edifices as the Patent Office, and wrote home, anticipating a later Prince of Wales, 'We might easily take some hints for our own buildings which are so very bad', and he made some drawings of them to take home.

At noon, the Prince was guest of honour at a hand-shaking reception, and later, at a grand dinner that represented the limits of the dour Buchanan's interest in festivity. A Royal again, rather than mere Baron Renfrew, and precluded by protocol from grasping each hand thrust at him, Albert Edward stood awkwardly to Buchanan's right as each person was named, and inclined his head slightly at each introduction.

The strait-laced President permitted no dancing in the White House. Although he also countenanced no card games, he made an exception for the Prince, as he recalled that such after-dinner recreation was expected by the Queen at Windsor. As guests departed, Buchanan discovered, after the royal entourage had been accommodated, that all White House beds including his own were occupied. He resorted to a sofa.

The next day, before another grand dinner, this time for the diplomatic corps in full dress, the royal party toured other Federal buildings, and then Miss Lane took her royal guest to Mrs Smith's School, an academy for young ladies in which she had an interest. For two hours he played ten-pins with Harriet and the girls. (As a result of her honour, in July 1861 Mrs Smith would sail to London and ask, unsuccessfully, to visit the Queen.) At half-past six, while a drizzling rain fell, the resident ambassadors and ministers sat down to dinner with the Prince. Then they gathered under the rear portico to watch fireworks.

On 5 October, a Friday, embarking on the Treasury Department's steam cutter *Harriet Lane*, the royal party, accompanied by the President, his Cabinet, and diplomats with their ladies, proceeded downstream on the Potomac to Mount Vernon, once the home of George Washington. Departing, they paid their respects at the General's grave, where the Prince placed a wreath and planted a tree marking the occasion. (The Prince also pocketed some horse chestnuts to plant at Windsor.) An artist fancifully recreated the scene. The slight young man stands bareheaded

*'The Prince of Wales has come over the wave – And planted a tree
upon Washington's grave.' Contemporary American engraving, 1860.
Collection of the author*

before the gated tomb while a black slave behind him sets the chestnut sapling into the ground, and before Bertie rises the spectre of Washington. The episode paralleled his paying respects, in Paris, at the tomb of Napoleon, but to his parents he wrote, without betraying any such emotion, that although Mount Vernon was 'a much revered spot by the Americans', the house was 'unfortunately, in very bad repair and rapidly falling into decay'.

Returning to the cutter, passengers found a splendid luncheon awaiting them on deck, and the atmosphere modified to enliven the return cruise. Since it was not the White House, Buchanan permitted a band to play, and Bertie danced the first number with the President's niece. As he seated her afterwards he was heard to whisper, 'Now, Miss Lane, who must I dance with next?' A *Punch* cartoon showed the Prince being introduced to an attractive young woman in ball gown and being advised, 'Now, my boy! There's your pretty cousin Columbia – you don't get such a partner as that every day!'

Salutes were fired from the Arsenal as the ship docked in Washington, and dinner for the diplomatic corps that evening was at the residence of the British Minister, Lord Lyons.

Only two months passed before a poem appeared anonymously in the press, 'Before the Grave of Washington', describing the 'stately, silent group' that gathered round the founder's 'holy dust':

> 'Twas gracefully and nobly done,
> A royal tribute to the free,
> Who, Prince, will long remember thee....

The next year the poetry competition for undergraduates at Cambridge University set 'The Prince of Wales at the Tomb of Washington' as subject. The winner was Frederick W. H. Myers, then eighteen and later a poet and essayist. His verses closed:

> Warrior and Prince, their former feud forgot,
> Have found a meeting here.

The unliterary prince evoked literary effusions everywhere he went. Harriet Beecher Stowe of *Uncle Tom's Cabin* fame described him as 'Young England' in the *Boston Independent*, Oliver Wendell Holmes penned a lyric, and Edmund Clarence Stedman in New York published a satirical volume in verse, *The Prince's Ball*, which went through four printings in less than four weeks.

The next morning the President and his niece accompanied the royal party along the Potomac by cutter to a rail link on the Virginia side to Richmond. After saying his farewells, Buchanan wrote to the Queen that her son 'has passed through a long ordeal for a person of his years, and his conduct throughout has been such as became his age and station.... In our domestic circle he won all hearts. His free and ingenuous intercourse with myself evinced both a kind heart and a good understanding. I shall ever cherish the warmest wishes for his welfare.'

When the Prince's itinerary was being worked out, a southern faction had prevailed upon Lord Lyons to arrange for a visit to a slave-holding state and showplace plantations. The British public, it was hoped, might concede that a chattel-based society was, at worst, merely paternalistic. As the journey involved only a weekend, including the obligatory church service wherever they were on the Sunday, going by rail to Richmond seemed safe enough, but taking no chances, the Prince's hosts arranged to cancel a large slave auction. This caused local resentment, the crowds milling about the Prince's hotel appearing openly hostile. (The *Herald* dismissed the unruliness as 'exuberance of good feeling'.) The next morning, as the Prince was being steered from church toward Haxall's Plantation, to tour the grounds from proprietor's mansion to slave quarters, Newcastle, recognizing that they were about to be politically exploited, politely refused. Rather, they went on to the less significant elements of the itinerary – the offices of the Mayor of Richmond and the Governor of Virginia, and the grave of President James Monroe. At nine on Monday morning the Prince's party returned northward to meet the chartered steamer *Powhatan*, then boarded a train for Philadelphia via Baltimore. At the wharf on the Potomac an Irish dockhand exclaimed to the Prince, 'May luck go wid you. And bedad, I only wish I'd an old shoe to fling afther yez, for it's not the likes of yez as come here every day.'

Philadelphia struck Bertie as 'the prettiest town I have seen in the United States'. In its red bricks and low buildings it resembled an English city, and he could at first stroll its streets unobtrusively because its inhabitants were busy celebrating the election for Governor. The posters and bonfires and torchlight processions were, happily, not for him. The Republican Unionist candidate, Andrew Curtin of remote Bellefonte in the centre of the state, appeared to have won, a foreshadowing of the turbulent presidential election and the aspirations of a minority Republican, the little-known Abraham Lincoln of Illinois. At the Academy of Music, nevertheless, where Friedrich Flotow's *Martha* was the bill, emotions were less Republican. The orchestra played 'God Save the Queen' as he entered, and the audience rose to his feet. A star at seventeen, Adelina Patti sang. She had already performed for the Prince in Montreal, and he wrote to his mother about Patti's 'not strong' but 'very pretty voice'. He also visited the newly modernized Eastern State Penitentiary, pride of the city, where he spoke to one of its most distinguished inmates, ex-Judge Vandersmith, convicted of forgery and corruption and with only eighteen months of a long sentence served. 'Talk away, Prince,' he said. 'There's time enough. I'm here for twenty years.' The Prince also toured the celebrated Girard College, an endowed school for orphans. There, asked to plant a tree, he had the help of a gardener who told Bertie that he had marched in Queen Victoria's coronation procession in 1838. At an asylum for the insane, a 'lunatic' danced a celebratory jig, and at a gravelly race course on the edge of broad Fairmount Park the Prince smoked a cigar while waiting for Rosa Bonheur (named after the famous French painter of horses) to begin – and win – a mile trotting race in one minute and forty-seven and a quarter seconds.

Accompanied by the local British Consul and General Bruce, the Prince and several younger members of the party, including Hinchinbrooke and Eliot, went to the German Club House on 12th Street, where they rolled ten-pins until midnight, the Prince, in his shirtsleeves, drawing on a sherry cooler. In the visitors book he signed himself as 'Albert Edward, London'. Presaging a later hazard to celebrities, a woman in black accosted him as he returned to the Continental Hotel on 9th and Chestnut Streets, followed by Lord Lyons and the Consul. 'Be you the Prince? Be you the Prince?' she badgered him as he tried to hurry up the stairs through 'another noble army of starers'. 'Yes, madam, I am,' he confessed, and she turned and exclaimed, rushing off, 'I'm happy! I'm happy! I've seen him, and was bound to touch him!' Everywhere apart from in Washington, where he slept in the White House, he was also the object of adoring trophy hunters. According to an observer, R. J. de Cordova, enthusiasts had already

> Torn his bed-clothes to strips, – every fool keeping one,
> To remember the linen the Prince slept upon.

They have stolen his gloves, and purloined his cravat;
Even scraped a souvenir from the nap of his hat.
In short, they have followed him, hustled and shoved him,
To convince him more fully how dearly they loved him.

In Boston, later, where he would have his hair trimmed, the barber would sell alleged locks of the Prince's hair.

At Perth Amboy, New Jersey, on 11 October, the *Harriet Lane* awaited the Prince's special train to ferry the party across the bay to New York, where the grandest reception in the New World was assembling. On board, General Winfield Scott, hero of the war with Mexico, headed the city's welcoming committee. Salutes were fired as the cutter entered the harbour, where at Castle Garden Mayor Fernando Wood received the Prince, who answered the welcoming address with his expectation that the people's hospitality would 'be worthy of the great city of New York'. It was indeed.

For the procession up Broadway in an open barouche, accompanied by 6,000 militia, His Royal Highness was hurried into a house near the wharf to don his colonel's uniform. During the pause, the 12th Regiment band gave a spirited rendition of 'God Save the Queen'. As the smartly clad troops proceeded at a walking pace, the Prince may not have been aware that behind each unit trotted a ragged black man with water pail and ladle to service the marchers, evidence that not all racial inequalities were Southern. The Prince, however, was distracted by the delirious throngs, estimated at 300,000, who crowded sidewalks, windows and roofs, and perched atop lamp-posts, trees and parked carriages. Banners welcomed 'Albert Edward', 'Lord Renfrew', and 'Victoria's Royal Son'. He was deluged with flowers. 'I never dreamed we would be received as we were,' he wrote to his mother. *The Times*'s correspondent reported to London 'an ovation such as has seldom been offered to any monarch in ancient or modern times'. Writing to the Queen's Private Secretary, Sir Charles Phipps, General Bruce described the reception in New York as beyond exaggeration, and the tour in general, 'with the exception of the Orange difficulty, ... one continual triumph'. (Richmond went quietly unmentioned.) The primary reason, he claimed, loyally, was widespread veneration for Victoria, 'but it is also true that ... the Prince of Wales has so comported himself as to turn it to the fullest account and to gain for himself no small share of interest and attraction. He has undergone no slight trial, and his patience, temper and good breeding have been severely taxed.'

Darkness fell before the marchers reached 23rd Street and the white marble façade of the Fifth Avenue Hotel. There the Prince bowed his acknowledgements from a balcony off his suite of rooms and then crawled into bed, exhausted.

The Grand Ball at the Academy of Music on 12 October was the emotional climax of the visit. Tickets, however expensive in order to defray costs, were restricted to 2,000 of the most socially eligible, as the fashion for expansive crinolines limited available space for dancing. Another 3,000 crashed through the barriers before the Prince arrived at 10.30, and by the time His Royal Highness opened the ball, to a fanfare, with the elderly and stout wife of Governor Morgan on his arm, the overburdened temporary floor was under strain. After several dances the crack of

THE NEXT DANCE!

*The Prince of Wales being introduced (by Mr Punch) to a dancing partner on his American tour (*Punch, *20 October 1860)*

splintering wood frightened some off the platform, but not enough, and the floor sagged, abruptly sinking three feet. Carpenters were called, and two areas were roped off.

Lawyer George Templeton Strong, of what he identified as the 'Prince-Catching Committee', detected 'a general sense of failure and calamity', but the Prince was conducted into the supper room, and others crowded in, while twenty carpenters 'were working for their lives'. The band continued to play, and guests promenaded, gossiped and engaged in opportunistic flirtations. Within two hours the dancers were again on the floor, the Prince determinedly going through his tally of eminent and bejewelled ladies. One of the younger women with whom he danced, Mrs Julia Field, 'noticed he was wearing white kid gloves that hung on his hands like wrappers – many sizes too big – and His Royal Highness explained that they had been sent to him anonymously, accompanied by a letter purporting to come from a lady who claimed that she was young and pretty, and was going to the ball, and declared that if she saw he was not wearing her gloves she would get close to him and shoot herself. Hence these enormous coverings on the Royal hands.' Vicariously, the unknown lady – not one of the élite on his crowded card – had danced intimately with the Prince of Wales.

A renewed outbreak of hammering interrupted the festivities: one of the repair crew had been inadvertently sealed under the new floor. While the frantic carpenter was being freed, and the Prince waited for his next partner, Mrs Camilla Hoyt, to push through the mob, an enterprising local bookbinder bustled up. He had a young woman on his arm and importuned, 'The lady with whom Your Highness was to dance doesn't seem ready. Allow me to introduce my daughter.' The Prince evaded the pair and danced steadfastly through his list until 5 a.m.

Another near-catastrophe was caused by Lord Hinchinbrooke's sudden nosebleed, stanched by some of the special towels on hand from the Fifth Avenue Hotel, embroidered with the Prince's 'Wales' plumes and royal '*Ich dien*' motto, which had been placed for him in a special dressing room. A snooping reporter chanced on the bloody towels in a basin and guessed wildly at an attempted assassination. Without success, General Bruce explained the prosaic reality. Even when Lord St Germans corroborated the story, the newspaperman would not be deprived of his sensational copy for the next morning's paper until the Prince was produced unscathed.

Despite little sleep, Bertie endured local tours which included P. T. Barnum's Museum, the Astor (now New York Public) Library, the Institution for the Deaf and Dumb, and Mathew B. Brady's photographic studio in 10th Street, where the camera recorded him and the thirteen in his suite, including its informal members, Eliot and Hinchinbrooke. Crowds clustered about their carriages, one ebullient Irishman, obviously untutored in American electoral law, waving his hat and shouting, 'Bedad! And come back here four years from now and we'll run you for President!'

After dark, from his hotel balcony, the Prince viewed an enormous torchlight procession of 5,000 men of the City Fire Brigade with their gaudily decorated and illuminated fire engines, some pulled by several men, some by horses, some steam-driven. The parade extended for several miles. 'For a fireman,' young Salomon de Rothschild explained to his family in France, 'his company's engine is everything; ... he spends everything he can to decorate it with jewels, painting, and gold and silver ornaments.' It was akin, he went on, to an expensive mistress. 'So these machines were covered with Venetian lamps, flowers, flags, torches; some were lit up by Bengal fire ... or by gas lights. When a company passed in front of the Prince's balcony, each fireman shot off fireworks which lighted up over an enormous distance the vast throng of people who were pushing forward to see this splendid sight.'

'This is for me! All for me!' Bertie exclaimed delightedly as the firemen, in black helmets, red flannel shirts and black pants with white belts, paraded before him, company by company, preceded by drum-pounding bandsmen. Then they vanished into the night. The extravaganza had indeed been for him – but also for the proud firemen themselves.

Sunday in New York meant Divine Service at Trinity Church on Fifth Avenue, from which, Strong reported, the Prince, as soon as the service was over, 'got up, looked warily down the aisle to see whether the coast was clear, and then pegged out of church as fast as his legs would carry him.... He showed much practical sense thereby.' (For the occasion, the chimes of the church had been tuned to 'God Save the Queen', and the choir habited in surplices.) Later he bade goodbye to his hosts and hostesses at a dinner at Consul-General Archibald's on 14th Street, and prepared for departure the next morning to West Point, up the Hudson on the waiting *Harriet Lane*. When expenses were later tallied, the New

York 'Four Hundred' (the local term for the cream of society) found a balance remaining. Each member who had contributed one hundred dollars was repaid $30.65.

Summing up the royal progress from New York, Harriet Beecher Stowe wrote fulsomely in the New York *Independent* that the Prince was to Americans 'an embodiment, in boy's form, of a glorious related nation' – that the England of Shakespeare and Milton had come 'modestly walking by our doors in the form of a boy just in the fresh morning of his days'. The Prince was to Stowe 'the proud remembrance of centuries of united Anglo-Saxon history'.

Old General Winfield Scott was the Prince's guide at the Military Academy, where, under a cold sun, the cadets paraded for the Prince, who was again attired as a colonel. Few of the marchers, however long their careers, would ever reach the rank the Prince had been gifted at nineteen. On leaving West Point to lusty cheers, the entourage proceeded to Albany on the river steamer *Daniel Drew*. There, while regiments of foot and cavalry cleared a path through the crowds, they went by carriage to the Congress Hall Hotel. On the morning of 17 October they entrained for Boston in a special 'State' car and, escorted by miles of grey, and blue and white, militia, they proceeded to fashionable Revere House. The next day was an official holiday in the city although the holiday atmosphere required no decree. Massachusetts Senator Charles Sumner wrote to London friend Evelyn Denison, then Speaker of the House of Commons, of the overwhelming welcome, 'I doubt if any description can give you an adequate idea of its extent.... At every station on the railway there was an immense crowd, headed by the local authorities, while our national flags were blended together. I remarked to Dr Acland that it seemed as if a young heir long absent was returning to take possession.'

There was, as elsewhere, a gala ball – this time for three thousand, at the Boston Theatre. Its interior was illuminated by a thousand gaslights. Trees, flowers and a waterfall decorated the hall; at the proscenium was a curtain resembling a huge American flag, and scene painters had created a façade of Windsor Castle. First on the Prince's dance card at ten was to be the young second wife of Mayor Frederic Lincoln, Emily Caroline. But before the band could even strike up 'God Save the Queen' a member of the ball committee, in his eagerness to meet the Prince, knocked over a large vase of flowers. The contents spilled over the guest of honour, again attired in his colonel's uniform with the blue ribbon of the Garter conspicuous across his breast. By now Bertie could cope with small catastrophes, and shrugged off the mishap. The music began, and, for the first time, most of the sodden Prince's partners were younger women, the daughters, granddaughters and grand-nieces of local worthies. One, tantalizingly unidentified by Kinahan Cornwallis of the *Herald,* was 'the most lovely girl I ever saw'.

At one in the morning, after seventeen waltzes, polkas, quadrilles and a lancers (a whirling quadrille first introduced in 1838), a tired Prince, pressed still by the curious, made his way into supper, but not before confiding enthusiastically to one pretty partner, 'I don't have half enough of this sort of thing [at home], you know. I hope to come to America again some time, without my nurses.'

At his hotel early the next day a bootmaker fitted the Prince and several in his party with newly fashionable, waterproof alligator-skin boots, to be delivered before they departed from Boston. He was photographed at the Revere by Jeremiah Gurney, who had missed his opportunity in New York (because Newcastle had selected Brady) and had pursued the royal party to Boston. The Prince met with the local intelligentsia, including Longfellow, Emerson, Oliver Wendell Holmes, and Mrs Stowe – a favourite of the Queen. On horseback he reviewed the Massachusetts Militia on Boston Common. Longfellow had alerted his friend Hannah Davie, 'It would be a thousand pities if such a true and loyal Briton, as you are, should not have a sight of your Prince!' He advised her that she would have an excellent opportunity to see him when he passed down Beacon Street to review troops on the Common, 'and you from a balcony can wave your handkerchief and say in your heart "God bless him"'.

That same Thursday, schoolchildren on holiday sang to him 'Our Father's Land', to the tune of 'God Save the Queen' and written for the occasion by Dr Holmes, who had first seen Victoria in London in the early 1830s as a young princess. It bade the Deity, in loving care,

> Guard thou her kingdom's heir,
> Guide all his ways.
> Thine arm his shelter be
> From harm by land and sea;
> Bid storm and dangers flee,
> Prolong his days!

At Bunker Hill on Friday the Prince viewed the hallowed rise where American rebels had first confronted his great-grandfather's Redcoats. In morning coat with royal purple gloves and cravat he visited Harvard ('no chance for ladies,' Longfellow warned Hannah Davie), where the senior class filed before him in stove-pipe hats and black coats, accompanied by the Germania Band which had played for the Prince in Canada. At the Harvard Library President Felton, accompanied by four former Presidents and distinguished members of the Corporation and Faculty, presented the Prince with an elegantly bound copy of ex-President Josiah Quincy's history of the college. He planted two trees. A Boston paper declared, 'He is fully qualified to shine even in Republican America.' But was it a Republican America that had taken to him, or an America now more nostalgic than it believed itself to be for the tradition and the pageantry it had rejected in its revolution?

In a special train of three carriages (which at noon on 20 October stopped briefly at Portsmouth, New Hampshire, where he bowed from the rear platform), Albert Edward reached Portland, Maine, at a quarter-to two. He would have one day to rest before embarking. A royal squadron of five ships awaited to convey his entourage to England.

The farewell party included the Governors of both Upper and Lower Canada, and of the state of Maine, and members of their Cabinets. Early on 22 October a last procession began, moving toward the Great Eastern Wharves, so christened when Portland was to be the cable link under the sea from England. A photographer took a picture of the stylish barouche drawn by four matching bays in which the Prince, in a tall beaver hat, leans forward as if into the camera. He was now comfortable in the camera's eye, one of the first celebrities whom photography had almost endlessly certified. Cannons boomed and people cheered; then they looked on in unfeigned sadness as, in a fresh breeze, the royal barge pushed off at a quarter-past three. The band on the *Hero* struck up 'God Save the Queen' as the Royal Ensign was run up to the maintop.

Carrying with him a number of limbs from American trees to be made into souvenir canes, and two grey squirrels and a mud turtle as gifts for his mother, the Prince embarked for home in his three-ship convoy, escorted out by two vessels of the British North Atlantic Squadron, the *Nile* and *Styx*. He was still recrossing the Atlantic on 9 November when he turned nineteen.

V

Higher (and Lower) Education

1860–1861

ALBERT EDWARD RETURNED to England to find his parents' perception of him unchanged. While storms still buffeted his ship on the
Atlantic his royal mother, informed almost daily of the Prince's celebrity
reception in reports still arriving from Lord Newcastle and General Bruce
by mail packet, gave Bertie grudging praise in a letter to Vicky in
Germany. 'He was immensely popular,' she conceded, 'and really
deserves the highest praise, which should be given him all the more as he
was never spared any reproof.' (She assumed that Newcastle and Bruce
had been as critical with him as his parents were at home.)

The press also heaped encomiums on the Prince's handlers rather than
on their charge. *The Saturday Review* allowed that 'By universal consent
he has discharged with unerring tact the pleasant social duties of the
street, the reception-hall, and the ball-room.' Albert Edward had to be
cautioned in the aftermath that 'even Royal life' was not a continual
exposure to 'stupid starers and loud huzza[h]s', and that English kings
did not 'exercise a political power proportionate to the deference which
attends their persons'. The individual to be congratulated on the success
of the tour, the column went on, the one upon whom the 'graver
responsibilities of the journey have necessarily fallen', was not the Prince,
but the Duke of Newcastle, who displayed 'dignity and judgment', and
whose 'Royal answers to loyal addresses' were 'put in the mouth of the
Prince'. Newcastle would be offered the Garter by Victoria. Dogged by
ill-fortune and ill-health, a wayward wife from whom he was divorced,
and embarrassingly unruly children, the Duke was considered by some

friends as the epitome of bad luck, and they were relieved that he had made it back with an unscathed entourage. 'I am so glad the Prince of Wales has arrived,' Emily Eden confided. 'I always thought they would have to put Jonah, Duke of Newcastle, overboard before the ship could make any way.' The windswept voyage had taken twenty-six days. It was, the Queen understated to Vicky on 17 November, 'very tedious. Last Thursday they were actually farther from England than the Tuesday before!! and a very rolling sea all the time.'

Bertie was still aboard when *Punch* published a cartoon in its issue of 10 November imagining a highly undeferential Prince, top-hatted although indoors, his feet on the fireplace fender and a cigar in his mouth, telling his indignant royal father in what was meant to be brazen Americanese, 'Now, sir-ee, if you'll liquor up and settle down, I'll tell you all about my travels.'

The journey, including the long voyages, had indeed been a learning experience. Although the Prince may have begun his progress only as a ventriloquist's dummy, he did not conclude it that way. When the *Hero*, *Ariadne*, *Nile*, *Flying Fish* and *Styx* had weighed anchor in Portland's spacious harbour to a 21-gun royal salute from Fort Preble, Albert Edward knew that he had accomplished something remarkable. He had not stumbled and he had acted with princely poise. He had encountered people from every station in life and not been found wanting, and he had taken well the waves of acclaim that were beyond his youthful due. By the Prince's birthday on 9 November, storms and adverse winds had pushed the *Hero* days behind schedule; it was running low on coal and even on rations. But to celebrate the day, the midshipmen turned out the marines from their gun room to set up tables for a birthday dinner, and the ship's band played 'The Roast Beef of Old England' although there was only salt beef left. Officers were sharing sea stories and laughter with the Prince and General Bruce when an icy swell rushed into the stern port, which had been left open, drenching the company. The seawater would not drain off, as the scuppers had been plugged for the party. The Prince was more delighted than dismayed. It was almost the last unscheduled moment he would experience for a year.

Punch had juxtaposed its irreverent cartoon of Bertie and his father, in which there would be a great deal more truth than anyone yet knew, with a serious verse in which a prideful United States asked 'John Bull' to

LATEST FROM AMERICA.

H.R.H. JUNIOR (TO H.R.H. SENIOR). "NOW, SIR-REE, IF YOU'LL LIQUOR UP AND SETTLE DOWN, I'LL TELL
YOU ALL ABOUT MY TRAVELS."

The Prince was sailing home, as a celebrity, from America, and Punch
*(10 November 1860) was prescient about his altered relations
with his father, Prince Albert*

… take back your Prince
From our superior nation,
Where he has been, for some time since,
Completin' education.

Windsor Castle, however, saw the need for resuming his interrupted schooling, and within four days of Albert Edward's return he was ordered to complete his term at Oxford in order to ready himself for the next term at Trinity College, Cambridge, as previously arranged. There was little time remaining. He went hunting with rich, raffish 'swells' from the Bullingdon Club, smoked a great deal (this was reported to Windsor Castle, whereupon Albert complained to General Bruce), and just before Christmas Bertie donned his Guards uniform once more to review the Oxford University Volunteers. *The Times* observed that the Prince had shown Americans 'a bit of the true stock …, what they have all come from'. *The Illustrated London News* deplored that 'As yet no occasion has arisen for giving him a personal welcome', and hoped for 'a public appearance' that would make England's gratitude known. Although King Leopold had written to Victoria, 'Bertie got well through his truly tremendous tour', the Queen and Albert had no such intention. Writing to her eldest daughter in Berlin, Victoria allowed that although Bertie was 'decidedly improved', and 'tells us a great deal of what he has seen', his complexion was 'a little yellow and sallow'. Reluctantly, he was given 'permission to smoke … only on condition he does not do so in public or in the house'. The Queen remained eager to marry him off, despite his youth, and urged Vicky to inspect available German candidates. From her photograph sent by Vicky, the Danish princess, Alexandra, was 'indeed lovely' – but given German and Danish territorial disputes over Schleswig and Holstein, she was an unwelcome choice: 'What a pity she is who she is!' Although Bertie knew of the matchmaking efforts he was not consulted.

The Prince arrived in Cambridge at 4 o'clock in the afternoon on 18 January 1861. The weather, General Bruce reported to Prince Albert, gave Bertie's new residence 'a cold and comfortless appearance but I hope that His Royal Highness will soon become reconciled to his new abode. The arrangements generally are satisfactory.' Bertie's matriculation (the formal enrolment of a student) took place the next morning. 'The Vice-Chancellor and the Heads of Houses', Bruce wrote, 'waited on the

Prince, after which the Mayor and Corporation [each] presented a short address. We then drove to the Vice-Chancellor's where H.R.H. was duly entered as a member of the University.'

Preparations for his stay had been under way for nearly a year. Dr Henry Philpott of Cambridge had been directed to find a residence for the royal student, and reported in March 1860 that Madingley Hall, four miles from the city, was 'in every respect well suited'. Lady King, who occupied it, was in financial difficulty. The building was spacious and the grounds 'remarkably pretty'. A rambling, redbrick, turreted edifice built in the sixteenth century and remodelled a century later, it had a large bedroom suite to be refurnished for the Prince of Wales and, advantageously for him, a tower stairway in an adjacent corner that would expedite covert exits and re-entrances. Charles Phipps, his Private Secretary, replied that the Prince was 'a little afraid of the distance', but General Bruce was 'less disposed to consider this an objection'.

While Bruce was pleased to have Bertie caged in the country, Dr William Whewell, Master of Trinity, realizing that the Prince of Wales would have to canter to college on a horse or be ferried in a phaeton, offered to bring him into closer contact with undergraduate life by making further rooms available in the Master's Lodge. There, Natty Rothschild, eldest son of banker Lionel de Rothschild, discovered, 'the different Regius professors come and lecture to him'. The Prince was 'not allowed to take any notes but has to write the lectures when he gets back to Madingley'. In theory this was the manner in which Albert Edward was to be educated.

The regimen at Oxford had been even more stultifying. Goldwin Smith, his history tutor, would open a text and stand by silently while the Prince attempted to read the book, Smith turning the pages. He made no effort to lecture, or to explain what the Prince of Wales was reading. 'I'm sure I bored him,' Smith accurately surmised. Cambridge was an improvement. The novelist, historian and Christian Socialist Charles Kingsley was a tutor at Trinity. Bertie visited Kingsley's house twice a week for a class in modern history, based on a syllabus prepared by Prince Albert, which a dozen other selected undergraduates eagerly attended. Beginning with the ouster of James II and the reign of William III (and Mary), Kingsley went on to George IV, encompassing such themes as Divine Right, the concept of national debt, the French Revolution, and the growth of Empire. Once each week the Prince came from Madingley for a private tutorial, Kingsley hoping, he recalled, to instil some 'sound literal principles' into 'that jolly boy'. The Queen wrote to Vicky that Bertie had 'taken to [Kingsley] very much'. To Bertie she complained, seeking any trivial reason to find fault with his behaviour, that he had 'got into the habit of sitting quite bent, on one side, or lolling on the table.... This dear child will NOT do for *any* person in your position.... I feel quite *pained* at what has the effect of ill breeding or nonchalance.' He replied dutifully that he was 'thankful' for the advice and would work at improving his posture.

Parental pettiness and the rigidity of the Oxford experience were both still fresh, and resented, a fact that General Bruce recognized. Without consulting Windsor, he became in practice far more flexible, although it took some time for Bertie to realize as much. Bruce, however, had his orders, and when specifically directed had to carry them out. Once he was warned that the Prince was neither at Madingley nor observed in college, and might have slipped away to London. He had indeed, and when met on the platform by the stationmaster, with a royal emissary waiting outside in a carriage (it was the new age of telegraphy), Bertie shrewdly instructed the coachman to convey him to Exeter Hall. The venerable meeting place in the Strand had been the site of his father's first speech in London – an attack on the slave trade – shortly after his marriage in 1840. No more righteous venue existed in England. Sabbatarians, teetotallers and even Quakers met there. Where the Prince had really intended to go is not known.

'I fancy', Natty told his parents, 'the little spirit he has is quite broken, as his remarks are commonplace and very slow.... He is excessively fond of the chase but Windsor does not approve of the national sport and allows him but one horse and does not even find horse flesh for his equerries. He is very fond of riddles and strong cigars and will I suppose eventually settle down into a well disciplined German Prince with all the narrow views of his father's family. He is excessively polite and that is certainly his redeeming quality. If he followed the bent of his own inclination, it strikes me he would take to gambling and certainly keep away from the law lectures he is obliged to go to now.' The self-assurance acquired in Canada and the US appeared to be fading.

From the start Bertie did his best to keep his father – Chancellor of Cambridge since 1847 – away, writing reassuring letters suggesting that arrangements according to Papa's plans were working well. He reported hosting a dinner party at which the Master and the Vice-Chancellor were guests, and also Albert's friend Dr Adam Sedgwick, Woodwardian Professor of Geology who, at seventy-six, seemed to Bertie 'very much aged'. The Queen and Prince Consort had recently seen a revival of Abraham Cowley's pre-Cromwell comedy *Cutter of Coleman Street*, about which Bertie attempted some humour on his parents: 'Cowley's play, I can quite imagine, must be a very original production & must resemble Mr Meyer's jokes, which generally leave out the point.' (Meyer was Albert's new German librarian.)

Albert, nevertheless, did visit on occasion, although busy with Victoria's affairs and his own aches and forebodings. The Queen's mother (Albert's aunt), ill early in 1861, died in March, and Victoria was seized by grief as well as by remorse, for she had kept the once-difficult Duchess of Kent at a distance. The Queen's mourning became so excessive that Albert feared for her sanity while conducting much of her business. Civil war had erupted in the US, and there were difficulties with France as well. The Queen's chief problem was with her Prime Minister, Viscount Palmerston, who paid as little attention as he could to royal prerogatives, while the Prince Consort insisted that she (and he) be informed, and consulted. Still, Albert found time to be at Cambridge on university affairs as well as to see Bertie, who had to cope with being a celebrity while attempting also to be as ordinary a student (of the nobleman category) as it was possible to be.

Solicitor Arthur J. Munby wrote of seeing the Prince that May at Parker's Piece at a military review, the 'Devil's Own' (the Inns of Court battalion) having come from the city to join the University unit: 'The Prince of Wales was on the field, in plain clothes, ... and was much cheered by the crowd as he rode away.' The next day, 19 May, was Scarlet Day, a sea of dress gowns in scarlet and pink, and purple and gold (the noblemen). While Munby was awaiting the recital of Grace at dinner in Trinity, where his brother Joseph was an undergraduate, he realized who the youth standing at his side was: 'a sudden likeness to his mother struck me: it was the Prince of Wales.... The full underlip, receding chin, and prominent eyes, are Brunswick all over.... He spoke to the dons he knew & shook hands; and was treated with respect, but no ceremonial whatever.... Presently the Master [Whewell] came up, his bearish old face warped into a courtly grin; and shook hands with the Prince, and led him to his own right hand, after himself taking part in the Grace. Two boys of the Prince's age – the Duke of S[t] Albans (who is strangely like Charles II) and Lord Pollington, were present: both far inferior in vigour & good looks to the Prince.'

Natty Rothschild wrote to his parents that May that he had seen the Prince Consort attending a lecture in the Senate House with his son. Albert had come up after reading press accounts that 'Wales' had been 'upset' from his punt into the Cam, not renowned for its cleanliness. 'Yesterday,' Natty explained, 'he [the Prince] went out in a tub with St Albans, Bourke, Sutton Weed & Fletcher and gratified the majority of his companions by throwing St Albans into the muddiest and dirtiest part of the river.... I must say I should have liked to have seen His Grace swimming about among the carcasses of dead dogs, etc.'

The young Duke of St Albans was among Bertie's titled cronies, and his family seemed to sense opportunity in the connection. Charles Beauclerk, the first Duke of St Albans, was the illegitimate son of Charles II by actress Nell Gwyn. At the University Races, Natty wrote, the Prince of Wales had 'scarecrow' duty, which resulted in their being left alone by proctors alert for infractions of the rules. A punt ('tub') which caught up with another could bump it out of competition. Crewmen surviving elimination would identify themselves by breaking off branches from willows overhanging the Cam and sticking them in their hair or their collars as 'scarecrows'. The Prince as a highly visible 'scarecrow' deflected discipline. The winners, Natty reported, included St Albans: 'I acted as judge and handicapper and was very pleased with the results.' Afterwards he went to the Master's Lodge, where 'I found assembled the party from Madingley, the [dowager] Duchess of St Albans, her [younger] son and daughter, L[or]d Falkland, the Beresford Hughes, the Vice Chancellor and Mrs Neville and a good many more. The other undergraduates besides myself were St Albans, Ld J. Hervey and Bourke.'

For the Rothschilds it was a social breakthrough. Oxford did not yet allow Jews to matriculate, and Natty, only the second in his family at Cambridge (after his uncle Mayer), had become a friend of the future king. Although Natty resented the unearned privileges he saw in practice all around him at Cambridge, he himself had become part of an exclusive circle. 'I cannot yet make out', he confessed to his parents, 'why noblemen and their sons ... can take their degree after seven terms and have no Little Go [the second-year examination toward the BA] to pass.* Both noblemen and fellow Commoners should be done away with, but I am afraid these things will never take place.' Later in the term, he described 'a grand Gala' on Whitsunday, at which 'the Dons appear in their scarlet robes, and the Prince of Wales and the [other undergraduate] Noblemen in blue and gold gowns. A stranger coming down here would take all the world for maniacs.'

The St Albans clan were invited to the Master's Lodge for dinner at 7.45, remaining afterward to talk about horses or to play whist. It seemed a special occasion for, unusually, young ladies were present. Bertie's crony, the young Duke, had a lively and attractive sister, Lady Diana Beauclerk, who possessed the same royal connection and was ostensibly trotted out for the benefit of the Prince of Wales as if grand dynastic considerations were of no consequence to the Queen. Earlier in the day the Duchess and Lady Diana, with her brother and the Prince and a crowd of curious undergraduates who merely tagged along, 'went down the river to Byron's Pool.... Lady Di shocked her mother by smoking one of the Prince's cigarettes.'

Later at the Lodge, 'the Prince sat between Lady Affleck and Lady Diana and the whole time at dinner he teased Lady Diana about her brother. After dinner the rooms upstairs began to fill and the guests played and sang and talked.' The atmosphere of cautious gentility was too much for Natty (now a regular attender at such gatherings). Guests with titles and degrees made for a dull evening, and he endured them impatiently in order to be within the Prince's orbit. 'The music and the company not being compatible with my tastes,' he confessed, 'I escaped at an early hour unnoticed.'

At other times the older dignitaries would leave early. Natty was the Prince's partner at whist on one such evening, and won twelve shillings and sixpence. 'We ought to have won three times as much,' confided the budding banker, 'but His Royal Highness threw away the game.' He was not much better at tennis or cricket, but improved as a horseman despite pennypinching at Windsor Castle, which allowed him only to ride 'old' and inexpensive Comus. 'No wonder that he gets so many falls and is

---

* Honours in the Little Go required knowledge of one of the Gospels in Greek, prescribed Latin and Greek texts, William Paley's pious *Evidences of Christianity*, the first three books of Euclid as well as the fourth and sixth books, elementary algebra and mechanics. Few aristocrats would have succeeded in the Little Go.

never up; someone ought to speak to the [Royal] Master of the Horse about it.'

On occasion the Prince was permitted to have his friends at Madingley without dons and clerics casting their shadow – for a lunch or dinner, or for billiards, or to make up a cricket eleven. ('I expect I shall have a fine leather hunt and a duck's egg,' Natty wrote pessimistically before one match.) Most dinners were full affairs, peopled by masters, professors, ministers, and a few outnumbered undergraduates. A special event was the journey to Cambridge by rail of Bertie's ten-year-old brother Prince Arthur. It rained the entire weekend, ruling out a look through the telescope at the Observatory, but the boy had lunch at Trinity, visited the great Chapel, and mingled with gowned undergraduates. Once he left, 'Papa' was to arrive, and in a letter to the Queen, Bertie professed himself happy in the expectation.

Albert arrived with further plans for the Prince. During the Long Vacation, which began late in May, Bertie would, finally, have the military experience he craved. With the civil war in America threatening to spill over into Canada, troops were being readied to bolster the thin contingents across the Atlantic. General Bruce had warned Windsor of 'the temptations and unprofitable companionship' that faced young subalterns, but Bertie had been promised an opportunity to train with the Grenadier Guards. He had resented his unearned and elevated commission, and craved the very camaraderie with young officers that Bruce feared. Through the Duke of Cambridge, the Army commander who, but for his being the Queen's cousin, would have been nowhere near Whitehall, Prince Albert Edward was ordered to ten weeks' duty with a battalion of the Grenadier Guards at the Curragh Camp in Kildare, west of Dublin. There he was to learn, by stages, 'the duties of every grade from ensign upwards'. By the end of this stay he was expected to have the competence to command a battalion and to 'manoeuvre a Brigade in the field'.

Wildly unrealistic though his assignment was, he was expected to conduct his training on the Oxbridge model. 'Having regard to his position both as a Prince of the Blood and Heir to the Throne', he was debarred from living in barracks with his brother officers and given private quarters. Twice a week he was to host dinner parties for senior officers – arranged for by his governors – and twice weekly he could dine in his own Regimental Mess. Once weekly he might accept an invitation to be guest of honour at the Mess of another regiment. On Sundays and the other open evening each week he was 'to read and dine quietly in his own rooms'. Nothing was specified about actual training and drill.

Even the Duke of Wellington would have found Bertie's requirements daunting. Yet Victoria and Albert made plans for a royal visit to Ireland in August so that the Prince Consort could be present at the Curragh to observe his son march at the head of a battalion. If all went well, Albert promised, when the Prince of Wales returned from Ireland he would be permitted to buy a country property out of his own accumulated funds of the Duchy of Cornwall. (Almost a year earlier, *The Times* had published a rumour that the Queen was about to purchase a Glengarry property as a future Highland retreat for her heir.) The intended Scottish estate was an element in the strategy to marry Bertie off and settle him down. He was less than eager for arranged and premature domesticity. Like his Cambridge cronies he wanted to sample some freedom.

The Prince was to arrive at the Curragh on 29 June. Had he known of the many letters passing between Windsor and Germany on the subject of his marriage, most of them to and from Vicky, he would have been shocked. One exchange had been between Albert and his brother Ernest, the Duke of Coburg, who had registered a protest that a Danish marriage alliance remained an option. A week before Bertie arrived at camp the Prince Consort wrote to Duke Ernest that he had no business intruding. 'Vicky has racked her brains to help us find someone [German], but in vain.... We have no choice.... Bertie wishes to get married soon, and it is also in his interest, morally, socially and politically to do so.... It is of the utmost importance that this marriage should not appear to be a Danish trump against us and Prussia.' Wedding schemes for Bertie, whose eagerness for matrimony was a parental invention, were almost the only effective therapy for Victoria, still deeply depressed and often hysterical with imagined guilt about her mother. Intending to be helpful, Albert examined a miniature of the Danish candidate, Alexandra, and assured Victoria the Princess was so attractive that, if he could, he would marry her himself.

On arrival in Ireland, the Prince of Wales was cheered by crowds as he drove through the streets of Dublin with the Viceroy, Lord Carlisle. Then came the dreary business of drill, with increasingly discouraging reports from General Bruce. The inexperienced Prince, only nineteen, was incapable of leading a company, let alone a battalion. Colonel Percy, commandant of the Guards, found that even Bertie's 'indistinct' voice could not convey the authority for command. 'I will *not* make the Duke of Cambridge think you are more advanced than you are,' he said in untoadying honesty. Bruce reported as much on 15 August, but the royal visit could not be aborted merely because the Prince had failed to meet unrealistic expectations. Bertie was ordered to appear in his colonel's uniform on 25 August to parade, but only, embarrassingly, in a subaltern's role. At atmosphere of urgency pervaded the camp because news had crossed the Atlantic of successive defeats of Union forces by the better-led Confederates, including a disaster at Bull Run in Virginia. There were concerns that if the South successfully broke free, a 'bullying' North might attempt to seize parts of Canada in compensation. Some of the troops on the Curragh might find themselves in action.

Victoria was later to commend Percy for treating her son 'just as any other officer', yet she was furious with the Prince of Wales for failing his family. All she could write favourably to Vicky was that Bertie 'holds himself much better'. To King Leopold she reported discouragingly, 'Bertie marched past with his company and did not look at all very small.' A newspaper dispatch reported innocuously that there was little to see from the distance reporters were obliged to stand. 'Beyond one or two Irish peasants who happened to be passing, there was hardly a single spectator in the plain [of Curragh].... Apparently it was only three mounted gentlemen looking on at a regimental drill. Yet even the country people present did not know that the Prince Consort was one of these three, or that the fair young officer with black crape on his arm at the rear of his regiment, who was so quick in obeying Colonel Percy's stentorian orders, and who stood at such rigid attention among the privates of his company, ... was the Prince of Wales.' (The black mourning band was for the Duchess of Kent, his grandmother.)

On 11 September he would report to his mother with some pride that 'with expert assistance' he had now drilled a brigade, but his military adventures were over. Having been shown Alexandra's picture, he was ordered to Germany to meet secretly with the princess chosen for him, to determine whether he could accept her. The cover for his trip would be that he was continuing his military studies by attending the autumn manoeuvres of the Prussian Army near Coblenz.

When he arrived a week later he learned that prying German newspapers had already 'taken it up', as he told Victoria, and were predicting an 'immediate rupture' between the Prussian and English courts if a Danish marriage took place. Vicky, now the Prussian Crown Princess, and already disliked in Germany as too English, had arranged the meeting, which took place at the cathedral at Speyer on 24 September. 'We were known immediately', Bertie wrote ruefully, but he would not give his impressions of the very young princess by letter. To her parents Alexandra cautiously reported feeling only 'the reverse of indifference'. No love match appeared in prospect although a match appeared inevitable unless another candidate surfaced.

When the Prince returned to Cambridge he found the talk more military than academic. As Natty Rothschild reported after a dinner party at Madingley, where the usual dignitaries outnumbered the undergraduates, 'The principal topic of conversation was the war with America. It seems that a large number of troops are to be sent to Canada, [including] two battalions of Guards, Ld Hinchinbrooke's battalion for one, the same with which the Prince did duty at the Curragh, one battalion of the Rifle Brigade, the 9th Royal Dragoons and ever so many fine regiments. The Prince is very anxious to join his own regiment.... They talked of our annexing Maine and Portland.'

While realizing that he would never be permitted to be in harm's way, Bertie may have dreamed of a military escape from his marital dilemma. But he only escaped into greater trouble. To his happy surprise he had found female consolation before meeting the very young and inexperienced Alexandra. General Bruce had warned of the corrupting influence of the randy young officers with whom the Prince would be thrown, however much he was sheltered. Nellie Clifden, literally a lady of the evening, knew her way about the Curragh camp and was known politely as an actress. Employed by Bertie's colleagues, after an evening of drinking had emboldened them, to force the facts of life on the Prince, she was in his bed when he got there. Nellie had proven talent to amuse, and the Prince of Wales saw to it that she continued to amuse him thereafter. He arranged to slip her into England from Kildare.

He returned to Cambridge on 15 October to finish the term. Whether or not he boasted of his bedroom prowess to his cronies, his seduction, once some of the subalterns from the Curragh returned with the tale to their London clubs, was the stuff of heady, gin-tinged gossip. His governors knew nothing. Nor did the Royals.

Only Scotland seemed to provide the therapeutic qualities which the

Queen had needed to recover from her unremitting grief for her mother. Pallid and worn, Albert was shattered by overwork, and by his sense of mortality. He agonized, too, about the often hysterical Victoria, who, he worried, might have inherited some of the 'madness' of George III. (The King's porphyria was only diagnosed as such two centuries after his death.) If this was the case, and if the Queen became a widow besides, the Prince of Wales might become a very young, and incapable, regent. The long nightmare of George IV could reoccur.

In that anxious state Albert waited until as late in October as he and Victoria could manage to return from Balmoral to Windsor, where the long succession of ceremonials which he had taken over from the Queen were to resume. There was also Bertie's twentieth birthday to mark on 9 November, and plans to work out further educational travel for him after Christmas. He was to visit the troubled Ionian Islands (acquired after Waterloo), 891 square miles in the Adriatic west of Greece, where an insurrection had failed in 1848. From the largest island, Corfu, he was to go on to Syria and Egypt. Albert intended to make the Prince of Wales a visible agent of Empire, which would continue the role he had tried out in Canada as well as keep him out of trouble in England.

As a further princely rehearsal, and to be surrogate for his chronically ailing father, Bertie was assigned the ceremonial opening of the new Middle Temple Library. The site dated from 1641, and the even more venerable Hall had seen early productions of *Twelfth Night* and *A Midsummer Night's Dream*. The Middle Temple, the ancient hive of the Law above Temple Bar in Fleet Street, held the huge oak table at which successful law candidates were 'called to the Bar', and Bertie, who had attended few university lectures on law, arrived at the stroke of two on 31 October attended by Bruce and Teesdale formally to open the new law library. A guard of honour of eighty men from the Devil's Own greeted him, and a band played 'God Save the Queen'. In the Parliament Chamber the Master Treasurer of the Middle Temple moved 'that His Royal Highness be admitted a member of the Middle Temple', and that he 'be called to the degree of the Outer Bar'. There being no opposition, the motions were carried unanimously, and the Prince was invested with the Bar gown and his name entered in the Call Book.

A further motion by the Treasurer, seconded by the Lord Chamberlain, was 'that His Royal Highness be invited to the Bench'. Again there was no opposition, and the Prince donned the Benchers' gown and took his seat as a Master of the Bench, at the right hand of the Treasurer. A procession formed to the new library, which was duly christened. The Prince declared it open, accepted his addition to the roll of Benchers, and prayed that further users of the library 'may succesfully emulate the fame of their eminent predecessors'. In Temple Church a choir sang the 46th and 72nd psalms and Handel's 'Zadok the Priest' to great effect, after which the 750 guests sat down in the Hall, and in an overflow pavilion erected in Fountain Court, to a banquet punctuated by loyal toasts. *Punch* would observe in verse about the cheaply earned toga and title of the callow new barrister:

> 'There's no royal road to learning',
> 'Tis a proverb [as] false as stale....

And it commiserated with his merciless Oxbridge 'course of cram' which whipped him from the Isis to the Cam, and

> ... whisks him to the Curragh,
> Camp experience to gain:
> Then to make confusion thorough,
> Back to civil life again....
> Hapless Prince! An age of cramming
> Owns its martyr-type in thee:
> Never brain-pan had such ramming....

Punch's lines appeared on 9 November, the day that Victoria, who never read anything not brought to her, wrote in her diary, 'Our dear Bertie's 20th birthday. May God bless and protect him and may he turn out well.' Three days later, after he had returned to Cambridge, George Byng, 7th Viscount Torrington, arrived at Windsor for a stint as a lord-in-waiting. Torrington, a garrulous *habitué* of London clubs and a purveyor of royal gossip and news to *The Times* as '*Your Windsor Special*', renewed his duties with deliciously calamitous news to impart to Albert. A 'story current in the clubs' linked Bertie and the Curragh with Nellie Clifden and claimed that he was continuing the relationship, which helped explain the Prince of Wales's reluctance to accept the Danish betrothal scheme. (In London, Nellie boasted of the affair, which boosted her stock with her clientele.) Albert waited until the next day, 13 November, to tell the Queen, at first keeping from her (she wrote in her diary) 'the disgusting details'. She left Albert to deal with the episode.

On 14 November Albert rushed off an anguished appeal to Baron Stockmar: 'I am fearfully in want of a true friend and counsellor, and that *you* are the friend and counsellor I want, you will readily understand.' Yet he knew that he was unlikely to receive any practical advice from old Stockmar, and perhaps no response whatever. Infirm and reclusive, Stockmar was unlikely to leave Coburg, but he confirmed that allegations about an Irish 'actress' had already surfaced in Continental papers.

With Torrington to tattle, Albert was quickly able to confirm the liaison, which in many great families might have been accepted with relief about the malefactor's proven manliness. For an Albertine king-in-waiting, however, it suggested weakness and potential scandal. Too heartbroken to confront his son in person, Albert waited until the 16th to write to Bertie 'with a heavy heart upon a subject which has caused me the greatest pain I have yet felt in this life'. From what Albert had learned, and anticipated, he foresaw the worst, in a scenario certainly coloured by his own premonition of inoperable illness and forthcoming death. The Prince of Wales was already the talk of the clubs; Nellie Clifden, he had learned, probably through Torrington, was a regular at London dance halls frequented by profligate gentlemen, and was now being burlesqued by the knowledgeable – to her amusement – as 'the Princess of Wales'. She might have a child by some other father, Albert admonished his son, but, 'If you were to try and deny it, she can drag you into a Court of Law to force you to own it & there with you ... in the witness box, she will be able to give before a greedy Multitude disgusting details of your profligacy for the sake of convincing the Jury, yourself cross-examined by a railing indecent attorney and hooted and yelled at by a Lawless Mob! Oh horrible prospect, which this person has in her power, any day to realise! and to break your poor parents' hearts!' To channel such wanton impulses, Albert warned, Bertie would have to be hurried into the marriage he had been resisting. The Crown had to be shielded from dishonour.

Bertie's response was shocked, contrite, and repentant. He owned to yielding to temptation but claimed he had ended the affair. Albert acknowledged that further inquiries were useless. 'The past is the past. You have to deal now with the future.' But to Victoria, who could be of little help after nearly a year of self-pitying grief and hysteria, and from whom Albert had hidden his own physical distress, the Prince of Wales was lost. His father would have to go to Cambridge to work things out:

Bertie could not be summoned to Windsor in such circumstances. Depressed and ill, troubled by sleeplessness, and exhausted from doing much of the Queen's work as well as his own, Albert told Victoria nevertheless that as soon as he could, he would visit Madingley. But, he confessed, '*Ich hange gar nicht am Leben: du hangst sehr daran ...*' [I do not cling to life; you do; but I set no store by it.] 'I am sure that if I had a severe illness,' he continued – in German, the language of their household since their marriage – 'I should give up at once; I should not struggle for life. I have no tenacity of life.'

In retrospect, his fatalism appears more like self-diagnosis than prophecy. He was in no condition, mentally or physically, to fulfil a commitment to inspect the new buildings for the Royal Military Academy for which he had long campaigned. He went to Sandhurst anyway, on 22 November, despite a drenching rain ('*entsetzlicher Regen*' in his diary). Albert returned to Windsor wet and exhausted, but despite feeling very wretched ('*recht elend*'), he was determined to settle his son's future, and on the 24th ordered a special train to Cambridge for the next morning.

At Madingley he could have remained indoors with Bertie for a heart-to-heart talk: a cold, intermittent rain was falling. Instead, he suggested that they talk outdoors, out of earshot, and Albert had to go on longer than he anticipated. During the apparently emotional exchange, they missed a turning off the St Neots Road. But Albert extracted assurances of appropriately princely behaviour henceforth, and forgave his son. In return, Albert promised not to search out the subalterns who had corrupted Bertie.

There was a Prince Consort's Room, decorated in green chintz, at Madingley, and Albert remained there overnight, talking to both Bertie and Bruce until nearly one in the morning. He returned to Windsor by an early train on the 26th, more ill than ever. To his wife he blamed rheumatism and insomnia. He was probably developing pneumonia. 'Dr Jenner', the Queen wrote unsuspectingly to Vicky on 30 November, 'said yesterday evening that Papa was so much better, he would be quite well in two or three days – but he is not inclined himself ever to admit he is better!' Her letter continued on the obsessive subject of royal match-making; Princess Alice, eighteen, was being betrothed to a mediocre Hessian prince. Victoria also aired a new concern: an American war-related outrage upon a British vessel. The mail packet *Trent* had been seized in order to remove Confederate envoys sailing to England to raise funds and buy weapons. From his sickbed, Albert would have to defuse the bellicose ultimatum to President Lincoln drafted by the Prime Minister, Lord Palmerston, and his Foreign Secretary, Lord Russell. Although the Queen considered the perpetrators 'ruffians', she sided with Albert about tempering the hawkish language, having written to Vicky only three weeks earlier, 'We are somewhat shocked at your speaking of "those horrid Yankees"' – when Bertie was received in the United States as no one has ever been received anywhere, principally from the (to me incredible) liking they have for my unworthy self.* ... Don't therefore abuse the 'Yankees' for their natural defects.' There was much, to her, about Americans that was crude and vulgar, but that did not make them the enemy.

With the threat of war dominating gossip as well as the press – the Atlantic cable was down, and offers to compromise over the *Trent* had to cross the Atlantic by sea – the Bertie scandal was still largely confined to his cronies and the clubs. (W. E. Gladstone's diary does not refer to 'The Prince of Wales & his misleading comrades' until the 21st.) Beyond them, William Hardman reported from Eton – an indication of how far the news had already travelled – that 'rumours ... have been freely circulated that [the Prince of Wales's] conduct is becoming loose'.

The Prince had no idea until mid-December that his father was dying (very probably of stomach cancer, exacerbated by pneumonia), as the daily routine at Cambridge had continued. On Thursday 12 December, Natty Rothschild wrote to his parents, he had been at Madingley for lunch 'and afterwards to go out with the harriers'. (All the participants should have been preparing for final examinations at Trinity.) 'We had a very jolly afternoon ... chasing the wily hare – till it was quite dark and the moon was shining quite brightly when we jumped the last fence. The Prince told me of the Prince Consort's illness, it seems they are afraid that gastric [typhoid] fever is epidemic at Windsor at present, and therefore they will not let the Prince of Wales return.' Bertie's news from Windsor was also that a favourable outcome was expected. He did not know that both reports were untrue. In reality no case of typhoid had been identi-

---

* The Queen was recalling Newcastle's claim from America that the lionizing of Bertie was actually popular affection for her.

fied at or near Windsor except for the alleged case of his father. The Queen did not know the dubiousness of the diagnosis and had to take the word of such physicians as Dr Jenner, who had told her two weeks earlier that Albert was rapidly recovering from something else, and two days earlier had assured her that the Prince was rallying from typhoid. Besides, she blamed Bertie for Albert's collapse after Cambridge, and thought that his sudden appearance at Windsor might suggest to Albert that he had taken a turn for the worse – which indeed had happened.

On Friday 13 December he was sinking fast, and his doctors finally confessed in a bulletin for the press that the Prince Consort's symptoms 'have assumed an unfavourable character during the day'. No malady was identified. His doctors drugged him with brandy every half-hour to mask his stomach pain; he had taken no solid food for two weeks. Princess Alice, who had assumed her father's care in the absence of professional assistance and in recognition of medical incompetence, took it upon herself to telegraph her brother, who, four hours after parting from his friends at the Elislie toll bar, and unaware of the anguish at Windsor, was (Natty reported) at 'a gay party' when he learned the dread news.

At the foot of Albert's bed early Saturday morning were Bertie and fifteen-year-old Princess Helena; Alice remained at one side of the bed, where she had posted herself, when awake, for days. Occasionally one of Albert's doctors checked his weakening pulse, but did little else. As the day wore on, Louise and Arthur came to the bedside. Alfred was at sea; the haemophiliac young Leopold was in the south of France for his health; the four-year-old Beatrice was kept away. In the darkened room, members of the royal staff gathered, stood uneasily, then slipped out. After her own exit, Lady Biddulph rushed to her husband's office in the castle – Sir Thomas was one of Albert's secretaries – and wrote to Earl Spencer, titular head of the Prince's Establishment, 'VERY VERY bad news. All the Household have been up to the Prince's room to see for the last time him who is *fast sinking*. The doctors say there is no hope not the slightest…'.

As the Prince's rapid breathing became alarming, Victoria hastened to the side of the bed across from Alice and whispered to Albert, '*es ist Fraüchen*'. Then she bent toward him and asked for '*einem Kuss*', and he kissed her. Then he slept again, and Victoria struggled to keep calm, clutching his thin, cold hand until her misery became overwhelming. She burst from the room and broke down.

At a quarter-to eleven, as Albert's children still clustered quietly at his bedside, their father's breathing began to change, and Alice recognized approaching death. She went for her mother. The Queen fell, weeping, upon the still, cold body and called her husband by every endearing name she could recall from their life together. Then she allowed herself to be led away. The children and some of the household officials followed to offer what comfort they could. For Bertie it was especially awkward. He understood that his mother blamed him for his father's death. Embracing her, he promised that he would do everything he could to help. 'I am sure, my dear boy, you will,' she said with more conviction than she would later feel. He did have two immediate responsibilities, neither of which he looked forward to. He had to assist with funeral and burial arrangements, as his mother, broken by grief, would be escorted to Osborne to mourn from a discreet distance. And he would have to leave Cambridge, which he had grown to love, to perform the boring ceremonial duties which the Queen might assign him as her surrogate.

Albert had died on a Saturday morning. By Monday, servants had begun packing for shipment to Windsor everything at Madingley that belonged to the Prince of Wales and his staff. By the next Saturday, General Bruce notified Lady King, her house would be completely vacated. 'The Prince returns for one night on Monday after the funeral – to put away some Papers &c wh[ich] his sudden departure prevented his doing before. I must beg you however not to mention this, as H.R.H. does not wish to be recognised at the Railway Station.' It had to be, for him, a quiet departure. To his closest friends, Charles Carrington and George Cadogan, he would write (on 19 and 25 December) that his father 'was always kindness itself to me, though I fear I have often given him pain by my conduct', and that he had lost him 'just at a time when I was most in need of his advice and counsel'.

The funeral took place at the Chapel Royal of St George's, Windsor, at 11.30 on Monday 23 December. It was sombre and simple, as Albert was said to have wanted it. Since the family did not want the obsequies to deny the people their Christmas, the ceremonies were to conclude well before Christmas Eve, leaving no time for the gathering of sovereigns and statesmen from abroad. The Life Guards and the Grenadier Guards took up their positions, and precisely at noon the mourners followed the velvet-draped coffin from the Castle into the chapel, the Prince of Wales walking behind the coffin, his small brother Arthur at his right hand, each wearing a kilt. The Dean of Windsor read the usual lessons, and

Albert's body was lowered from the bier into the Royal vault at twenty minutes to one. Only the creak of the machinery supporting the bier broke the profound silence. His face in his hands, Bertie wept.

Once the mourners had left, he returned to the vault to lay flowers from his mother, sent from Osborne that morning, on the coffin. Later, as quietly as he could, he took a train to Cambridge, to arrive after dark, and to return the next day. His father and mother had both wanted him to develop into a second Albert. Suddenly he had to replace Albert, but whether any of the Prince Consort's functions would fall upon Bertie remained, to him, unknown.

VI

Bachelorhood

1861–1863

'*M*Y FIRM RESOLVE, my *irrevocable decision*', Victoria vowed to her Uncle Leopold ten days after Albert's death on 14 December, '[is] that *his* wishes – *his* plans – about *every* thing are to be *my law!* And *no human power* will make me swerve from *what he* decided and wished.... I apply this particularly as regards our children – Bertie, etc – for whose future he had traced everything so carefully.' To General Bruce she declared, in the usual royal third-person, 'that she alone would decide, in conformity with her husband's counsels, to which none but herself had been admitted, the future of the Prince of Wales'. In effect she would do exactly what she wanted while claiming that it was the 'object' of 'our beloved Prince and Master, our Guide and Counsellor'. When Mary Anne Disraeli would suggest innocently that the Prince of Wales must be a great comfort to her, Victoria demurred 'Comfort! Why I caught him smoking a fortnight after his father died!' She would 'try to employ and use' Bertie, she wrote to Vicky on 27 December, 'but I am not hopeful. I believe firmly in all Papa foresaw.' Her son had suffered a 'fall' akin to original sin: 'Oh! that boy –' she insisted, 'much as I pity [him] I never can or shall look at him without a shudder as you may imagine.'

Vicky would protest gently, 'Pity him, I do.... But more you cannot ask.' Yet her mother was adamant that Bertie had to repent at a distance, and marry as quickly as possible in order to contain temptation to the marital bed. 'B[ertie]'s journey is all settled,' the Queen explained on 11 January 1862 while noting vaguely that she had overridden protests from the Cabinet about her handling of her heir. 'Many wished to shake my resolution and to keep him here – to force a constant contact which is more than ever unbearable to me.... And though the intentions [of Bertie] are good, the tact, the head, the heart are all lamentably weak. The marriage is the thing, and beloved Papa was most anxious for it.' Stockmar, however, had written sardonically to Albert before the Prince Consort's last appeal to him (he had already learned of the Nellie Clifden affair) that the 'main reason' given to him for the betrothal to the very young Alexandra was 'that it is hoped that the defects of spirit and mind of the one person' [the Prince of Wales] 'should be made up by the strength of the other person. How daring it would be to take part in this lottery of possibilities.' Further, Stockmar had alleged, he saw nothing in Alexandra's family to warrant confidence: 'One of the heads of the family is supposed to be insignificant and imbecile and the other head is of lax principles.' (The Queen understood that Stockmar was referring to the Princess's weak father and allegedly immoral uncle, King Frederick VII.) Nevertheless, all that kept the impatient Victoria from formalizing the match was a decent interval of mourning, while her son was beginning to recognize that he could purchase his personal and financial freedom from his mother only by marrying and distancing himself in his own establishments.

On 29 January the Queen saw her Prime Minister at Osborne. It was 'the first time since my great misfortune'. Viscount Palmerston discussed his concerns about the future of the Prince of Wales. 'The country was fearful we were not on good terms,' she noted him as saying. She insisted that Bertie could not live with her as his 'doing nothing' in such circumstances 'was not a good thing'. But she proposed nothing for him to do, although he might have assumed some of the ceremonial functions she was unwilling, as mourning widow, to perform herself. Palmerston conceded that, having no duties, the Prince should travel, and should indeed marry, and he was unconcerned about the political ramifications in Germany of a Danish marriage, since 'They did not affect THIS country.' Bertie was, she acknowledged in her diary, '*the* difficulty of the moment', and she 'would hardly have given Lord Palmerston credit for entering so completely into my anxieties'.

Encouraged (for no obvious reason) by his discussion, the Prime Minister then suggested by letter the symbolism of having the Prince of Wales succeed Albert as Master of Trinity House, the charitable foundation that supported lighthouses and harbour safety, and which had as trustees 'Brothers' from the élite in government and society who gathered annually for a prestigious dinner punctuated by toasts and a major address. To Victoria her callow son was, at twenty, an impossible choice for such a visible public responsibility, and might prove impossible for it at any age. Sir Charles Phipps was instructed to inform Palmerston that both she and her late husband shared objections 'to HRH being put for some years, into any position lately held by the Prince Consort'. That she meant, literally, 'some years' was clear two years later when she ordered Phipps to write to Sir William Knollys 'that she thinks that the Prince of Wales had better decline the Royal Academy dinner this year, and ... that it is a meeting which his father attended only very rarely'. Embarrassed by her heavy-handedness in shutting Bertie out of public roles, Phipps added his own comment in closing, 'I am bound to obey the commands which are laid upon me.... My functions however are purely ministerial.'

Charles Dickens, who from the beginning had disliked Prince Albert as an upstart German and even in death dismissed him as 'commonplace', had to admit that there was no replacement for the Consort at Court. The Queen, he gossiped to a Swiss friend, William de Cerjat, 'applies herself to all sorts of details appertaining to the [Albert] Memorial, all the morning, and cries the rest of the day'. Her state of mind was so 'unhealthy' that 'she persists in striking out the word "late" from all formal mention of him in documents that come before her'. Dickens even unkindly suggested (it was then 16 March, three months after the Prince Consort's death) that Albert may have left her 'in the family way', which was baseless. At most a half-truth was his assertion that there was 'no doubt of her setting her face strongly against the Prince of Wales (a poor dull idle fellow). I *know*', he continued erroneously, 'that at the present time the Exhibition Commissioners are beginning to despair of her allowing him to open the Building.' A commercial and cultural sequel to the Great Exhibition of 1851 had been planned by Albert, to open on the eleventh anniversary of the spectacular original, 1 May, but Dickens should have known that the Prince of Wales had already left for the East, and would not be back in time to have any ceremonial role. Nor was Bertie to have any hand in the laying of the first stone of the mausoleum at Frogmore, Windsor, where Victoria intended to sleep side by side with Albert, in death as in life. That ceremony was scheduled for 15 March, while Bertie was travelling in the Mediterranean. As for the

Exhibition, she asked the King of Prussia to permit Crown Prince Frederick, Vicky's husband, to do the honours. 'My own grief', she explained, 'makes it impossible for me or my children to participate at all in the opening festivities.' Fritz dutifully came, but the public was not pleased at the importation of yet another German to perform an English function.

The Prince of Wales's purchase – from funds accruing to the properties of the Duchy of Cornwall – of the Norfolk estate of Sandringham had been arranged by Albert. Since the property was run-down and renovations had begun, the Prince would have to begin life as a country squire in absentia. Yet he was now a wealthy young man and would soon have complete control of his funds, if not of his life. The 8,000 acres of Sandringham, far to the north-east of Windsor above King's Lynn, near the coastal area known as the Wash, would furnish his private doings with a domestic screen from his prying mother. Some psychological distancing came with the delivery to the Queen early that January of dedicatory verses by Alfred Tennyson, the Poet Laureate, to his *Idylls of the King*, which, Tennyson explained, Albert himself 'had told me was valued by him'. The blank verse tribute to 'my own Ideal knight', who would be 'hereafter, thro' all times, Albert the Good', published the next month at the head of a new edition of the Arthurian cycle, may have made it easier for the Queen to ponder Bertie's confession to her, just beginning, that he could never succeed to the throne as Albert. No human being after his father could life up to the Prince Consort's qualities. Bertie, in his own private reckoning, was henceforth to be Edward; he would sign his 'A.E.' initials rather than 'Albert'. Victoria was aware that the last King Edward, the teenage son of Henry VIII, had been a mere cipher; but the idea of a succession of sovereigns named Albert was something she would not relinquish easily, and it would emerge again and again.

The Prince's travel plans were announced as one of the last wishes of his father. The tour gave editor John Delane of *The Times* opportunity strongly to suggest that in the period of mourning, and even after, Albert Edward could be of service to the sovereign as he had been in North America and, to a lesser extent, in Europe. His past performance and his further seasoning abroad would establish his credentials 'to greet the friends of England in his own country' and to perform 'many public or semi-public duties' that the Prince Consort had managed for the reclusive Queen. She would not take the hint.

Bertie had departed on 6 February, to travel at the Queen's instructions 'in the very strictest incognito', which meant limiting the trappings. He knew he was being exiled, and understood his mother's deep depression, which he hoped would pass. She spent much of her time disconsolately in Albert's small Osborne study, maintained as if he were alive and where she felt his presence most strongly. Bertie had entered to say goodbye, then returned for a second farewell, she noted in her journal, 'and was low and upset, poor Boy. So was I.' As usual, General Bruce was to head the entourage, which included three equerries and a doctor. As both chaplain and guide, the Queen asked the reluctant but dutiful Arthur Stanley, at forty-seven the Regius Professor of Ecclesiastical History at Oxford, to take leave and act as mentor to the party in Egypt and Palestine. It proved no sacrifice. Canon Stanley was to enjoy the journey, make good friends of both Bertie and Bruce, become Dean of Westminster on his return and, a year later, become engaged to Lady Augusta Bruce, the General's sister and the Queen's most intimate lady-in-waiting.

'Incognito' for the Prince was very loosely observed. After a brief stop-over in Paris, the 'Baron Renfrew' entourage entrained for Darmstadt, where Albert Edward was to meet the Grand Duke of Hesse, whose second son, Ludwig (now *Louis* by Victoria's fiat), was soon to marry Princess Alice. In Vienna, *en route* to the Ionian Islands, the royal party was hosted by Emperor Franz Josef, and in Venice by his beautiful young empress, Elizabeth, who seldom spent any time with her husband. At Trieste the travellers boarded the royal yacht *Osborne*, sent to meet them by Victoria, to sail down the Adriatic to Corfu. Joining them as guide in Adriatic waters was the thirty-one-year-old writer–adventurer Laurence Oliphant, who found Bertie no intellectual but wrote, 'I think his development will be far higher than people anticipate.... His defects are rather the inevitable consequences of his position which never allows him any responsibility or forces him into action.' According to the London publisher George Smith, Oliphant already had a reputation as a fount of gossip – 'a sort of human and animated newspaper'. Then also a secret agent for the Foreign Office, he joined the Prince's entourage as cover while he snooped about Austrian-held Venetia and the restless Ionian Islands. In later years Bertie was to look to Oliphant for inside information on foreign affairs – and on attractive women, another subject in which they would share an interest. When in England after the voyage, he was to see a lot of the Prince, as a guest at Sandringham or at Marlborough House, or at the Cosmopolitan Club.

Corfu's Greeks, Bertie found, were eager to be linked legally to their mainland countrymen, and made the minimum of fuss over him by any title. With little reason to remain in Corfu, the party crossed the Strait of Otranto to Turkish-held Albania, where, to hunt wild boar, Bertie wrote in his diary on 22 February, they had 'an escort of Albanians with their long guns, fez & white petticoats'. Two days later they were in Alexandria, where Said Pasha, the Viceroy of Egypt, ignored the Baron Renfrew charade and ordered a 21-gun salute fired to welcome the heir to the throne of Britain. General Bruce was indignant but Said shrugged and explained that his subjects would permit nothing less. The Viceroy put them up in a splendid palace in Cairo as a base from which to see the sights. Mail awaited the party, and early in March Bertie replied to Charles Carrington at Cambridge, suggesting that he should dispose of Nellie Clifden, whom Carrington had apparently inherited from his crony, and also that he should '*occasionally* look at a book'. The lifestyle of his entourage, Bertie, boasted, would be 'especially well adapted to a gay fellow like you'. From London, Henry Adams, son of (and secretary to) Charles Francis Adams, the American Minister, wrote to a friend on 15 March, garbling his gossip, 'The Prince of Wales is in Egypt. He is said to have taken to women lately, and they point out at the Argyll Rooms the woman whom he came to London to see, a visit which made a great row with his father and mother. It is currently reported that on parting from this female he gave her a sovereign, saying that he would be happy to increase the sum but he must put it down as lost at cards or else his father would find him out.'

That the Prince even mentioned reading a book was unusual itself, but when at a loose end on board ship he had turned the pages of Ellen (Mrs Henry) Wood's best-selling *East Lynne*. He was seldom to mention a novel again. Canon Stanley carried a guidebook about, and lectured to the party (as well as sermonizing on Sundays), but confessed that he found it nearly impossible to produce 'any impression on a mind with no previous knowledge or interest to be awakened'. Albert Edward preferred a rifle to the printed page, and fired at almost anything but chickens and goats, endangering quails, vultures, lizards, rabbits, even Nile crocodiles. Stanley's one ministerial achievement was to persuade Bertie to forgo shooting on Sundays.

To see the Sphinx ('very curious and interesting') and the Pyramids required camping nearby – the Viceroy provided tents complete even to Persian carpets – so that they could rise by dawn and begin climbing in the chill morning before the sun baked the area. The Prince refused assistance up the Pyramid of Cheops and noted in his diary on 4 March that 'the ascent is rather tedious & difficult, but you are rewarded by a fine view'. (The Bedouin boy denied his opportunity to assist the Prince's ascent had Bertie pointed out to him and exclaimed, 'What, that little chap!') *The Times* on 17 March reported his feat, and *Punch* versified:

> For youth like yours exertion hath its charms,
> And you repulse those Arabs' dingy arms,
> You climb alone, and swift the height you gain,
> Your panting suite toil after you in vain....

Below, Francis Bedford, a photographer once employed by Prince Albert, unpacked his camera equipment at each site and recorded the tour in 180 albumen prints.

For sailing up the Nile to inspect tombs and ruins and statuary, Said supplied two sumptuously appointed dahabeeyahs. Armed with *Murray's Hand-Book*, the Prince claimed to have studied the temple at Edfou 'excessively', and tolerated the awesome ruins at Karnak, although Canon Stanley chose to offer a sermon from a corner with good acoustics. But when Bruce announced the ruins at Thebes as the next site, the Prince objected, 'Why should we go and see the tumbledown old Temple? There will be nothing to see when we get there.' 'Well, Sir,' said the General, 'you need not go – but some of us wish to go and shall go.' Reluctantly, His Royal Highness went and, in Stanley's description, 'treated the pillars, and the sculptures, I will not say with interest or admiration, but with the most well-bred courtesy, as if he were paying a visit to a high personage'. It was a courtesy, however misplaced here, that was to become the hallmark of the Prince's personality.

Returning north to board the *Osborne*, they steamed for Jaffa, which they reached on 29 March. Recognizing no incognitos, Suraya Pasha, the Governor-General, met them in style, furnished fifty servants as attendants en route (by horseback) to Jerusalem, and a hundred cavalrymen to supply security. At noon each day the cavalcade halted for a fine luncheon and a two-hour siesta. Bertie smoked at the entrance to his tent, and fingered the beard he was cultivating. As they proceeded eastward,

Canon Stanley wrote, 'In front is usually the Prince, in his white robe, with his gun at his side. Close by him, also [hooded] in a white burnous, is the interpreter (Noel Moore) who must always be with him as we approach any town, to be prepared for the arrival of some petty governor coming out to meet us, and falling on his knees to kiss the Prince's stirrup.... Around, or behind, or before, but usually as we approach the encampment scampering over everybody in violent haste to be close to H.R.H., the long array of fifty mounted spearmen, their red pennons flashing through the rocks and thickets.'

At Jerusalem, Jericho and Bethlehem, Canon Stanley offered historical and biblical lectures, but at Hebron the party was denied permission to enter the Cave of Machpelah, legendary burial place of Abraham and the other early patriarchs and their wives. No Christian had been permitted to set foot there since 1187. Stanley, however, refused to heed warnings of adverse Muslim reaction, and asked Bruce to claim the Prince's 'extreme displeasure' and intercede with Suraya Pasha. On 7 April, Suraya duly arrived with supporting cavalry, and personally escorted the party into the tomb. 'Well, you see,' the Prince boasted to Stanley, 'exalted rank has its privileges, after all!' Very likely the Turkish Sultan, recognizing crucial British aid against Russia in the Crimean War only six years earlier, had ordered that his provincial governors be accommodating to the Queen's heir.

By Good Friday the entourage had reached Nazareth; on Easter Sunday they arrived at Tiberias, on the western edge of the Sea of Galilee. Each night their attendants set up a tent city and each morning they took it down. Near Mount Gerizim they encountered the Samaritan observance of Passover. (A nearly extinct and isolated community of Jews even then, the Samaritans base their religious observance only on the Torah, the first five books of the Hebrew Bible.) At the foot of Mount Tabor on 19 April they halted at the encampment of Sheik Agyle Agha, who, the Prince wrote in his diary, 'is a celebrated man in Syria, & protected the Christians during the recent massacres. He is a tall, good looking man & he and his brother received us in their tent.... Agha gave us luncheon, which was placed before us in wooden dishes, & we had to eat with our fingers à l'Arabe. I gave him a revolver before leaving with which he was very much pleased.'

Before embarking from Beirut they visited Sidon, Tyre, Tripoli and the Roman ruin of Baalbek, shattered by an earthquake in 1759. (The Queen had insisted that Bertie's stay in 'Sodom and Gomorrah' be as brief as possible; however, Sidon was not Sodom, which was one of the legendary 'cities of the plain' below the Dead Sea.) Nothing could keep Canon Stanley from preaching in exotic places, and on 4 May he sermonized amid the fallen blocks of a second-century Ptolemaic temple.

They anchored in the Dardanelles where the British ambassador to the Sublime Porte, Sir Henry Bulwer, came aboard with high-ranking Turks who, despite the official incognito, invited the Prince on 20 May to an audience with the Sultan, Abdul Aziz, in Constantinople. Bulwer primed Bertie with appropriate subjects and responses, and was impressed by the Prince's performance. He had a way with people, cultivated during his transatlantic travels, that was to make him an effective diplomat. Stanley thought that Bertie also had an 'astonishing memory of names and persons'. In Constantinople he received both a surprisingly affectionate letter from the Queen (who liked him more from afar), and a Foreign Office rejection of his request to go on to the Crimea to visit battle sites of the recent war with Russia, on the grounds that it was likely to be provocative rather than diplomatic. The Prince was disappointed, but on 29 May embarked for Athens, en route for home.

General Bruce, who had been ailing when in Turkey, collapsed in Athens with a fever apparently contracted in Syria or Palestine. Dangerously ill, he had to be evacuated to England. (To fill his place temporarily, the Queen hastily arranged for Sir Charles Phipps to meet the party in France.) Greece was in political turmoil as a result of the unpopularity of King Otho, a Bavarian sovereign foisted on the country and soon to be deposed. Bertie politely accepted Otho's award of a souvenir bauble, the Order of the Redeemer of Greece, and sailed on to Marseilles. Arriving in France on 10 June, he travelled overnight by train to Paris, where Phipps cautiously had him put up at the British Embassy. Bertie happily visited Napoleon III and Eugénie and their entourage at Fontainebleau, renewed his enchantment with Paris, purchased jewellery there for Alexandra, and, beardless again, was reunited with his mother on 14 June at Windsor. She thought he looked 'so improved'. Even a fortnight later he remained 'greatly improved', and offered (Victoria referred to Albert as if alive) 'to do whatever his Mother and Father wished'.

On 27 June, in London, Colonel Bruce died. He was fifty-nine. As he had paid less and less heed to the Queen's restrictions, the Prince had grown to like him more. Two weeks later Victoria informed her son that since he was 'too near 21' for a new governor, she would name Sir William Knollys, sixty-five and a retired general, as his 'Comptroller and Treasurer'. The Prince was learning to bide his time. Dutifully and diplomatically, he replied, 'As you feel sure that dear Papa would have approved of the appointment, that will make it doubly my duty to like and get on well with him.' He did, and the general's son Francis was later to be the Prince's Private Secretary. But when the Queen told Bertie that she felt she had to acquaint Knollys with what had happened at the Curragh, Bertie exploded, then apologized, 'I have reflected and now think that it is certainly better that General Knollys should know. Hoping that this may be the last conversation that I shall have with you on this painful subject.' The Prince knew that he had to get through the dwindling months without mishap until marriage would set him free.

The Queen had shared her concerns with Vicky after Albert's death that Alexandra's family should not be kept unaware of Nellie Clifden, for 'were the poor girl to be very unhappy [after the marriage], I could not answer for it before God had she been entrapped into it'. While she dithered about it, the Duke of Cambridge, her cousin, attempting to sabotage the betrothal because he himself had a daughter to bestow, wrote to Alexandra's mother about the Curragh embarrassment. Vicky learned of the treachery through her lady-in-waiting, Walburga Paget, a German countess who had married a titled Englishman. 'Wally', Vicky told the Queen, had discovered Alix's mother 'in floods of tears with this letter from Uncle George in her hands and in great distress about it.... She had not heard a word of all of this before.' The Queen asked that her view of the matter be conveyed: that Bertie was a 'poor innocent boy' led into 'a scrape' by 'wicked wretches'. Vicky explained further that Queen Victoria was '*very* confident' that the Prince of Wales, having regretted his dereliction, '*would* make a steady Husband', and that the Queen 'looked to his wife as being his Salvation', and was 'exceedingly satisfied and pleased with him since his return to England, and thought him immensely improved'.

With that apparently settled (Alexandra's family in any case knew they were making a great match, and were the envy of Protestant Europe), Victoria arranged to meet the future bride, and for Bertie to renew his brief acquaintance. Travelling as the Countess of Balmoral, an unconvincing incognito, the Queen, with an entourage far too formidable for any countess, left for the country palace of her uncle, King Leopold, at

Laeken, near Brussels. She intended to continue on to revisit Albert's birthplace in Coburg. Prince Christian and his wife, through whose line he was heir apparent to the Danish throne, were already in Laeken with their daughters Alexandra and Dagmar (who would become, as Marie, the consort of the future Tsar Alexander III of Russia). The Countess of Balmoral arrived on 2 September, remaining only two days. She noted in her diary on 3 September that Alexandra, still seventeen, but carefully attired for the interview, given Victoria's morbid mourning, in a plain black dress without jewellery, 'is lovely, such a beautiful refined profile, and quiet ladylike manner.... How He [the late Prince Consort] would have doted on her and loved her.' In a private talk with Alexandra's parents Victoria hoped that 'their dear daughter' would 'accept our son' – not their future son-in-law but Albert's child, and her own – 'with her whole heart'. The next day she travelled on to the scenes of Albert's child-hood, intent on not giving him up to fading memory.

The Danes returned to Ostend, where they claimed to be at the seaside on holiday, to await Albert Edward, who reacquainted himself with his bride on 5 September and drove over each day from a hotel in Brussels, where Alexandra's family joined him on 8 September for the formal proposal. Bertie went through the accepted routine, calling Prince Christian to his rooms (as the more elevated Royal). 'Then I told him', Bertie wrote to his mother, expectantly awaiting the news in Coburg, 'how I loved his daughter and how anxious I was that she should be my wife. I told him that I had quite made up my mind, and that I knew you had told him the same. I don't think I ever saw anybody so much pleased as he was.' King Leopold arranged a dinner at Laeken, at which Bertie sat between Alexandra and her very deaf mother, falling, he claimed, 'in increasing love'.

The next morning they returned from the hotel in Brussels to Laeken, where the Prince of Wales took Alexandra into the garden alone, 'and then', he told Victoria, he 'offered her my hand and my heart. She immediately said *Yes*. I then kissed her hand and she kissed me.' He cautioned her, Bertie went on, knowing his audience, that she would find her 'new home' in England 'very sad after the terrible loss we had sustained. I told her how *very* sorry I was that she could never know dear Papa. She said she regretted it deeply and hoped he would have approved of my choice. I told her that it had always been his greatest wish; I only feared that I was not worthy of her.... I only hope it may be for her happiness and that I may do my duty towards her. Love and cherish her you may be sure I will to the end of my life…. You may be sure that we shall both strive to be a comfort to you.'

They rode together by day; in the evenings Alix, as appropriate, played the piano and sang. At Victoria's insistence, when they sat alone, the mother of the bride-to-be sat in the next room with the door open. On 14 September, again on the Queen's instructions, the Prince left for Coburg to rejoin Victoria, and Prince Christian and his family returned to Copenhagen. Bertie could not offer to visit there. The Queen declared there would be implicit support of Denmark in its dispute with Prussia over hereditary claims to Schleswig-Holstein. A war had already occurred (1848–50) over the largely German-speaking duchies (only northern Schleswig was Danish), and another conflict loomed. Pro-Danish but fettered by the Queen's familial Germanism, the Prime Minister, Lord Palmerston, explained the complications of the territorial dispute by observing that in his long involvement with European politics only three men in England had ever understood the Schleswig-Holstein question: Albert, the Prince Consort, who was dead; Mellish, a mythical ministerial appointee in the Foreign Office, who allegedly was mad; and he himself, who had forgotten the formula.

Barred from Denmark, Bertie sent to Alix in his place a hand-coloured photograph taken the year before, when he appeared far more callow. In a tail coat and holding a top hat, he leaned against a pillar. It was a safe and reassuring picture for her parents.

Victoria had her own quarrel with the Danes within days of her meeting Alix's mother and father, as Frederick VII wrote to the Queen (she reported to Vicky) 'that he rejoices at the marriage and wishes that it should take place in England as it would then be performed with more ceremony!!! How impertinent. No answer will be given.' Victoria would not have *her* heir married on the bride's petty soil. Her response was not to invite the King to the wedding. His private life in any case did not bear scrutiny. (He was married morganatically to a third wife after two divorces.)

Vicky and her husband were under fire in Prussia for having conspired in the betrothal of the Prince of Wales to an enemy of the state, and Victoria offered her daughter and son-in-law use of the *Osborne* for a Mediterranean cruise to escape their bad press, orchestrated by Count Bismarck. In a Machiavellian move, the Queen insisted that Bertie go with them, at the same time inviting – in effect ordering – Alexandra to England. The only stipulation by her parents was that she return for her eighteenth birthday on 1 December. Victoria was attempting to control the marriage even before it occurred.

Alexandra was to arrive on 5 November, after a brief ceremony on 1 November (morbidly 'in darling Papa's room', the Queen wrote to Vicky) formally announcing to three peers representing the Government that the Prince of Wales would be married on 10 March, 1863. (She chose the date and venue without consulting the future bride and groom, and ignored the Anglican clergy, who frowned upon weddings during Lent. 'Marriage', declared the Queen sternly, 'is a solemn and holy act *not* to be classed with amusements.') Alix's father, Prince Christian, who had accompanied her from Denmark, was not displeased. Although the childless Danish King's designated heir, he lived, for someone of his royal expectations, in relative penury and could not have brought off a grand wedding. He and Alix arrived on the Isle of Wight to fireworks off the pier and a band playing the Danish national anthem. Yet the only Royal to greet them was the nine-year-old Prince Leopold, who gave Alexandra a bouquet. According to Lady Augusta Bruce, who accompanied little Leopold, Alix 'took the great representative of the House of England in Her arms and kissed Him'.

Barred from England while Alexandra visited, Albert Edward was exiled to the other *Osborne*, then pitching in stormy seas off Tunisia, Sicily, Malta and southern Italy. Vicky and her brother were both seasick. A paddle-wheel shaft broke breasting a wave and the yacht had to be towed to port for repairs. On 9 November Bertie had to mark his coming-of-age on board ship in the Bay of Naples, a deliberate down-playing of the date's significance, although Victoria, as a birthday gift, had him emptily promoted to general. In London, Benjamin Moran, Secretary of the American Legation, took a carriage to Buckingham Palace to sign, on behalf of Minister Adams, the customary visitors' book for congratulating the Prince of Wales on the occasion, but found there was none. From Osborne, the Queen wrote about Alexandra to Vicky in Italy, 'She is so passionately attached to me! It is, my dear child, such a blessing.'

With Victoria's permission, Albert Edward, en route home by train from Marseilles, met Alexandra at Calais on 28 November, remaining overnight with her father, who had returned for her, as chaperon. While in Paris to change trains, he again stayed at the British Embassy and, to the concern of Sir Charles Phipps, was once again entertained at Court by Eugénie, who introduced him to some of the most intoxicating (but for the sake of propriety, married) young countesses and duchesses in her circle, and even a voluptuous princess, Jeanne-Marguerite Seillière de Sagan, who let it be known that she had a faithless husband. The Prince of Wales filed the information away in his excellent memory.

The Prince had less success with at least one attractive but unmarried Parisian, according to an account given to Princess Marie Louise by the marquise d'Harcourt, who at 101 was still sharp in memory. At a ball in his honour in the early 1860s in one of the great houses, the unworldly Bertie began a flirtation with a charming guest who was remaining overnight. He would like to continue the acquaintance, he murmured. After the other guests left, he would come up to her room. Surprised, and unsure how to dissuade him, she told the Prince that she would place a rose outside her door so that he could identify it. Later, HRH found his way upstairs, and discreetly knocked on the door identified by the rose. A voice whispered '*Entrez*', which he did. Sitting up in bed was a kitchen-maid.

After Calais, Sir Augustus Paget, acting for Victoria rather than the Prince, negotiated a marriage treaty in Copenhagen to formalize the nuptials. On 3 December, from Windsor, the Queen wrote to Vicky that Bertie had returned 'really very much improved'. It did not, however, improve his disposition – though he kept it under control – that his managerial mother, making all the wedding arrangements herself, informed him that he might invite only six friends to the ceremony. More would unduly crowd St George's Chapel, where no nuptials had been celebrated since the marriage of Henry I to Adelaide of Louvain in 1121. Victoria claimed, as she was often to do, that her decision was Albert's wish, but she considered herself in indefinite mourning and would not participate in a public spectacle in London. (Ostensibly also at his posthumous behest, only Alexandra's immediate family was invited.) Bertie put on his modest invitation list Lord Carrington, the Duke of St Albans, Lord James Hamilton (an Oxford friend, later the 2nd Duke of Abercorn), Lord Henniker, Lord Hinchinbrooke (later the Earl of Sandwich), and Charles Wood (later Viscount Halifax). He arranged to have his former tutors invited as honorary chaplains.

As the wedding day approached, the Prince's Comptroller, Sir William

Knollys, began to establish what Albert Edward's actual income and property was, on his reaching his majority. From the income of the Duchy of Cornwall he had an annual £50,000. The rent roll from the Sandringham properties brought in an additional £15,000. In the Commons, the Chancellor of the Exchequer, W. E. Gladstone, argued that the heir's income should be at least £100,000, in order to maintain an appropriate lifestyle. It went unsaid that the Prince would also have to maintain a substitute Court out of his inadequate funds for as long as the Queen remained unwilling to end her seclusion and mourning. Although Radical MPs objected, Parliament voted £50,000 annually for the Prince of Wales, £10,000 of which was designated as 'pin money' for his Princess, who had no funds of her own. Learning of the grant to his daughter, Prince Christian confided to Lord Russell, still the Foreign Minister, that as heir to the Danish throne he possessed an annual income then equivalent to £2,000, and that it had once been only £800.

Bertie was not marrying an heiress, as some of his titled and spend-thrift cronies were free to do. On his own, however, he could now pay repeated visits to his fashionable tailor, Henry Poole of Savile Row, and also acquire a fine new horse. Natty Rothschild saw the Prince riding on 16 January and wrote cattily (and ungrammatically) to his parents, 'They make a first-rate pair; if anything the new horse is the best of the two.'

Despite parliamentary intervention and the substantial buying power of the pound in 1863, the Prince's income was only a fraction of that of the great territorial, industrial and mercantile magnates. He was never to live within his resources and, later in his life, would call on the discreet – and sometimes indiscreet – help of friendly financiers often (from his mother's standpoint) socially beyond the pale. Unable yet to spend freely, and not yet immediately identifiable, as he was now cultivating clipped whiskers for his wedding, he could slip in and out of the public gaze. 'The other day just before his marriage,' Sir William Hardman wrote, 'he was smoking in a first-class railway carriage (ordinary train) and the porter, not recognising him, asked him to show his ticket. A lady residing at Windsor told a friend ... he had gone up to the bookstall and bought a copy of *Punch* and actually paid for it himself.'

The Queen's unwillingness to furnish her heir with anything to do benefited Bertie in at least one respect: the press was reluctant to moral-ize about his neglect of his princely duties. But for taking his seat in the House of Lords at four in the afternoon of 5 February – an insignificant privilege of his majority – he had no public occupation, though in recognition of his forthcoming marriage the Queen allowed him to preside over her levées, the first on 25 February. St James's Palace, Benjamin Moran wrote – Victoria kept Buckingham Palace in mourning – was 'tremendously crowded, there being 1000 presentations'. (A huge backlog of aspirants for such social cachet had built up during her seclusion, and the invitations announced that all presentations were to be considered as if made to the absent Queen herself.) 'The Prince looked remarkably well & shook hands with almost everybody at first in true American fashion.'

Until the Queen lost interest in the custom late in life, after the wedding he would preside at dozens of further levées with Alexandra. The forthcoming royal wedding and the continuing withdrawal of Victoria made Albert Edward highly, if temporarily, popular. The audience at the Olympic Theatre, there to see the comedian Frederic Robson do a burlesque *Robin Hood*, discovered the Prince in one of the boxes when someone shouted, 'Long live the future King of England!' Still gauche, the Prince responded in embarrassment to the cheering by slipping out of sight.

Deprived of the wedding itself, Londoners planned to celebrate the arrival of the Princess and cheer her passage through the city en route to Windsor. *The Times* would publish Tennyson's Laureate verses, 'A Welcome to Alexandra', as bathetic as they would prove ironic, about

> The sea-kings' daughter as happy as fair,
> Blissful bride of a blissful heir ...

and Welsh composer and organist Brinley Richards turned out '*Bendith ar ei Ben*', or 'God Bless the Prince of Wales', with English lyrics by A. G. Prys-Jones, asking that Divine 'guidance' furnish the Prince with 'strength and wisdom'. (Richards was rumoured to be up for a knighthood for his efforts.) Young Arthur Sullivan prepared a *Princess of Wales's March*, incorporating Danish airs, for a Wedding Festival Concert at the Crystal Palace in Sydenham, across the Thames. Albert Edward was awarded the Freedom of the City of London, citizenship *honoris causa*.

While London prepared triumphal arches, bunting, flags and illuminations, its entrepreneurs fashioned souvenirs to sell. Seats on scaffolding along the parade route escalated in price. Indoor spaces were hawked in the press, and on the front page of *The Times* of 28 February

1863, a Saturday (when classified advertisements traditionally occupied the first several pages), someone offered, with obvious *double entendre* and a typographical error either accidental or – more likely – hilariously deliberate,

> ROYAL PROCESSION. – FIRST FLOOR, with two large widows, to be LET, in the best part of Cockspur-street, with entrance accessible behind.

Copies of the paper, after the discovery, fetched premium prices, and the advertisement, allegedly placed by a Mr Lindley, did not reappear. Arthur Munby heard of shop windows let for the day at '22 guineas each; and of men at Windsor who have let their houses – opposite the Castle – for the four days, for £150'. His mistress, a scullery maid, told him that her employer had 'given near £100' for a room along the route. American envoy Charles Francis Adams had a seat 'with a lot of greasy coats on an itinerant platform, at a cost of two shillings'. His more cynical son (and secretary), Henry, wrote to his brother Charles, Jr, a Union Army officer, about the 'bother and fuss', that 'it seems as though a temporary bee has lodged in the bonnet of this good people', and saw only a 'determined, ponderous and massive hilarity'. Robert Browning, eager nevertheless to secure a seat for himself and his son, wrote to friends in America, 'Everybody is crazy – literally – about the entry next Saturday of the Princess: the crowd will be enormous. I heartily wish I were out of it all – but must place Pen, and, being caught in the current, may as well see it with good grace.' Dickens would claim to be 'be-princed to the last point of human endurance', but nevertheless hired a carriage to take his younger children to the festivities.

The classified columns of the dailies advertised marriage medals ('unrivalled works of art') at a shilling; 'riband rosettes' to wear at wedding events for a shilling, 'wedding favours' adorned with Prince of Wales plumes for a shilling, mounted photos of the couple at thirteen shillings-and-sixpence; miniature portraits of them to fit *carte de visite* albums ('the most exquisite and refreshing novelties ever issued') at a half-crown, and Alexandra hair curlers at a shilling per pair. For viewers with seats remote from the procession, there were souvenir binoculars at two guineas, and medallions with 'unrivalled likenesses' of the pair at one guinea in silver, ten guineas in gold. (In New York, Bertie's old friend Tom Thumb had just been married, and card photos of 'Gen Tom Thumb and Mrs. Gen

Tom Thumb' were also advertised – at one shilling-and-sixpence each.) Copies of 'The Fair Maid of Denmark', a forgettable new song by W. H. Bellamy and J. L. Hatton, were on sale for a shilling-and-sixpence. The anthem 'God Bless the Prince of Wales' was offered in sheets arranged for four voices at a shilling-and-sixpence, but only at Brewer and Co., 23 Bishopsgate, could one buy, in a new wedding edition, the Charles Jeffreys ballad (set to music by B. Nelson) 'Oh! Take Her but Be Faithful Still', known familiarly as 'The Bride', for two-and-sixpence. And Messrs Garrard, the Crown jewellers, advertised their display of 'the costly presents manufactured for the Prince of Wales for his bride' in diamonds and pearls, open to 'fashionable visitors'.

The royal yacht *Victoria and Albert* had been sent to Antwerp to convey Alexandra, her parents, her two brothers and three sisters, and two of her uncles (but not the Danish King) across the North Sea and up the Thames to Gravesend, where the yacht was surrounded by dozens of private boats crammed with cheering well-wishers. Despite the flotilla's slow pace, the Prince of Wales was late getting to the dock on Saturday morning, 6 March, but he ensured that his unpunctuality would be forgotten. Abandoning all decorum by running up the gangway from his carriage, he embraced Alexandra and, to the delight of the adoring crowds, kissed her. It was probably the most popular public act he ever performed. Even *Punch* lost its satiric edge in rapturous verses about the bells and bunting and the boom of cannon proclaiming that 'Her foot is on English ground!'

By special train the bridal party and the Prince's staff travelled to the Bricklayers' Arms railway station in Southwark, on the south bank of the Thames, where they were met by the Lord Mayor, his sheriffs and other officials in their medieval regalia. There a carriage procession formed to cross London Bridge and, to the blare of bandsmen and the urging of outriders from the Life Guards, and led by troops from every contingent within marching distance from London, the Prince and Alexandra drove toward Paddington Station via Fleet Street and the Strand, Pall Mall, St James's Street, Piccadilly and Hyde Park. Tiers of seats on the eastern and southern sides of St Paul's held 10,000 spectators, many of them waving Danish flags, while below the seats the proprietors of the Freemason's Tavern ran 'an extensive buffet, with unlimited champagne'.

Londoners were charmed by the slight young Princess, who braved the drizzle and cold and, finally, a wan sun, in an open carriage, attired in a grey silk dress and violet jacket, with only her white bonnet a concession to the nuptials. (The muted colours were a tactful gesture to the mourning Queen.) She and her mother sat side by side, the Prince and her father opposite, their backs to the horses, tipping their tall hats. 'Hats off!' shouted the men as her carriage approached. 'Here she is!' women called out. In an age before electronic media, the reality of the royal wedding lay in its preliminaries, in the processions, the banners and the bunting, the external panoply that made the monarchy accessible to the masses. Newspapers covered every aspect of the affair, from Alexandra's arrival to her exchanging of vows. Thousands of ordinary people – even many of the privileged – who had no seats in St George's Chapel (which could squeeze in only 900), nor any way to get to Windsor, gathered at railway stations and on carriageways that took the bejewelled and beribboned celebrities, in Court dress and full uniform, to the wedding. In such ways, unticketed celebrants seized a further morsel of the nuptials. While they, but for their souvenirs, enjoyed the party atmosphere at no cost, the Queen's parsimonious Household officials estimated the cost of the wedding at £4,500 – including £50 for Alexandra's temporary use of rooms at the Castle.

'I *dread* the *whole* thing *awfully*,' the Queen underlined to her daughter Vicky before she left Berlin for the wedding, '& wonder even how *you can rejoice* so much at *witnessing* what *must* I should think be to *you*, who loved Papa so *dearly*, so *terribly sad* a wedding.' Vicky's 'ecstasies' were 'incomprehensible'. It would be important, the Queen warned, that she herself be protected from '*noise & joyousness*'. For her the important day was the day before the ceremony, 9 March, when the Queen visited the newly completed mausoleum at Frogmore in the Windsor grounds, escorting Bertie and Alix to Albert's tomb. 'I opened the shrine,' she wrote in her diary, oblivious to the impact of the melancholy setting upon a probably rather frightened young girl, 'and took them in. Alix was much moved and so was I. I said, "*He* gives you his blessing!" and joined Alix's and Bertie's hands, taking them both in my arms. It was a very touching moment and we all felt it.' It made explicit the Queen's intention. The wedding guests at St James's Chapel might be glittering and gaudy, and their excitement electric, but she was determined to overspread it with gloom.

On the day of the wedding, the *Daily Telegraph*, after insisting that it would not philosophize on such a celebratory morning, cautioned the

Prince to listen carefully during the marriage service and seize 'all the solemn notes which sound for HIM in the music of the Wedding March'. He was to be aware that 'never yet in its ample scope did graver fears and graver hopes cluster about the Heir of the Empire', and that while 'Victoria has made it *queenly* to be good, pure and faithful', it would be his charge to make such qualities 'princely'. The Radical, Republican *Reynolds's Newspaper* scorned such adjectives, and saw praise of the Prince as the hope of England and the Princess as the fairest of the fair, as 'loathsome' and 'ludicrous'. Behind the sentimentality it saw cheap commercial exploitation of the wedding. The young newlyweds 'have been [inadvertently] employed to advertise the nostrums of quack doctors, puff the work of slop tailors, [of] short-measuring and adulterating grocers'. Unthinking national enthusiasm, it claimed, had nothing to do 'with the unselfish loyalty of English tradesmen', and *Reynolds's* feared that the pretty Princess of Wales, only eighteen, would become a commercial icon – an 'inanimate doll, for fashion to ape and extravagance to deck'.*

Although the wedding was the social event of the decade, the Queen attempted to mute its pageantry in every way. Her model was the marriage of Princess Alice to Prince Louis of Hesse the year before, which was private in the extreme, set on the Isle of Wight in the dining room at Osborne House before the grand portrait of the royal family by Franz Winterhalter, in which the late Prince Consort appeared young and slender in Court breeches, crimson neckband of decorations, and blue ribbon and badge of the Garter, while Victoria was regal and radiant in tiara and white lace. Sixteen years later the Queen, in black, had sat stiffly in an armchair, oblivious to the ceremony, gazing only upon Winterhalter's portrait of Albert. The Archbishop of York, himself a widower, wept as he read the service. There was no wedding cake, no confetti, and afterwards the married couple had had to lunch alone with Victoria.

Now, with her ladies-in-waiting discreetly about her but feeling 'lonely and desolate', she sat out the medieval ceremonies in Catherine of Aragon's balcony overlooking St George's Chapel, visible to everyone in her black silk and crêpe in a recess above and (from the congregation) to the left of the altar. Upon her widow's weeds she had pinned the Prince

* Paradoxically, *Reynolds's Newspaper* shared its offices with *Bow Bells*, a pro-royal paper, blatant evidence that newspapers were products to be marketed as well as purveyors of information and ideas.

Consort's own Garter star with blue ribbon, as well as a jewelled miniature of Albert she wore as a brooch – which made it possible for Albert (since the sum of her theology was a belief in a hereafter in which she would be reunited with her husband) to be present at the wedding. The Bishop of Oxford preached the marriage sermon, proposing the theme, 'Rejoice with them that do rejoice', though Victoria had insisted on adding the words, 'and weep with them that weep'. C.T. Longley, the Archbishop of Canterbury, conducted the service, and the 'Swedish nightingale' Jenny Lind, in her soaring soprano, accompanied the organ and choir in a chorale composed by Prince Albert – a performance during which the Queen was seen to look upward, then become stricken, after which she was dramatically assisted out to recover herself. To Gladstone (in his diary) the ceremony was 'the most gorgeous sight I ever witnessed, & one of the most touching'. For his political rival Disraeli, it was like a fairy tale, and 'the only pageant which never disappointed me'. The Queen was a consummate actress, and made certain there were more eyes upon her than upon Albert Edward and Alexandra. As the royal person-ages passed her cabinet to the strains of Mendelssohn's 'March of the Priests' from *Athalie* (rather than his Wedding March from *A Midsummer Night's Dream*, first performed at a marriage when the Princess Royal was wed in 1858), they looked up, paused, and bowed. 'I had never seen the Queen since the catastrophe,' Disraeli recalled, 'and ventured, being near-sighted, to use my glass. I saw H.M. well, and unfortunately caught her glance.' Scolded by her frown, he did not repeat the error.

As the ceremony proceeded with clockwork precision and dignity, with Albert Edward in general's uniform under velvet Garter robes and Alexandra in white and silver satin, and a long silver train borne by eight bridesmaids, W. P. Frith sketched the scene for a large, crowded picture. Learning that Frith had accepted the commission, Sir Edwin Landseer exclaimed, 'So you are going to do the marriage picture! Well! For all the money in this world, and all in the next, I wouldn't undertake such a thing.' Frith had been offered a modest (given the painter's usual fees) £3,000 by Sir Charles Phipps in the Queen's name, and sat happily in Court dress ('suit, sword, etc.') while working – musing, he noted, upon what a 'glorious subject for pageantry and colour' it was. But he would have to retrieve dresses and uniforms from afar, paint some participants from photographs, others from substitutes, and some from imagination. The ten-foot canvas took a year to complete, and to get four-year old

Prince William of Prussia, Vicky's eldest son and the future German Kaiser, to pose – during the ceremony he had crawled about looking for kilts and biting bare knees – Frith had had to let him 'paint a little on the picture'. A master of crowd scenes, Frith could populate his canvas convincingly, yet the true drama, but for the comedy of savage little Willy, remained hidden from him and his sketchbook in the Chapel.

At the altar with Bertie, who now showed signs of self-indulgent plumpness under his robes, were his brother-in-law, the tall, whiskered Crown Prince of Prussia, and his uncle (and Albert's brother) Ernest, Duke of Saxe-Coburg-Gotha. Prince Frederick was in difficulty at home for abetting the Danish marriage, and Duke Ernest, more Prussian than the Prussians, had tried to sabotage the betrothal. None of Alexandra's attendants, all of them British, had been chosen by her. She knew no one at the ceremony beyond Bertie's family and her own. Acknowledging that morning to Crown Princess Victoria, her new sister-in-law, that she was marrying someone she barely knew, she told Vicky nonetheless, 'You may think that I like marrying Bertie for his position; but if he were a cowboy I would love him just the same and would marry no one else!' (A cowboy then was simply a boy who tends cows, not a mounted cattle-ranch hand.) It was probably the most forceful remark she would make over a long life not given to asperity.

Perhaps loveliest of the bridesmaids chosen for her, about whom she knew little or nothing, was the animated Lady Diana Beauclerk – who may fleetingly have entertained a hope of standing where Alix now stood.

The Queen, in her mourning clothes and lace-covered widow's cap, did not mix with the throng at the post-wedding breakfast. By the time all five hundred guests gathered under a marquee it had become a late lunch. Briefly, the newlyweds, in their going-away clothes, slipped away at the Queen's instructions to pose with her for a family picture photographed by John Jabez Mayall, in which the central figure, to the Prince's left, was a marble bust of Albert. Afterwards, Bertie and Alexandra came to bid her goodbye, a farewell she had arranged, theatrically, on a staircase; then the couple left by special train for Southampton, and the waiting royal yacht which would ferry them to the Isle of Wight. At Osborne House they would finally be unchaperoned.

At their departure there was chaos at the small Windsor railway station. A group of Eton boys led by the fourteen-year-old Lord Randolph Churchill tried to keep the train from leaving, and broke

through a small police cordon and wooden barrier while a band, oblivious to the commotion, played 'God Save the Queen'. As the train finally
pulled out, young Churchill, his prized top hat lost, saw the Prince at the
carriage door, shouting 'Hurrah!' in relief at getting away.

The confusion became worse as sun changed to rain and bejewelled
ladies in their swirling gowns, separated from their escorts in the confusion, tried to squeeze into the crowded and inadequate railway cars of the
single return train to London. There was a frantic scramble for seats.
Disraeli managed to rescue the regal wife of the Austrian ambassador,
Countess Apponyi, swathed in sables and diamonds and blue velvet
embroidered in gold, and assist her aboard. 'I think I had to sit on my
wife's lap,'; he remembered. 'When we got to Paddington [Station] in the
rain there was no ambassadorial carriage; but ours was there, and so we
took home safe this brilliant and delightful person.'

While the wedding guests began leaving Windsor in the late afternoon, London was festive with bells ringing, banners and hangings
everywhere, illuminations prepared to turn night into day, fireworks at
the ready and all theatres open and offering free seats. Every town and
village had its own equivalent, from public dinners to military parades.
In every port, the masts of ships were resplendent with pennants and
flags. With her daughter Helena, then sixteen, the Queen made her way
back to Frogmore and what she would always call the 'dear Mausoleum'.
No crowd noises penetrated the silence. 'Ah, dear brother, what a sad and
dismal ceremony it was!' Victoria wrote to King William of Prussia.

VII

Falling out of Love

1863–1868

'FOR MY PART,' Disraeli wrote to the Tory leader in the Lords, the Earl of Derby, 'I think even Princes should sow their wild oats, and not step out paterfamilias from the nursery or the middy's berth.' He was thinking of the recently married Prince of Wales, who had had little opportunity beyond the services of Nellie Clifden for what was often referred to as a sentimental education. His Princess, an innocent eighteen, had had none. In the near privacy of Osborne they learned together, and since abstinence was the only form of contraception they knew, Alix was soon pregnant.

Court officials planning the formal introduction of the couple to the *haute noblesse* arranged an evening reception for them at St James's Palace, the great brick mansion at the corner of St James's Street and Pall Mall which had not been used for such an occasion since the reign of George III. While an orchestra played, the young Princess, wearing a coronet of diamonds, was escorted about the illumined saloons by her radiant husband. The Queen, sequestered from joy, was nowhere to be seen.

From Osborne the bride and groom had returned to Windsor as a courtesy, then had gone by train to King's Lynn, and on to Sandringham on 28 March to observe the expensive renovations. On 7 April they moved into Marlborough House to initiate what Disraeli called a public honeymoon. There would be weeks of celebration, unlike anything London had ever experienced, including a review of Volunteers in Hyde Park, a march-past of 22,000 in which the Prince was assisted by his brother-in-law, Louis of Hesse, who was almost as inexperienced at arms as was the twenty-one-year-old honorary general. On the day of the review, 28 May 1863, Dickens wrote to Etienne Carjat, 'The Prince and Princess of Wales go about (wisely) very much, and have as fair a chance of popularity as ever prince and princess had. The City ball in their honour [at the Guildhall] is to be a tremendously gorgeous business.' On 14 June, Disraeli wrote to his elderly friend Sarah Brydges-Willyams, in Torquay, 'This royal honeymoon, of many months, is perfectly distracting. Nothing but balls and banquets, the receptions, and inaugurations and processions, so that one has not a moment to oneself, and lives only in a glittering bustle.'

Victoria spent much of the festive period at Osborne, explaining to Queen Augusta of Prussia, her daughter Vicky's mother-in-law, 'I feel so very shattered, and my time is very occupied, as everything is such a burden to me.' Her chief burden remained Bertie, to which she added Alix, whom she saw now as frail if pleasantly pretty, pious to the point of having tracts at her bedside, shallow in intellect – her competence in French was embarrassingly limited – and almost as hearing-impaired as her mother. From Osborne the Queen wrote to Vicky during an April interlude in the balls and receptions, 'Bertie and Alix are here since Saturday. He has let himself down to his bad manners again. She is dear and good but I think looks far from strong and will never be able to bear the London [social] season unless she has but few late nights.' To Vicky in May she worried that she saw no signs yet of a pregnancy, and feared, if the event occurred, that the parents could only produce 'unintellectual children', yet 'It would be very sad if they had none.' Alix, she claimed, now disenchanted, 'has the smallest head ever seen.... I dread that – with his small empty brain – very much for [their] future children. The doctor says that Alix's head goes in, in the most extraordinary way just behind the forehead: I wonder what phrenologists would say.' Soon she complained to Vicky that Alix was sallow and losing her freshness, and 'Alas! She is deaf and everyone observes it, which is a sad misfortune.' She was anxious, too, about Affie, now nineteen, who seemed 'smitten' with Alix and would have to be kept away from Marlborough House. Prince Alfred did not have the 'character' to resist the temptation, 'and it is like playing with fire'.

Despite her splendid isolation, Victoria was well aware of her world, though the world outside assumed otherwise. In the *Boston Journal* in July 1867, an article from its anonymous London correspondent (most reportage then was unsigned, and the writer might even have been, as Lord Torrington long was, a person with royal entrée) exaggerated her retirement only slightly. In 'The Daily Life of Queen Victoria' the London informant observed that she was 'seldom seen', even in the privacy of Windsor:

> Servants complain bitterly of the quiet and inactivity of everything royal. The horses are unused, and the stablemen yawn in indolence. Little company is received. The state [dinner] plate has never been used since the death of Prince Albert. Her private apartments are under the charge of a Highlander, named [John] Brown. He is the Queen's domestic prime minister, and has more influence over her than [Lord] Derby. He attends her Majesty ... and gives orders with imperial grace. He holds his position to the intense disgust of the royal household. On state occasions he goes bare-legged [in a kilt].... The Queen does not attend the royal chapels, either in London or Windsor, as she dislikes being gazed at. She has her private chapels.... Even the crowd of men who wear the royal livery and sleep under the same roof do not see the Queen from one year's end to the other. Her drives are all private. The Home Park has a drive of six miles.... The elegant state horses champ and snort in the stables, while the Queen, in a low-backed wagon, a low-wheeled carriage, and her stubby pony, takes a drive.

The Queen was a secluded, perpetually mourning, widow, more and more dependent upon Brown, whom the royal children, especially Bertie, heartily despised; nevertheless, her eyes were sharp and her informal intelligence system – which included Brown – was peerless. Diplomats and Ministers kept her informed via her locked red boxes of Cabinet messages, and courtiers vied to offer confidences gleaned from the comings and goings of visitors and from their connections outside. To Vicky she wrote frankly in June of her fear that Alexandra could never live up to her small potential with 'a very weak and terribly frivolous' husband. 'Oh! What will become of the poor country when I die! I foresee, if B[ertie] succeeds, nothing but misery – for he never reflects or listens for a moment and he [would] ... spend his life in one whirl of amusements as he does now. It makes me very sad and angry.' But she did not leave the matter there, as an empty complaint. As Lord Stanley, a Disraeli ally and son of Lord Derby, noted in his diary that June, 'Much talk in London about the extraordinary way in which the Queen undertakes to direct the Prince and Princess of Wales in every detail of their lives. They may not dine out, except at houses named by her: nor ask anyone to dine with them except with previous approval or unless the name of the person invited is on a list previously prepared: and the Princess, after riding once or twice in the Park, was forbidden to do so again. In addition, a daily and minute report of what passes at Marlborough House is sent to the Queen. The parties most concerned make no complaint, but others do for them, and the whole proceeding is ill-judged.'

The couple – Bertie in particular, had to outwait her. He was now of age, and – albeit through a comptroller – in charge of his finances and his life. (Knollys was not to divide his loyalties for long. His career was caught up with that of the Prince.) Still counting on Knollys to be her deputy rather than the Prince's, Victoria wrote to him as late as June 1866, in a letter he was instructed to show the Prince of Wales, that the London social élite (the personal inference was unmistakable) had become 'so lax and bad' that the Waleses had a duty 'to deny themselves amusement in order to keep up that tone in Society which *used* to be the pride of England'. The Prince was to show his disapproval by 'not asking them to dinner, nor down to Sandringham – and above all, by not going to their houses'.

On the surface the Queen was generous and supportive, holding what was for her a rare drawing-room reception at Buckingham Palace on 16 May to introduce Alix to the right people in London. Nearly 3,000 ladies were presented, and the pale Princess became so exhausted that at one point the doors had to be closed to afford her some rest. The Danish Minister, Forben de Bille, commented to American Legation representative Benjamin Moran that Alexandra needed 'some of the roast beef and ale of England to give her more flesh and development'. More perceptively, Victoria noticed that Alix's waist had thickened and her clothes were being 'let out'. The Queen had not yet been told that the Princess was pregnant. That was a delicate matter to broach to the Queen, and it seemed inconsistent with her complaint to Vicky on 24 June that Alix and Bertie were becoming 'nothing but puppets, running about for show all day and all night'.

George Meredith wrote to William Hardman on 4 July that the *Court Circular*, usually the least informative location for significant revelations about royalty, had reported, as Meredith summed it up, 'The Prince took

a ride [on horseback]: the Princess took a drive. *Verbum sap.*' Her delicate condition became the talk of London. *Punch* published a cartoon,
'What the Nation Hopes to See', showing a proud Queen holding a
swaddled infant in her arms behind her stood the new royal parents. An
heir ensured the succession into a third generation.

For a time, Alexandra did little to accommodate to her pregnancy.
Having lived in aristocratic penury, she delighted in the parties, the
operas, the balls, the hostessing which she could do in her own
mansion, in which they spent most of their time while Sandringham
was being renovated. Both princely properties required new coach
houses and stables to fit their own style. The Prince also contracted for
a luxurious smoking room for each home. In London, Alix, who in
Denmark had shared a single bedroom with her sister, had a suite of
sumptuously decorated rooms for herself, and three pianos. With her
personal allowance from Parliament she could now order her gowns
from Charles Frederick Worth's stylish establishment in Paris, made
fashionable by the patronage of Eugénie, rather than making, or
mending, old ones. Among the eighty-five servants in Marlborough
House (dozens more looked after the stables), four polished and repol-
ished the silver, much of it wedding presents. In the kitchens, aside from
maids, were a chef, two cooks and a confectioner for delicacies. The
stables employed an additional forty servants – coachmen and grooms.
Bertie had his special brougham; Alix had her choice of a landau or a
victoria, the latter a low, four-wheeled carriage for two with collapsible
hood and high, forward seat for the driver, named after her mother-in-
law in 1844.

The English *haut monde* had long craved a royal personality around
whom its social activities could revolve, and the Prince of Wales, with
only the most nominal ceremonial functions decreed by his mother, and
those largely the dedication of memorials to his father, filled the vacuum.
He could do so even when the Princess, often absent in the later child-
bearing months as convention demanded, was unavailable. At the time
of Bertie's twenty-second birthday, in November, Alix had filled out
enough to withdraw discreetly from public view though not from such
family events. Among his birthday gifts was a rug worked by his sister
Louise, then fifteen, together with a statuette which he declared was
'admirably modelled'. He prophesied that she might some day become
'an eminent sculptress'. The Prince's loyalties to his brothers and sisters

WHAT THE NATION HOPES SOON TO SEE.

*An heir to the heir is expected, and the succession is guaranteed. The
Queen with the still unborn grandchild, and young
Bertie and Alix behind her (Punch, 23 January 1864)*

were absolute, and remained so, and he was sensitive to their need for
self-esteem. Such professions came rarely if ever from their mother, who
saw her children almost always in terms of how they could support her
as Queen. As she would confide to her diary (8 July 1871), 'After '61 I
could hardly bear the thought of anyone ... standing where my dearest

had always stood; but as years go on, I strongly feel that to lift up my son and heir and keep him in his place, near me, is really what is right.' The greatest happiness of others, she felt, should come from their exertions in her behalf, as became clear just after Bertie's birthday, when Lady Augusta Bruce, her favourite lady-in-waiting, and now forty-one, announced ('most unnecessarily', Victoria felt) that she would marry Canon Stanley. It was, the Queen wrote to her uncle, Leopold, 'my greatest sorrow and trial since my misfortune'.

Other loyalties began to divide mother and son before the year ended. Prussia and Denmark had long fought, by words and by arms, over the possession of the duchies of Schleswig and Holstein. With the accession of Alix's father to the Danish throne as Christian IX late in 1863, the issue of inheritance of the territories came up again and Denmark formally incorporated Schleswig into the kingdom. For Bertie, despite his eldest sister's status as Crown Princess of Prussia, his wife and his father-in-law were Danes, and the duchies, despite a complicated history of claims and counter-claims, belonged with Denmark. Managed by Prussia under Count Bismarck, the German states (Holstein was part of the German Federation) threatened invasion, and the Queen told her Ministers that she would never consent that England should go to war with Germany to support Danish ambitions. The issue simmered into 1864, when, early into the new year, the Waleses, visiting Windsor and staying in the grounds at Frogmore, drove on 8 January to Virginia Water, now frozen over, so the Prince could play ice hockey. Alex watched from a sledge but, feeling increasingly unwell, was driven back to Frogmore with her lady-in-waiting, the Countess of Macclesfield. Since the Princess's labour was premature, no preparations had been made. A local physician, Dr Brown (subsequently to be knighted and given an honorarium of £1,000), was summoned, and came at a gallop, arriving barely in time for the birth, at which he was assisted by Lady Macclesfield, who wrapped the baby, only four pounds and very pale, in one of her flannel petticoats and some cotton-wool, and laid him in a basket near the fireplace. Victoria, who did not arrive until the next day, exaggerated only slightly in her diary that Lady Macclesfield, who had borne twelve children, had acted as nurse 'in every sense of the word', and that there were 'no clothes for the poor little boy, who was just wrapped in cotton wool'.

The Queen hovered over her grandson for four days, increasingly unwelcome as she ticked off her instructions for '*names, sponsors,* and *christening*. The parents were to have nothing to do with it, although from Osborne she announced her permission to have the christening at Buckingham Palace rather than at Windsor, conceding that 'the people of London ... should *not* be deprived of having *some event* in town'. Because the baby was premature she wanted the ceremony delayed until it was 'full size'. And she intended to hold the child herself, although it would be 'trying' to go to London. She insisted on naming the sponsors, although some, in the climate of Danish–German animosity, might cause 'heartburnings', and she insisted on her names for the baby, beginning with Albert Victor and including Leopold. Hinting at earlier arguments at Frogmore she added, 'I would advise reserving *Edward* for a second or third son.' (The child was in fact named Albert Victor Christian Edward.) 'Respecting your own names, and the conversation we had,' she went on imperiously, and invoking Albert, 'I wish to repeat that it was beloved Papa's wish, as well as mine, that you should be called by *both*, when you became King, and it would be *impossible* for you to *drop* your Father's [name]. It would be monstrous, and *Albert alone*, as you truly and amiably say, would *not do*, as there can be only *one* ALBERT!' The '*two united names*', she insisted, would be the way of the future, first in him, and then in his son.

   With adroit amiability, Bertie reminded his mother that 'no English Sovereign' had ever borne two names, and 'it would not be pleasant' to be in the titular company of Victor Emmanuel and Louis Napoleon – 'although no doubt there is no absolute reason why it should not be so'. The Queen dropped the matter, and Bertie formally kept his Albert Edward identity, and his 'AE' initials, yet exactly a month later, 15 March 1864, American papers were reporting via some opportune leak which the Prince could, if he wished, deny, 'The name by which the Prince of Wales will ascend the throne will be King Edward the Seventh.' And almost immediately after the christening, the infant Prince Albert Victor Christian Edward began to be known within the bosom of his family as Prince Eddy.

   On 1 February, Prussia (with its Confederation allies) had invaded the disputed Danish provinces, and the differences between mother and son were exacerbated by their conflicting loyalties. Although Victoria claimed neutrality, in order to keep England out of war and to be available as mediator, the Prussians had no interest in a brokered settlement, realizing that they could easily overpower Denmark, a process made easier by England's refusal to intervene. Members of Palmerston's Government were furious with what John Wodehouse – the future Earl of Kimberley – called 'a miserable vacillating undignified policy'. Alexandra was miserable and Bertie furious, and the Queen wrote obtusely to Vicky, whose husband was off clearing the Danes from Schleswig and Holstein, 'It is terrible to have the poor boy [Bertie] on the wrong side, and [it] aggravates my sufferings greatly.'

Although Lord Russell, the Foreign Minister, was anxious for the Prince of Wales, as heir to the throne, to see official dispatches relating to the crisis, Victoria told Russell that she would not permit the Prince to have a 'separate and independent communication with the Government'. Rather, she would show him what she wanted him to see. General Grey explained 'confidentially' to Russell on her behalf, 'that His Royal Highness is not at all times as discreet as He should be'. Bertie protested that he ought to have access to the traditional red boxes in which Cabinet papers were sent (he had been sworn in as a member of her Privy Council in February 1863 and had a seat in the House of Lords) but she turned him down, writing, 'You could not well have a Government key, which only Ministers, and those immediately connected with them, or with me, have.' Her intransigence would spur him to develop his private ministerial and diplomatic contacts – and with some success – but the very method led him to further indiscretions. A later Foreign Minister would tell the Queen's Private Secretary, Sir Henry Ponsonby, that one evening he received messages from four friends all reporting that 'One of my first notes to him had been handed round a dinner party.' It may have been indiscreet bragging, or the Prince's realization that the avenue to information was often someone's assumption that the heir was already knowledgeable.

When defeat came for the Danes, the Prince agitated for permission to go to Denmark with his wife, and to take their child, ostensibly so that he could be seen by his other grandparents, but it was clear to the Queen that any visit would demonstrate covert solidarity with Alix's homeland. Reluctantly, she acquiesced, but with the proviso that the baby be sent home after three weeks, that the Waleses observe the strictest incognito (an absurdity in the circumstances), and that they return via Germany to demonstrate royal impartiality. The young Royals, however, were as popular in England as was the Danish cause, and cheers for them wherever they went were also anti-German manifestations. At

Cambridge they were the guests of honour at Trinity College's May Ball, traditionally held in early June, where – the press reported – the Prince bowed 'one thousand eight-hundred and seventy-six times' receiving guests who had been practising walking backwards in order to be at their best as they retired from the royal presences. He shook hands with each of the young 'old boys' who were 'up' in his time, and the undergraduates sang 'For he's a jolly good fellow'. In London they often rode in Hyde Park, with a cluster of the fashionable eager to trot nearby in their finery. One, for whom it was a busman's holiday, was the curvaceous American star of the hit melodrama *Mazeppa*, Adah Isaacs Menken. As the 'Naked Lady' she rode bareback in flesh-coloured tights during the afternoons and evenings at the Victoria Theatre in Waterloo Road, but gave up her mornings to be seen with HRH. 'I had an engagement to ride horseback in the Park today at 12,' she wrote to New York newspaperman Edwin James. 'And you know the Prince is again in Rotten Row, and what woman of spirit, or taste, would keep away if she could possibly get out, and more especially if Poole had just sent home her new and beautiful riding habit?'

After the social season in London, in which Alix was now perceived as the beautiful princess in distress, the public continued to sympathize with Denmark. Many saw the Queen, despite her ostensible seclusion, as the tool of her German relatives. Making a family visit as well as a political statement, the Waleses sailed for Denmark in the *Osborne*, with the infant Prince Eddy. Alix, who had not been up to all of Bertie's diversions, had gone, nevertheless, to race meetings and balls with him, and they had entertained and been entertained. But the Prince could not bear a quiet evening, and when he did not go out with friends to sample London night life he had them to the smoking room at Marlborough House for cards, a 'baccy' (baccarat, as gambling, was unlawful but played privately by the privileged), and a midnight supper. Some of his guests, however, came from the political and diplomatic worlds, and he saw himself, particularly after the wilful pro-Germanism of his mother, as someone who should learn more about, and even influence, foreign policy. The Danish connection was a spur, since Alix's brother, as a naval cadet of seventeen, had become George I of Greece after the expulsion of ineffective King Otho and the inability of the Greeks to secure a more senior (but safe) Royal from the courts of Europe. And Alix's sister Dagmar ('Minnie' to her family) was about to be betrothed to the Tsarevitch of Russia.

Influenced by the helplessness of Denmark and the timidity of other nations, Bertie saw Prussia as the aggrandizing enemy likely to alter the balance of power in Europe. Without permission from Windsor Castle, and pursuing his own objectives, primarily then to demonstrate that he could not be tyrannized, he called on the visiting Italian revolutionary hero, Giuseppe Garibaldi, on 12 April, earning the outrage of the Queen, who was loudly unhappy at Garibaldi's presence in Britain, and his being lionized by some of the aristocracy she counted now as false friends. Even Palmerston and Russell, the political leadership of the Liberals (the renamed Whigs), had Garibaldi to dinner, which Victoria saw as an affront to Austria, still a territorial power in the north of Italy.

On 23 April the Prince responded to his mother that he had met Garibaldi '*quite privately*', and saw him as '*uncharlatanlike*' and as an Italian patriot. In their talk, Bertie made it a point to note, he had indeed 'referred to Denmark'. Rather than rail again at him, she chastized Knollys for not reining in her son, and warned that 'for the future she must *insist* that no step of the *slightest political importance* shall be taken [by the Prince] without due consultation with the Queen'. Knollys replied politely, but Bertie, obviously made aware of her message, wrote on his own behalf (27 April) that General Garibaldi had been hailed by her subjects, and sought 'the Unity of Italy, which is the avowed policy of the present Government'. Apparently Prince Albert's political lessons prior to young Bertie's first trip to Italy had not failed after all. (At a dinner for the French ambassador the Prince even attempted a diplomatic pun, wearing a cravat with the colours of the winner of the Derby and announcing, 'This is an additional tie between France and England.')

Knollys, the Prince added bluntly to his irate mother, 'is not, and cannot be, responsible for my actions. I have now been of age for some time and am *alone* responsible, and am only too happy to bear *any* blame on my shoulders.' It was his declaration of independence, but he would learn that in a monarchy, even a constitutional one, the heir to the throne was less than independent. In the clash of wills, the Queen still had the heaviest artillery. But one can guess what lay behind Gladstone's enigmatic diary entry on 25 June, 'Dined at Marlborough House: both Prince & Princess were [anti-Prussian] as usual, & this is saying much.' The Chancellor of the Exchequer had been involved in Cabinet discussions on Denmark, which were to continue the next afternoon, and had decided to take no action unless the nation's very existence were threatened. Bertie and Alix were doubtless hotly indignant.

The price of temporary freedom from his omnipresent mother was, for Bertie, that in Copenhagen, where dinner was at five and he had no friends, he missed the frenetic life he loved. Since the Russian Tsarevitch – the Grand Duke Nicholas – was due in Denmark to solicit the hand in marriage of Alix's sister, Bertie offered to be absent, and sought a hunting invitation from Charles XV of Sweden for the ten-day wooing period. Learning of the unplanned trip, Victoria instructed the Waleses to visit Stockholm incognito and stay at a hotel, or at the British Legation, but the Prince was in no mood to accept such instruction. The couple were guests at the palace in Drottningholm, from which Bertie went out to hunt elk, while the Swedish press covered his visit for what it was. (There were even rumours that he had been attentive to several attractive Swedish women.) Reproaches came from Victoria, and Bertie wrote to her from Copenhagen, 'The King was immensely gratified by our visit, and what would have been the good of annoying him by not going to the Palace? … You may be sure that I shall try to meet your wishes as much as possible, but … if I am not allowed to use my own discretion we had better give up travelling altogether.' Yet as *Punch* had already politely warned, anything he did or was alleged to have done became the inevitable target of scribblers. 'Yes, my dear Prince,' *Punch* wrote, 'things will grow worse and worse.' He could not 'even take a bath without a paragraph being published recording that event, and telling us at what temperature you bathed'. He might detest the attention, 'But I assure you once more that you must bear it. A cat may look at a king, and a toad may look at a prince.' It was a lesson left unread.

Victoria had already ruled out any princely intervention in German–Danish affairs, brushing aside earlier his suggestion that the British fleet enter the Baltic to protect Denmark from attack from the sea, and then rejecting his offer to be an intermediary to assist a settlement. His mother allowed him no access to Cabinet information, which he could only extract at second hand in the conviviality of smoking rooms and at dinner parties, and he did not know that she had offered herself to King William as intermediary, but in vain. She then called the Prussian King's Government obstinate and ambitious, and he denied all allegations as slander. Nevertheless, Victoria insisted that in the interest of amity Bertie and Alix were to return home via Germany, on the pretext of visiting family. He was 'to show that he is not only the son-in-law of the King of Denmark, but the Child of his parents', and he was to cancel his plans to return via Paris, travelling instead through Belgium. As she well knew, denying Bertie a sojourn in Paris was the worst of punishments.

Alarmed, the Foreign Secretary, Lord Russell, hinted politely that her dictation of the Prince of Wales's every move abroad could have unforeseen consequences for her. Undeterred, and determined to tame her brash son, she had the unhappy Sir Charles Phipps lecture Russell on her behalf (17 October) that it was 'of the highest importance' that the Queen's authority 'should be distinctly defined and constantly supported and maintained by the Government', and that its policies – in effect, her own – should not be 'associated in the Prince of Wales's mind with her Majesty's authority'. For Victoria, the Prince was to 'feel nothing but confiding affection'. Bertie duly visited relatives in Hanover and Darmstadt, and met his sister Vicky and her husband in Cologne, waxing furious afterward (to Lord Spencer) that Crown Prince Frederick was in Prussian uniform complete with 'a most objectionable medal ribbon which he received for his *deeds of valour???* against the unhappy Danes'. Vicky voiced complaints (to her mother) about Bertie's partisan behaviour, and the Queen explained that he had 'become quite unmanageable' under the influence of 'that most mischievous Queen of Denmark', and that 'Alix, as good as she is, is not worth the price we have had to pay for her in having such a family connection. I shall not let them readily go there again.'

The public was of a different opinion. Soon after their return the royal couple went to the Princess's Theatre to see Dion Boucicault's sentimental hit play about urban poverty, *The Streets of London*, which Dickens had derided as 'utterly degraded and debased'. (He had never had a stage success equivalent to the popularity of his novels.) Anti-German feeling had not abated. The audience cheered the royal pair in what was obviously a gesture of solidarity with Denmark.

By the time the Prince and Princess were reunited with Victoria at Osborne, the Queen had calmed down and found Alix (to Vicky on 19 November 1864) 'really a dear, excellent, right-minded soul.... I often think her lot is no easy one, but she is very fond of Bertie, though not blind.' The implication was that both mother and daughter had already heard tales, including fresh reports from Sweden, that Bertie was displaying, at the very least, a roving eye. Yet Alix was again pregnant, and before she had to sequester herself she and the Prince enjoyed, with no signs of rift, further London opera and theatre, hosted elaborate dinners and were guests of honour at others. At Marlborough House they hosted a party that November at which the entertainment was Tom Thumb, whom he had last seen when a child at Buckingham Palace more than twenty years before. 'General Tom' – he still appeared in Napoleonic uniform – had wed Lavinia Warren, twenty-one and 32 inches high. P. T. Barnum was touring them about Europe, and in each country they would borrow an infant (the smaller the better) and claim it as their own. While the Prince's entertainments were talked about, his guests were often unwelcome at Windsor as incompatible with the Queen's mourning.

The Queen, and sometimes her courtiers, continued to deplore the raffish, if aristocratic, company the couple kept, and even some distinguished and influential personages were sniffed at as the wrong sort. Earl Spencer advised that the Prince and Princess should not attend a Rothschild ball, given by the baronial parents of Bertie's Cambridge friend, as 'the Prince ought only to visit those of undoubted position in society'. Lionel and Charlotte de Rothschild were 'very worthy people', he conceded, 'but they especially hold their position from wealth and perhaps the accidental beauty of the first daughter they brought out'. (Their daughter Leonora may have been ravishing, but she was also a Jewess.) The Prince of Wales paid no attention to such prejudices, and, while the Princess was still active early in 1865, she asked Lady Ely to invite three of Baron de Rothschild's children, Natty, Alfred and Evelina, and Evelina's husband Ferdinand, to a ball at Marlborough House. Since the Prince was still presiding at royal levées which the Queen refused otherwise to hold, he invited both Natty and Alfred to one that March; and their mother, Charlotte, was able to report sardonically to her son Leopold that 'the Prince was gracious, as usual, smiled and shook hands – but H.R.H. has accustomed them to much kindness and cordiality; what amused them, however, was the rebuke he gave to Lord Sydney, who fine gentleman and jew-hater as he is, announced Natty [as if a foreigner] as Monsieur "Roshil" – "Mr de Rothschild" was the correction he received from royal lips.'

Without Alix, but with 'fast' friends, and using cabs rather than his own more recognizable equipages, Bertie went, hardly unseen, to *louche* music halls, and to clubs like the Jockey and White's, where he could – and often did – lose more than a hundred pounds in an evening at whist to politicians and peers like the Duke of St Albans, Lord Methuen, and the younger Sir Robert Peel, all far more acceptable socially to the 3rd Viscount Sydney, Master of the Queen's Household. More properly, yet reflecting his style, he presided at the opening of London's first grand hotel, the luxurious Langham in Portland Place, then the largest building in the city and instantly the fashionable place in which to be seen. At the height of the social season, on 2 June 1865, the Prince and Princess went to a concert by Sir Charles Hallé's orchestra, after which Alix returned too fatigued to be hostess at a late supper party. She retired, and soon after midnight she gave birth to her second son, precipitating new conflicts with the Queen.

'I can't deny', she confided to King Leopold, 'that I am glad that I am spared the anxiety and fatigue of being with Alix at the time.' Still, she found cause for anguish in the baby's names. His parents preferred George to Albert. 'We like the name and it is English,' Bertie explained. 'I had hoped for some fine old name,' Victoria returned, holding out for Frederick. 'We are sorry to hear that you don't like the names we are giving to our little boy,' his father wrote to Balmoral, 'but they are names that we like and have decided upon for some time.' Offering to compromise, the Queen withdrew her objections to George, but added, 'Of course you will add Albert at the end. We settled long ago that all dearest Papa's male descendants should bear that name.' The future George V was christened George Frederick Ernest Albert. That was enough to mollify Victoria, and she paid a rare visit to Marlborough House to visit Alexandra, writing afterward (17 June) to her Uncle Leopold that her new grandson was 'very small and not very pretty', and that Alix was 'much *verblüht*' – faded. Then she went off to Coburg for the unveiling of a statue of Prince Albert.

Although Alexandra employed a wet-nurse to breast-feed the new prince, she also enjoyed being a mother sufficiently to bathe and dress her children. A lengthy lying-in was then required after a birth, and, intolerant of even the slightest inactivity, Bertie chafed at her delay in going out again with him into society. Without her, he continued his card-playing visits to clubs and frequented the races, inspiring a letter to Knollys from Phipps, obviously dictated by the Queen, observing that it was a 'general opinion' that the Prince of Wales 'overdoes the visiting and going about'. Even their elaborate dinners at Marlborough House and weekend house parties at Sandringham were far from the staid, monochromatic functions, intended to raise the tone of the tarnished monarchy, which the Queen had insisted upon during her marriage with Albert. The Waleses had their carpets rolled back for dancing; horseplay and practical jokes were encouraged; and the recent invention of the soda syphon entered into their frolics as guests doused each other with jets of soda water. Tray-tobogganing down the carpeted stairs was popular, although the challenge may have been daunting to ladies in stays and crinolines. The fun often went on until dawn began to break, and Alix, never punctual anyway, would sleep until nearly noon. The concern from Windsor Castle was that newspapers would call attention to Bertie's 'unceasing and inconsiderate pursuit of pleasure', thus losing him the good feeling which the press was chronicling. As Victoria's surrogate, Phipps even claimed to have heard the younger generation saying that 'the Prince of Wales is flying about rather too much'. Nevertheless, the Queen still refused to give the next-in-line for her throne anything useful to do.

A new and unexpected diversion in the Prince's life arose when he plunged into the nursery to warn that Marlborough House was aflame. In days of fireplaces, gaslight and candles, blazes were common. The Waleses were fortunate that the flare-up was quickly under control, Bertie assisting by chopping at burning floorboards and organizing the servants to form a human chain to convey buckets and jugs of water. Given the eminence of the householder, Captain Eyre Massey Shaw of the Metropolitan Fire Brigade was on the scene in person. Excited by the affair, the Prince asked Shaw to let him know about any big fires in London so that he could lend a royal hand. The exuberant Eyre Shaw, thirty-six and one of the most popular figures in London (even to the extent of having lines sung about him years later in Gilbert and Sullivan's *Iolanthe*), agreed. Soon after, the Prince joined the firemen at the blazing El Dorado music hall in Leicester Square. If possible he would race to the scene with one or more of his friends, including the eccentric playboy Duke of Sutherland, about whom the Queen carped (to Bertie) that 'he does not live as a *Duke ought*'.

In the autumn of 1866 Alix was again pregnant – her third pregnancy in less than four years of marriage, and unhappily inopportune as she could not travel to Russia for the splendid wedding in St Petersburg of Princess Dagmar to the Tsarevitch. Although Grand Duke Nicholas, who had come to Denmark to court her, had since died of tuberculosis, no diplomatic difficulty arose. Minnie was fully prepared to marry his brother, Grand Duke Alexander, who needed a royal bride as much as Minnie wanted a throne. Bertie had been restless at home with his pregnant wife although his clubs in Pall Mall were only a short walk from Marlborough House, and was delighted when Alix suggested that he go to the wedding without her. He explained to the Queen, 'I should be only too happy to be the means in any way of promoting the *entente cordiale* between Russia and my own country.' He added, 'I am a very good traveller, so that I should not at all mind the length of the journey.'

Victoria invited – indeed ordered – Alix and her children to stay with their 'Gan-gan' until Christmas. 'I own', the Queen had confessed to her son on 16 October, 1866 about the junket to Russia, '[that] I do *not* much like the idea.' She did not want him to be in St Petersburg and Moscow in early winter, or to lend his support to what would appear to be a Danish occasion. Her real reason, she admitted, after dismissing the political importance of his presence, for Britain, was his 'remaining so *little* quiet at home, and always running about. The country, and all of *us*, would like to see you a little more stationary.... However, if you are still very desirious to go now, I will not object.'

In fact the Prince of Wales did very little running about in his own country, as his mother offered him few ceremonial opportunities and he was too public a figure for opportune private diversions. (Gladstone felt that she should furnish £50,000 from her funds to support his royal appearances, especially as she continued to press Parliament for grant allowances and dowries to her other children, from whom nothing was expected.) One function materialized late in October, just before he left for Russia. At Norwich, where he arrived with the popular Princess, John Wodehouse, representing the Cabinet, voiced his vexation in his diary: 'The Norwich people out of sorts because the P. of Wales did not look graciously enough at them. H.R.H. has not the talent of pretending to look pleased. When he is bored, he looks it. Not a good quality in a Prince.' Bertie took him off, at the reception, to the smoking room to ask advice on how to get out of travelling with his brother-in-law Fritz, the Crown Prince of Prussia, to St Petersburg, claiming that it was 'a dodge of Bismarck's to secure the Crown Prince a good reception', though Bertie was probably attempting to evade what he saw as the presence of a family watchdog. Further, there were political difficulties straining relations with his Prussian brother-in-law who had not only led troops against the Danes but had been a general in the swift defeat of Austria in the fratricidal war of June 1866. Then, Bertie had told the French ambassador in London that he prayed for an Austrian victory – despite his 'Prussian' sister, Vicky – to contain German militarism. Wodehouse, however, wondered: 'Was not the whole conversation a pretext to get out of the ball-room to smoke?'

With a full beard now cultivated in place of side-whiskers, the Prince of Wales left for St Petersburg looking appropriately Russian, and travelled by rail most of the way with a small entourage including his crony Lord James Hamilton, the future 2nd Duke of Abercorn. The lavish wedding took place in the chapel of the Winter Palace on the River Neva on 9 November, the Prince's own twenty-fifth birthday, after which he telegraphed affectionately to his mother that all had gone well. He had been received with warmth, attended grand parades and banquets, and gone on a frozen hunt where seven wolves were bagged. He did not add that at a ball he had worn his kilt and danced with alluring damsels in deep *décolleté*. Had she seen the scandal press in London she would have learned of the Russian beauties, but her ladies-in-waiting read no such gossip to the Queen. (The Prince was learning, in both St Petersburg and Moscow, that he could bed almost any woman he wanted, even if he chose only to enjoy the titillation afforded by the possibilities.) The pregnant Alix, in the interim, delayed accepting her mother-in-law's invitation, arriving at Windsor only on 13 November 'looking', the Queen informed Vicky, 'very thin and pale; but I think a little larger than last time'.

Returning, Bertie travelled via Berlin to pay his respects to his sister, who wrote to the Queen, 'I shall be quite glad when he gets home, as I think it is very trying for his health to spend so many nights in the railways in the cold, have such different eating and times of meals and be stuffed into overheated rooms.' For the Prince, however, it was an adventure to be preferred to a dreary country Christmas in the rain at Sandringham with Alix in the last stages of her confinement.

Before they returned to Marlborough House they spent a country weekend of the sort Bertie liked at Holkham Hall, the seat of the Earl of Leicester, where among the guests were Prince Alfred (now the Duke of Edinburgh); Bertie's friend George Leveson-Gower, the 3rd Duke of Sutherland, and his wife; and Charles Gordon, the 11th Marquess of Huntly, whom John Wodehouse – now much in Bertie's company –

called 'an impertinent young puppy from Cambridge'. On Thursday 3 January, 1867 at Holkham sixteen gentlemen killed 1,683 fowl, 'a stupid massacre on the whole', according to Wodehouse 'and horribly cold. The ladies including the Princess picknicked in a tent, & walked about in the snow (the Princess in a sledge) to see the shooting.' The 'amiable' Alix was nearly seven months' pregnant.

The Prince of Wales, Wodehouse thought, looked ill. 'He is ruining his health as fast as he can – eats enormously, sits up all night [at cards], smokes incessantly, drinks continually 'nips' of brandy; he has only to add as I fear he will gambling and whoring to become the rival of the "first gentleman in Europe",' (a reference to the increasingly open excesses of Napoleon III). That evening, Wodehouse wrote, 'we had a dance but this was too quiet for the Prince who prefers some romping game. We had a specimen of this the next night. It was a melancholy exhibition – at once puerile and *mauvais* [wicked] too. Add to this that the other chief amusement was putting brandy cherries &c. in tail[coat] pockets, Harvey sauce* in flasks &c. and you have some picture of the tom foolery which we very unwillingly took some part in. L[or]d Leicester would have stopped it if he could, but he could do nothing but look on in disgust and contempt.' Writing in his diary of another 'romp', like most of them probably alcoholic in inspiration, Charles Carrington boasted, 'We had roaring fun, and ended by carrying the Prince of Wales in triumph round the house in my Grandmother's sedan chair; one of the old poles snapped in two, and he had a tremendous spill.'

The Waleses returned to London for the birth, and for Bertie's social convenience. The Queen was preoccupied with the new Tory government led by Derby and Disraeli, and early in February for only the second time since Albert's death – and at the request of the ingratiating Disraeli – she opened Parliament in person. (As Chancellor of the Exchequer, Disraeli had provided £1,000 to help finance the Prince of Wales's Russian junket.) Rather than remain home to await the accouchement, Bertie went off with his brother Affie to Ireland for more shooting. At Marlborough House, Alix's aches and pains were dismissed as the precursor to labour, and despite her complaints of chills and fever

---

* Harvey Sauce, concocted by the innkeeper of the Black Dog in Bedfont, Middlesex in about 1760, was a bottled brown sauce recognizable, like Worcestershire Sauce, by its essence of anchovies.

on 15 February, 1867, the Prince, on his return, could not bear to be absent from the Windsor Races. He was away when a physician was sent for, and diagnosed Alix as suffering from rheumatic fever. That immunological reaction to a streptococcal infection was extremely threatening in a pre-antibiotics era. Her most serious symptoms were inflammation of the heart, with irregular heartbeat, followed by further fever and painful migratory arthritis. Three days later a medical notice was posted at Marlborough House declaring that the Princess of Wales was acutely ill but not in danger, and observers, who understood that such bulletins were not issued casually, flooded the royal residence with recipes and nostrums and wishes for her recovery.

Alix was very ill indeed, but only a third telegram, each message increasingly urgent, persuaded Bertie to return to Marlborough House. There on 20 February, without the aid of chloroform (which doctors felt was too dangerous to administer in the Princess's weakened state), she gave birth to Louise Victoria, named after her two grandmothers. For a time the Prince demonstrated an affection and concern that counteracted rumours of his callousness. He had his desk moved into her spacious bedroom suite, so that he could write letters at her bedside, and chat with her. But then the Queen of Denmark came to be at her daughter's sickbed, and remained for two months, furnishing Bertie with opportunities to escape.

Lady Macclesfield, who was helping to nurse Alix, wrote in her diary about his growing neglect, 'The Princess had another bad night, *chiefly* owing to the Prince promising to come in at 1.00 am and keeping her in a perpetual fret, refusing to take her opiate for fear she should be asleep when he came! And he never came till 3.00 am! The Duke of Cambridge is quite *furious* about it and I hear nothing but general indignation at his indifference to her and his devotion to his own amusements.' Urged on by General Grey, the loyal Knollys (very likely writing indirectly for the Queen) tried to persuade the Prince that he was eroding his public reputation by flouting the proprieties, but his sickroom appearances remained minimal.

Even in the United States, reports arriving via the Atlantic telegraph suggesting that while Alexandra was 'at the point of death' and the English public unaware of the crisis, 'the Prince haunts the theatres as usual'. (By 'theatres' the newspapers implied the indecorous music halls.) The American press speculated, as their London counterparts could not, whether 'he haunts the theatres to allay public anxiety respecting his wife, or that he does it out of brutal indifference to his wife'.

Not even the Princess's critical illness curtailed Bertie's entertaining at Marlborough House, where Alexandra lay, flushed with fever and pain, in her suite above the busy entrance hall, library and state dining room. On 10 March, the day after a typical princely dinner, the editor of *The Times*, John Delane, described the occasion to his mother, from being received by 'four scarlet footmen' at eight to his late departure. The twenty gentlemen guests – dinner parties for the Prince's high-living friends were smaller and informal – ranged from his mother's cousin, the Duke of Cambridge (the stodgy commander-in-chief of the Army, whom he thought of as an uncle), to the Danish Minister and Members of Parliament. The dinner itself, Delane wrote to his mother, was 'not better than many others', but the wine was 'good and abundant', the better, perhaps, for uninhibited conversation. Such occasions were virtually Bertie's only means of securing information and offering his own views. 'There was plenty of talking both during dinner and afterwards,' said Delane, 'and I had my share, and rather more.... Indeed, the Prince had so many afterthoughts as I was going away that he actually shook hands with me four times.'

As Alix's convalescence proceeded, she could be wheeled out into the spring sun, but walking was a painful effort. One knee remained permanently stiff. She would learn to walk with a gliding movement to limit what became known as the 'Alexandra limp'. She was also becoming increasingly deaf, and had nothing to occupy herself. 'The melancholy thing', Lady Frederick Cavendish observed in her diary about the couple, 'is that neither he nor the darling Princess ever care to open a book.' One of her few public appearances with her husband in the months of her slow recovery was at the christening of their daughter in early May – as Louise Victoria Alexandra Dagmar. From Osborne, the Queen complained to Vicky, her pride still wounded, 'The child ought to be called "Victoria". But upon those subjects Bertie and Alix do not understand the right thing.' In August, after some extended dissipations which her intelligence system had not reported to her, Bertie visited his mother alone at Osborne, and she observed ingenuously that Bertie was 'very kind and amiable – but I think he wants change of air and scene. Poor Boy, it is very sad to think of his whole existence changed and altered and *dérangé* by this lamentable illness. Please God that poor Alix may recover her health, but I own I fear very much she will never be what she was.'

Bertie had already organized his change of air and scene. Having remained in England for his daughter's christening, he left immediately afterwards, in transparent incognito, for Dieppe, where the future Lord Salisbury (then still Lord Cranborne) provided a villa. There the Prince enjoyed the company of Gaston Gallifet, a womanizing marquis and a youngish general, who liked to show the ladies the small silver plate that patched an abdominal wound he had received in France's failed effort to keep Mexico in 1863. (Later Gallifet and the Prince were to share a mistress.) Then they went to Paris, where lusty musical comedy soprano Hortense Schneider, whose favours were bestowed on many admirers, was appearing in a sell-out operetta by Jacques Offenbach, *La Grande-Duchesse de Gérolstein*. One after another, sovereigns and statesmen arrived in France for the lavish Universal Exhibition meant to flaunt the grandeur of the Empire – the Tsar of Russia, the Khedive of Egypt, the Sultan of Turkey, the King of Sweden, the Chancellor of Prussia, the eccentric king of Bavaria, as well as assorted princes and dukes. In *défilade*, however, they occupied adjacent boxes, some each evening for weeks, delighting in performances in which difficulties of language seemed inconsequential. The Prince of Wales was more attentive in the Duchess's dressing room than in his *loge*. Set in a petty German dukedom with a token army and insufferable aristocrats like Prince Paul, Baron Grog and General Boum, the operetta suggested parallels with Coburg to the Prince. In mythical Gérolstein (first invented in a novel by Eugène Sue) it is the Duchess rather than the Duke who conducts her amours with indiscreet abandon, and it is obvious that the librettists, Henri Meilhac and Jacques Halévy, were satirizing at a safe distance the hollow vanity of Napoleon III's parvenu and corrupt aristocracy. A line from one of her songs, '*J'aime les militaires*', about the '*sabre de mon père*', was suggestive enough to become identified with her easy indulgence of privileged admirers.

Ever since the opulently endowed Mlle Schneider had performed her aphrodisiac cancan in Offenbach's *Orphée aux enfers* the year before, reclining on a banqueting table in the scanty costume of a Bacchante, then bounding off and kicking up her heels to frantic applause, the Prince had anticipated admiring her backstage at the Théâtre des Variétés, and had begun taking her to private midnight suppers at which they may have done more than dine. He had already offered his attentions, in London, to the sexy Finette, who performed her own inflammatory version of the cancan at the Alhambra in what became the traditional French costume – long black stockings and frilly white panties, with an expanse of bare thigh showing between. 'Nadar' (Gaspard Tournachon) photographed her with a beauty spot above her lip, and spit-curl on her forehead, both of which advertised her naughtiness. The verb 'to kick', said an observer of Finette's troupe, 'had never been so actively conjugated before'. Agreeing, the Middlesex magistrates briefly withdrew the Alhambra's licence.

In Emile Zola's daring novel of Second Empire show business, *Nana* (1880), set in 1867, the Prince of Wales appears, transparently renamed the Prince of Scots, as a backstage admirer of a voluptuous demi-mondaine Vénus, celebrated for her 'Amazonian bosom' and her ability to turn even crowned heads into her slaves. The frock-coated Prince is 'largely and strongly built, light of beard and rosy of hue, ... a sturdy man of pleasure'. In her rose-coloured dressing room at the Variétés under the 'hot flare' of gaslight, he and the 'half-naked' Nana – obviously Hortense Schneider, though Zola makes her younger than Hortense would have been – clink champagne glasses to 'Your Highness' and 'the Army' (a reference to the actual Offenbach *opéra bouffe*), and to 'Vénus'. 'Well, then, it's agreed,' says the Prince from her divan, looking at her as the actual Prince of Wales often did, 'though half-shut eyelids', as she makes up for her role. 'You will come to London next year, and we shall receive you so cordially that you will never return to France again.'

So extravagant was Schneider's fame, and so interwoven were reality and fantasy in Paris then, that when she ordered her carriage to the Exposition in the Champ de Mars and attempted to enter through the Porte d'Iéna, reserved for heads of state, she declared, 'Make way! I am the Grand Duchess of Gérolstein!' The guards lifted their hats, bowed low, and let her pass.

The next autumn she was indeed in London to perform her signature role at the St James's Theatre. The Prince of Wales would see her thereafter at her home in the avenue de Bois-de-Boulogne, but not again on the stage, which she abandoned in 1869 for an extended visit to an even more extravagant worshipper, Ismail Pasha, the spendthrift Khedive of Egypt. It was the year of the opening of the Suez Canal, which Ismail celebrated by commissioning Giuseppe Verdi to compose *Aida*, lavishly premiered at the Cairo Opera in 1871. (Bankrupt in 1875, Ismail had to sell his Suez shares.) Hortense Schneider would not have another Parisian success until 1874, with Offenbach's *La Périchole*, and the next year, at forty-two, she retired.

The more daring London papers connected the Prince's name with the alluring Mlle Schneider, but wrote nothing about the audacious Versailles favourite, the princesse de Sagan. Thanks to the enterprising Eugénie, he had rediscovered Jeanne-Marguerite de Sagan, daughter of a wealthy banker and separated from the monocled dandy prince Boson de Sagan (a model for Proust's baron Charlus), in Versailles in 1862. The princesse had signalled that she was available, but for Bertie her mansion in the rue St Dominique was too accessible to prying eyes. He preferred her sprawling Château de Mello, south of Paris, where he would call whenever he could slip away, her servants greeting him like a visiting monarch. When, in 1866, nine years after her first son was born, she again became pregnant, her continuing relationship with the Prince of Wales was so acknowledged in her elegant circle that she found it necessary to keep up appearances by a façade of a reconciliation with her husband. (Her second son would be prince Hélie de Sagan.) Each spouse then returned to previous infidelities, but the elder Sagan boy, later to become the duc de Talleyrand-Périgord, had recognized even earlier that His Royal Highness was more than just a frequent guest for a private luncheon. Once, on slipping curiously into his mother's boudoir, the boy found the Prince of Wales's garments draped on a chair. Snatching them, he hurled the royal finery out of a window into one of the elaborate fountains in the gardens below. When the Prince emerged from his lady's bedroom his sopping clothes were being rescued by agonized servants. In his coach-and-four he had to leave the Château for Paris in ill-fitting borrowed apparel.

Alix's illness and convalescence also created opportunities for princely diversion on his own side of the Channel. Like his aristocratic cronies he looked for illicit romance among safely married women – though, like his friends, not always so. In the same year he offered what was at first sincere consolation to Lady Susan Vane-Tempest, widowed daughter of his old mentor the Earl of Newcastle, his senior official on the voyage to Canada and the US seven years earlier. The Prince had visited Newcastle's country seat at Clumber and knew Lady Susan, who, contrary to her father's wishes, had married the unstable Lord Adolphus Vane-Tempest, son of Lord and Lady Londonderry. A notorious drunk, Lord Adolphus had attacks of delirium tremens as well as fits of madness unrelated to

alcohol. When he died in 1864 leaving Lady Susan distraught and penni-
less, the Prince began making sympathy calls. By 1867 he was consoling
her between the sheets, but as a widow she had no one with whom to
stage a reconciliation when biology left her in the same precarious condition as the princesse de Sagan.

The Prince of Wales returned from Paris for Ascot week, which he
spent without Alix. She reappeared publicly after his return from the
races for a banquet at Marlborough House for the visiting Khedive of
Egypt (despite their rivalry for Mlle Schneider), who had come up from
Paris. Then came the Sultan of Turkey, another species of potentate the
Queen preferred only to receive formally at Windsor before retreating to
Osborne. Suddenly the Prince of Wales was needed as host – although he
had planned to return to France, ostensibly for the Exhibition. 'I think
it is very hard that I should be obliged to be back on the 3rd [of July],'
he complained to Princess Louise, who was acting as her mother's social
secretary, 'which will give me no time at all in Paris, [and] only affront
the people there by my short stay and I think it will probably be hardly
worth while to go at all. I have never shirked any public duty yet, and
have been *always* ready to do anything State or Public for Mama, and I
think it is very hard that the first favour I ask should be declined.'

Bertie was back from Paris in time to greet the Sultan on his arrival at
Dover after even more reluctantly meeting Queen Augusta of Prussia
and, at Victoria's instructions, accompanying Augusta back to London
after tea at Windsor. At one dinner the Prince hosted at Marlborough
House, Princess Alexandra asked writer and man of mystery Laurence
Oliphant if it were true that he had hawked fruit at railway stations along
the ramshackle line in Armenia. Yes, he said; he did it because it was
necessary, and to keep his pride down. For *that*, the Prince of Wales
remarked, all he had to do was to take a short walk to Buckingham
Palace. (It made his point, even if the Queen issued her orders from
Windsor.) For an antidote to pride he might also have opened the pages
of *Tomahawk*, a London satirical magazine despite its suggestive
American name, which on 20 July 1867 published a bogus report of a
speech he was said to have delivered at the University of London.
Tomahawk gibed that the Prince intended to follow up his address on
education with one on philosophy, 'and as of this date he has almost mas-
tered the pronunciation of the more difficult names and gotten the
general headings memorized'.

When the London social season ended, Alix appeared able to travel with her husband to the *Kurhaus* spa at Wiesbaden for further recuperation, accompanied by their three small children, two doctors, Bertie's equerries and twenty-five servants. With wheel-chair and walking stick, she did little at the rented mansion near the Hotel de la Rose but watch over the children with their governesses and occasionally descend into the murky, yellow-brown medicinal baths. The Prince dieted and steamed away some of the pounds put on during the season, drank the tepid, disagreeable mineral water, dabbled at the gaming tables then a feature of every spa, and on afternoon and evening promenades without Alix he enjoyed the attentions of eager ladies. He also went to the races, despite the Queen's warning that the racing clientele was disreputable and his public character would suffer. Bertie responded sharply on 27 August, refusing to deny himself the Sport of Kings, which he was attending with his equerry, Christopher Teesdale, and crony, Charles Carrington: 'I know that Vicky has written to you on the subject,' he wrote, 'but one would imagine that she thought me 10 or 12 years old, and not nearly 26.'

One of the 'other subjects' about which she wrote was the imminent visit of her father-in-law, King William, to Wiesbaden – not for the baths, but to pay a courtesy call on the recuperating Alix, who still viewed him as the Enemy. Depressed and increasingly deaf, she had no interest in seeing most visitors, especially William, and vented her rage at the accommodating Bertie, who was under orders from his mother to receive the King of Prussia. 'A lady may have feelings which she cannot repress,' he explained about the weaker sex to Victoria, 'while a man *must* overcome them.' When the Queen, who had shirked her own royal responsibilities with claims of mourning and physical incapacity, insisted that Alix could not let her private feelings conflict with her 'duties', the Prince of Wales conceded defeat and telegraphed William to come to breakfast the next day, first showing his message to the unhappy Alix. With a night to reconcile herself to diplomatic necessity, she was composed and civil the next morning. Pleased, King William invited himself to remain for luncheon, and Bertie took it as a foreign affairs success. Cultivating the powerful from outside the policy-making sphere remained his only avenue into politics.

When Lord Carrington returned to England he received a jewelled tie-pin from the Prince to celebrate 'two or three lucky coups' at the gaming tables. He mentioned no other coups. What was public knowledge about the Prince's indiscretions prompted *Reynolds's Newspaper* to excoriate the heir 'whose whole life is consecrated to fashionable recreation'. Simultaneously scolding Victoria, who by then (6 October 1867) was in Scotland, the paper carped that neither monarch nor heir were earning their incomes nor having any perceptibly useful impact upon the nation. 'Though the Queen were to take up her permanent abode at Balmoral, … and the Prince of Wales were to devote himself for the remainder of his days to the beauties of Wiesbaden and the delights of its "hells" [the gambling dens], neither England nor Ireland would be one farthing the worse.'

The Prince's watering-place weeks, which became annual pilgrimages ostensibly to shed the avoirdupois from the gargantuan dinners of the season, were followed by the usual months of visits to such grand country houses as Woodnorton and Houghton and Buckingham Tofts. Both for appearances and to inhibit his straying, Alix accompanied her husband, looking grand in elegant clothes that emphasized her hourglass waist and nine-strand pearl choker that dramatized her slender throat. Nevertheless, châtelaines of stately country seats anticipated the complex ritual of sex by discreetly arranging bedroom suites to locate a likely *amoureuse* within nightly stalking distance of the appropriate gentleman. Such sinning required a complaisant husband who slept, for the occasion, in an adjoining dressing room or padded off to tumble another lady. By morning, with decorum restored, the chatter at breakfast was brightly irrelevant.

The Prince's employment at pleasure was almost the only occupation available to him. He could pursue it in England, or in France or Germany, and when abroad he was a little less visible. Since Alix could not be abandoned as regularly as he might have wished, when the long country house autumn ended with the onset of winter, the Prince, with the frail Alix still leaning upon a walking stick, remained briefly at home into the new year. Yet gratification beckoned. *Bell's Life*, a sporting paper, reported that at Badminton, the Duke of Beaufort's estate, late in February, he had gone fox-hunting in Charlton Park on Ash Wednesday, which caused, locally, 'no small amount of indignation'. On 2 March 1868, oblivious to the uproar, he led a run with the Royal Buckhounds after releasing a carted deer from the Queen's herd at Bate's Farm, near Harrow. A party of horsemen pursued it with him for twenty-four miles through Wembley and Wormwood Scrubs to the Goods Yard at

Paddington Station. There, before the eyes of horrified porters and railway guards, thirty gentlemen dispatched it, after which the Prince left his mount to his handlers and in shooting garb took the train back to Windsor, surprising travellers on the platform. Delane's *The Times* merely reported that he 'hunted with Her Majesty's staghounds yesterday'. Papers like the *Pall Mall Gazette*, in more lively reading, criticized the wretchedness of the chase. One paper alleged that the Prince had ridden with his friends from Paddington across Hyde Park to Marlborough House, which suggested a further public affront.

Disraeli, then Prime Minister, wrote to the Queen four days later that it would be useful to send the Prince of Wales on a royal tour of Ireland, and enclosed a letter he had solicited urgently from the Marquess (soon to be Duke) of Abercorn proposing the visit. In the third-person language of protocol, but without disguising the need to repair her heir's public image, Disraeli humbly explained

> that, should your Majesty approve … , the consequences, in his opinion, would be highly advantageous. The moment is very suitable, and to seize the *à propos* is generally wise.
>
> There is no doubt a real yearning in Ireland for the occasional presence and inspiration of Royalty.
>
> Mr. Disraeli would venture to observe that, during [the last] two centuries, the Sovereign has only passed twenty-one days in Ireland.
>
> If your Majesty approved the suggestion, his Royal Highness, from whom a visit of a week is only now contemplated, might make a longer visit later in the year, hunt, for example, in the counties of Kildare and Meath, and occupy some suitable residence....
>
> This would, in a certain degree, combine the fulfilment of public duty with pastime, a combination which befits a princely life.

Victoria minuted an acid response the next day – through General Grey – that she objected strenuously to any hint of a home, or role, for the Prince in Ireland. She wanted no precedent of royal residences in any of her dominions, even Wales. 'And in the Prince of Wales's case, *any encouragement* of his constant love of running about, and not keeping at home, or near the Queen, is *most earnestly* and *seriously* to be deprecated.'

Then she wrote a strong 'Dear Bertie' letter to her heir. He could visit Ireland if he chose, and her Government wanted it, but no more than that. And she regretted that the occasion chosen should be the '*Races*', as it strengthened the belief 'already far too prevalent, that your chief object is amusement'.

On 11 March 1868 the Prince replied in a 'My Dear Mama' letter that if he went to Ireland it would be as a duty to the Government, and that he would 'be ready to do anything that is required of me when I am there'. As for the Punchestown Races, his presence would be valuable 'because such a large concourse of people would be gathered together from all parts of the country, who look upon those Races as a kind of annual festival, and would have a better chance of seeing me there than at Dublin, and give them an occasion to display their loyalty to you and our family, if (as it is to be hoped) such a feeling exists'.

It was a shrewdly written appeal. Bertie's education had not all gone for naught. Still, he would be offered no responsibility in Ireland, or anywhere. The supposed Sport of Kings found no adherent in the Queen.

VIII

The Sport of Kings

1868–1871

THE PRINCE NEVER allowed prying newspapers to inhibit his amusements. While Disraeli was attempting to make him disappear temporarily to Ireland, Bertie was off on another local hunt, this time to baron Mayer de Rothschild's Buckinghamshire estate at Mentmore. With the sun hardly up, his party gathered at Euston Station to board the Duke of Sutherland's private saloon carriage. Heavy rain and a north-west wind threatened to mar the morning, but there was more to do on arrival than rush out into the soggy field. To celebrate the Prince's first visit to Mentmore, Baron Rothschild served for breakfast what Natty de Rothschild described modestly as 'delicacies of and out of the season'. HRH, he wrote to his mother, Charlotte, indulged 'as if he does not mean to go out hunting'. Yet the deer were loosed into the Vale of Aylesbury on schedule and, Natty reported with awe, although 'the best riders fell on every side', the sturdy Prince, despite 'his sitting up night after night smoking, etc.' kept up the pace.

A few days later, on 10 March 1868, Natty and his brother Alfred were at Marlborough House for a concert the Prince gave to mark his fifth wedding anniversary. Publicly he and Alix shared a storybook marriage; the Princess appeared with him at royal levées four times during March, always looking radiant, and again on 25 March at a grand reception in the new Foreign Office building overlooking St James's Park, where Disraeli was celebrating his climb up the greasy pole to Prime Minister on Derby's retirement. (Even Anthony Trollope lobbied for a place at a princely levée, claiming to Lord Houghton – Monckton Milnes – that it would improve his prestige as a postal bureaucrat at a convention in America.)

Ireland came next. Disraeli had won his point but only barely, as the Waleses arrived at Kingstown (now Dun Laoghaire), south of Dublin, in mid-April just in time for the Punchestown Races, where 50,000 spectators gathered to greet them. The Prince unbent to shake hundreds of hands. Irish newspapers forewent their nationalism to praise Alexandra's 'peculiar charm' and to plead with the Prince to build a Balmoral in Ireland and stay for a season each year. *Punch* followed up that suggestion, which Victoria had already privately vetoed, with a cartoon, 'The Irish Balmoral, or a Vision of 1869', showing the Prince, hunting rifle on his shoulder, crossing an Irish stream with Alix, side-saddle, on a white mare, and devoted countrymen, including a barefoot boy, following behind them. It was a utopian dream.

THE IRISH BALMORAL, OR A VISION OF 1869.

The oft-voiced solution for an occupation for the Prince was an honorific lieutenancy in Ireland. Punch *(2 May 1868) sees it as an idyll for the Waleses. Bertie saw it as exile. Both Queen and Prince dismissed it as unacceptable*

On their way to Holyhead for the boat to Ireland, the Waleses took their children to the Queen at Osborne. On the railway platform at Basingstoke, Alfred Munby 'found myself', he noted in his diary, 'standing next to the Prince of Wales, whose three fair children were laying their faces to the carriage window close by, while the Princess sat within: all going by our train to Osborne. The Prince, in billycock hat, smoking [a] cigarette, loudly laughs, jauntily walks up & down in the crowd, talking to this man and that. Thus does this Prince represent to us the long result of his race, the outcome of 800 years of English history.' HRH enjoyed such immersion in people, and recognized its value for him. When his mother had once complained about how bad the noise of London was on her nerves, the Prince had suggested (26 February 1869) that if she sometimes took a turn in Hyde Park ('where there is no noise') and then returned to Windsor, 'the people would be overjoyed – beyond measure. It is all very well for Alix and me to drive in the Park – [but] it does not have the same effect as when you do it; and I say thank God that is the case. We live in radical times, and the more the *People see the Sovereign* the better it is for the *People* and the *Country.*'

It was often ruinously burdensome to be honoured by the heavy presence of the Prince. His chief host in Ireland was the Lord-Lieutenant, the Duke of Abercorn, who worried only about the Prince's habit, now becoming the practice in his set, of smoking at his table after dinner. How could Abercorn prevent the fouling of his dining room without discourtesy to his royal guest? The Duchess rose to the occasion, informing the Prince as he was shown about Dublin Castle that a room near the dining room had been specially fitted up for him for his post-prandial cigar.

A few unearned honours were still missing from the Prince's plenitude, among them his installation as a Knight of St Patrick, which was arranged with great pomp at St Patrick's (Anglican) Cathedral. To mark the event nearly all of the Fenian prisoners in Irish jails were released, but their cells would soon be occupied by others of their persuasion. The Queen was far from happy at the parole of the Fenians, since, while Bertie was in Ireland, his brother Affie, in Australia, had been shot and wounded by an assailant named O'Farrell, who claimed Fenian sympathies. Victoria hoped he was an 'American Irishman' and claimed to Vicky in Germany that visits to the colonies by Royals would have no 'permanent, good effect'.

By then Alix's fourth pregnancy was far advanced, and the Prince, having returned from Dublin, had to make do with entertainments close to home, including a ball for the social season at Marlborough House only five weeks before the Princess was due. The Queen deplored the 'miserable, puny, little children (each weaker than the preceding one)' Alix bore. 'I can't tell you', she confided to Vicky, 'how these poor, frail, little fairies distress me for the honour of the family and the country.' She was addressing the wrong audience: the Prussian Crown Princess was herself still in the process of producing her eight children, few of whom were to accrue much credit to family or country.

All the Prince could manage in the way of duty, when invited, was to open an exhibition, or a building. He did both that May when he travelled to the Leeds Exhibition of Fine Arts, held in the new Gilbert Scott-designed wing of the West Riding Infirmary. (Scott had designed St Pancras Station and the Albert Memorial.) The Prince also visited the magnificent long seventeenth-century gallery at Temple Newsam, lit entirely by candles. Suffering from a head cold and the allegedly stifling atmosphere, HRH complained of the heat. While Lord Houghton, who was with the party, gaped in disbelief, their host, Hugo Meynell Ingram, promptly had several venerable windows smashed open to afford his royal guest sufficient air. (Suggesting a cause for the Prince's discomfort, Houghton observed that he was 'getting terribly fat.')

Apart from public events, he spent little time with Alix as she gloomily awaited another birth. Whether in London or in the country, he often had his companions in. At Sandringham after his usual huge breakfast, eaten alone in his suite while his guests dined downstairs, he would turn up at 10.30 in boots and tweeds for a late morning's shooting, halting briefly in a clearing for hot soup brought out in china tureens by attendants. A painting by Thomas Jones Barker, *A Big Shoot at Sandringham*, now at Windsor, shows a pause in the hunt, with a shotgun in the crook of the Prince's elbow. Gathered round under the gnarled trees are the Prince's two equerries, Major Teesdale and Captain Ellis, and a cluster of the Prince's cronies.

Four hours into the hunt his servants would have a large lunch ready in a covered marquee. Like his mother he could ingest a substantial meal in a short time, after which the heated containers of food were removed, whether or not the others in the party were finished. After that, bearers of liquid sustenance kept pace, struggling along with the baskets of iced champagne as the party continued whatever chase there was. Shouts from the thirsty Prince of 'Where's the boy?' would lead to the London fashion of summoning waiters for 'a bottle of the Boy'.

Shooting would end in time for tea, which was always much more than tea, and later there followed a ten-course dinner, usually with oysters, prawns, beef and lamb, at which Alix often presided. The Prince recovered his appetite after midnight and often had another large repast. Such gourmandizing got him through the duller days.

Princess Victoria Alexandra Olga Marie was born on 6 July – 'a mere little red lump was all I saw', the Queen wrote dismissively to Vicky, making a derisive allusion to 'the rabbits in Windsor Park'. Then she left for a holiday in Switzerland under her transparent pseudonym of Madame la comtesse de Kent, taking with her the kilted Scot ghillie John Brown, who had become notorious as her attendant, even giving rise to a scurrilous report in a Swiss paper that Victoria (in her fiftieth year) was sequestering herself abroad to give birth to Brown's child. Despite her strict instructions to be referred to by her incognito abroad, and to have her mail addressed that way, with the feisty Brown and his kilted brother Archie in tow, she carried her own limelight.

The Prince was at his most discreet in 1868, slipping away only rarely, and being obsequiously attentive to the Queen, in the hope of securing some role as king-in-waiting. For him the real sport of kings did not involve horseflesh but, rather, the kind concealed under crinolines and *décolletage*. His mother knew he had not reformed, but her intelligence system had not always found him out. Unlike Affie, who womanized openly and was 'a great grief', as she confided to Vicky, Bertie was 'so loving and affectionate, and so anxious to do well, though he is some times imprudent – but that is all'. The Crown Princess was encouraged, because, she wrote in return, it was 'an *idée fixe* all over Germany that he is not a good son to you – and that you cannot bear him near you'.

Bertie seemed indeed a better son when he was far away. The Queen fondly imagined that his every move abroad was chronicled by the press and by embassy observers – and that when Alix was with him he had a further restraint on his fancies. After the Derby, which he would not forgo despite an earnest plea from the Queen, and his mollifying visit to her at Balmoral in May ('to spend my sad birthday with me'), he discovered how great a mistake his presence at the Derby really was. His old Cambridge chum Lord Hastings ('the Wicked Marquess'), mired in racing debts, had risked everything on the favourite, Lady Elizabeth, which lost. He was rescued from criminal proceedings for debt by friends who came together to deal with the creditors. The press deplored the folly of the spendthrift Harry Hastings, who had squandered a family fortune; and attention then shifted to the sporting Prince of Wales and his irresponsible Marlborough House set. Hastings vanished from Bertie's guest list, but the damage was done.

The Prince began urgently to plan an extended tour abroad to assist the public in forgetting. The most difficult aspect to arrange in view of the Queen's hostility to Denmark was Alix's leaving the three eldest children in Copenhagen with her parents. Victoria described all the little ones, despite her impatience with tots, as priceless 'Children of the Country', best left in her safekeeping. Almost at the last moment she yielded, keeping only the royal infant as hostage in England. And after an early autumn round of country house visits with Alix, and a ball they gave at Abergeldie Castle, the family property near Balmoral, the Waleses began their six-month junket, minus baby, to the Continent and the Middle East.

When they left on 18 November for Paris, to be hosted first by Napoleon and Eugénie, their entourage included a doctor, thirty-three servants, half-a-dozen retainers and the Prince's bachelor playmate Lord Carrington. During the exotic portions of their travels they would also have the company of members of the press corps, few of whom ever had an unkind word for the Prince, who was their bread-and-butter – and future sovereign. The Emperor's ball at Compiègne was a triumph for Alexandra, who had recovered as much as she ever would, yet a hunt there was nearly a tragedy for the Prince. He prided himself on his horsemanship (which was excellent despite his increasing girth), and on his willingness to take risks. *The Times* on 23 November reported that two days earlier, 'having advanced somewhat beyond the general rush of riders', the Prince 'found himself between two stags, which charging him simultaneously, knocked over his horse and passed on. The Prince escaped with a slight abrasion of the skin on the leg, and was so little affected by the shock as to be able to dine at the Imperial table in the evening.'

From Copenhagen they travelled to Stockholm, where the Swedish King inducted Bertie as a Freemason. He had rejected Masonic membership more than once in England, at his mother's request, and when the news came by telegraph to Osborne she was shocked, attributing it to his inveterate love of honours, baubles and uniforms. 'I quite agree', he explained to her on Christmas Day 1868, 'that secret societies as a rule are to be deprecated, but I can assure you that this has unpolitical signification.... I feel convinced that I shall have many opportunities of doing great good in my new capacity.' What he craved, and what the Queen continued to deny him, was a role in the political realm, and he saw opportunities for that through the connections afforded by Freemasonry. In 1875 he would become Grand Master of the Order in England, broadening his contacts and justifying for himself what the Queen deplored. One way or another, however shut out by his mother, he wanted to count for something.

Still another bauble came his way after the children were packed aboard the royal yacht for home and the Waleses went on to Berlin. The King of Prussia invested Bertie with the Order of the Black Eagle, offered usually to heads of state. At the ceremony he met and chatted with Bismarck, von Moltke and von Wrangel, the architects of Prussian military expansion. Alexandra remained unbending to the enemy of Denmark. When she addressed the Queen of Prussia as 'Your Majesty' rather than 'Aunt Augusta', the Queen turned her back on the Princess – who was in any case not her niece although instructed by Victoria to pretend as much. Austria was a relief, although court rigidity was such that the Prince and Princess had to call formally on all twenty-seven Archdukes in Vienna, hoping that many were not in the city. None, however, had to be called 'Uncle'.

The colourful phase of the tour began in Egypt, in February. There, the Queen learned, the *bon vivant* Duke of Sutherland and the 'unprincipled' (Victoria's description) Sir Samuel Baker – an adventurous African explorer who had married a Hungarian lady – were waiting to join the Waleses. 'If you ever become King,' Victoria warned, 'you will find all these friends *most* inconvenient, and you will have to break with them *all*.' Baker, he replied firmly on 26 January 1869, had discovered the source of the Nile, 'and, whatever his principles may be, he is unlikely to contaminate us in any way. Besides, he will not be on the same boat with Alix and me.' Bertie held few high cards aside from his position as heir, but he had his limit when it came to enduring indignities from his royal mother.

Awaiting the Prince's party in Alexandria was W. H. Russell of *The*

*'Forty Centuries Looking Down Upon Him': the Prince of Wales
in Egypt (Tomahawk, February 1869)*

Times, famous since his uncompromising coverage of the Crimean War. An assortment of Nile and Suez experts, diplomats and additional friends would also join the entourage, one of them Prince Louis of Battenberg, who had been a midshipman on the *Ariadne* on the American voyage. 'You will doubtless think', Bertie wrote to the Queen, 'that we have too many ships and too large an entourage.' In the East, he explained, 'so much is thought of show, that it becomes almost a necessity'.

On 8 April 1869 *The Queen's Messenger* put that argument into perspective, to the Prince's advantage. 'Our future King', it continued, 'will have the inestimable advantage of knowing both the friends and the enemies of his country from personal experience. Turkey, Egypt, Russia and the Holy Land will not be to him merely geographical terms as they have been to all our former sovereigns since Richard the First.'

The party travelled in the utmost luxury, pointed shotguns at everything that moved, from crocodiles (Bertie bagged one) to waterfowl, brought back with them thirty-two mummy cases and, in a lapse of judgement, a ten-year-old Nubian orphan boy, Ali Achmet, who had attracted the Prince with his shining smile and colourful garb. Along the Nile the boy had survived by stealing. At Sandringham, despite earnest Christian instruction, he would continue his depredations at a higher level until he was removed to a clergyman's care – in effect, house arrest.

After weeks on the Nile and an inspection of the new Suez Canal, they went on to Constantinople, the Crimea, Athens, Vienna and Paris. In the Sultan's realms as they began turning homeward, they found the excess of state courtesies and the lack of privacy exasperating. A full orchestra played at breakfast, multi-gun salutes punctuated each sightseeing stop, and 'God Save the Queen' – with an ornate Ottoman flourish – was heard everywhere. Further, everyone even remotely connected with the Sultan's court expected expensive gifts, and HRH felt obliged to purchase, to satisfy minimal expectations, an enormous quantity of gold and jewelled snuffboxes, while objecting about the necessity to his mother's ambassador. From Osborne she telegraphed to the Prince (4 May 1869), 'You will, I fear, have incurred immense expenses, and I don't think you will find any disposition (except perhaps as regards those which were forced upon you at Constantinople) to give you any more money.' She also confessed that she had begun to enjoy the previously disappointing Wales children, returned to her from Denmark, 'and I shall be very sorry to lose them. They ... are very fond of Grandmama. You must let me see them often ... as I should not like them to become strangers to me.'

At Sebastopol, General Kotzebue, the Governor of the shattered fort he had helped to defend during the Crimean War, showed the Prince and Princess about, Bertie writing afterwards to Victoria that the former battlefield furnished him with 'one of the most interesting days that I can remember'. He was saddened that over 80,000 combatants had died there '– for what? For a political object! I could write you many pages more on the subject.' The junket was proving to be an education.

The Prince had responded (7 May) to his mother's concern about the expenses of the journey that 'it won't ruin us'. She had warned, too, that if Alex spent extravagantly on clothes in Paris en route for home it would be immediately known, and would encourage Republican feeling. She – the Queen – had set the opposite example: 'everyone points to *my* simplicity'. (Of course she did virtually nothing and went virtually nowhere but for her country homes.) The 'frivolity of Society', she added pointedly, '. . . reminds me of the Aristocracy before the French Revolution'.

He had 'given' Alix in Paris, Bertie explained, two 'simple' dresses, 'as they make them here better than in London'. They had heard on their travels, he confessed, sad stories from London about 'scandals in high life'. They were earnestly 'to be deplored', but so too, he contended, was 'wash[ing] their dirty linen in public'.

Back in London on 12 May, Bertie soon became bored. Having nothing better to do, he picked a fight with the committee managing White's Club, to which he had swiftly resorted. With a cigar or cigarette almost always in hand, he had proposed, for his convenience, that smoking be permitted in the Club's morning room. When traditionalists opposed the change, he resigned, coaxing moneyed friends into opening a competing club, the Marlborough, almost opposite Marlborough House, at 52 Pall Mall. In effect it was an extension of his mansion, and a massive smoking-room. His friends had to join, and despite a payment of £100 toward the purchase of the lease (at £18,000) and a 30-guinea initiation fee plus membership and expenses, he assumed ultimate power of veto over membership. The club flourished.

Tobacco was more than an addiction for the Prince. It was even more crucial to his existence than food or drink, as smoking was his principal leisure activity. Turkey to him was the land of the tobacco leaf, and when he learned that a Russian émigré named Marcovitch was living in an attic where, assisted by his wife and daughters, they also made the strong Turkish cigarettes that were offered to him by a friend, he determined to visit the source. Together with a handful of his cronies, he trudged up the several flights of stairs and asked permission to watch the process. Marcovitch offered the gentlemen samples of both varieties of his product, and the Prince, delighted, urged that Marcovitch open his own shop to sell them. The Russian pointed to the bareness of his garret and explained that he had no money to start a business. 'Do it,' said the Prince, 'and I will see that you succeed.' He placed his card on the table, and, with his friends, left.

Once the door closed Marcovitch examined the card, and realized that with it he could borrow on the confidence of royal patronage. He set up a tiny shop in narrow Air Street, off the lower end of Regent Street, and the Prince and his Marlborough Club companions were among the first purchasers. Soon after, came Carlo Pellegrini, known as 'Ape' the famed caricaturist of *Vanity Fair*, who permitted his name to be used for Marcovitch's 'Pellegrini' cigarettes. The firm was soon Marcovitch & Co., Ltd.

The social season began for the Prince with Ascot Week, for which he rented a nearby estate, Cooper's Hill, for his convenience. After his annual ball at Marlborough House on 5 July he announced that Alix needed therapy for her knee, which required their returning to spa country, this time at Wildbad, on the River Enz below Karlsruhe. It was close to other resorts the Prince frequented, and he did not allow Alix's presence to restrict his movements. As in France, Bertie felt liberated from his mother's scrutiny. Then came Scotland, where he intended to shoot grouse and deer in the Highlands, but Alix, again pregnant and close to the onset of labour, needed to be back in London. Unable to remain inactive and without the use of Sandringham (which he was turning into a grander structure), he rented Gunton Hall, near Cromer. Alix remained at Marlborough House. In London on 26 November, she gave birth to her fifth child, Maud Charlotte Mary Victoria. Before Alix had even completed the lengthy obligatory lying-in, her husband had her on a run of country house visits, for he insisted on going to Holkham Hall for New Year's Day, 1870, and then, after interludes at Gunton Hall, to other seats of his moneyed friends, some of whom risked bankruptcy for the honour of entertaining him in his grand style.

The visit to Kimbolton Castle, the Duke of Manchester's seat, almost proved too costly for the Prince himself. While, on the afternoon of 14 March, the Duke's Light Horse Volunteers were drawing up at the station and the Huntingdonshire Volunteers were forming at the Castle, the 3.50 train from King's Cross was shunted off at Hitchin to permit the 4.25 royal train to pass. Empty carriages from the earlier train, separated from the front section, slipped off the rails, obstructing the Prince's oncoming train, nearly due. Frantically, workmen tried to clear the line, and the crowd on the platform, according to *The Times*, sensing the 'imminent danger', exhibited 'intense excitement'. The royal train, approaching at full speed, appeared to miss the spilled carriages 'by six inches'.

The next day *The Times* contritely printed a letter from the irate Superintendent of the Great Northern Line, Francis F. Cockshott, contending that track signals had indicated safe clearance, which had in fact been four feet by the time the royal carriage passed. He deplored 'alarming the public'.

After his country house visits and presiding over eleven levées for the Queen (the only 'work' she considered offering him), the Prince made his usual plans for Ascot – despite entreaties from Victoria that racing and wagering drew only the worst in society. Offering a compromise in a letter of 1 June 1870, she proposed that he attend only on two days, as had her uncle William IV. 'Your example can do *much* for good, and may do an immense deal for evil, in the present day.'

'I fear, dear Mama,' he returned, 'that no year goes round without your giving me a jobation* on the subject of racing.' He was, he insisted, attempting to elevate 'the great national sport of this country'. Shunning the races 'should no doubt win the high approval of [the Sabbatarian] Lord Shaftesbury and the Low Church party', but the character of the sport would decline from 'pleasant social gatherings' to something worse. It would also 'look both odd and uncivil … if I suddenly deviated from the course which I have hitherto adopted'. He regretted when they were 'not quite *d'accord*', but he reminded her that he was 'past twenty-eight and have some considerable knowledge of the world and [of] society'. He intended to use his own discretion – 'and whatever ill-natured stories you may hear about me, I trust you will never withdraw your confidence from me till facts are proved against me. Then I am ready to submit to anything.'

His own confidence – arrogance, even – about emerging from moral scrapes unscathed had been bolstered by the events of the previous February and March. His friend Charles Mordaunt, a Conservative MP from Warwickshire, had filed for divorce from his twenty-one-year-old wife, Harriett, a dark-haired beauty whom he had married when she was seventeen and he was thirty. In 1869, she had given birth to a sickly, premature son who had a minor eye infection which she did not realize

---

* He meant 'jaw-bation', a lecture.

SIR JONATHAN FALSTAFF.

*Although ostensibly about the US post-Civil War Alabama
claims for compensation from Britain for outfitting a Confederate
raider,* Punch*'s cartoon (29 May 1869) covertly conveys the image
of the Prince as a roistering Prince Hal*

would clear up in three weeks. Distraught that the baby was threatened
with venereal blindness, she became hysterical. In panic she asked her
nurse, Elizabeth Hancox, 'Is the child diseased? ... Is it born with the
complaint?' Deep in postpartum depression, Lady Mordaunt claimed to
her husband that the ailing infant was not his – that she had committed
adultery with Lord Cole, Sir Frederick Johnstone, and other admirers.
'Charlie,' she allegedly confessed, 'the child is not yours at all. I have been
very wicked and have done very wrong with more than one person.'
Among those she identified was the Prince of Wales. Her lovemaking had
occurred, she claimed, even 'in open day'.

Rifling her desk, Mordaunt found seemingly innocent letters from the men she had named, including eleven in the Prince of Wales's hand that were at best mildly affectionate and unrevealing – and a valentine. His letters, signed blandly, 'Ever yours very sincerely', and at worst hoping 'that perhaps on your return to London I may have the pleasure of seeing you', did not palpitate with passion. Placed into evidence although not read in court, the harmless if embarrassing texts were soon in the newspapers. Acting for her father, Lady Mordaunt's lawyers defended her on grounds that her statements were those of someone unsound in mind and innocent of actual adultery, and had served the Prince with a subpoena. Bertie's appearance on the stand in the Court for Divorce and Matrimonial Causes in Westminster Hall would be the first time since the reign of Henry IV that a Prince of Wales had appeared in a court of law.

Since his letters suggested little other than indiscretion, the Queen telegraphed her sympathy and support, and the Prince replied effusively, 'I cannot sufficiently thank you for the dear and kind words you have written me.' Both Mordaunt and his butler, Henry Bird, testified on 20 February 1870 that the Prince was at Mordaunt's house in London as often as once a week in 1867 and 1868, even while Mordaunt was away shooting in Norway. Once on returning to Walton Hall from a trip abroad Sir Charles had found his wife showing the Prince her driving skills with ponies and cart, hardly a clandestine activity. Angrily, Mordaunt had dismissed the Prince, then dragged Harriett to the lawn to watch as he had the ponies – her symbols of independence – shot. 'I told my wife', he testified, 'not to receive [further] visits from him.' The episode apparently made her more wilful, for Henry Bird confessed, 'Lady Mordaunt gave me directions that when the Prince called, no one else was to be admitted.'

Evidence was produced that on one occasion the Prince took her to dinner at a hotel, which implied much but established little. The public learned from court transcripts that the Prince had known Lady Mordaunt for several years, seeing her even in Scotland, but his even closer connection to her family remained unrevealed in testimony. Sir Charles and Lady Forbes of Newe were intimate friends of the Prince and often seen at Abergeldie and Balmoral. Helen Forbes, born a Moncreiffe, was an elder sister of the unfortunate Harriett. Married in 1864, she had a second child in March 1868, a daughter christened Evelyn Elizabeth but known as 'Evie' all her life to a doting Prince, who may have suspected he was her actual father. Evie's son, the surrealist poet and art collector Edward Jones, would claim that the Prince of Wales was his grandfather; at the very least he was Edward's godfather.

Newspapers devoted spicy columns to the Mordaunt proceedings, about which Harriett Mordaunt knew nothing. (Court transcripts of scandalous divorce cases and sanguinary murder trials were legally publishable, and the nearest the English press came to printing unregulated soft porn.) Sequestered under medical care, she had to be washed and dressed like a child, her nurse testified, sometimes smeared herelf with excrement, and appeared to be descending into irrecoverable insanity. Her husband charged that she feigned hysteria and madness to avoid pleading to the petition for divorce.

Although Victoria had intervened indirectly with Mordaunt to keep her son from testifying, nothing availed. The Prince of Wales went into the witness box on 23 February and was examined by Serjeant Thomas Bellantine's associate counsel, Francis Deane. The interrogation was phrased – perhaps out of deference to the Queen – to permit innocuous responses from His Royal Highness in two or three words, and the Prince was quoted as saying, unmemorably, 'I was', 'I did', 'I did also', 'I have', 'I do', 'There was', 'I believe so', 'She was', and 'It is so.' One question, however, dealt with whether he sometimes used hansom cabs – presumably to avoid identification. Finally, as the spectators in the packed courtroom held their collective breath, Deane, a QC, said, 'I have only one more question to trouble your Royal Highness with. Has there ever been any improper familiarity or criminal act between yourself and Lady Mordaunt?'

In a firm voice the Prince answered, 'There has not.' The spectators burst into applause and had to be admonished by Lord Penzance, the presiding judge. The Prince's escape from opprobrium had taken seven minutes. But, Sir Henry Ponsonby claimed, 'London was black with the smoke of burnt confidential letters.'

Other respondents under subpoena also denied improper familiarities, and the evidence of her diaries, which validated their visits, proved only that Harriett Mordaunt – clearly an abused spouse by contemporary, if not nineteenth-century, standards – acted indiscreetly before succumbing to madness, or to feigning it.

To demonstrate public support of the Prince, the relieved Queen sent for him to be received at Windsor, with Alexandra. According to *The Times*, which reported the call upon Victoria, 'The Queen's sympathy with Lady Mordaunt's family has been warmly and constantly expressed through the Dowager Duchess of Athole.' To show his confidence that he had been vindicated, the Prince made himself visible nearly every day, skating in Regent's Park, driving along Rotten Row in an open carriage, and going to the theatre. Alexandra usually accompanied him, and to suggest further that she took the matter lightly – probably not the case – in writing a letter congratulating the gossipy Princess Louise on her forthcoming marriage, Alix referred to Bertie as 'my naughty little man'.

Early in March the case would turn upon whether Lady Mordaunt's apparent insanity was a bar to the further prosecution of the suit by the petitioner. Lord Penzance ruled that further proceedings had to await proof by Sir Charles that his wife had recovered her mental capacity. On 22 March he was ordered to pay the respondent's court expenses. Five years later Mordaunt was granted a divorce on grounds of her incurable insanity. She survived in a private asylum until 1906.

The Queen could do nothing but deplore in her journal that her son's 'intimate acquaintance with a young married woman' had been 'publicly proclaimed', evidencing 'an amount of imprudence which cannot but damage him in the eyes of the middle and lower classes, which is most deeply to be lamented in these days when the higher classes, in their frivolous, selfish and pleasure-seeking lives, do more to increase the spirit of democracy than anything else'. For the first time in his life he was even booed in a theatre – at the Olympic on 1 March. Victoria had also done her share for Republicanism by doing almost nothing at all. Nearly a decade had passed since her descent into purdah. Radical politicians and papers questioned what Britain was receiving for its investment in monarchy. Discredit to the monarchy – which Prince Alfred was abetting with open liaisons with married women – offered impetus to a noisily active Republican movement in which the most visible proponent was populist Liberal MP Sir Charles Dilke, who was seeking cause for reducing parliamentary grants for royalty.

While the Mordaunt affair emboldened the Radical press in Britain, its attacks on the heir and his ways were still mild compared with an article by the Irish journalist and politician Justin McCarthy, who had been writing from the safety of New York since 1868. In his 'The Prince of Wales' in the March 1870 *Galaxy*, McCarthy ostensibly defended the

Prince from the worst of the excesses attributed to him while actually accepting most of them as fact. And he marshalled an impressive array of evidence. Still, as he observed, 'the public must not expect all the virtues of a saint to belong to the early years of a prince of the family of Guelph'. (The Hanoverian Welfs, who traced their ancestry to a brawling tenth-century Saxon dynasty, had provided England with its first four Georges.) McCarthy contended that those who had seen the Prince of Wales on his visit to America 'would surely fail to recognize the slender, fair-haired, rather graceful youth of that day in the heavy, fat, stolid, prematurely bald, elderly-young man.... When his eyes and features lapse into their habitual condition of indolent, good-natured, stolid repose, all light of intellect seems to have been banished.'

McCarthy went on to describe the Prince's tastes as not for 'high art' but for 'little theatres where vivacious blondes display their unconcealed attractions' in the '*pièce aux jambes*'. Night after night during the 'long and lamentable illness of his young wife', he allegedly patronized theatres where he could gaze upon 'prodigies of myriad nakednesses', particularly the performances of '[Hortense] Schneider, that high priestess of the obscene, rich with the spoils of princes'. No other lady was identified by name, but in a litany of scandals of which the Divorce Court matter was only the latest, McCarthy gave primacy to a 'brilliant and beautiful' aristocrat 'moving in the court circles of the French capital' who loved ball costumes 'which left the company no possibility of doubting the symmetry of her limbs and the general shapeliness of her person.... This lady received the special attentions of the Prince of Wales. He followed her, people said, like her shadow.' McCarthy claimed that 'a smart pun was soon in circulation, which I refrain from giving', as it identified 'the lady in question'. Possibly the salacious pun was, given the French tendency to drop final consonants, along the lines of '*Sagan est son gant*'. 'Sagan is his glove' leaves little to the lubricious imagination. No sophisticate in upper-class Paris would have doubted that McCarthy meant the princesse de Sagan.

As for the 'profligate' Prince, who was 'dull, stingy and coarse', and 'deeply immersed in debt', McCarthy predicted that a stubbornly royalist England would put up with his improprieties, and when he became king, 'screen the throne against scandal'. It was to be preferred by Englishmen to the dangers of 'organic change', unless his faults became 'grosser and more unmanageable with [the] years'. Distant in New York,

McCarthy underestimated the level of disenchantment. Even at Ascot, identified then as the playground of the Prince, Bertie was hissed on 13 June as he drove up the course. For crowd insurance he had invited, and sat with, the aggressively pious Prime Minister, W. E. Gladstone, who earlier in the year had noted approvingly in his diary the Prince's 'natural intelligence'. Only when a horse in which the Prince was rumoured to have an interest won the last event of the day, was he cheered in the royal stand. Uncowed, he growled, while appearing genial, 'You seem to be in a better temper now than you were this morning, damn you!' He raised his hat and then lit a cigar, and the crowd, his aspersions unheard, cheered him again.

European crises as well as his own kept the Prince close to home in 1870. As was his practice, he spent some summer days at Lord Londesborough's shooting lodge near Scarborough, where in 1869 the fashionable photographer Oliver Sarony had taken the Prince's portrait. Copies went on sale at a shilling, which was only the beginning of HRH's unwitting exploitation. Sarony's studio artist, Thomas Jones Barker, it was advertised, was executing a large canvas of the Prince of Wales walking on the Spa Promenade at Scarborough (where in reality he never felt it was suitable to his dignity to appear), and 'those who would like their portraits included in the subject should lose no time in giving their orders as we understand that positions in the picture are being rapidly appropriated'. Up to a hundred guineas were paid to have one's likeness, adapted by Barker from Sarony's photographs, placed on a figure strolling close to the Prince. Although a commercial fraud, it was innocuous. Had the Prince been photographed with more compromising companions, most of whom were female, and French, he might himself have had to pay the cameraman to desist.

The rush of events in 1870 abbreviated the Prince's diversions in France. Alix had departed for Denmark without him that summer, intent after the Mordaunt affair on prolonging her nearly annual visit to her parents. With scant excuse, however, France declared war on Prussia on 15 July. Hoping to extricate his faltering Empire from economic difficulties and find a cause to rally an increasingly disillusioned people, Napoleon III had counted upon a quick victory, but Bismarck had actually lured the Emperor into initiating a war for which militarist Prussia was more than prepared. The conflict would quickly turn sour for France. Before it did, the Prince hurried to Paris, ostensibly en route to Copenhagen to bring

Alix home. For some of the courtesans of the Second Empire, the war marked the close of their careers; others would be survivors and the Prince would patronize them again. Two would reappear in England, Cora Pearl and Catherine Walters, better known as 'Skittles'. The extravagant Cora liked to exhibit herself wearing only a string of pearls or a sprig of parsley tucked into an obvious part of her person. She was sometimes carried into a room of gentlemen on a large silver platter as the main course – *Cora Pearl à la nue*. Skittles, introduced to the Prince by 'Harty Tarty' Hartington, Liberal leader in the Lords, carried on her business in both capitals and was not dislocated by the war. Then there was Giulia Beneni ('La Barucci'), The self-described 'greatest whore in the world', who was introduced to both Bertie and Affie during the Exhibition season of 1867 by the duc de Gramont, and to whom the Prince of Wales, rendered indiscreet by her passion (or her ability to simulate it), wrote letters very different from those he sent to the pathetic Harriett Mordaunt.

The Prince's indiscretions were becoming more and more alarming. He felt impervious to criticism, whatever the quarter. At a dinner party at the French Embassy in London on the eve of the declaration of war, he apparently expressed to the Austrian ambassador the hope that Austria, still bitter after its defeat by Prussia five years earlier, would join France. The Prussian ambassador learned of the remark and telegraphed it to Berlin. Vicky complained to her mother, 'The King and everyone are horrified at Bertie's speech which is quoted everywhere.' Before long the Prince had changed his mind. The French, he confessed to his mother in a very different kind of letter sent on 20 July from Paris, were, this time, 'quite in the wrong'. With so many of his relations in Germany 'it is not likely that I should go against them'. He would not, however try to alter Alix's feelings, which would never change. Shortly after his return from Copenhagen the French were overwhelmed at Sedan and the Emperor soon captured; Eugénie and her son would flee to England.

'What an awful state of affairs in France now,' the Prince wrote to Charles Carrington. 'The Emperor a Prisoner, and virtually abdicated, and [Marshal] MacMahon's army surrendered. I fear there will yet be a fearful carnage in Paris, if peace is not made and revolution [is] the final and invisible result. It is a sad business, and so unnecessary. France will not recover from this shock and humiliation for years to come. I pity the poor Empress and Prince Imperial very much, and I wonder how the former will ever get out of Paris.' When she did, Bertie, without consulting his mother or anyone in the Government about the political consequences, impulsively offered Eugénie suburban Chiswick House to live in. The property of the Duke of Devonshire, it was ostensibly not a royal residence, but the Duke had loaned it to the Prince of Wales. Bertie's gesture was entirely one of friendship, but was deplored at Whitehall as interference with the granting of asylum.

A 'Society for Aiding and Ameliorating the Condition of the Sick and Wounded in Times of War' – one of the precursors of the Red Cross – was formed as the French Army was falling apart. The Queen became its patroness and the Prince its largely nominal president. He also volunteered to mediate a settlement, but no one took him seriously. Exasperated, Gladstone called the offer 'Royal twaddle'. The Prince did not seem committed to regular work, and the French wanted no more of Louis Napoleon.

Not needing Paris to declare victory, the Prussians proclaimed a German Empire on 18 December in the Hall of Mirrors at Versailles. A republic sprang up in defeated France, and in Britain Republican clubs in cities from Aberdeen to Plymouth took heart from the example. The Radical new mayor of Birmingham, Joseph Chamberlain, declared that he would not be surprised if a republic soon emerged in England. To the Foreign Secretary, Earl Granville, Gladstone had written on 3 December that royalty still had 'a large fund to draw upon', but 'the fund of credit is diminishing'. He blamed both mother and son. 'To speak in rude and general terms, the Queen is invisible and the Prince of Wales is not respected.'

Since the Queen's ceremonial duties were nearly all that were left to her, her failure to perform them left the monarchy without apparent public value. Gladstone again proposed to Granville the oft-rejected role for the Prince as representative of the sovereign in Ireland. Eventually the Prime Minister would collide once more with Victoria on the matter, as she would have none of it. As Gladstone put it to Granville, 'The Queen has [again] put an extinguisher upon my proposals.' At Hawarden, the Prime Minister's home near Liverpool, Gladstone confided to Lord Spencer, Groom of the Stole to the Prince,* that he 'pitied the Prince of Wales, and felt the necessity of an effort to give him responsibility and work', but Spencer realized that the effort was futile.

* Head of his Household.

The Government was increasingly nervous about growing Republican sentiment, and hoped that the wedding of Princess Louise to Lord Lorne, son of the Duke of Argyll, on 21 March 1871, at Windsor, would create some proprietary national joy. A rarity among spousal candidates, Lorne was not a foreigner. The Prince of Wales, who had disapproved of a non-dynastic match but had failed to get his way, made special efforts to point out positively that it was a British event. Underlining that, Lorne's kinsmen at the nuptials would wear kilts of Campbell green. The cavernous Albert Hall had been opening in South Kensington the day before, with large crowds to greet the Queen, who was so seldom in London, but the Prince presided. At the wedding, however, claiming that she was only substituting for the Prince Consort, who somehow was only absent, the Queen would not let Bertie give the bride – his sister – away, traditionally a male prerogative.

Alexandra had been present at both events, yet she was shortly expecting her sixth child, who was born on 6 April 1871. Prince Alexander John Charles Albert survived only a day, and was buried quietly in the churchyard at Sandringham. Nothing else about his arrival and departure was quiet. Headed in large type 'A Happy Release', *Reynolds's Newspaper* – described by George Meredith as 'Reynolds's putrid paper' – declared callously, 'We have much satisfaction in announcing that the newly-born child of the Prince and Princess of Wales died shortly after its birth, thus relieving the working classes of England from having to support hereafter another addition to the long roll of State beggars they at present maintain.' The outrage at Windsor Castle was compounded by the reprint of the piece in the *Pall Mall Gazette* on 24 April under the heading, 'Another Inauspicious Event'. The Queen banned the *Gazette* from Windsor.

Unreasonably, Victoria and others blamed the Prince for neglecting the Princess's health, and therefore the infant's chances, by keeping Alexandra at his side too long. (Alix herself had felt that she could monitor her husband's movements only by keeping him close at hand.) The Queen deputed the Dean of Windsor to talk to her son about it and reported 'that he will be more careful about her in future'. Although the death of the child had nothing to do with Alexandra's public appearances, she had been intent upon showing herself to defuse speculation about the state of the marriage. Besides, Bertie wrote to his mother, he and the Princess had many duties 'as your representatives. You have no conception of the quantity of applications we get, in the course of the year, to open this place, lay a stone attend public dinners, luncheons, fêtes without end.... I certainly think we must be made of wood or iron if we could go through all they ask.' Yet the costume 'Waverley Ball' at Marlborough House went on as scheduled as the peak of the London social season. The Prince appeared as Sir Walter Scott's 'Lord of the Isles', in kilt and tall-feathered cap; the Princess was regally costumed as Mary Queen of Scots. They contrived, as always, to look more loving than they were. But there were to be no more pregnancies for Alix, who was only twenty-six. The only legal barrier to babies was abstinence, and it is likely that marital sex for Alix ended with the conception of Prince John. For the Queen's heir, however, fornication was the true sport of kings.

At home the Prince had to begin to plan the upbringing of his small sons. The Queen expected Prince 'Eddy' to be Albert II, but he had inherited Alix's deafness and was at best slow to learn – even more so than his father. The choice as tutor fell on John Neale Dalton, the thirty-two-year-old curate at Whippingham church, near Osborne, who had a booming voice and radiated authority, and was to supervise the education of Prince Eddy and Prince George for eleven years. Despairingly, Dalton reported to the Prince of Wales that Eddy lacked 'all physical and mental tone', and that only the presence of his younger brother, who was hardly a scholar himself, gave Eddy 'any incentive to exertion'. The outlook for the succession seemed doubly bleak.

After the Paris Commune insurrection ended in failure on 28 May 1871, the Prince arranged to see the battlefields of Sedan and Metz that August, then to meet Alix in Germany on family visits. The Tsar was also visiting with his brood in order to permit the Duke of Edinburgh (Affie) to pay court to the Grand Duchess Marie. While that charade went on, Bertie could not keep himself away from the gambling tables at Homburg. There he was far more conspicuous than at Sedan or Metz, and inevitably *Reynolds's Newspaper* reported (24 September) that the 'Heir-Apparent to the British Throne' was staking gold 'obtained from the toil and sweat of the British working-man' on 'the chances of a card or the roll of a ball'. Learning of it, Gladstone sent for a copy of the paper, then wrote to Granville, 'These things go from bad to worse.' Gladstone had engaged the Queen in a long, and ultimately futile, conversation at Windsor on 23 June about his obsessive desire to see the Prince of Wales installed in a 'Royal Residence' in Ireland. Soon after, Earl Spencer confided in his diary, 'I think the Queen is right in fearing that flatterers would gather round the Prince [in Dublin] and he would be exposed to dangers difficult for him to resist.'

While the Prince was unintentionally encouraging Republican sentiment by everything he did, Victoria was bedridden at Balmoral. Her condition was largely hidden from the press – an easy task in the Highlands. Yet it aborted a family conspiracy conceived by Vicky and Bertie at a gathering at Osborne to present to 'our adored Mama and our Sovereign' a diplomatically phrased plea (drafted by Vicky) that she confront the Royalty Problem by showing herself more often to her people. As senior male sibling the Prince of Wales claimed the right to determine when a propitious moment to serve the ultimatum had arrived. That moment was not to be. The Queen fell seriously ill in mid-August yet would not delay her scheduled railway journey overnight to Scotland. Exacerbating a streptococcal infection in an age before antibiotics, she developed a large axillary abcess that required the services of the eminent surgeon Joseph Lister to open a six-inch incision under anaesthesia. As she healed slowly, an attack of rheumatic gout in a foot ('almost a *third* illness') kept her virtually immobile and in pain for another month. The public learned little about her condition until she was almost recovered, but her illness derailed what the Prince described to Princess Louise as 'Vicky's celebrated letter' recalling their mother to her duties. He predicted that conditions might soon change. They would, but not as he anticipated.

Returning from Germany, he visited his mother at Balmoral and then went to nearby Abergeldie, where Gladstone called as part of his unremitting yet doomed campaign to rehabilitate the heir apparent. 'Dined with the P. of Wales', Gladstone wrote in his diary on 29 September. Grasping for something positive to add, he noted, 'Played whist, against him. He showed great memory.'

It required no feat of memory on the Prince's part to understand why, while at Abergeldie, he received a letter from Mrs Harriet Whatman, who identified herself as the closest friend of the desperate Susan Vane-Tempest, the widow of the insane Lord Adolphus. Mrs Whatman wrote, she explained, out of 'a sense of duty and loyalty to your person', and from her 'deep and sincere affection and pity for a most unfortunate and unhappy lady'. Lady Susan was pregnant with HRH's child, as he had been informed earlier that summer, and she was now within two or three months of 'the crisis'. Her situation was 'most pitiable' and 'dangerous for all parties'. Without funds to 'meet the necessary expenses and buy the discretion of servants, it is impossible to keep the secret'. The dire prospects were affecting her friend's 'health and mind'.

By the same post Lady Susan herself appealed to the Prince. 'I cannot tell your Royal Highness how *utterly miserable* I am', she wrote, 'that you should have left London without coming to see me. You have shown me *so much* kindness for the last four years that I cannot understand your having twice been in London in two days without coming to see me. What have I done to offend you?' She confided that she had done her best 'to obey the orders your Royal Highness gave me the last time I had the happiness of seeing you, but the answer was, "*too late* and *too danger-ous*".' Guardedly, she explained that at his instructions she had gone unsuccessfully to 'Dr C' – his physician, Oscar Clayton – for an abor-tion. Now she needed money to rent a house somewhere where she could complete her pregnancy safely and secretly, suggesting that Ramsgate as 'a seaside place … might be the safest'. She did not want to be remote from London as she was 'so afraid of being in the hands of a country doctor.' Only Mrs Whatman and a mutual friend, Lady Augusta Gordon-Lennox, now married to a minor Saxon prince, knew of Lady Susan's straits.

'Don't *please* be angry', she closed, 'if I *entreat* you to come and see me before I go away.' Her only hope to avoid disgrace, Lady Susan added, was that 'My little maid's event will be about the same time as my own.' (The maid's timely pregnancy seems suspiciously like an invention to deflect identification.)

The Prince left the problem, and the distraught Lady Susan, to the loyal and discreet Francis Knollys. It was not the only potential scandal Knollys had to deal with that September. (The son of General Sir William Knollys, he had become the Prince's embattled Private Secretary.) On the 11th, the Prince had received a letter from Pirro Beneni in Italy, reporting that his sister, known as Madame Barucci, had died of tuberculosis, and that all her correspondence with '*votre Altesse est en mes mains*'. His Highness could reclaim these intimate letters from those brotherly hands for approximately twelve hundred pounds. The Prince wrote to Knollys that the 'scoundrel' Beneni was also threatening the Duke of Edinburgh, another Barucci client, and that the safest route for negotiation was through a Monsieur Kanne, a royal courier in Florence who had performed confidential assignments before.

Since no one had replied to Beneni, who knew nothing of schemes that ranged from proposing theft (the Prince's suggestion), to contentions that the letters were forgeries, to bargaining the price down, he wrote on 27 October of his proposal to hold a public sale of his sister's effects in Paris, at her house in the rue de la Baune, on 9 November. Two days before the auctioneer's hammer went down, Knollys acknowledged despondently to the Prince about the burglary proposal that the days for 'those sort of things are past', and urgently telegraphed Kanne to 'buy everything with signatures'. That evening Kanne reported, 'Letters are 20. Have today seen them all. They are not signed but have A.E. Most are of delicate nature. B. wants £400. Have offered £40. No use.' Having examined them, Kanne wrote to Knollys, 'I came to the conclusion that the nature of them precluded every possibility of their being such [forgeries]. The writing, the intimate gossip, are sufficient proofs of identity and of being originals. At the risk of offending HRH, I *privately* for that reason mention it to you, and I have good reason for doing so, that the Prince can *not* be *too careful* with his writing.' Every scrap of it, he pointed out, 'becomes every day of more value and importance.' On 9 November, the date of the sale and coincidentally the Prince's thirtieth birthday, the invaluable Kanne arranged for a birthday present for him purchased with the Prince's own pounds. For 6,000 francs, about £240, the letters exchanged hands.

Although most private embarrassments did not become public, the *Sheffield Daily Telegraph* went too far in reporting that the Prince of Wales was about to be cited as co-respondent in a divorce case between Lord and Lady Sefton. That August the paper was condemned for libel at the Leeds Assizes. Not long before, the Prince had been mortified by an alleged exchange of letters between him and his brother Prince Alfred, who had been in India, printed in the *Madras Mail* and then reprinted in such European papers as the *Indépendence Belge*. He hoped one day to go to India himself, he told Affie, 'if la mère approves'. Referring to the Mordaunt case, he was quoted as saying that 'la mère begged Mordaunt to leave my name out of the proceedings'. He complained that 'poor father's name is constantly held up.... Here nine years after poor father's death I am expected to sit in sackcloth and ashes to his memory.' The letter contained much else that was known to few others than Bertie and evidenced his style, but the Queen dismissed it to Vicky as a fiction 'invented abroad', and *The Times* loyally declared the letters 'forgeries'.

In the anxious September of Lady Susan and the late La Barucci, the Prince went off to Cavalry Brigade manoeuvres – his second opportunity in two years. An honorary colonel or general of several regiments despite his lack of requisite military skills, he loved uniforms and fancied that but for his heir-apparent burdens he could have been a career soldier. At the least he was an experienced horseman. Fenian leaders organized a protest to his visit in Phoenix Park, Dublin, and police had to use force to break up the demonstration, exaggeratedly labelled 'riots' by the press. By the time the Prince arrived in Ireland, the crowds appeared loyal. In any case, he saw little of them. 'The military life agrees very well with me,' he wrote to the Queen (18 September), 'and I enjoy it very much.' Life in a tent as a senior officer was far from stark, and the distractions of 'moving troops, camp equipment, stores, food, forage, etc.' occupied him very little. Under the prevailing conditions of Army incompetence, he reported, as if he had not contributed to them, 'it is a perfect wonder to me that everything goes off as well as it does'. His own maladroitness – in one war game the umpire declared the Prince's unit as rendered ineffective by cannon fire and the survivors taken prisoner – was satirized in a less-than-mediocre screed by the pseudonymous 'Captain Pipeclay', *The Battle of Foxhill, The Prince of Wales in a Mess, or, The Mill, the Muff and the Muddle.*

Towards the end of October HRH travelled to Scarborough to visit his friend the Earl of Londesborough for some shooting with their set. The Prince returned as the looming Barucci scandal was being defused abroad, in order to be home for his birthday. That he had been in the north of England, and often hunted there, gave a political opening to wealthy screw manufacturer Joseph Chamberlain, campaigning for re-election to his city council seat in Birmingham by appealing to working-class Republicanism. His businessman opponent, William Ellis, Chamberlain charged, was assidously a Royalist. 'If Mr Ellis likes,' said Joe Chamberlain, who cultivated the common touch by using his Christian name, 'when next the Prince of Wales comes down to Warwickshire to shoot cows out of a cart' – and he was interrupted by voices shouting, 'Just like Joseph', 'Keep your temper, Joseph', and even, with sarcasm, 'Monarchism for ever' – 'when that interesting event next takes place, I shall have no objection to Mr Ellis illuminating his warehouses as much as he likes, ... But Mr Ellis has no right to take the taxes from the people, who have great difficulty in earning their weekly wages, and to expend that money upon that tomfoolery.' (Chamberlain kept his seat by seventy-two votes.)

Soon after, on 6 November, Sir Charles Dilke, MP for Chelsea and one of the most outspoken Radicals on the Liberal benches, harangued a working-class audience in Newcastle about the Prince, attacking his ineffectuality during the autumn manoeuvres. On the grounds of the heir's palpable unfitness he went on to advocate a British republic on the new French model. 'There is a widespread belief', he concluded, 'that a Republic here is only a matter of education and time. I say, for my part – and I believe the middle classes in general will say – let it come!' The speech seemed to herald Republicanism as a serious political force, but much of the censure came from politicians criticizing the costs to the nation of supporting a monarchy, rather than arguing the benefits of change. Even earlier, an anonymous pamphlet, *What Does She Do with It?* (actually by George O. Trevelyan), which acquired a large readership, had dealt with allegedly unseemly cost of a vacant throne, and the Queen's salting away money she did not spend on ceremony. Dismissing the charges, the Tory *Daily Telegraph* argued,

> If we are to frame a bill of indictment against the House of Hanover, would it be a mere petty list of kitchen expenses, and butler's pantry accounts? When we put the Throne of England in the British Museum, we will, please God, have a nobler reason than because it cost us a million sterling; that is to say sevenpence three farthing a piece.... The purpose of England in history is more than that the working-class should draw high wages and drink cheap beer, than that the Peers should shoot pheasants, or that the middle classes should learn the piano and make money.

On 14 November, a Tuesday, the daily *Court Circular* reported the indisposition of the Prince of Wales – that he 'continues to be unable to pay his proposed visit to Maharajah Dhuleep Singh at Elvedon Hall, Thetford'. Singh was a favourite as well as an exasperation to the Queen. (Deposed from his princely state as a boy after the Indian Mutiny, he had lived in England since and often visited Victoria as almost a surrogate child.) After a visit to London later in the week for the theatre, the Prince felt feverish, consulting his doctors as well as Victoria's physician Dr William Gull. They identified typhoid fever, which had also struck Lord Chesterfield, and Chesterfield's groom, both of whom had been at

Londesborough Lodge with the Prince. Although the Scarborough area had long been known for its salubrious waters, both were gravely ill. The physicians blamed Londesborough Lodge's drains. Everyone had damnable drains.

At first the cautious *Court Circular* described the 'febrile attack' as 'unattended with danger'. By 23 November the indisposition was acknowledged to be typhoid, but with 'no unfavourable symptoms'. A ball scheduled for Sandringham on 1 December was, however, postponed. The Prince's condition was reported the next day as continuing 'favourable', and on the 25th, despite 'a rather unquiet night … the course of the fever continues uncomplicated'. As usual the physicians lied: Bertie was actually very sick. The *Daily Telegraph* published three columns on the 27th interpreting the reports from Sandringham as disquieting and recalling the fatal case of Prince Albert exactly ten years earlier. (Allegedly the Prince Consort had died of typhoid fever but his doctors had concealed the true nature of his illness for as long as they could.) Bulletins, some of them alarming and others bland and uninformative, began to be issued morning and evening.

The severity of the Prince's illness became clear to the public when, on the 29th, a special train was ordered from the South Western and Great Eastern Railways to take the Queen at 3.30 p.m. to the little station at Wolferton built for visitors to Sandringham, where there was one tiny shop that sold (a paper reported) 'tobacco and oranges'. Major newspapers were beginning to send their star reporters for what soon seemed like a death watch. (Indeed, on 1 December, both Lord Chesterfield and his groom, William Blegge, died.) Quick to capitalize on a sensation, newspapers rushed out special editions to meet the demands of a public that had never warmed to alien Republicanism. Victoria had avoided Sandringham, to her a sink of iniquity second only to Marlborough House. Now, although wan and weak after her own serious illnesses, she came, making demands for her entourage that overwhelmed the Prince's guest quarters and forced the eviction of lesser eminences to nearby inns and country houses. At Sandringham itself, Princess Louise and Princess Beatrice had to share a bed.

Bulletins remained vague, but *The Times* reported on 2 December that 'the worst fears have gained ascendancy'. The Queen was reported to be in tears as she departed to await further news at Windsor. Stealing a march on the competition, a reporter for the *Daily Telegraph* bribed a servant for titbits from the sickroom and reported that the Prince, in delirium, maundered about 'the Camp' at the Curragh, the 'sham-fights', and 'the charging'. He also called for the Revd William Lake Onslow, the resident vicar. 'He never comes to see me now,' the Prince muttered, 'Poor Onslow, I am afraid he is dead.' (A retired naval chaplain, Onslow had served on HMS *Racoon* until recruited to tend the souls of the 160 parishioners at Sandringham, from princes to stableboys.) Raving, the Prince shouted, whistled, sang, and heaved pillows at his despairing doctors, who did little but issue cautious, even optimistic, bulletins. The fever was 'severe', but its progress was 'satisfactory'. 'The symptoms continue without change.' 'There is a regular though gradual decline in the symptoms.'

Even less illuminating were the efforts of a future Poet Laureate, the mediocre Alfred Austin who, in one of his most bathetic couplets produced over an inglorious career, wrote:

> Flash'd from his bed, the electric tidings came,
> He is not better; he is much the same.

Weekly papers issued guarded reports, concerned that their information would become obsolete before publication. Despite its tradition of burlesque, *Punch* published a cartoon, 'Suspense', showing Britannia waiting anxiously at the sickroom door. Interest was worldwide. Earl Granville, the Foreign Secretary, received a telegram from Monsignor Francis Stonor in Rome, 'The Holy Father charges me to ask for news of the Prince of Wales. He prays for his recovery.'

On 8 December, London dailies shocked readers with 'Serious Relapse of Prince of Wales', following with a physicians' bulletin admitting a 'considerable increase in febrile symptoms'. The *Telegraph's* special correspondent declared that 'the worst fears are entertained'. He followed on the ninth with 'Dangerous Relapse'. The Prince continued 'in a precarious state'. The Home Secretary arrived; the Queen prepared to return. 'Deep emotion' was reported throughout England, and premature reports of the Prince's death surfaced. Political attacks on the Prince evaporated. Railway workers meeting at the Lambeth Baths in south London to air grievances passed, instead, a resolution 'that this meeting of two thousand workingmen, having heard with deep sorrow of the death of His Royal Highness the Prince of Wales, desire the chairman to express their great grief at the irreparable loss sustained by Her

Majesty and Her Royal Highness'. Newspapers unable to confirm the death offered only 'a glimmer of hope'. Family members continued to arrive at Sandringham as doctors declared grimly, 'nothing more unfavourable to report'. On Sunday 10 December churches across Britain filled with parishioners praying for the Prince. (The day before, the Western Synagogue in London was led in prayer to grant the Prince 'length of days to pursue his life's journey worthily and happily'.) In Hereford, a curate, Francis Kilvert, noted in his diary, 'We do not know whether the Prince of Wales is alive or dead ... and we did not know whether to mention the Prince's name in the Litany or not. Mr. Venables read prayers, and when he came to the petition ... for the Royal Family he made a solemn pause and in low voice prayed "that it may please Thee (if he still survive) to bless Albert Edward Prince of Wales".' Before the afternoon service began, 'a form of prayer for the Prince came down by telegraph from the Archbishop of Canterbury, the first prayer that I ever heard of as coming by telegraph'.

In Sandringham at half-past five that Sunday morning the Queen was awakened by a message from Dr Jenner that the Prince had come through a dangerous 'spasm' and again by a second message that there had been an even more severe recurrence. Returning, Sir William advised the Queen 'that at any moment dear Bertie might go off, so that I had better come at once'. She put on a dressing-gown and found the Prince motionless, but for laboured breathing, with candles burning nearby as if he lay on a catafalque. All she could do was sit helplessly behind a screen. When his breathing slowed, she, Princess Louise, and Bertie's three brothers, all of whom had gathered in the room, were asked to leave. Dr Gull told the Queen he was 'much alarmed'.

The Cabinet met the next day, 11 December, a Monday, to consider whether any alternative action need be taken as the Prince was legally regent in the event of the Queen's incapacity or death. City by city, newspapers published Sunday prayers from churches across Britain. Tuesday papers reported 'Increased Danger of the Prince of Wales', and 'fresh access of grave symptoms'. While the Prince seemed nearly comatose, the Queen, discouraged from remaining in the sickroom, walked about the Sandringham grounds on the arm of Princess Louise. On Wednesday the noon medical report was 'condition unchanged'. At five, doctors could report only 'no abatement of the symptoms'. Contradicting the doctors, who seemed to have abandoned hope, the *Daily Telegraph's* canny special correspondent, aided by a house informer with better intelligence, it seemed, than Dr Gull or Dr Jenner, reported that although the Prince was not sinking further, he had 'a good deal of muttering delirium, and is still feeble and feverish'. That seemed an improvement, for 'he has ... been able to take freely the necessary stimulants, and has even manifested a very distinctly expressed preference for a draught of ale, which was gladly indulged [him]'. Grasping at remedies, the physicians had ordered the sinking patient rubbed down with 'old champagne brandy', and he slept, perhaps overcome by the fumes. On awakening he was offered a glass of ale by Affie, greedily gulped it down, and asked for another, then lapsed again into sleep. But he was turning the corner.

In Bath, the charismatic Evangelical divine Dr John Cumming, who had a huge following despite a series of failed prophecies of celestial Armageddon, declared that the events at Sandringham were, somehow, evidence that 'all Republicans must be silenced'. He was unaware yet of the powers of drink, against which he also preached.

What appeared most ominous to a sensation-hungry press, if one believed medical prognoses, was that the patient's fever (already 104 degrees) was predicted to crest on the 14th, the tenth anniversary of Prince Albert's death. 'It is now ten years tomorrow', the *Pall Mall Gazette* observed, 'since the Prince Consort died of a similar affliction. As long as the world lasts, there will be superstition in it, and however foolish the feeling, there is real anxiety about tomorrow.' Gladstone wrote to the Queen with sanctimonious sincerity that he would not 'mock the sorrow of this moment by assurances which ... must seem so poor and hollow; but he earnestly commends the sufferer and the afflicted round him, most of all the Mother and the Wife, to Him alone who is able either to heal or to console, and who turns into mercies the darkest of all His dispensations'. Loyal prayers emanated from pulpits everywhere in the isles where, only weeks before, their occupants had privately, if not publicly, deplored the Prince of Wales's immorality and uselessness.

Almost no one in Britain expected the Prince of Wales to survive through the fatal 14th. At his bedside, Princess Alexandra, Princess Alice (who had earlier tended her father) and the Queen gathered in the sickroom for the end, Victoria recalling, 'Alice and I said to one another in tears, "There can be no hope." I went up to the bed and took hold of his poor hand, kissing and stroking his arm. He turned round and looked wildly at me saying, "Who are you?" And then "It's Mama."

SUSPENSE.

*As the heir lay apparently dying, attitudes about him largely changed (*Punch, *23 December 1871). However he did not*

"Dear child," I replied. Later he said, "It's so kind of you to come," which shows he knew me, which was most comforting to me.' His physicians issued a bulletin at eight on the morning of the 15th cautiously noting that 'the debility is great, but the general conditions are favourable'.

The next day the Prince was given less brandy (the soporific for the dying) and more milk, and was moved, the papers reported, from his sickbed 'which has been the scene of so much suffering' to 'a fresh couch'. The Queen wrote to Vicky on the Saturday that she remained sceptical of the 'marked improvement'. With more optimism, the Queen's Private Secretary, Sir Henry Ponsonby, noted to Francis Knollys that he 'assumed that the Prince of Wales … will [now] gladly accept the advice of those who think that employment is desirable for him; and that the present may be a turning point in his life, if properly managed'. He suggested (as alternatives) philanthropy, the arts and sciences, the military, foreign affairs, and Ireland. Knollys (on 19 December) saw little hope of any of them. His 'intimate knowledge' of the Prince's 'character and tastes' led him to eliminate all but foreign affairs, as Ireland would be rejected by the Queen, while the others required a 'special aptitude' which was non-existent. Foreign affairs, Knollys admitted, 'have afforded occupation to even the most indolent of Princes'. Gladstone in any case would not be budged from his untenable Irish solution.

At Sandringham on Sunday 17 December, before returning to Windsor, Victoria attended services at the little church of St Mary Magdalene, where Mr Onslow, recalled by the Prince of Wales in his delirium, prayed for His Royal Highness's 'renewed health and strength'. To universal amens, the Queen the next day awarded Dr William Gull an instant baronetcy. Later, Mark Twain would remark, with Genesis in mind, 'When the Prince seemed dead Mr Gull dealt blow after blow between the shoulders, breathed into his nostrils, & literally cheated Death. It startlingly reminds us of the earliest incident in the history of the human race.'

From Windsor on 20 December, the Queen explained to Vicky that Gull was 'a fashionable doctor; but he is a very clever man besides, and a good, religious, courageous one – who is as anxious for dear Bertie's moral welfare as for his physical well being. We all feel that if God has spared his life it is to enable him to lead a new life – and if this great warning is not taken, and the wonderful sympathy and devotion of the whole nation does not make a change in him, it will be worse than before and his utter ruin.' Yet she realized, she confided, that he was 'adored by his people for his frank, kind, hearty manner to them all'.

Throughout what remained of December, wherever 'God Save the Queen' was sung, tearful audiences followed with 'God Bless the Prince of Wales'. Although, predictably, *Reynolds's Newspaper* claimed that the Prince's condition had been 'purposely exaggerated' to create 'a sham panic got up for the occasion to serve a political end', Republicanism seemed all but dead. 'What a sell for Dilke this illness has been!' Lord Henry Lennox, MP for Chichester and the younger son of the Duke of Richmond, wrote to Disraeli. Dilke and other Republican orators suddenly found themselves facing hostile crowds, while the public swamped Sandringham with gifts, most of which were returned with thanks – all but a barrel of home-brewed beer, which was set in a dark, cool cellar to await the Prince's recovery.

In South Kensington, A. J. Munby called upon Theodore Martin, then working on a life of Prince Albert authorized by the Queen. Martin was not at home, but his wife, the graceful Helen Faucit, who had just retired from the stage, invited Munby to stay and chat. Soon two other friends arrived, the Revd Charles Kingsley, once the Prince of Wales's tutor, and the historian J. A. Froude. When they began discussing the inevitable subject, Froude observed that the usually silent multitudes had been showing 'what the real feeling of the country is; and the few malcontents have been cowed'. Even the working classes, which had mobilized to support reduction of the working day to nine hours, he noted, had been enthusiastically supportive of the Prince. Kingsley expressed hope and confidence in the Prince of Wales's character, and Mrs Martin exclaimed, so Munby noted in his diary, 'After such a burst of enthusiasm, and from such a nation, what a King he ought to be!'

'I have heard it said', Froude observed 'in his half-cynical yet gentle way', as Munby wrote, 'that no one ever got good from an illness.'

IX

Relapse

1871–1875

OBSESSED WITH 'RESCUING' ladies of pleasure, pursuing them on what he called 'night walks', and often flagellating himself afterward, Gladstone found a very different kind of rescue challenge in the Prince of Wales. There was also a political bonus in setting the Prince on the path to virtue. The increasingly unpopular Liberals would appear as the rescuers not only of the Prince's tarnished reputation but of the throne itself – all, of course, as Gladstone understood, in the High Anglican style for which Victoria had no sympathy. His proposal, about which the Queen was as dubious as he expected, was to stage a grand thanksgiving service for the heir's recovery at St Paul's. The extravaganza would be preceded by a grand procession through London from Buckingham Palace at which the Queen and Prince would be seen by the ordinary people for whom there would be no pews in St Paul's.

The Prince of Wales's relapse on 27 December nearly ended the Prime Minister's ambitions. For a third time the Queen rushed to Sandringham, where, on New Year's Day 1872, she penned a prayer into her journal, 'May our Heavenly Father restore him and let this heavy trial be for his good in every way!' Two weeks later the Prince was recovering sufficiently for Gladstone to offer plans to Victoria for his spectacle, set for 27 February. To that he added his renewed entreaties for the Queen's 'determination of the Prince of Wales's future'. In anticipation of the event, an effusively pious and sentimental booklet *The Prince and the Prayer*, was printed anonymously, celebrating Albert Edward's recovery, and attributing it solely to God's intervention. It was 'a life given back,

... full of energy, nobleness and self-sacrifice'. Alexandra sent copies to friends, one to a Mrs Thomas, possibly an extra nurse during the illness, 'in remembrance of the sad time of sickness she spent at Sandringham'.

In many ways the Prince's illness rescued what remained of his reputation, or at least postponed its further disintegration. J. R. Green, a Lambeth librarian whose *Short History of the English People* (1874) was to become an influential textbook, scoffed that the Prince's recovery would 'deliver us from a deluge of that domestic loyalty which believes the whole question of republicanism [is] solved by the statement that the Queen is an admirable mother and that her son has [had] an attack of typhoid'. That domestic euphoria insulated the Prince from responsibility. Among other things he could ignore the entreaties of Lady Susan Vane-Tempest, soon to bear their unwanted child. On 3 February 1872 she wrote pathetically to the discreet Francis Knollys from a London address that she had felt so '*very* unwell' after Christmas that she had returned to consult the Prince's doctor, Oscar Clayton. 'He has not allowed me to leave my room since I returned as I may not even put my foot to the ground. He is *most* kind in coming to look after me and says that [the pregnancy] is going on all right but that I must not return to Ramsgate.... I am *too* sorry to be obliged again to have recourse to the kindness of One who has already been so generous to me, but the expenses of two houses and the extra servants have been *very* great.... I cannot enter into all particulars but Dr Clayton will explain all to Him.'

To the Prince himself Lady Susan wrote on the 8th thanking him for his thoughtlessly offered tickets to the thanksgiving service. 'Alas!' she said, cautiously, 'I could not go to the Cathedral but you can well believe *my heart and my thoughts were there*.' In a plaintive postscript she added, 'Forgive such a *scrawl* my dear sir as I am a cripple on two sticks and cannot move about!!!!' The Prince indiscreetly kept her letters but never saw her again. Three years later she was dead.

As the thanksgiving extravagance approached, the Queen's advisers and Gladstone's Cabinet timidly offered her new proposals for giving the Prince a royal role. His most visible duty to date had been to open the Albert Hall for his mother, on 29 March 1871. (She claimed to have felt 'giddy' on the dais before the 8,000 in the audience, and handed her written remarks about admiring the beautiful structure to Bertie, who said, simply, 'The Queen declares this hall now open.') The former Chancellor of the Exchequer and Secretary for India Charles Wood –

Viscount Halifax – told Victoria through Colonel Ponsonby 'that [for the Prince] now to lead an idle life would be very calamitous', and he earnestly trusted that the future sovereign 'would have some occupation'. As always the suggestion was 'employment in Ireland'. While brushing aside all such proposals, the Queen awaited public reaction to the thanksgiving festival, perhaps as some index to national feeling about the Prince. Working-men's groups had already complained about the cost – an estimated £13,000.

Throughout the United Kingdom 27 February 1872 was declared a legal holiday to free people to crowd the route of the procession or to attend the excesses of thanksgiving arranged in churches across the kingdom. On the appointed morning Victoria rode in a state landau drawn by six horses, with Alix at her side and 'Bertie opposite'. Seven open carriages preceded them, and fifteen bands stationed at intervals along the route played 'God Save the Queen' and 'God Bless the Prince of Wales'. Victoria saw 'millions out', demonstrating 'wonderful enthusiasm and astounding affectionate loyalty.... Bertie was continually with his hat off'.

To the Queen the interior of St Paul's was 'stiflingly hot', and the service, during which the Prince knelt (with some difficulty) in prayer and endured a *Te Deum* by a monster chorus and a tedious sermon by the Archbishop of Canterbury, was 'too long'. The ceremonies ended at a quarter-past two, after which the royal family returned to the Palace amid 'deafening cheering', arriving at twenty minutes to four. From Marlborough House that evening the Prince wrote to his mother that he was 'touched ... by the feeling that was displayed in those crowded streets to-day towards you and also to myself'. He was tired, and plagued since his illness by a painful, swollen leg. He could not yet walk unaided. But to mark the event, the busy Poet Laureate added an epilogue to his *Idylls of the King*, shrewdly referring to the 'crown'd Republic's crowning common-sense' in maintaining its traditional loyalties. The lines, addressed to the Queen, made it clear that Republicanism was no longer a serious political force:

> When pale as yet, and fever-worn, the Prince,
> Who scarce had pluck'd his flickering life again
> From halfway down the shadow of the grave,
> Passed with thee thro' thy people and their love,
> And London roll'd one tide of joy thro' all
> Her trebled millions ...

" THANKSGIVING. "

Gladstone's prayerful thanksgiving for the Prince's recovery,
staged at St Paul's, as viewed in Punch, *2 March 1872*

Englishmen – according to Tennyson – recognized the 'poisonous honey
stolen from France' by the likes of Dilke and Bradlaugh and Chamberlain
as not for them. Even *Punch* published a two-page drawing imagining the
Prince at St Paul's kneeling in prayer. Accompanying verses railed at
cynics and scoffers who had questioned the pageant, which had enriched
'stagnant lives of toil and gain', and was a triumph for 'Queen, Prince and
Folk'. In untimely fashion Sir Charles Dilke arose shortly in the House
of Commons and moved for an inquiry into the Civil List, from which
the Queen and various Royals drew stipends, and was howled down. The
motion was rejected by 276 to 2.

The Prince's slow recuperation made reconsidering an occupation for him still premature, yet two days after the thanksgiving ceremonies, on entering the Palace grounds from Constitution Hill, the Queen was nearly shot at by a young Fenian. Seeing someone unknown lurking at her carriage door, John Brown sprang at him, jarring loose a pistol which proved unloaded. Only a heartbeat separated an unprepared Bertie from her throne, but Victoria would do nothing about it.

At first the Prince seemed, to the Queen, reborn from his near-death experience. Recuperating at Osborne in mid-February, just before the excesses at St Paul's, he appeared to his ever-hopeful mother cleansed of his sins. 'It is like a new life,' she claimed to Vicky in Berlin, '– all the trees and flowers give him pleasure, as they never used to do, and he was quite pathetic over his small wheelbarrow and little tools [of childhood] at the Swiss cottage. He is constantly with Alix, and they seem hardly ever apart!!!' It was an opportunity for a kingly apprenticeship, but Victoria and the Cabinet failed to find a formula to make that possible. Disraeli had tried with equal lack of success. Now Gladstone reviewed proposals to acquaint the Prince with the Foreign Office, the India Office, and the War Office, as well as other roles that mirrored Bertie's father's interests rather than his own. Yet none attracted the Prime Minister as much as his perennial panacea of an Irish solution, which the Queen stubbornly found unacceptable. And she could count upon at least one ally in keeping her son from establishing what she felt could be a rival viceregal court in Dublin: Bertie himelf.

In a conversation with General Ponsonby, the Marquis of Hamilton, Lord of the Bedchamber to the Prince and his close friend, agreed that 'some congenial employment' had to be found for HRH, but warned that he 'dislikes any suggestion about Ireland, and would positively refuse to go there officially in any capacity' unless ordered by the Queen. That indirect objection did not close the subject, as Gladstone was unable to let the idea go. It took an objection in writing from the Prince himself. He would be glad to talk to the Prime Minister, Bertie explained to his 'dear Mama', about 'useful employment which I could undertake as your eldest son'. Gladstone even went to Sandringham for a weekend later in 1872 to propose a glorified Lord-Lieutenancy – in Ireland. (In his diary Gladstone confided how much he enjoyed the atmosphere of Sandringham, which did not have 'the stiffness of a Court'.) But anything involving even minimal paperwork, the Queen warned Gladstone, was beyond her son's capacities. 'The P. of W. has *never* been fond of reading, and from his earlier years it was *impossible* to get him to do so. Newspapers and, *very rarely*, a novel, are all he ever reads.'

In August a cabinet photo of the Prince and Princess of Wales was issued for general sale, showing the Prince looking reassuringly hale and serious and Alix, as youthful and beautiful as ever, devotedly clutching her husband's arm. However Gladstone made no headway over the matter of serious work. Chafing in frustration, he predicted in his diary that 'the bitter fruit will be reaped hereafter', and that 'the illnesses of last year' had been 'a golden period', now wasted, to reform the Prince of Wales. All the Prince seemed to want was to travel as a very important person, which never bored him, and the opportunity to wear colourful foreign uniforms as honorary colonel of an élite regiment. When his brother Alfred finally found a wife, marrying a daughter of the Tsar, and would wear, on occasion, the uniform of a Russian cavalry officer as the sovereign's son-in-law, the Prince of Wales longed to accept a similar colonelcy. Victoria remained obdurate. It was 'wiser and better' for the future king to keep free of foreign uniforms, however attractive. He would have to set styles some other way – and, indeed, did so all his life. He invented creased trousers when his valet mistakenly put creases in the front and rear, rather than the sides. He was credited with the blazer and the dinner jacket, and the bottom button of a jacket has traditionally been left undone ever since the Prince left his that way to relieve pressure on his protuberant paunch. Few years would go by when the Prince did not inaugurate a new style, largely out of boredom with the usual, or for his own convenience.

On 9 March 1872, the day that Gladstone had offered a memorandum to a Cabinet committee to justify his pursuing the Prince with the Irish 'rescue' scheme for the rest of the year, the Prince and Princess of Wales left for a Mediterranean holiday. He visited the Jockey Club in Paris, which had survived the Prussian siege, then called upon President Louis Adolphe Thiers to legitimize his stay in the capital. In Cannes they boarded the royal yacht and were conveyed to Rome, where, to the consternation of die-hard Protestants in England, he called upon the Pope. The Waleses then went to Florence, Venice, and Lake Como, returning to London on 1 June, thus missing still another national thanksgiving for HRH's survival, this time at the Crystal Palace. (Gladstone stopped at nothing in joining religiosity to rescue, ostensibly on the Prince's behalf.)

For the grand event on 1 May, Arthur S. Sullivan, identified in the programme as a music teacher in the 'Ladies' Division' of the School of Art, Science and Literature at the Crystal Palace, composed a gigantic *Te Deum* to be sung by a chorus of 2,000 to an audience of 26,000. Victoria permitted the work to be dedicated to her 'in consequence of the particular circumstance of the case', Sir Thomas Biddulph wrote to Sullivan. The diva Thérèse Tietjens led the cheering masses at the end of the concert in 'God Bless the Prince of Wales'. Whether or not the intercessions with the Almighty helped, the Prince was stouter than ever on his return, and ready to resume his former lifestyle.

He was hardly back when Knollys and Henry Cole, who had helped Prince Albert stage the Great Exhibition at the Crystal Palace, exploited a projected princely visit to the South Kensington Museum, a legacy of the 1851 Exhibition, to promote his renewed popularity. The day before the much-publicized progress, 23 June 1872, Cole sent a message to Knollys, 'The district is all alive and near the Museum it is a sky of flags and mottoes.... The simple loyalty of the poor people is a thing which our Botany Bay Chancellor of the Exchequer* cannot understand.' After the Prince of Wales's appearance Cole boasted happily, 'Communism, Republicanism, and Citizen Dilke beaten hollow by loyalty, thank God.'

In Rome, HRH had purchased two marble nudes for Marlborough House, to accompany a small marble nymph by Princess Louise's sculpting master, J. E. Boehm, for which Catherine Walters – Skittles – had modelled. The Prince knew her body only too well but he had no need to explain that to Alix. It was placed in a niche in his library. He had little acquaintance with the volumes there, but Skittles was an open book. So were other '*doubtful* characters', as the Queen scoffed, through Sir Henry Ponsonby, when Gladstone suggested that the Prince could compensate for her abdication of social influence by leading 'the higher society of London'. Her son's 'fashionable set', she retorted, did him nothing but harm. Walter Bagehot had written in *The English Constitution* (1867), observing the current Prince of Wales and aware of the historical disjunction between monarchs and their heirs, 'All the world and the glory of it, whatever is most seductive, has always been offered to the Prince of Wales of the day, and always will be. It is not rational to expect the best virtue where temptation is applied in the most trying form at the frailest time

* The Australian-born Robert Lowe.

of human life.' It was no different with Prince Albert Edward, whom Bagehot dismissed as 'an unemployed youth'.

That nothing had changed was apparent from *Beeton's Christmas Annual* for 1872, the popular holiday season potpourri. More displayed on drawing room tables than read, it featured a long and often flabby but sometimes on-target parody of Tennyson's *Idylls of the King. The Coming K——* transparently skewered the Prince of Wales – 'Prince Guelpho' in the anonymous verses.* Alluding to the Mordaunt trial and to the Prince's brush with death, Guelpho confesses ruefully:

> I would not that such trouble came again,
> And much more careful am I than I was; —
> One illness and one witness-box's enough.

Guelpho is described as 'a favoured guest of him who lost Sédan' – Napoleon III – and someone who 'knew Schneider, and large-eyed Judic', the latter very likely the kohl-lidded Sarah Bernhardt, of Jewish ancestry. When at home, although he 'enjoyed an evening at a London fire', Guelpho concerned himself more with 'comfortable ease' –

> To dress in well-cut tweeds …,
> To smoke good brands; to quaff rare vintages;
> To sport with Amaryllis in the shade....
> How well he liked to flirt, how well to dress,
> How well to dine, how well to pigeons shoot … ,
> The worthy leader of our every game.
> He sets our fashions.

To an innocent aspirant Guelpho explains that his gentlemen were 'carpet knights', not the legendary Arthurian sort who avenged misdeeds and undid evil:

> '*My* knights are of a very different kind.
> We don't ride forth redressing wrongs; we find
> It is enough to dress ourselves, young man....
> We do not rescue maidens in distress –
> Our motives might, you see, be misconstrued.
> Mine *have* been, once or twice unpleasantly.'

---

* The authors were Samuel Beeton, Evelyn Jerrold, and Aglen Dowty. Victoria's family line on the Continent had been the Guelphs.

Had Guelpho's 'Papa' lived, the authors speculate, 'He might ha' got into a different set', but 'his Pa was nipped in the bud', and rather than work at 'fattin' pigs and sheep' on the royal model farm, Guelpho 'sowed a tidyish crop … of wild oats'.

The verses even exposed the Prince's involvement in sponsoring

> … fisticuffs and acts of prowess done
> In many a prize-ring …,
> The noble art of self-defence.

Prize-fighting was illegal at mid-century. Advertised only by word of mouth, bouts evaded detection by being staged just after sunrise. A pugilist describes

> … [how] we pitched
> The ropes, and fix'd the stakes into the ground.
> The seat of honour were the Coming K——'s,
> And beaming he gazed upon the scene,
> And whispered in my ear afore the fight,
> 'The belt will be for thee.'

Jewelled winner's belts had come into fashion as a substitute for – sometimes a supplement to – unlawful purses. Wagering on fights was as illegal as were the breaches of the peace, but Prince Guelpho 'booked a bet of four to one' and in the most vivid lines in the verses, the rivals strike at each other with 'windmill arms, … not heeding blows', until at the close of the seventeenth round, one of the bloodied, groggy combatants falls

> Like to a log, and lay upon the turf. …
> Then did gay Guelpho clap his hands with glee,
> And pat the Nobbly one upon his back;
> 'O noble man,' he said, 'and chivalrous;
> Almost I feel inclined to dub thee knight;
> For grandly hast thou fought thy fight to-day,
> And well have I pulled off my bets on thee.
> Who says the days of knightly deeds are done?'

Albert Edward had returned, as the verses implied, to the preoccupations of his predecessor as Prince of Wales, the future George IV, whose favourite pugilists served as ushers at his coronation. Prize-fighting had since become a furtive sport, harassed by the police. Although it had undergone a temporary renaissance with the notorious Tom Sayers – John Heenan fight in 1860, royal patronage seemed unthinkable, but the Prince was generous with his favourites. Julian Osgood Field, whose American mother had danced with young Bertie in New York, recalled, as a fourth-form Etonian who had slipped away to the ringside, seeing HRH presiding (in traditional top hat) at Angelo's in St James's Street when the nimble Guardsman Charley Buller gave 'very much the worst of it' to the brawny but fading Jem Mace. Delighted, the Prince 'gave Charley a very handsome pair of sleevelinks and invited him down to Sandringham on the strength of it.... There were not a few other memorable feats at Angelo's presided over by the Prince.' The raffish Buller was not much use in the Life Guards but was a pet of the Prince.

Least favourite of courtiers was 'that brute J.B.' – as Bertie called the Queen's personal servant John Brown in a letter in November 1872 to Princess Louise. Brown's ascendancy over their mother diminished their own access and increased his arrogance. The royal siblings were constantly scheming to rid the Court of him, Bertie as chief plotter, but nothing would work. Still, it represented one responsibility which the Prince had assumed for himself – spokesman for the family. He complained to the Lord Chamberlain's Office, for example, when the Court Theatre in Sloane Square premiered a burlesque, *The Happy Land*, by Gilbert à Beckett and 'F. Tomline' (covertly W. S. Gilbert). The play not only depicted Gladstone and his Cabinet, but joked about the stinginess of the Queen. 'Which of the royal palaces is placed at his disposal?' a character asks about a visiting king. 'Claridge's Hotel', says another. The Examiner of Plays closed the theatre for a night while the script was cleansed.

As heir apparent he wanted to be consulted on royal betrothals, and took it on himself to expand the social horizons of his siblings by conferring respectability on former outsiders. The English and the French Rothschilds became good friends. Marlborough House had already been open to them; and the Prince had hunted with them. The French branch of the banking firm had survived the war with Prussia, and the Prince met Alphonse de Rothschild (with Natty), in 1873 at an entertainment at the home of the duc de la Rochefoucauld-Bisaccia, who was pressing the claim of Louis-Philippe's son, the comte de Paris, to the vacant throne. One of his hostesses, at her mansion in the faubourg St Honoré, was the baronne Alphonse, Leonora de Rothschild, with whom he was rumoured to have had a liaison. The Queen was dismayed by her son's French acquaintances, yet he somehow maintained friendships with Republicans, Royalists, and Bonapartists, charming them all.

Napoleon III and Eugénie had always been kind to him, and the Prince determined, after the exiled Emperor's death on 9 January 1873, to attend the funeral. The royal presence, however, could have offended the new Republic, and the Queen, after consulting with Gladstone's Foreign Minister, Lord Granville, objected. 'One cannot be wrong in showing respect to fallen greatness,' the Prince insisted, and Gladstone in responding to Granville contrasted HRH's 'good nature and sympathy' with his lack 'of political judgment, either inherited or acquired'. Ignoring criticism, the Prince of Wales attended the lying-in-state on 14 January, accompanied by Prince Alfred and their brother-in-law (Helena's husband) Prince Christian. Then they paid their respects to the former empress, who sat, veiled in black, in a shuttered upstairs room. The next day, with thousands of curious onlookers crowding the village for the spectacle, Napoleon III was buried at the church of St Mary on Chislehurst Common. Again the Prince of Wales was present, as were dozens of his Parisian friends.

Until he could indulge himself again in Paris, he accommodated his erotic itch in London. Hotels, however discreet, and private upstairs rooms in restaurants, were inconvenient. Francis Knollys wrote to the twenty-six-year-old Earl of Rosebery on the Prince's behalf to request the use of his London house as a rendezvous for HRH and his brother Alfred – soon to marry Grand Duchess Marie of Russia – and their 'actress friends'. Rosebery found excuses, but there were others eager to remain in the Marlborough House set and who had discreet town addresses.

For the Queen he was often forced to play royal host. The future Tsar Alexander III and his family visited at Marlborough House from mid-June into mid-August, while the unwelcome Shah of Persia arrived soon after the Tsarevitch, but was put up in Buckingham Palace, which Victoria would not visit while the 'brusque and rough' Nasr-ed-Din remained. On 20 June she gave the bejewelled Shah a formal luncheon at Windsor, during which he struggled with knife and fork, and drank from the spout of his teapot. Then she returned the 'strange' visitor to London, to be entertained, along with 3,000 guests, by the Lord Mayor at the Guildhall, and by the Prince of Wales, who took him once, overnight, to Trentham, the vast estate of the Duke of Sutherland. (In the palace, the Shah's retainers roasted a lamb in his rooms, then pulled it to pieces with their fingers. After he left, Victoria asked the frugal Gladstone for funds to restore the guest suite.) Royal visits were also occasions for parades, and at Windsor the Shah and the future Tsar were in the same procession, on horseback, the visitors cantering on either side of the Prince. The three were arrayed in the colourful sashes and medals each had awarded the other, or which had come from the Queen, who rode in an open carriage behind them, accompanied by the ubiquitous John Brown.

His Royal Highness's favourite cavalcade was always at Ascot during Race Week, a spectacle which in 1873 Mark Twain had come to cover. His notes refer to the 'fiery liveries' of the postilions mounted on each of the four horses drawing the Prince's carriage, and to the loud cheers of the throng, toward which the Prince and the 'trim graceful' Princess in a dress with a row of bows down the front 'bowed continually'. Although Twain had clambered hazardously atop a grandstand to get a good view of the balding Prince, enthusiastic spectators impeded his view. 'But when [he] took his hat off got good top of his head. No hair – otherwise I had that climb for nothing.... Gray coat & stovepipe hat.'

When the Prince was freed from the Queen's diplomatic leavings to travel again, A. J. Munby's scrubwoman–mistress, Hannah Cullwick, saw a crowd gathering at Charing Cross Station as a red carpet was unrolled for the Waleses. The Prince, she wrote ungrammatically in her diary on 22 September, 'was much stouter & bigger nor i expected to see after such an illness as he had lately. It did me good watching the crowd & to think o' the different grades o' people there is in the world, that even gentlemen had to bow & scrape to the royal family.' Expert Savile Row tailoring normally concealed HRH's paunch, as his first appearance in *Vanity Fair*, on 8 November 1873, evidenced. In the 'Spy' caricature, he wore a jaunty cap, and a striped shirt and polka-dot tie under a jacket that did not match his trousers. Lolling on an elbow with both hands in his outer pockets, he looked more Left Bank than London.

Early in 1874, the press resumed its scepticism about the rehabilitation of the Prince, opening with Beeton's *The Siliad*, which continued the scurrilous themes of *The Coming K——*. To Earl Granville on 5 January Gladstone argued that to take any action to suppress it would only publicize its charges. In one episode the Queen upbraids Guelpho for the vices alleged in *The Coming K——* but her son points out, realistically,

What can it matter, even if 'tis true,
I wouldn't be so glum if I were you.
Suppose I am all that they say I am,
I'm better so than [to] live a priggish sham.

However he lived no sham, as became obvious to Constance Rothschild, who spent a weekend at Sandringham that January. Among the guests were Benjamin Disraeli, Dr Magee (the Bishop of Peterborough), and Disraeli's Private Secretary Monty Rowton. Between tea and dinner, with Rowton as accompanist, the Princess of Wales sang a number of her favourite hymns. As the lugubrious music continued until midnight, the Prince, glancing at his watch and bowing toward the Bishop, remarked, 'Sunday being over, we may resort to the bowling alley.' (Few had licence to respond to the Prince's disregard of convention. The next year, visiting Aston Clinton, Sir Anthony de Rothschild's estate in Buckinghamshire, the MP Bernal Osborne was seated at the card table with the affable Prince as his partner. When HRH asked whether the stakes should be half-crowns, Osborne answered cheekily, 'Certainly, Sir; we could hardly play for crowns.')

The Prince was looking forward to Disraeli's return as Prime Minister. There was a congenial raffishness about Dizzy's respectability, and general election polling was to begin on 1 February 1874. Confidence in Gladstone's Government had dwindled. As the campaign warmed, on 10 January the Waleses, remote from any domestic role, left for St Petersburg for the marriage of Alfred, the Duke of Edinburgh, to Marie of Russia. Russian hospitality was lavish. For the Prince and other noble guests, a boar 'hunt' (to the press a pig-sticking) was arranged in which eighty animals were slaughtered. While abroad the Prince was pleased by Disraeli's courtesy in telegraphing that his Conservatives had decisively defeated Gladstone's Liberals. On his return, the Prince of Wales, to his delight, became a welcome guest at Disraeli's official entertainments, and at one dinner, after the Prime Minister had devoted himself to the beautiful American wife of Lord Randolph Churchill, the Prince asked Jennie, 'And tell me, my dear, what office did you get for Randolph?' She had hinted at none, and told the Prince as much, which represented to him politics too subtle to understand. At another reception, the outgoing Gladstone observed to the Princess of Wales (so he noted in his diary), 'D[israeli] complained of my absence: said they c[oul]d not get along without me.' Neither Prince nor Princess understood the rules of politics which required an opposition that could be demonized. The concept seemed at the moment too subtle, even, for Gladstone.

Disraeli's early months in office, which led into the London season, saw the apogee of the masked ball in England. In June, Lady Marian Alford, daughter of the Marquis of Northampton, held a ball at Alford House, Prince's Gate, for which HRH, who loved costumes, was delighted to dress up. To Lord Spencer of the Prince's Household, his former Private Secretary Courtenay Boyle wrote, 'Most of the people struck me as being rather new at the game; not pretending to any powers of chaff, I went about watching and listening.... I do not fancy the English temperament suited the thing.... Still it was decidedly amusing, and when everyone unmasked the comparison of notes was by no means uninteresting. Very few people recognized their Royal Highnesses, who must have thoroughly enjoyed themselves. [Lord] C[harles] Beresford called him a jolly old Cardinal.' In July the Prince held a *ballo in maschera* of his own, for which 1,400 invitations to Marlborough House were sent. Lord Rosebery wrote to Sam Ward that he came 'in rose-coloured satin, blazing with hired jewels, as Bluebeard'. Alexandra, bejewelled just short of coronation excess, appeared as a Venetian lady, and her husband was costumed as Charles I, dancing until dawn in a satin and velvet suit embroidered in gold, with a wig of Cavalier curls under a wide-brimmed black hat trimmed with a tall white feather. The cost of the entertainment and the post-midnight supper, served in two scarlet marquees out of doors, was enormous, but rather than deplore the extravagance, *The Times* praised the 'well-ordered magnificence' which proved the Prince's descent 'from Kings whose Courts have never been wanting in splendour'. Ceremony was sadly lacking under Victoria.

Although the Prince handled little money himself publicly except when gambling, one story accepted by such later intimates of his as Viscount Esher was that, in 1874, an Oxford Street dealer in silver and porcelain found a gentleman in his shop who wanted to sell a piece of jewellery and asked for a hundred pounds for it. Could the Prince have been sufficiently hard up to chance recognition? The proprietor asked where his caller got the piece. 'Never mind about that,' said the visitor, who did not identify himself. 'It's mine and I want to sell it. Will you give me a hundred pounds?' Looking at the owner more than the object, Joseph Joel Duveen, a Jewish immigrant from Holland and once a lowly lard salesman, objected, 'No. It's worth much more than that. I'll give you five hundred.' The discreet, casual contact led to royal patronage of the firm, which became Duveen Brothers in 1879. (Sir Joseph Joel Duveen was knighted after the coronation for later services rendered to the King.)

Acting for the Queen, who badgered her staff about press reports of the Prince's financial difficulties, General Ponsonby wrote from Balmoral to Sir Arthur Helps, the journalist who had assisted Victoria in preparing her *Highlands* journal and in editing the speeches of Prince Albert,

> Paragraphs have lately been appearing about the Prince of Wales's debts.... The *World* has published three leading articles stating that his Royal Highness owed £600,000, that he applied to Mr Gladstone to bring the matter before Parliament, and that he refused, that Mr Disraeli was to be asked to do so, and finally that the Queen had paid off these debts.
>
> There is not a word of truth in any of the above statements.

Ponsonby insisted that on any occasion when the Prince exceeded his income, he fell back on his capital, but that such occasions have been 'very trifling'. Repetition of such calumnies – especially an article in the influential *Times* – could lead, however, to their 'being believed'. Since Helps had connections at the *Daily Telegraph*, the Queen wanted a 'friendly hint' given to its editor. To Victoria, Sir William Knollys and the Prince himself both denied unpersuasively that the Rothschilds had settled any princely indebtedness, but Knollys confessed that he had tried to keep the Waleses from visiting Paris and Baden, where they spent a great deal of money, and – in Baden – the Prince gambled without success. They had departed London on 27 August, and Alexandra had gone on to Denmark to visit her parents. That further upset Knollys, who acknowledged to the Queen that any separation of the Prince and Princess on the Continent 'cannot be otherwise than most undesirable'. Disraeli was enlisted to persuade the Prince to exercise great discretion when in Paris. But the Prince's French companions were themselves – depending upon one's social and moral lenses – both desirable and undesirable, and (thinly disguised) virtually the cast of characters in Marcel Proust's *Remembrance of Things Past*.* ('Swann dared not add [to Dr Cottard]', Proust writes, 'that one of these friends was the Prince of Wales.')

* *À la Recherche du temps perdu.*

The Times had observed, in condoning the Prince of Wales's debts, that while the Queen remained in seclusion he had been representing the 'Royal House of England for ten years in visits to the chief courts of Europe, and has been burdened with the expenditures required to discharge these duties'. In a domestic aspect of that role, on his return from France he visited factory towns in the Midlands, again doing what was no longer expected of the Queen. In Manchester, he and Alix toured Gillott's pen factory, and at Elkington's firm the Princess electroplated a vase. Now Mayor, the dapper, monocled Joseph Chamberlain, a screw manufacturer until his election, toasted the royal couple at a luncheon with words belying his earlier Republican demogoguery and suggesting higher political ambitions. Praising their 'spontaneous visit', he prophesied that it would 'draw closer the ties between the Throne and the people, and increase the popularity already enjoyed by members of the Royal House – a popularity based quite as much on their hearty sympathy and frank appreciation of the wishes of the nation as on their high position and exalted rank'.

The Times praised Chamberlain's 'courteous homage, manly independence, and gentlemanly feeling'. Clearly he had a larger political future ahead. *Punch* published a cartoon in its issue of 14 November, 'A Brummagem Lion', representing the Princess of Wales, scissors in hand, clipping the claws of the Republican lion (with the Mayor's face), while the Prince, in the background, watches in evident satisfaction. In accompanying verses *Punch* punned that the Mayor 'has behaved himself less like a Republican than a Chamberlain'.

After Birmingham, the Prince and Princess went to Coventry for further factory inspections. There they were accompanied by the Liberal leader the Marquess of Hartington, known as Harty Tarty for his consorting with such demi-mondaines as Skittles – arrangements that did not foreclose his long and public liaison with the Duchess of Manchester, who was with the party. The Prince's circle loved practical jokes, and HRH asked an equerry to include a bowling alley in their Coventry itinerary, and to inform the Mayor that the Prince had especially wanted it included because of Hartington's enjoyment of the working-class game of skittles. In his address there the Mayor announced in all innocence, 'His Royal Highness asked especially for its inclusion, in tribute to your lordship's love of skittles.'

In his own way, often at his own hazard, the Prince of Wales was

A BRUMMAGEM LION

The anti-monarchist Mayor of Birmingham, sensing the Prince's
new popularity after his illness, gives way to personal political ambition.
Joe Chamberlain, Princess Alexandra and
the Prince of Wales in Punch, *14 November 1874*

keeping the monarchy visible – which was the mixed assessment of the
authors of *The Coming K——* in their 1874 Christmas satire, on sale
priced one shilling that November. The new pamphlet, *Jon Duan*, was
aimed primarily at the allegedly malingering Queen and her controversial heir. *The Leeds Weekly News* had reported on 6 June 1874 that at
Balmoral the evening before 'Her Majesty danced for the first time since
the death of the Prince Consort. She danced with [her small grandsons]
Prince Albert Victor and Prince George … and afterwards took part in a

reel with John Brown, her attendant, and Donald Stewart, game-keeper.'
Jon Duan was irate. Victoria was wasting herself in private on 'stalwart
grooms and keepers', while the Court was 'bound in virtuous chains'. All
England would sing a *Te Deum* if she would lock Albert's Mausoleum,
'leave in peace the dear departed shade', and resume being a queen. If she
were unwilling, 'Abdication' was the only remedy, and – in a pun on
'shade' – 'let the Son appear…!'

Recalling the 'heartless, soulless wretch' (afterward George IV) who
was Prince Bertie's titular predecessor, *Jon Duan* predicted:

> Our Heir-apparent will not be like this –
> He mayn't be brilliant, but he is not brutal;
> He may be simple, but it's not amiss
> If that is all he is … : it is well, we wis –
> … Since kings are now for us but gilded toys,
> To have one who won't make a fuss and noise.

He wouldn't be 'meddling', either, 'like his sire', the Prince Consort,
which *Jon Duan* thought fortunate, as 'a bailiff on the throne we don't
require'. Further to his credit, despite the aspersions on his spendthrift
ways,

> No one can say that our A.E. is stingy –
> Indeed, his failing lies the other way;
> Yet, though he on his capital infringe, he
> Spends his money in a British way.
> The coming Court will not be quite so dingy
> As that o'er which his royal mamma has sway.

Perhaps in exasperation at the Queen's self-imposed purdah, the press
let her heir's incognito visits to Paris go unremarked, however conspicuous there the increasingly portly Prince had become. But even dinners
and demi-mondaines had begun to bore him, and he began to explore a
change of scene. He had no interest in visiting the parched domain of the
Shah, whose visit had diverted him and created considerable newspaper
coverage in England. (Anthony Trollope satirized it in his masterpiece
The Way We Live Now, in the visit of the 'Emperor of China'.) But beyond
Persia lay India, and the press had praised the Prince for travels that
enlarged the world view that would be advantageous for him as king.
With the opening of the Suez Canal in 1869, voyages to the Indian

sub-continent had become more feasible, and he began now to toy with that prospect. In India he might be received as if he were already the king, and hunt legendary beasts, meet exotic people, and include as entourage his pick of his Marlborough Club cronies. He would find ways to exclude Alix, whose presence would complicate itinerary, protocol, and – possibly – pleasure.

While continuing his routine of public appearances and private amusement, the Prince instructed his librarian at Sandringham, who cared for HRH's thousands of unread books, to acquire if necessary, and set aside, volumes about India. Grounds had to be established for the

WORK FOR THE NEW GRAND MASTER.

Brother Punch (*log.*). "NOW, THAT YOUR ROYAL HIGHNESS IS HEAD MASON, I HOPE YOU'LL DO YOUR BEST TO IMPROVE OUR PUBLIC ARCHITECTURE ; AND, ABOVE ALL, THE DWELLINGS OF THE POOR."

Mr Punch satirizes the practical insignificance of the Prince's appointment as Grand Master of the Masons (Punch, *1 May 1875*)

long and expensive spree, and for Disraeli's new Government to pay for it. What the Prince did not know was that on Disraeli's taking office earlier in 1874 he had begun discreet enquiries about purchasing for England some of the French or Egyptian Suez shares, to establish some stake in the new lifeline to India. A royal journey through the Canal to the subcontinent would help establish the Ministry's case.

Early in the new year the Prince's proposal came quietly to the India Office, and Lord Salisbury worried to Disraeli about the cost. The journey would have to be made in what *The Times* would call 'well-ordered magnificence' – a royal progress. Salisbury was also sensitive to the prerogatives of the Viceroy, who was the Queen's representative in India and entitled to the honours due to her. Legalisms aside, there was also the potential for embarrassment with women and with native rulers, as the Prince intended to take with him some of his playboy friends. The only way to limit the risk was to increase the opportunity for supervision – including in the entourage a personal chaplain, government officials, civil servant aides, even newspapermen.

While the India voyage was still under discreet discussion, the Prince made some effort to establish an appearance of propriety, going so far as attending a huge prayer meeting in March 1875 held by the spellbinding American revivalists Dwight Moody and Ira Sankey. However curious about the evangelists as a phenomenon – they claimed a total audience of 335,000 in England – Victoria declined to go, ostensibly because Moody and Sankey offered sensationalism rather than religion. Had she attended, Disraeli would have goaded her into yet more queenly appearances. But the Prince slipped away again to Paris afterwards, where émigrée art student Marie Bashkirtseff, a precocious fifteen, saw him at the Comédie-Française. He took his seat toward the end of the first act of Offenbach's *Madame l'Archiduc*, she wrote in her diary, 'and I blushed with pleasure. The Prince of Wales has charming manners, but one cannot say that he is good-looking. He is below average height, quite fat, and has a rather beautiful oval face with grey eyes, an aquiline nose, a short, thick beard, and ... very little hair.... It was a very agreeable evening – an amusing play and a future king! Some minutes after he sat down, he picked up his opera glass and directed it at me. At first I thought he was looking next to us, but having fixed my eyes on his binoculars, I was sure he was looking at me.' The Prince may have been scouting for new amusements.

The next day Marie was at the Gare d'Est seeing relatives off to Russia when her aunt Nadianka Romanoff shouted over the snorting and hissing of the locomotives, 'Here's the Prince of Wales!'

'The adorable Prince', Marie wrote, 'was preceded by two cocottes. That's practically nothing for him – this playboy, this Lovelace, this Don Juan. To be what he is, is only to be better loved, and I am altogether certain that he is in every divorce court. Women play around with all kinds of rascals, and wouldn't it be absurd for them to resist such a prince?' The fashionable Alexander Bassano had just photographed the Prince top-hatted, heavy-lidded, bearded, with a cigar jutting arrogantly from his downturned lips. He seemed the epitome of the wealthy Parisian *roué*.

It was also the post-war moment about which Proust wrote in *Le côte de Guermantes*, wherein the Prince appears only passingly, although friends he had known since the lush days of the Second Empire are evoked – the old nobility and the *nouveau riche*. Among them, the prince de Foix, who is captivated by Oriane de Guermantes (an amalgam of Parisian beauties), may be based on the womanizing Prince Constantin Radziwill, with a suggestion, too, of the Prince of Wales. The princesse de Sagan becomes the princesse de Luxembourg, while her complaisant husband, prince Boson de Sagan, is in part (with the comte Robert de Montesquiou) the baron de Charlus. One of his hostesses at her home in the rue d'Astorg, and at the apex of Parisian society, was the comtesse Elizabeth de Greffulhe, often a guest at Sandringham and a model for the duchesse de Guermantes. She entertained on a sumptuous scale at her mansion in the rue d'Astorg. Hélène (Mme Henry) Standish, born a patrician des Cars (and also in part the princesse de Guermantes), was once lover of général Gallifet as well as of the Prince of Wales. Grandson of a wealthy Englishman, the complaisant Henry Standish furnished his house in the avenue d'Iéna as if it were in London, and he and his wife (who were childless) were frequent visitors at Marlborough House and Sandringham. Mme Standish – who strikingly resembled Alexandra – even wore '*le chic anglais*' clothes that suggested the Princess of Wales, which must have made the intimacies between lovers especially curious.

Dalliances with aristocratic ladies never seemed enough. When in Paris the Prince also sought out expensive *grandes cocottes* and *grandes horizontales*, even notorious actresses like the exotic tragedienne Sarah Bernhardt – to the dismay of his Comptroller and the delight of voyeurs

1. Albert Edward, Prince of Wales (*left*) and Prince Alfred in 1852

2. Opening the Great Exhibition: Victoria, Albert and children at the Crystal Palace, Bertie at the Queen's right hand (*Illustrated London News*, May 1851)

3. The two young princes with their companions, the Hon. V. Dawson, Frederick St Maur, Lord Arthur Clinton, Stanley Dawson, Maitland Dawson, John Athlone Farquarson, Henry Farquarson and Charlie Phipps, in Buckingham Palace gardens, June 1854

4. Albert Edward in 1858: pastel by
George Richmond

5. The Prince at Louise Hosmer's studio in Rome in 1859, learning about Art (*Harper's Weekly*, 7 May 1859)

6. The Prince's Ball at the Academy of Music, New York (*Illustrated London News*, 1860)

7. The Prince of Wales as a very young Colonel (*Harper's Weekly*, July 1860)

8. The funeral of the late Prince Consort in the Chapel Royal of St George's, Windsor: Bertie and Arthur (in kilts) walk behind the coffin (*Illustrated London News*, 1861)

9. The Prince of Wales (*centre*) and his party at Capernaum, on the north shore of the Sea of Galilee, April 1862

10. The Prince of Wales and his bride leaving for the railway station at Windsor *en route* to Osborne (*Illustrated London News*, 1863)

11. A bust of the Prince of Wales reproduced as a wedding remembrance in 1863

12. Among other wedding souvenirs was an equestrian pair in Staffordshire china of the Prince and his Princess

13. Queen Victoria in mourning dress with the Prince and Princess of Wales and a bust of the late Prince Consort, 1863

14. View of Sandringham House across the lake, 1864

15. The Prince of Wales (*right*) playing whist at Abergeldie, October 1871. Prince Alfred is opposite. Drawing by Zichy

16. *Vanity Fair* (8 November 1873) depicts a dapper, Frenchified Prince of Wales. There is a subtle sense of dissipation conveyed

17. The Prince of Wales in 1875, photographed in raffish elegance by Bassano

18. Max Beerbohm's later vision of one of the Prince of Wales's rare visits to Queen Victoria

19. Ceylon: the Prince atop a dead elephant (*Illustrated London News*, 1875)

20. India: the Prince's first tiger (*Illustrated London News*, 1875)

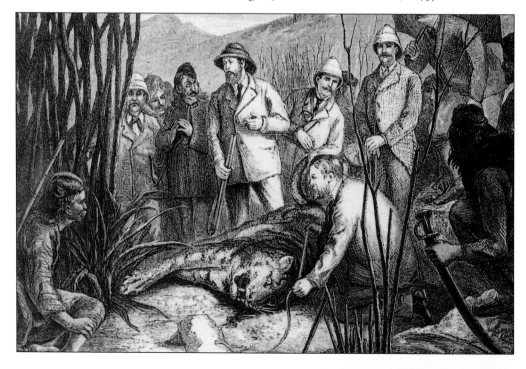

21. The Prince of Wales's entry into Baroda on an elephant, November 1875 (*Illustrated London News*)

22. The Prince in Calcutta in December 1875, being entertained by Indian music and dancing (*Illustrated London News*, 1876)

23. Prince Albert Victor and Prince George of Wales on board HMS *Britannia*, December 1877

24. The Prince and Princess of Wales and their family at Marlborough House, 1889. *Left to right*: Prince Albert Victor; Princess Maud; Prince George (seated); the Princess of Wales; Princess Louise, Princess Victoria (seated); the Prince of Wales

25. Alberta Olga Caracciolo, the Prince's ostensible godchild, drawn by Jacques-Emile Blanche in Brighton, November 1887. From the scrapbook of Alberta Olga, later Baroness Olga de Meyer

26. The *Pall Mall Budget* in June 1891 depicted the Prince of Wales sitting impassively but too conspicuously at the Tranby Croft slander trial. Lord Coleridge presides at his right. In the box is Gordon-Cumming; behind him is Sir Francis Knollys

27. A full-page advertisement for Bushmills Whisky in *The World*, depicting the
Prince of Wales escorting the Shah of Persia round the Paris International
Exhibition of 1889. Identification with this popular drink was an excellent if
unsought piece of public relations

28. The Prince of Wales opening the Underground Railway's Stockwell Station, City and South London Railway, 4 November 1890 (*Illustrated London News*)

29. The Prince opening the Tate Gallery in 1897 (*The Graphic*, 31 July 1897)

30. Four generations: Queen Victoria with the Prince of Wales, George Duke of York (later George V) and Prince Edward (later Edward VIII) in August 1899

like Marie Bashkirtseff. The press reported, however, only his visits to grand estates like Rambouillet, seat of his friends the duc and duchesse de la Trémouille, where, despite the wretched weather, the gentlemen in the party managed to shoot 1,100 pheasants on a Monday morning, nearly 300 of them credited to His Royal Highness. When papers noted his dining in Paris at the élite Jockey Club, their reports fell silent about the hours thereafter.

On 30 March 1875, while the Prince was again on his priapic rounds in Paris, Disraeli sent a letter to his Secretary for India, Lord Salisbury:

> The Indian Expedition!
>
> It seems that our young [Prince] Hal kept it a secret from his wife and induced his Mother to give her assent on the representation that it was entirely approved by her Ministers.
>
> The Wife insists upon going! When reminded of her children, she says, 'The husband has first claim.'

Disraeli's reference to Shakespeare's hero, also waiting in the wings, had a plethora of implicit meanings behind it, with at least one of them with a positive twist. In Prince Hal's words in *Henry IV*, Part 1:

> If all the year were playing holidays,
> To sport would be as tedious as to work.

Although Salisbury urged the Queen, without much confidence, 'The Indian Council think it will have a highly beneficial influence upon the minds of Your Majesty's Empire in particular,' she refused to provide a penny from Crown funds to finance the venture. She insisted that the venture should be '*very carefully considered* and weighed in the Cabinet', and looked with 'much anxiety and apprehension to so long and distant a voyage'. She might die, she suggested, while her heir was abroad. Further, the Prince took 'little care of himself', an observation that had more than health overtones. The venture was, she wrote to Vicky, 'quite against' her desire.

Long fascinated by India, the Prince had taken it on himself in 1870 to cable across the Atlantic to General Ulysses S. Grant, then the American President, 'I feel sure you will rejoice with me on the completion this evening [23 June] of submarine telegraphic communication between Great Britain & America with India.' Puzzled, and uninterested in the subcontinent, Grant asked his aide, Horace Porter, to send the message to the Secretary of State with the legend, 'The President is not certain whether this is genuine or a hoax. If considered genuine please send a reply in his name.' While they pondered the Prince of Wales's cable, another arrived for Grant, from the Earl of Mayo, then Viceroy of India. Responding to the 'Vice Roy' – rather than the Prince, who had no official role – the President drew attention to 'the union this day completed between the Eastern & Western World'.

Disraeli tried his own special brand of persuasion about India, explaining to the Queen that if the Prince were out of England *under supervision* for six months, the investment would be worth the price, and if HRH learned something about the Empire in the process, that would be a bonus. He needed some kind of work. While Radical opposition grew to the use of any public funds to finance what appeared only to be another pleasure-seeking jaunt, Disraeli undertook the management of the Queen, the Prince, and the royal progress itself. In that, he had the backing of political theorists like Walter Bagehot, who wrote, 'If the Prince is to travel at all, especially in countries penetrated by traditions as to the significance of external symbols of power, he must travel in a manner becoming his position.' Liberal MP A. J. Mundella, speaking in the Commons, agreed that if a monarchy were to exist at all, 'it should not be a cotton velvet or a tinfoil one'.

Since the Prince had no way to finance the trip – described extravagantly by the Prime Minister as a fact-finding royal progress – out of his own depleted funds, Disraeli and Salisbury manipulated the India Council into 'cordial willingness to make the requisite financial arrangements'. As the Prince could be expected to receive gifts of great value – which he would keep for himself – from Indian rulers, and had to supply something significant in return, the Indian Government was persuaded to offer £100,000 – raised from an initial £30,000. With that as a beginning, Disraeli secured a grant of £112,500 from Parliament, to be paid from the Treasury and from Admiralty funds, the latter because a ship had to be refitted as a floating hotel.

By telegraph, plans went back and forth in great detail between England and India, while the Prince complained to everyone he could in the press and in public life that he was being treated penuriously. At a dinner at Greenwich, where the Prince was among the guests (so Disraeli reported to his confidante, Lady Bradford), the Duke of Sutherland, one of HRH's closest cronies, remarked scornfully, 'What a shabby concern this vote [in the House of Commons] is! If I were you, Sir, I would not take it. I would borrow the money of some friends at 5 per cent.'

'Well, will you lend it [to] me?' the Prince asked the surprised Sutherland, one of the wealthiest but least liberal men in the kingdom. The question, Disraeli claimed, 'shut the Duke up'.

George Sutherland was nevertheless on the Prince's list of friends to accompany him to India, along with Viscount ('Sporting Joe') Aylesford, Prince Louis of Battenberg, Lord Charles Beresford, Lord Carrington, and Lieutenant Augustus FitzGeorge, the Duke of Cambridge's illegitimate son. All were ostensibly aides-de-camp. The Queen was furious, writing from Osborne to Vicky on 14 July 1875, 'I am trying all I can to get some better and more eminent persons added to this list which I sent you, ... But the difficulty is very great and I fear dear B. has a number of stupid, *soi-disant* friends who put all sorts of ideas into his head. The whole thing is very full of difficulties.' Francis Knollys had already informed Sir Henry Ponsonby – mother and son were discussing India only through their secretaries – that the Prince was exasperated by her interference, after having all his life tried to be obedient to her wishes. Since 'the idea of this visit emanated *entirely* from the Prince of Wales', it was reasonable, 'as far as practicable, ... to keep the arrangements connected with it in his hands'. To Victoria herself, Salisbury explained diplomatically that 'his Royal Highness's great kindliness of disposition' has led him 'to treat with too gracious a manner persons not deserving of such a treatment'.

Trapped between, Disraeli had to endure an emotional visit from the Prince at Downing Street, where he refused to eliminate any of his eighteen boon companions. The Prime Minister advised the Queen to give way. Others on the voyage would legitimize the tone, if only as service personnel and observers, and Victoria could choose a personal representative from her gentlemen-in-waiting. Also, the veteran *Times* correspondent W. H. Russell was listed as honorary secretary to the Prince as well as tour historian, and Sydney Hall was to be press artist. (Other newspapermen would follow in a chartered steamer.) Aboard would be a doctor, a chaplain, a zoologist, a botanist, a senior clerk from the India Office, and a host of servants, including three chefs and the Duke of Sutherland's piper. The Admiralty was luxuriously to refit a troopship, the *Serapis*, for the voyage, Disraeli pressing his conviction that the trip was a serious diplomatic opportunity. 'I am fully alive to the importance of my trip to India,' the Prince wrote to him earnestly, 'and hope that neither you [n]or anyone else in my land will have cause to regret that the honour of my country has been placed in my hands whilst in India. Am I saying too much in stating this?'

The loyal *Mail* defended the trip as a 'great public ceremonial' of exactly the sort HRH should perform, and *The Times* agreed. *Reynolds's Newspaper* condemned the trip as 'supremely ridiculous' – an expensive folly. 'Albert Edward, the hero of the Mordaunt divorce suit, the mighty hunter', it charged, was interested in 'pig-sticking and women' and had no other motives. Ponsonby agreed in Salisbury's hearing that the object seemed 'amusement' and nothing else. The Secretary for India added, 'And to kill tigers'.

X

Embodying the Raj

1875–1876

ATTIRED IN THEIR medieval habiliments of office, the corporate officers of the City of London marched early in October 1875 in procession to Marlborough House formally to bid the Prince of Wales godspeed before he sailed to India. Once they were received, their Recorder read the address, which approved of the Prince's seeking to become personally acquainted with the country, the customs, and the sympathies of the many millions of 'Her Majesty's subjects, over whom, if God so will, you are one day destined to rule'. Prepared for the delegation, the Prince replied, 'If the result of my visit should conduce to unite the various races of Hindostan in a feeling of loyalty to the Queen, attachment to our country, and of goodwill toward each other, *one* great object at least will be gained.'

On the Sunday before the departure, Dean Stanley told a capacity audience at Westminster Abbey in language intended for the Prince and his party, 'We pray that they may not forget the high and noble work they have undertaken. We pray for them, and give them our sympathy in all that is good, and in the detestation of all that is base.' In a plea from the pulpit that suggested his Royal Highness's censorious mother, he exhorted, 'Wherever they may go, may they see that the name of England and English Christendom shall not be *dishonoured*; that morals shall not be *relaxed*; that the *sensual flag* shall not be raised; and that *the standard of national morality* shall not be lowered, but raised aloft.'

Sceptical that the Prince would see anything of the 'abject nakedness' of the real India, the Bombay *Native Opinion* proposed pointedly that 'live specimens of poor natives of all castes should be shown to the Prince', that 'the future ruler of India' be presented native cooking utensils and implements, that he see how ordinary Indians earn their livelihoods, and that he spend a night in 'a specimen hut or house, in which the poor Indian finds rest and protection from the sun, rain and cold'.

While the Disraeli Government struggled to find funds for the trip, the Prince of Wales went about his usual business, expecting Sir Bartle Frere of the India Office, the senior official accompanying the party, to work everything out. Disraeli was particularly incensed when he discovered that, at Bertie's request, Frere had allocated £300 from the trip budget, an enormous sum in contemporary purchasing power, for each of the party to purchase cotton tropical underwear. All of them, Frere and Disraeli both knew, were independently wealthy. Biding his time, the Prince made a round of ceremonial appearances, presiding at the opening of the New Merchant Taylor's School, accepting his installation as Grand Master of English Freemasons, attending the first race meet of the Four-in-Hand Club (which competed in carriages), opening the Margate Deaf-and-Dumb Asylum, escorting the Sultan of Zanzibar to Aldershot, and participating in token fashion in the final summer exercises of troops at Sandhurst.

It made no difference to the Prince which viceroy of India he would upstage; that was another problem left to Disraeli to untangle. Lord Northbrook, Gladstone's viceregal appointment, was eager to depart, as the only way to separate his son from an inappropriate relationship with a lady in Simla, but the Prime Minister could find no Tory worthy suitable for the trophy assignment who was willing to accept it. The climate was extreme, the distances formidable, the isolation from cultivated English society unappealing, and the drain upon the appointee's personal funds appalling. Northbrook agreed to remain for a few more months.

At home, the refitting of the *Serapis* for the voyage was becoming more expensive daily. The royal apartments on the upper deck of the 6,200-ton former troopship had a reception room, a drawing room and a dining room divided only by curtains so that they could be thrown open to become a spacious saloon for state functions. They were decorated in white, blue and gold, with mirrors in oak-and-gold frames, and mahogany fittings. The furniture was solid oak. The rooms were fanned by a double set of punkahs manipulated from without by the human machinery of six Chinese seamen. Two sets of private bedrooms and baths, one on each side of the ship, afforded the Prince the more comfortable windward side at all times.

Space was also made for the Prince's private stud of horses, and a menagerie of farm animals was hoisted aboard for fresh milk and meat. (Some were intended as a gift for Alexandra's young brother, who had replaced the ousted Otho as king of Greece.) Since hundreds, if not thousands, of gifts and awards had to be presented ceremonially, gold and silver medals with the Queen's profile were struck and loaded in large quantities. The lavish and complex arrangements alone seemed sufficient to revive Republican sentiment. Yet, although *Reynolds's Newspaper* and other Radical publications objected to the 'useless expenditure of money which could easily be better employed, even if only in lightening our national burdens', few readers thought that their future sovereign should travel in unimposing style.

On the afternoon of 11 October, the Prince, with Alix, left Marlborough House in an open carriage for Charing Cross Station. Crowds gathered to watch the much-publicized beginning of the journey. On the platform the brass band of the Scots Fusilier Guards played 'Hail to the Prince and Princess of Wales', a forgettable anthem composed for the occasion by J. P. Clarke, the regimental bandmaster. Then an elegantly fitted and decorated train of locomotive, royal saloon, two saloon carriages, two first-class carriages and two guards' vans took the party on the two-hour trip to Dover, where the Princess of Wales, tearful (it was said) at parting, may have been far more unhappy at being excluded. Robed ceremonially in cloaks over which were medallions on chains, and carrying maces, the Mayor of Dover and his Council offered an address which closed with wishes for 'a safe voyage and a happy return'. The Prince responded succinctly through the noise of rockets fired from ships in the harbour, 'I am much obliged to you, Mr. Mayor.'

At Calais, Alexandra took leave of her husband. The next morning, accompanied by Prince Alfred, she returned on the same Channel steamer that had ferried them. The Prince of Wales's party entrained for Paris, remaining overnight incognito to avoid formalities, then proceeding to Brindisi in the boot of Italy. The royal train arrived at 8.30 in the morning on the 16th, and a sumptuous breakfast was served on board, with the Italian Minister of Marine and local officials as royal guests.

At 11.15 a launch returned the Italians to shore. A crowd at the dock

"BON VOYAGE!"

"GOOD BYE, MY DEAR BOY! AND MIND YOU GIVE MY LOVE TO INDIA."

The Prince of Wales en route to India. The Serapis *is in the
background (*Punch, *16 October 1875)*

cheered. The *Serapis* quivered as its screw began turning, and it moved
slowly seaward in the wake of the *Osborne*, which was followed by the
Hercules and the *Pallas*. Not everyone sat down to the first dinner under
steam. Seasickness afflicted the party, and W. H. Russell reported cautiously that in several cabins there was 'hidden but audible suffering'. In
the prescribed *Serapis* dress – blue jackets with black silk facings (the first
dinner jackets), black trousers and black necktie – the Prince went round
the decks before dinner to inspect 'the Farm', and his horses from
Sandringham, but he, too, failed to appear at the table. A lusty sirocco
was blowing in from the southern Mediterranean. Later the Prince
reappeared in the *fumoir* on the quarter-deck, a glassed enclosure

panelled in white and gold, and fitted with sofas, which he had ordered as his *al fresco* smoking lounge.

The first port of call, the Piraeus, near Athens, was reached under a cloudless, windless sky, but the *Serapis*, taken in at twice the recommended speed by its captain, Carr Glyn, lost both its anchors as he tried to slow it down. Calling for full astern, he lost control and carried away the bowsprit of the King's waiting yacht before mooring in confusion. Although the habour was crowded with beflagged boats greeting the Prince, no one was injured. The shaken celebrities took launches to a royal train to Athens at ten minutes before noon, while a military band played 'God Save the Queen'. The next day the travellers returned to a breakfast on deck for 100, including the Greek delegation, and King George of the Hellenes (once Prince William of Denmark) decorated the members of the Prince's party, including Canon Duckworth, with various degrees of the Order of the Saviour. Having recovered both anchors, the crew got the ship going again at five in the evening on 21 October, and steamed south toward Egypt.

In a calm sea under a bright moon, the pace of the ships was slackened in order to arrive at Port Said on schedule. The Prince passed some of the time studying a large relief map of India, engaging in pistol practice, and joining in such deck amusements as quoits. As the temperature rose in the afternoon, many escaped to siestas. At 7.30 a.m. on the 23rd the flags of shoreline consulates at Port Said were visible. An hour later the convoy entered the breakwater at the northern end of the Suez Canal. Bands on anchored Egyptian frigates began playing what was allegedly 'God Save the Queen', and cheers came from the crowded deck of the *Pekin*, which carried correspondents from London and other papers to Bombay. The royal stop-over in Egypt would enable the press to reach India ahead of the Prince.

Ismailia was reached at 5 p.m. There the Khedive's three sons greeted the Prince and escorted his entourage to a special train, equipped with an American saloon carriage, which ran at a breakneck – for Egypt – forty miles an hour. By nine they were at the Shoubra Road Station, where the Khedive stood in a uniform of blue and gold, decorated with jewelled ceremonial orders received on his visits to other potentates. Although the Prince had visited Cairo twice before, he was escorted yet again to the historic wonders of the city and put up at the elaborate Gezireh Palace, built to receive the Empress Eugénie. At eleven on 25 October, in his field marshal's uniform despite the heat, appropriately augmented by the chain and collar of the Star of India, His Royal Highness conferred on Prince Tewfik, eldest son of the Khedive and his heir apparent, the Order of the Star of India. The staff surgeon on the *Serapis*, Dr Fayrer, read the warrant authorizing the award, and the ribbon and Order were carried in on small pillows by General Probyn and the Prince's equerry Colonel Ellis. HRH read an address in English confirming that the presentation was by 'will of the Queen', and the Viceroy replied in French and affixed the ribbon and Order on the breast of Tewfik. It was in effect a rehearsal for dozens of similar presentations in India.

In the afternoon the Englishmen visited the Pyramids and dined nearby under a large marquee, watched a performance by dancing girls 'voluminously clothed from the waist downwards' (according to Russell) and otherwise covered with necklaces of gold coins, bangles and bracelets. The Pyramid of Gizeh was illuminated as darkness fell, and the royal party returned to Cairo for a French comedy, *Les trente millions de gladiateurs*, at the Opera, where a full house cheered the late-arriving celebrities.

The next day the Khedive decorated everyone in the Prince's party with one degree or another of the Order of the Medjidié. Following the ceremony, the Viceroy and the Khedive and their staffs escorted the Prince's entourage to a special train to Suez. There, since the blazing sun, 'round as a shield', had already set with desert abruptness, the *Serapis* was loaded and reboarded under the torchlights of rows of soldiers. Shrewdly, Russell wrote of the operation (which would be repeated often), 'When the Prince of Wales comes and goes, everything for his coming or going seems as if it happened in the order of nature; but could one only see the anxious faces, and the calculations, and the consultations, and the pre-arrangements, he would be able to judge how far those who are hidden behind the folds of the Purple have to do with the arrangements for its complete effect.'

Aboard the gleaming white-and gold *Serapis*, while the unseen punkah wallahs swept the sultry air over the Prince's dinner table and he ceremonially toasted the Queen, a telegram arrived for him with news from London announcing the winner of the Cambridgeshire, a race run only a few hours before. (His staff in London knew what was important.) Little news after that, until they reached India, would be as up to date.

A tireless traveller, Bertie was not prostrated by the heat of the Red Sea or by the tedium of ceremony. 'He sits mopping away', his secretary, Albert Grey, wrote in a letter home, 'as we steam along with the thermometer at 88 on the bridge at midnight.' To Alix the Prince wrote, in a letter to be mailed from their next destination, 'It was 109° in the sun yesterday, and I went down to the engine-room just before dinner where it was 118° and in the stokehole 129°!' While punkahs fanned him in his shaded quarters he neglected to note that seamen worked entire shifts in such furnaces.

Aden, at the southern tip of Arabia, was reached at dawn on 1 November. Somali boys surrounded the *Serapis*, swimming close, shouting to onlookers on deck, and diving for coins. The Prince debarked at nine to fanfares from the band of the resident British garrison, received and rewarded local Arab chiefs, lunched with the Resident, participated in the renaming of a curving street set back from the sea as Prince of Wales Crescent, and was driven out to inspect the enormous masonry tanks that stored and supplied the colonists with water in a land where rain seldom fell. At 5.30 in twilight he reboarded the *Serapis*, and at 10.30 the ships steamed out into the placid Indian Ocean toward Bombay.

Just after two the next afternoon the engines failed. Crews found a condensing pipe malfunctioning. It was pumped clear, but an hour later the screws again stopped, and the ship's machinery expert descended into the engine room, removed his coat, and proceeded to re-examine the pipes. Immediately after him came two adjunct London firemen – the Prince of Wales and the Duke of Sutherland. In an hour and a half the ship's screws turned again, the blame this time placed on intrusive jellyfish.

For several more days, in a glassy sea, the voyage's monotony had to be eased by circuits of the Duke of Sutherland's piper, small-arms practice on scavenging sea birds, an outdoor concert, and amateur theatricals, until a headwind blew the smoke and clinkers from the funnel into the faces of those on deck. Disraeli had arranged with Lord Carrington to have independent dispatches sent from the *Serapis*, and one written at sea suggests more than meets the eye. 'I am glad to be able to say', he wrote, 'that the P. of W. is wonderfully well; in fact better than he has been for the last twelve months – he takes great care of himself and goes to bed earlier than he does in London. He seems very much impressed with the importance of the journey.' The Queen, however, was disturbed by a report to her of practical joking being played by the Prince's intimates, as if the *Serapis* were a country house on their weekend circuit.

As 5 November was Guy Fawkes Day, the crew prepared a villainous-looking effigy to represent him, and, to the sounds of foghorns and struck pots and pans, sentence was pronounced, and he was dropped into the deep, to be exploded by attached rockets and flares. The dampened charges refused to ignite and the instigator of the Gunpowder Plot of 1605 was lost in the darkness.

On the morning of 8 November the *Osborne* and the *Serapis* rounded Malabar Point, the first landfall approaching Bombay, sailing between rows of saluting warships. On the dock were British colonial officials and Indian nobles in robes of state glittering with jewels. At three the Viceroy and his party took a launch to greet the Prince on board and escort him ashore. In the late-afternoon heat he set foot on Indian soil, accoutred sweatily in the inevitable field marshal's uniform with the collar of the Garter and the sash and jewel of the Star of India, and plumed helmet wrapped with a red puggaree, or turban. To the Indians he was an impressive figure. Although barely five-feet seven, he weighed nearly two hundred pounds, and the great dinners on his tour would add to his girth. The next day would be his thirty-fourth birthday.

For two hours in the dusk the combined entourages of the Prince and the Viceroy toured Bombay in open carriages while bands played, people on the dusty torchlit streets cheered, and women waved handkerchiefs and scarves from their balconies. A motley queue of native carts and carriages followed, increasing in numbers as they continued on. Canopies erected along the route to shelter the more important residents harboured at one spot a group of robed Muslim elders. Above them, incongruously, could be seen a sign in large square letters, lit from behind and apparently erected by English colonists, 'TELL MAMA WE'RE HAPPY.' The procession ended at Government House, where a crowded and colourful reception was followed by a splendid dinner, the first of dozens of similar events where, with low salaams, the Prince was presented to a bewildering number of maharajahs and lesser nobility, each grandly arrayed and bejewelled. Several hereditary 'ruling' princes, enshrouded in diamonds, were mere children of ten or eleven, evidence of the mortality rate in torrid, unsanitary India.

In the tree-lined park of Government House, an elaborate tent city was set up for those attending the Prince of Wales. Beyond, on the main street, were tents for extra servants, an artillery battery and a detachment of the 2nd Queen's Royals. Because of the damp soil, all tents were affixed to unstable wooden platforms, which pitched and swayed as if the occupants were at sea. Security for the Prince was obsessive, not only because of the assassination three years earlier of the Earl of Mayo, then Viceroy, but because India remained a barely governable chaos of languages, races and cultures. 'Our orders', Carrington wrote to Disraeli, 'are always to be with him – always round him on all occasions. He is never on any pretence to take any petition or address from a native's hand, and not to be out on any occasion after dusk except in a carriage.' Despite safety concerns, the temptation to sample the Indian night was difficult to resist. W. H. Russell was awed by the extravagant light. To greet the Prince, the long, narrow streets were 'rivers of fire'. One was 'blinded by the glare of lamps, blazing magnesium wire, and pots of burning matter'.

The next day at noon all India celebrated his birthday with the firing of cannon, and the Prince was obliged to receive twenty-four distinguished native guests in carefully researched precedence, after two hours of previous audiences in heat that no quantity of punkahs could allay. Further, he had to appear yet again in full field marshal's uniform for the presentations, buttoned up to the throat. The Rajah of Kolhapoor was entitled to a nineteen-gun salute; the portly Rao of Kutch received only seventeen; the Gaekwar of Baroda, only twelve years old and new to his throne, his robes and arms glittering with diamonds and emeralds, was entitled to twenty-one. The Prince assured the child that he would watch his career with interest, and urged that he study English – and horsemanship. And to Earl Granville, Disraeli's Foreign Minister, HRH wrote, 'The little Gaekwar of Baroda who is as old as our oldest boy, seems a really very intelligent youth, though only six months ago he was running about the streets adorned with the most limited wardrobe.' As the Prince had been briefed, when the last Gaekwar had been deposed for corruption, his predecessor's childless widow, on being asked to name a successor, idiosyncratically chose a beautiful boy she had seen playing, half-naked, in the alleyways.

At the beginning of the Prince's day, Sir Bartle Frere had brought him a gift from the Princess of Wales that had been concealed aboard the *Serapis* – her framed portrait. The press might make something romantic out of the gesture: Alix may have had some other meaning in mind.

She would now accompany him throughout India while, through the telegraph and undersea cables, the world went with the Prince. The hostile *New York Irish World* wrote, 'Millions of eyes are vigilantly fixed upon his slightest movements, and it behooves him if he be a man to respect himself, even if he despise and scorn mankind. To a person in his position, it requires more audacity – more unblushing impudence – to indulge in turpitude than to the ordinary members of society, and faults which are venal in the humble are unpardonable in a prince.... Now the character of the Prince of Wales is as notorious as the sun at noonday. It is not the whispered scandal of private malevolence; it is blazoned to the four winds, and known to the whole world.'

Although the editorial deservedly excoriated the shortcomings of the Prince, it took no note of the contributing factors, among which were his lack of a state role, and – since he lacked the intellectual rigour of Prince Albert – there being little for him to pursue but pleasure. His advising the young Gaekwar of Baroda how to grow into a ruler was a poignant irony, since Bertie had failed his own father's rigid course of instruction, and he still displayed symptoms associated with his childhood inability to focus, deficient control of impulses, and hyperactivity. These tendencies would resurface at times in India, yet the subcontinent proved from the first days of his royal progress to be a learning experience beyond what might have been expected, and demonstrated princely strengths and sensitivities that would emerge again and again in parallel with his shortcomings.

While His Royal Highness was receiving princelings in Bombay, one of his own was insisting upon his precedence at home. Prince Albert Victor – 'Eddy' – was slow as a scholar but apparently quick to perceive *lèse majesté*. Crossing from Osborne to Portsmouth in rough weather on the royal yacht, he noticed that the Royal Ensign was not displayed, and complained about the slight to his and his brother's rank. The Officer of the Watch explained that in the squalls the silk flag could be ripped apart. 'Never mind that,' insisted the eleven-year-old Eddy. 'When any of the royal family are on board it ought to be flying. I beg it may be hoisted immediately.' Loyal papers praised his spirit.

To his younger son, George, the Prince of Wales wrote of some 'very curious' animal combats that had been staged for the party's amusement. Elephants, rhinoceroses, water buffaloes and rams had been sent against each other, 'but none was hurt, excepting one buffalo who had his horn broken, which I fear must have hurt him a great deal'. Newspaper reports deplored the spectacle and claimed that the Prince left the arena 'highly delighted'.

The Prince, who knew few Jews in England other than Natty Rothschild and his siblings, encountered in Bombay 'the Rothschilds of the East' in the exotic Sassoon family. In Toledo until the expulsion from Spain in 1492, and Sephardic merchants in Baghdad for generations thereafter, they had shifted operations to the Raj in 1832. The swarthy Sir Albert Abdullah Sassoon had endeared himself to the Prince of Wales before he had even met him, having substantially endowed the Elphinstone High School in Bombay in 1872 in recognition of the Prince's recovery from typhoid. Local economic pre-eminence had already earned Sassoon the Star of India, and in 1873 a knighthood. On a visit to London in 1874 he was given the Freedom of the City of London. In Bombay he laid on a lavish entertainment for the Prince, and recommended to him his half-brothers Arthur and Reuben Sassoon, who had established themselves in London and Brighton. Both would become close companions despite being on the social margins.

Even more than the Queen, her heir was without racial or religious bias, yet he quickly encountered both among the smug British political and military authorities. As early as 13 November, in his first days in India, he wrote to his mother to complain about 'the rude and rough manner with which the English political officers ... treat the princes and chiefs upon whom they were appointed to attend'. He protested to Lord Salisbury about the 'disgraceful' usage of 'nigger' by the colonials. 'Because a man has a black face and a different religion from our own,' he wrote to Lord Granville on 30 November, 'there is no reason why he should be treated as a brute.' He, was unaware of the first explosion of resentment by Indians, which occurred during the laying of the foundation stone in the port of Bombay for Elphinstone Docks, done with Masonic honours because the hero of the Mutiny after whom they were named had been a Mason. The Parsee, Muslim and Hindu guests were out of place, and the colonials, in the robes of their order, concealed the Masonic rites from them. Unaware of this, the Prince spoke idealistically of the way in which the Masonic lodges in India – which in practice did no such thing – 'fulfil the objects of their institution by uniting together men of various races and creeds in the bonds of fraternal brotherhood'. As he went on, the indignant Indians walked out.

Another affront to amity occurred at the Elephanta Caves, on an island just east of the harbour. Although the site was considered sacred because of the immense stone carvings of Hindu deities, the Prince's civil hosts insensitively arranged a banquet for 160 guests in the largest cave, serving improper food and drink and illuminating the interior with hundreds of lights that also sullied the dignity of the setting. Again he was the victim of bad advice, as he would also be in Calcutta when he asked, inappropriately, to see the interior of a Bengali home, and was entertained – reluctantly – in women's living quarters. His curiosity was satisfied, but the local press was livid.

Critics abroad took more offence at his wholesale hunting carnage – the original reason for the journey. Shooting expeditions were sandwiched into the diplomatic protocol. He made ceremonial visits to some of the maharajahs who had greeted him in Bombay, including the little Gaekwar, with whom he climbed up into a howdah for a ride upon a gold-caparisoned elephant. When the beast dropped down in a succession of convulsive heaves and jerks, the Prince gripped the rail before him. The elephant re-established itself on its forelegs, and led a procession of colourfully painted, mountainous pachyderms, each with great tusks decorated with silver rings. Bands played and troops followed – the Gaekwar's Baroda Horse and the perspiring 3rd Hussars, who had travelled for eighteen hours from Bombay.

The next morning the royal entourage was off at dawn by rail to a hill station, to hunt cheetahs lured by the blood of deer killed by an advance party. Several days of shooting followed from a tent camp. The big event, on 23 November, was a pig-sticking, as beaters drove boar into a fusillade of spears and guns. When further shooting south of Bombay, at Mysore (which had already spent tens of thousands of pounds preparing for the Prince's reception), was ruled unhealthy because of fever in the area, the Prince insisted on hunting across the Gulf of Mannar in Ceylon (now Sri Lanka). An itinerary was hurriedly arranged. En route, the *Serapis* touched at the Portuguese enclave of Goa, once a great city but falling into neglect and ruin. Greeted there by the colonial Governor, and – in W. H. Russell's description – 'smooth, well-bred, amiable ecclesiastics', the group visited a vast and crumbling cathedral, now nearly empty of worshippers, listened to a native musical performance mainly of drums and cymbals, and saw the shrine of St Francis Xavier, a dark chapel haunted by a single beggar who was offered nothing for his persistence.

The Portuguese Governor was given lunch aboard the *Serapis*, and, on his debarking, the ship weighed anchor for Ceylon.

The lights of Colombo were visible just before daybreak on 1 December. Dozens of small craft swarmed around the *Serapis*, all offering exotic local merchandise for sale. A crush of local officials and expatriate citizenry from all over the island had gathered on the docks by dawn, but it was nearly four in the afternoon before the Prince, his field marshal's uniform now adapted to Indian latitudes, disembarked. (In Colombo's heat, seven degrees above the Equator, he wore a white suit and plumed pith helmet.) The streetside population was wide-eyed with awe. Nothing more momentous had happened on the island within living memory. As the Prince was driven along the sea-wall and through the city, the Ceylonese, 'not much weighted with clothing' (in Russell's description), 'ran, shoved, leaped up to get a view even of the waving plume and white helmet'. At Kandy, the inland capital, the Prince mingled with men of 'the upper ten thousand', attired in 'enormous stiffened white muslin petticoats.... I doubt if anything so unmasculine, uncomely, and unbecoming was ever devised.'

The Governor, William H. Gregory, whom the Prince was to knight the next day, entertained the leading notables at an outdoor state dinner. 'Lamps and lanterns were waving in the perfumed breezes. Rows of cocoanut-oil lamps [were] climbing up the hill-sides to join with the stars; streamers floating from elevated masts; [the] clang of music, beating of native drums, blowing of horns, sound of gongs and mighty cheering ... rolled away like thunder.' The entertainment was a troupe of 'devil dancers' in masks, followed by a promenade of elephants in single file, their adornments shining in the light of torches. 'The better bred of these animals ... salaamed, and uttered a little flourish of trumpets through their probosces, as they came opposite to the place where the Prince was standing; some knelt down and made obeisance before him; but the propriety of the procession was somewhat disturbed by the cupidity of one [elephant] which, finding that the Prince had a small store of sugar-cane and bananas, ... could not be induced to go on without difficulty.'

The party pushed through the exuberant Ceylonese growth, wading past palms of stupendous size, elephant creepers which could strangle huge trees, through expanses of gigantic reeds and avenues of rubber trees, beyond a bewildering variety of orchids and exotic flowering plants.

To satisfy local feeling they also visited a perfumed temple which held the South Asian equivalent of a fragment of the True Cross – a Sacred Tooth of the Buddha. It proved to be 'nearly two inches long and one inch round'. Sceptically, Russell wrote, 'If the article was ever in [the] Buddha's mouth, and if he had a complete set to match, he must have possessed a wonderful jaw.' The bell-shaped shrine of copper was about seven feet high, with six interior cases of rubies and diamonds. First reciting a long prayer, then lifting the golden lotus leaf on which the alleged tooth rested, and holding it for the Prince to admire, a venerable monk in spectacles, the Hereditary Keeper, quivered with emotion. HRH duly looked at it.

On 5 December, once torrential tropical rains ceased, the party took a new rail line to a hill-station at the 6,000-foot level, beyond jungle scraped for coffee plantations into deep forest. Above them about 1,500 men were hastily constructing a kraal for the Prince's elephant hunt, for which his shooting garb included sola topee, stout knickerbockers, and 'leech gaiters' under high boots to thwart the island's most populous and persistent creatures. (He would write to George that the jungle leeches 'are very bad, and climb up your legs and bight you'.) After five hours in his stand, he watched the beaters drive an old tusker toward him. He fired and hit it in the head, but it lumbered into the forest. Local hunters led him through the dripping heat, and his party followed, losing hats and ripping coats. Suddenly the wounded elephant appeared. The Prince tried another shot, and the elephant dropped as if dead. While he hacked its tail off, the symbol of victory according to the Ceylonese, his crony Charles Beresford, a sailor by profession, climbed up its rump to dance a hornpipe. Refusing to die, the stubborn beast struggled to its feet, pitching Lord Charles to the ground. As it plodded off with its stump, the party watched in surprise.

Other elephants emerged, were fired upon, and disappeared into the bush, but for one great pachyderm which heaved on its side in a stream. There it dammed the flow, and the Prince, assisted by other hunters, pushed through the muddy water and climbed on to the inert hill of flesh. Natives and Europeans pressed forward from trees and stockades, again cheering for the Prince to take the customary souvenir. Streaming with sweat, his clothes torn to shreds, he sawed off the tail. Afterwards the pleased bearers also cut wedges from the elephant's ears as trophies.

Since darkness was approaching, they hurried to their horses at the edge of the jungle, and then to a road where carriages awaited. Crossing the edge of a ditch, one carriage overturned, tumbling out Lord Aylesford, General Probyn, Lord Charles Beresford, Augustus Fitz-George, and the Prince. No one was hurt, and the Prince crawled about to retrieve the spilled tail – perhaps not so curious a bag from Ceylon as his flying fox, which Russell jokingly called *Pteropus Edwardsii*, further confirming the name by which everyone long understood HRH would be known. A sharp-toothed, red-haired bat with a five-foot wingspan, repellent black mammalian face, and nocturnal habits, it was a rare creature to be seen in daylight. Like strange fruit, the bats hung from a high branch by a hind leg, their heads hidden in the hairy membrane of a wing. It took a borrowed fowling-piece to bring them down, as on the first shot they flapped to higher altitudes, but the Prince wanted a personal specimen (although he could have found them in the London Zoological Gardens).

Before departing Ceylon he attended the inevitable ball for Europeans at the Colombo Club, received deputations from native leaders and learned Buddhists, received gifts and distributed ceremonial medallions. The band of the 57th Regiment played him to the water's edge, and he held a farewell dinner on the *Serapis* for local civil servants in the evening heat, as lanterns and fireworks lit up the harbour. On the morning of 9 December the *Serapis* weighed anchor for Tamil country in the Indian south-east. At landfall the Prince's exhausted party took a special train up the coast toward Madras.

The Duke of Buckingham as Governor of Madras, with municipal and military dignitaries, greeted the Prince at 8.10 a.m. on 13 December, and a state procession made its way to Government House. Tens of thousands of spectators who had come from afar and camped overnight watched respectfully with crowds of Madrasi. Only the gold umbrella held above the Prince's head at the Duke's suggestion let the throngs perceive instantly who was the Prince and future king. A rajah complained to a minister of another native state after a further round of greetings and addresses, 'Think what a way I have come to see the Prince! Think what distances we have journeyed, and yet we are permitted to gaze on his face [only] for a moment!'

'Very true,' said the official, 'but just think what a way the Prince has come to see you!' And that Indian perspective on the heir's itinerary, which included all-night journeys on rumbling railways and days of wallowing at sea, numberless addresses and entertainments that required immense reserves of patience, and receptions and presentations that introduced to him a blur of rajahs, bureaucrats, military officers, holy men, native ladies, schoolchildren, merchants, farmers and hunters, made the Prince's progress far more of a triumph than anyone might have prophesied. Not so, however, to *Reynolds's Newspaper*. 'The fact is', alleged the working-class weekly, 'that the hopeful heir to the British throne does not see India at all. He happens merely to be hurrying from one province to another, feasting, giving state receptions, dancing, patronising idolatrous temples, witnessing the burning of human bodies, and favouring sports of the most revolting and barbarous kind.' It quoted the correspondent of the *Daily News*, writing from Bombay, as charging that the Prince 'is not seeing India as India really is, but India swept, garnished, decorated, after the manner of a transformation scene in a pantomime'. Meanwhile, each hunting episode was a 'sickening spectacle' of 'gross amusement'. (It was a rare occasion when the Queen's viewpoint coincided with that of *Reynolds's*.)

In Madras the first defection from the Prince's party occurred. Impatiently, the Duke of Sutherland, who wanted to see more of the country and less of ceremony, decided to continue overland. Wearied of levées and banquets himself, the Prince announced that he would spent 14 December in seclusion at Guindy Park, the country seat of the Governor, eight miles from Madras, as it was the anniversary of his father's death. Victoria would have been surprised. It was the first time that the Prince had ever called such posthumous attention to Albert. The next morning, nevertheless, HRH was up at five – in the Indian climate everything began early – for the races nearby, which ended at eleven, when the heat was already intense. Only the horses recalled England. Some jockeys sported turbans, or white petticoats, or colourful robes, and many native spectators perched in trees.

To accept an honorary Doctorate from the University of Madras, the Prince appeared at three, in academic cap and robe, at stifling Government House, after which he paid one of his return visits – to the widowed Princess of Tanjore. She sat with ladies of the Duke of Buckingham's family, behind a screen. When introduced, the Prince could thrust in his hand to be shaken, and it was tactfully supposed that he could not see her face. Although an English officer translated for her, she said, in English, 'I am glad to see my Royal Brother.' The Prince properly referred to her as his 'Royal Sister', and there was little more to say. Had he known how little she knew of the world outside he might have brought up Disraeli's purchase, since the voyage began – and through a Rothschilds' loan of £4 million – of the Khedive's Suez Canal shares, which had captured the public imagination in England as ensuring the passage to India; or that India was about to receive a new viceroy, Robert Bulwer Lytton, the diplomat son (he was Minister at Lisbon) of the late novelist. But such intrusions of mundane reality did not impinge upon a widow lady of the ornamental nobility who revealed only her bangled brown arm.

The Suez shares purchase had become public on 25 November, and the news had reached India by telegraph the next day. The Prince of Wales heard about it personally only when a letter from Disraeli dated 11 December arrived by sea mail. To impress the Prince that it was an out-witting of France, which might have acquired a monopoly over the Canal, the Prime Minister explained that the London Rothschilds had to put up the entire price rather than share the risk with the Paris branch, for Alphonse de Rothschild 'is *si francisé* that he wd. have betrayed the whole scheme instantly'. Bertie may have felt that he, too, had been out-witted. Again he had learned of crucial news about the realm over which he would be sovereign by reading it in the newspaper.

The Indian paper *Shubba Suchak* had just asked editorially what benefit the country was likely to receive from the tour of a prince without powers to redress grievances, alleviate discontent, or remove injustice. The Prince of Wales understood his limitations. All he could do was observe as much as he was permitted to see, and await the day when he would have as much of a role as Parliament, practice and personality made possible. Meanwhile he watched native entertainments laid on for him; sampled curries at tiffin in the Madras Club, where the only Indians were the cooks and waiters; listened to Indian children sing 'God Save the Queen' in the People's Park; reviewed troops and received rajahs; and saw the eerie 'illumination of the surf' by small floating craft lit into blue-and-white phosphorescence, which billowed on the waves and drifted shoreward. Crowds watched until midnight.

A 'Native Entertainment' had been scheduled for ten in an immense railway station now converted into a vast theatre. He was two hours late, but the audience rose to salute him, and he accepted yet another formal address while the entertainers waited to continue. Held for his pleasure were the 'nautch girls', Indian dancers colourfully adorned from throat

to ankles, with their bare arms and fingers encircled by dozens of bracelets and rings. He had already been bored by their like. Soon he rose to
retreat to the supper room, then called for his carriage to Government
House. It was already two hours into the new day. At six he was up again
for a jackal hunt.

When the Prince left Madras on 18 December, the crowds that had
greeted him earlier were nowhere to be seen. A polite native gentleman
explained to W. H. Russell with typically Indian courtesy, 'There are so
many thousands sorry for the prince's leaving that they cannot bear to see
it, and so stay away.'

The 166 miles northward to Calcutta were accomplished by sea, and
delayed by a cylinder failure that woke everyone at two in the morning
on 20 December. On 23 December the *Serapis* arrived to a greeting of
cannons, crowds, dignitaries on the dock, and loyal addresses. Calcutta
was the winter seat of imperial government, and the pageantry lived up
to it. The outgoing viceroy, Lord Northbrook, presided over receptions,
banquets and the inevitable presentations, and the Prince as usual
avoided sitting on the throne prepared for him. On the day before
Christmas he greeted the Maharajah of Kashmir, who had travelled many
miles south-east to see him, and from another corner of the subcontinent
the Maharajah of Johore, sovereign of a Malayan province north of
Singapore. Each was entitled to nineteen guns, but in the confusion,
some salutes were missed altogether or wrongly numbered, and, in the
announcements of dignitaries, the Begum of Bhopal and the Maharajah
of Rewal may have had their sexes reversed. Salaams were exchanged and
most patricians departed pleased. The Prince was a warm host and made
his guests, however powerless within the Raj, feel important.

In tropical climes, or below the Equator where the northern winter is
summer, Christmas Day is a peculiar holiday. On the *Serapis*, the deck
was transformed into a winter scene with cotton wool for snow, and
improvised holly wreaths. Even a Father Christmas appeared at dinner,
where the Prince proposed the health of Captain Glyn, and an enormous
number of additional toasts left almost no one out. It would be many
months toward the next Christmas before they would see England again.

A ball on New Year's Eve for the local European contingent of 2,000
was not over until four in the morning, but HRH was up a few hours
later for a ceremonial Durbar at 7.45 described as a Chapter of the Star
of India. Rajahs and Europeans alike were housed in columns of tents

that went on for a mile from Government House, and outside the Prince's large tent were rows of chairs for the presentations. Stars and collars and ribbons were placed round the necks of kneeling rajahs; a grand march was struck up, salutes fired, arms presented by a guard of honour, and a procession of ornamented elephants furnished local colour. As the Prince was returning to Government House in his carriage, an Indian with something in his hand rushed alarmingly toward him. It proved to be a petition to redress a grievance. A guard plucked it from him, and the Prince went on to unveil an equestrian statue of the assassinated Lord Mayo.

New Year's Day 1876 was one of the Prince's longest and busiest in India. He watched a polo match on the maidan in the late afternoon, attended a banquet at Government House, observed a fireworks display by the fleet, and, at 10.15 p.m. saw veteran actor Charles Mathews in a performance of his farce *My Awful Dad,* which the Prince had already sat through in London at the Gaiety. The polo match, Russell wrote, was 'an exciting contest between the Calcutta and the Munipuri players; the former big [English]men, on well-fed, well-groomed ponies; the latter light [turbaned] men on ragged, poor-looking tats. The contest was rendered equal by the skill of the Munipuri men.' For the theatrical evening, boxes went for £100, and takers among maharajahs – for whom the cultural gulf was too great – were few.

On 4 January, the party began a tour by train of northern India and Bengal. At Patna, on the Ganges in Bihar Province, the avenue to the Durbar tent was lined by 380 elephants, which then passed in procession with the 109th Regiment. Something else may have impressed the Prince more. 'It was surprising to see', Russell wrote, 'what an assembly of [English] ladies, in the most charming bonnets and most correct costumes, were waiting to welcome him.' Yet India was no test of the Prince's celibacy. In seven months abroad there would be little temptation and no opportunity. As Carrington had written frankly to his mother, Lady Carrington, at the start, 'We are more like a lot of monks than anything else.' And of the Prince's eighteen companions in the party, there were always one or two, or an equerry, who stood guard outside the Prince's bedroom or tent every night to ward off danger which might have come from within or without.

While in Benares the Prince affixed the cornerstone of a hospital, and in Lucknow laid the foundation stone of a memorial to the native heroes of nineteen years earlier who had defended the Residency against 60,000 mutinous Sepoys. When the ceremony was over the Prince suggested impulsively that some of the veterans in the audience be presented to him, and a group was escorted to the platform by Major Cubitt, under whom they had served. One preparing to air a complaint about his pension, muttered, 'Fourteen rupees a month, *Shahzadah!* – It is not much, is it?' Another, nearly blind from a wound and supported by his sons, exclaimed, 'Let me see him!' The prince asked guards to let him approach, and the old man raised his hand to his turban in salute, peered closely and sighed, 'I thank Heaven I have lived to see this day and the Prince's face!' When he felt that the Prince of Wales had taken his hand, his emotions overflowed and, sobbing, he had to be led away, so that each of the men, however ragged, could have a turn to speak to the Prince. It was a rare encounter with the real India.

In the city of Vizianagaram he visited the Golden Temple and Sacred Pool (now polluted, and covered with green scum). Nearby in a shop selling brass idols and flowers offered to local deities, 'among the prints on the walls was recognised, not without merriment, the portrait of a celebrated French actress, who might be doing duty for the terrible helpmate of Shiva'. Russell did not identify her, but the description fits the Prince's kohl-eyed friend Sarah Bernhardt.

Before they entrained for Delhi, another pig-sticking opportunity was arranged for the royal party. The trapped boar were fierce, inflicting injuries on the horses and spilling some of the men; the General-in-Chief in India, Lord Napier, fell with his horse and fractured a collar-bone, as did Lord Carrington. The Prince of Wales rode hard, but safely, and got his pig. With shoulder and arm in a sling, Carrington was back on 10 January, the special train stopping for him near Onao, as they approached Delhi. There, another grand Royal Camp was set up, with tents and streets and outdoor lamps, and even a greensward that was newly laid and almost green. Napier was back to lead a grand review of troops, and the Prince perspired heavily in his field marshal's uniform, as the cool highland nights were followed by dusty heat at noon.

Delhi was the headquarters of the Army of India, which fielded as many troops as the rest of the Empire combined, together with thousands of elephants and camels as well as horses. A monster parade preceded the formalities of tours and banquets, illuminations and pageantry, and at a Durbar, visiting potentates blazed with jewels. Last to be introduced, Sir

William Gregory recalled, was the Chief Minister of the Nizam of
Hyderabad, Sir Salah Jung, who arrived 'all in white and absolutely
devoid of ornament save a magnificent diamond in his turban'. (He had
been shrewdly advised by Laurence Oliphant.) Impressed with Jung's
dignity and air of authority, the Prince impulsively invited him to be his
guest in England.

On 17 January the party boarded another train, and the city of canvas
in Delhi was struck. On the 18th they arrived at Lahore, to the north-east
of the Punjab. To the travellers, the dusty city looked much like Cairo,
although the city fathers greeted the Prince in gold-threaded turbans,
brocaded robes, and with chains of emeralds, rubies and pearls round
their necks. At the salutes and presentations the Rajah of Nabha, a Sikh,
received eleven guns, as did the rajahs of Faridkot, Chamba, and Sukkut.
Not entitled to any guns and reduced to a few minutes of ceremony were
the equally picturesque Sirdar of Kalsia, Nawab of Loharu, Nawab of
Dujana and Rajah of Golar.

The nights were now chill as the party travelled by special train and
then by elephant upland toward Kashmir, stopping to dedicate a bridge
across the Chenab in Alexandra's name, and visiting with great pomp the
fabled Taj Mahal at Agra on Sunday 30 January. (It had been built as a
memorial for the wife of a Mughal emperor who had died in childbirth
in 1631.) A colonel's wife, among the thousands there to look at the Prince
looking at the temple, exclaimed in awe, 'I would die tomorrow to have
such a tomb!' A lone voice soared upward in prayer toward the vaulted
roof as the party entered. On the Jumna River to the north, tiny earthenware prayer boats no larger than a coffee cup, each lit with an oil wick,
drifted into the darkness.

A convoy of carriages the next day took the party to the elaborate
palace of Scindia, the Maharajah of Gwalior, where the Prince's bedstead
and bath were of solid silver, and the reception hall panelled in gold leaf.
For entertainment a sham battle was staged by the Gwalior militia attired
in chain mail and jewels. Afterward the young Maharajah vowed his
loyalty to the Queen, adding, 'I have nothing to show worthy of his Royal
Highness. My palace, my troops, what are they to him? His attendance
at my parade this morning in the heat and dust, the interest the Prince
took in it, were out of his consideration for me. I am an ignorant man,
almost without education.... When the time comes for the Prince to
ascend the throne, I hope he will remember Scindia.' The Prince replied

that he would never forget Gwalior, and that he knew he had a friend in Scindia.

At a boar hunt twenty-five miles from Agra on 3 February, young Prince Louis of Battenberg was thrown from his horse, fracturing a collar-bone. At the earlier pig-sticking, where Carrington had suffered a similar spill, Beresford had lost some teeth, and his Norfolk friend Lord Suffield had been injured by his own spear. No less involved, HRH, who still rode well despite his weight, came through each hunt unscathed.

Still-distant Kashmir would be the venue of a grisly entertainment put on in Jammu for the Prince and much reported by the press corps that followed him. As the correspondent for the *Daily Telegraph* observed wryly, 'To be a sportsman in Kashmir, as in Spain, you must not be burdened with sensitive feelings.' In an 'amusement' far more sanguinary than a bullfight, a cheetah mauled a penned black buck, clawing the animal's throat as it cried out in terror and pain. Inevitably it was reported in *Reynolds's Newspaper*, and an irate Cornishman – the Prince was Duke of Cornwall – then wrote that although HRH had been asked to preside the previous August at an agricultural fair and had consented, within a week of its opening he had cancelled, on grounds that he was busy preparing to go to India. 'That was about three months before he went away, and in the interim he could find time to go to horse races [and] … watering places, &c. But he could not spend a single hour in a county from whence he receives forty thousand [pounds] a year. I suppose, sir, it was because they had no pigs for him to torture, no wild beasts to … tear each other to pieces for him whilst he was there.'

'Bertie's progresses lose a little interest and are very wearing – as there is such a constant repetition of elephants – trappings – jewels – illuminations and fireworks,' the Queen wrote sourly to Vicky. Yet none of it was the Prince's doing. The maharajahs laid on what was expected in their settings. The Prince of Wales was a captive to the culture of the sub-continent.

For much of the remainder of the trip, the Prince would be able to eschew pomp and unlimber his guns. Tiger-hunting was still to come, in Jaipur, where the big cats had to be driven by beaters toward the 'sportsmen'. As with some elephant and boar hunts, the sportsmen were safely ensconced on platforms, in trees, and upon howdahs, and *Punch*, in its almost weekly satires on the tour, described such tiger-hunting in extravagant Indian malapropisms. According to its fictitious representative in

India, a bullock was killed, then steeped in rum to befuddle a tiger which would feast upon it. Once groggy, the well-fed tiger was tied up in an empty forty-gallon cask, whereupon the *Punch* reporter sent messengers with the news, 'and presently my Noble Sportsman and the Suite [came] in carriages, armed to the teeth.... However the natives did the thing in style. They erected a wooden tower, into which my Royal Companion could climb, and from which he could shoot at his ease.' When the cords were loosened, however, and the tiger's tail pulled, he was still 'sleeping off the fumes of the rum'. Roused with buckets of water, the beast padded out of the tub with a growl, yawned, and proceeded toward the jungle. 'Another tug of his tail from me sent him off toward the Royal box, whence he was very soon saluted with two or three shots that immensely astonished him. He gave one roar, bounded off, and disappeared, much to the disappointment of the gentleman in the wooden tower.'

Eventually the inventive man from *Punch* finds the groggy tiger, fells it with a silent shot from an air pistol, and inserts a cartridge appropriated stealthily from the arsenal of the 'Noble and Distinguished Party'. Bending over the carcass, a native locates the bullet, 'which being handed round (like the shoe in *Cinderella*), to find out to whom it belonged, was at last discovered to fit *exactly the bore of His Royal Highness's rifle!!*'

On 5 February the Prince bagged his first tigress, fat and pregnant with three cubs, an untimely discovery which did not dampen the party's jubilation. He then returned for another look at the Taj by moonlight, and on 8 February set out by train for a shooting camp which appeared to be at the foot of the Himalayas. Lit by the setting sun, the snowcapped mountains were actually hundreds of miles away, but appeared so high and enormous in the cold, clear sky that the great plains to the south seemed almost beneath them. The land swarmed with game, from tiger and leopard to winged and burrowing creatures, and the vast shooting camp set up for the Prince, maintained by 2,500 persons, included a Gurkha military band which played Verdi, Donizetti, Offenbach and Mozart, 119 elephants, 550 camels and 100 horses. Coverts were beaten daily, but no big game emerged until Valentine's Day, when two bears were shot, one by the Prince. The next day Carrington felled a tigress that must have been nursing her young, as milk flowed from her paps as she rolled over with a growl and lay still. On the 18th a ten-foot tiger charged the elephants, and, to give the Prince a shot, someone shouted to the others, 'Do not fire!' Nevertheless a worried hunter fired from the other side of the loop, and with that kill, the shooting excursion in British territory ended. The party continued into a corner of Nepal on 20 February, 600 coolies carrying storage boxes labelled 'Agra Ice Company'.

As the royal travellers crossed the Nepalese frontier to Jumoa, letters from home awaited them which threatened embarrassments up to the highest level, exposing an affair between Edith, the wife of 'Sporting Joe' Aylesford, and another of the Prince's London circle, Lord Blandford, heir to the Duke of Marlborough. Indiscreet letters also surfaced from the Prince to the lady, whose affections ranged widely. The Earl of Aylesford was with the shooting party, as was Lady Aylesford's brother, Colonel Owen Williams. Hoping that Williams had some influence over his sister, the family in England urged his immediate return, and he had left hurriedly on 13 February. Soon after, a message to Aylesford from Edith announced that she was leaving him for Blandford, who was deserting his wife for her. On 28 February Sporting Joe left by elephant for the railhead at Bareilly, to the south in India, hoping to keep a lid on the scandal. Two days later Carrington wrote to his mother of the 'disgrace' and 'misery' brought to the camp. 'Our party is much reduced now, as we have lost the Duke of Sutherland, [Albert] Grey, Owen Williams and Joe Aylesford. Old Alfred Paget, too, is dying to get home …'.

Although the Prince, under threat himself if he were subpoenaed to give evidence in a divorce suit, condemned Blandford as 'the greatest blackguard alive', he could hardly cancel the ebbing days of the tour. Nepalese authorities resolved that the Prince should not draw a blank in their country, and the next day trapped a tiger and kept it blockaded by elephants until HRH could fire three shots into it. Seven more tigers fell that afternoon, six credited to the Prince, who was shouted such instructions as 'Fire just before you, Sir! There he is in front!' His unflagging enthusiasm and energy amid the plethora of wildlife drew the expected encomiums from his hosts; and the tour historian, visualizing an endless supply of jungle cats, predicted, 'It will be many a long year before Nepal ceases to keep up a breed of tigers.'

In almost every case the Prince sentimentalized and improved upon the realities in letters to his sons. 'Since I last wrote to you,' he told them on 23 February, 'I have had great tiger shooting. The day before yesterday I killed six, and some were very savage. Two were man-eaters.' (At least one had been found near human remains.) 'To-day I killed a tigress and she had a little cub with her.' (He added that he hoped to bring some cubs back to England.) 'Two little bears and an armadillo got loose in [zoologist] Mr Bartlett's tent last night and frightened him so that he did not know what to do.' (It was very likely a Carrington prank.)

On 25 February, mounted on Arabian horses, the dwindling party set off on a search for wild elephants, and, after a long run, a wounded elephant fell behind and was secured by a rope round a hind leg. Breaking loose, it was penned by four hunting elephants and secured by a rope round the other hind leg. From his howdah, the Nepalese Prime Minister, Sir Jung Bahadur, observed that the defenceless pachyderm, sunk to its knees, was blind in one eye and bore a broken tusk, both old injuries. 'I will let him go,' Bahadur offered, 'if the Prince expresses a wish that he be set at liberty, but I hope to be able to offer his Royal Highness the [other] tusk.'

The Prince accepted the bargain, and the elephant was raised and tethered to a large tree. As it lost its remaining tusk, the tormented animal trumpeted a long, bitter cry, then refused a consolatory sugar cane held at arm's length. At a campfire that night, Sir Jung presented the tusk, and the next morning the elephant was released into the bush.

Following a tiger hunt the next day, during which the Prince's group bagged nothing, a pious Sunday intervened. The next day the camp was raised. A Gurkha band played 'God Save the Queen' and 'God Bless the Prince of Wales'. On Leap-Day, 29 February, the party moved to Bahadur's private preserve, Bahminie Tal, from where HRH asked the party's physician, Dr Fayrer – who had injured himself in a fall during an elephant hunt – to start with aides for Lahore, as he would need more travel time. Fayrer left on a howdah for Bareilly, where he ordered a special train to return the party.

On 5 March the Prince held a final Durbar, offering his Nepalese host several English rifles, a silver statuette of himself in the uniform of the 10th Hussars, and other gifts. Sir Jung's family and associates also received royal tokens. The next day baksheesh was distributed liberally. After breakfast, farewells were exchanged, and the Prince remarked to the surprised Sir Jung that, through the magic of the telegraph, what the Prime Minister had said at the Durbar the day before had already appeared in the London papers.

Also making news in London papers was the ruffled progress through Parliament of the controversial Royal Titles Bill, which would style the

Queen as Empress of India. Even Disraeli's own party was lukewarm about altering the traditional title, but the status-sensitive Victoria was insistent. Once Prussia took on imperial trappings as the German Empire in 1870, she had been concerned about being outranked in protocol by her own daughter in Berlin. Disraeli's purchase of Suez Canal shares while the Prince was away, and the Prince's much publicized tour of India as her heir, seemed to Victoria and her Prime Minister an opportune moment for the move. Never consulted, the Prince of Wales learned about the new royal style from *The Times of India*. Since airing his grievances to his mother was useless, he wrote to Disraeli with a sense of having been abused, 'As the Queen's eldest son, I think I have some right to feel annoyed that the announcement of the addition to the Queen's title should have been read by me in the newspapers instead of [my] having received some intimation of the subject from the Prime Minister.'

The Prince's hectic schedule left little time for frustration about distant events. At Bareilly the next day, below the south-western corner of Nepal, Lord Northbrook arrived to escort his royal guest by rail toward Bombay, and departure. A final Chapter of the Order of the Star of India was held at the Lieutenant-Governor's residence, and Major-General Sam Browne, VC, who had lost an arm in the Mutiny, was knighted, along with Major-General Dighton Probyn and Surgeon-General Joseph Fayrer. Just before midnight the royal party left on the East Indian Railway for Jabalpur, then via the Great Indian Peninsula Railway to Khandwa, a tedious journey of several days and nights, punctuated by stops for receptions, inspections, breakfasts, lunches and dinners. At Jabalpur they inspected the prison, where seven Thugs – a fraternity of Hindu murderers – had already spent thirty-five miserable years. The Prince asked the wickedest-looking of the prisoners how many lives he had taken. His hands clasped in a deprecating gesture, the Thug admitted to sixty-seven. When HRH was preparing to leave, they began chattering among themselves and the Prince was told, 'They beg, Sir, that you will be pleased to order that instead of three rupees a month, their present allowance, each of them shall receive four. It will make them quite comfortable.'

If it could be done, said the Prince, he hoped the increase would be granted. 'Very few of them would live to enjoy it.' The elderly prisoners were delighted.

At Khandwa, where the royal train arrived at 8.40 p.m. on 10 March, a banquet was scheduled – 'that is,' William Russell wrote, 'there was a remarkable bill of fare: but the dishes set forth thereon were by no means to be found on the table'. The party was jaded with food and with travel, and no one cared. Lord Suffield toasted the health of the Princess of Wales, and the Prince returned thanks for the success of the trip. At eleven the next morning, again after travelling all night, what remained of the group arrived at Churchgate Station, Bombay. A guard of honour had been drawn up, but the sun was already very hot, and the parade route to the dockyard gate was largely a collection of umbrellas under which knots of people watched quietly. Over one portal was a sign, 'God Speed You!' A steam launch took the party out to the *Serapis* while thirteen warships saluted with volleys. Since the next day was a Sunday, sailing was scheduled for Monday, and at eleven, the inevitable church service was held on the quarter-deck in the muggy heat. Later in the day Admiral Macdonald gave a farewell dinner to the Prince on board the *Undaunted*, and the next afternoon, with loading of the Prince's haul accomplished, the *Serapis* raised anchor and sailed into the Indian Ocean toward Aden, Alexandria and Gibraltar. It had been seventeen weeks since their arrival in Bombay. Three days later, on 16 March 1876, the Royal Titles Bill passed its second reading in the Commons.

In India alone the Prince had travelled nearly 7,600 miles by land and 2,300 miles by sea, and met more governors, maharajahs and local chiefs than anyone before him. Also, perhaps, no visiting hunting party had ever bagged twenty-eight tigers and captured fourteen elephants, numbers quickly seized upon negatively by the Radical press. A menagerie of eighty animals crowded the steamy deck of the *Serapis* as it headed home.

'Now that the nation's resources have been idly squandered upon a vain journey, and that the "grand tour" is all but wound up,' *Reynolds's Newspaper* challenged, 'it behooves us to ask, "What has been the result, and what has the country got in return?" The result has been pernicious in every sense.' It excoriated the tour as an orgy of 'pig-sticking, tiger-hunting, viewing elephant fights, and similar bloody and cruel sports', and 'a wearisome, monotonous round of levées, fireworks, banquets, addresses, illuminations, receptions, visits, and so forth. That British royalty must have cut a contemptible figure is manifest.' Yet the Prince of Wales had represented the previously remote monarchy with éclat, performed dull and repetitive ceremonies with dignity, treated native rulers shorn of power if not wealth with warmth and sensitivity, tolerated

THE "STAR" OF INDIA.

Punch *on the perceived success of the Prince's tour of India (13 May 1876)*

unwelcome entertainments with courtesy, and played the sportsman – despite the enervating heat and humidity – with energy and gusto. Even before he left Bombay, the Prince ordered by telegraph that an exhibition be prepared at the India Museum in South Kensington (one of the forerunners of the Victoria and Albert Museum) of the exotic presentations in enamel and gold and jewels made to him by the maharajahs. The artefacts would be shown several times thereafter, including at the Paris International Exposition of 1878. They would be also be pictured in a two-volume illustrated catalogue, and become a source for design and manufacture. This commitment to public display was itself a diplomatic gesture toward India. A year after the visit the new viceroy, Lord Lytton, would note, with some wry exaggeration, to the Under-Secretary for India, 'The fact is, the whole of Anglo-Indian society is mortally offended with the Prince of Wales for not having sufficiently appreciated its superiority to everything else in creation.' In the Anglo-Indian mind was 'an idée fixe that I came out with secret instructions from his Royal Highness to snub and aggravate the whites, and pet and spoil the blacks'.

Further, although a leading Bengali poet, Chandra Bandopadhgaya, had written satirical verses, *Bajimat*, attacking the Prince and his visit, and a farce, *Gayadananda*, mocked the Prince of Wales in Calcutta theatres before being closed by the police, their thrust would prove at odds with the realities. There were no royal scandals in India, and no indignities. The heir's high-profile tour had represented the Raj well, and implied a commitment to the subcontinent that was a cautionary message to expansionist Russia. Even *Punch*, in a column titled 'When the Prince Comes Home', proposed without tongue in cheek 'a triumphal march called "The Hero of India"'.

XI

The Mixture as Before

1876–1881

O N THE FIRST day of 1877, the Queen was proclaimed Empress of India at a Durbar in Delhi stage-managed by Lord Lytton. At a celebratory dinner at Windsor, Victoria startled Bertie and Alix, who were accustomed to seeing her in bleak black, by wearing masses of jewels given to her by acquiescent Indian princes and maharajahs. Seventy ruling chiefs came to England for the occasion, their spokesman the Maharajah of Gwalior, who saluted her in the name of his peers as *Shah-in-Shah Padshah*, or Monarch of Monarchs.

On Victoria's stout figure the profusion of baubles was incongruous, and the Earl of Beaconsfield – as Disraeli had become – asked with some irony whether she was wearing all her new Indian diamonds and pearls. 'Oh, no,' said the Queen; 'if you like I will have the rest brought in after dinner for you to see.' Chests of jewels duly arrived.

Not present, although the Prince of Wales had invited him to England, was Sir Jung Bahadur. Before sunrise on a holy day in February he had gone to the Bagmati River, below Katmandu, the Nepalese capital, to bathe. Later he was found dead on the bank, an apparent suicide. He had known he was fatally ill. His three widows had quietly immolated themselves on the Prime Minister's sandalwood funeral pyre. Soon after, the Prince received a letter from the senior widow – the post took nearly a month in transit – to announce their already realized intention to perform *suttee*.

Tragedy seemed to cling to Sir Jung's family. A nephew of the reigning Maharajah had died just a month after the Prince had left Nepal, and the widow, Bahadur's daughter, had vowed *suttee*, officially illegal since 1829 but still practised by the devout. Deploring the widow's intention, in which she was supported by Brahman priests, the Maharajah notified the British Resident at his court, Charles Girdlestone, who explained diplomatically to Sir Jung how the Prince of Wales, whom he had hosted, would feel about an act illegal under the Raj. Rather than forfeit the future king's good will, Nepalese authorities rescued Sir Jung's daughter from her vow. The Secretary for India, then Lord Salisbury, was kept informed, and on 25 June 1876 wrote to the Prince, 'I feel sure that your Royal Highness will be interested to know that your presence in India, besides all the other benefits it has caused, has had the effect of materially checking this horrible crime in its last retreat. I think it would be desirable that your R.H. should express to Sir Jung Bahadur your aversion to *suttee*, and your hope that it may be entirely suppressed.... Such an expression of opinion would probably be far more effective than any pressure which the government of India could bring to bear.' Yet the ghastly mourning practice would be carried out threefold for Sir Bahadur himself.

The Prince had learned of the Royal Titles Act only after he left Nepal on 5 March; also, in what seemed another snub, his mother had not waited for his return to order the opening of the completed Albert Memorial on 9 March, curiously without ceremony. He would have officiated – which may have seemed awkward to the Queen amid an untimely new scandal. The Aylesford affair had followed the Prince home from India. Aylesford had returned to demand a divorce from Edith and duel with Blandford. By the time the Prince reached Egypt, his Private Secretary, Francis Knollys, had learned of a compromising packet of letters from Bertie to Lady Aylesford. HRH had casually flirted with her as he did with many married women who attracted him, and he had indeed penned impulsive trifles. As usual, the Queen accepted the innocence of Bertie's blandishments while observing that 'the publication of any letters of this nature would be very undesirable as a colouring might easily be given and injurious references deduced from hasty expressions'. She urged the Prince to keep distant from the aggrieved parties.

To head off a divorce, which would exclude Lady Aylesford from society (an open liaison in their circle was acceptable if the parties remained married), she called on the Princess of Wales at Marlborough House. The Prince was still at sea, returning via Malta, Gibraltar and Lisbon. Lord Randolph Churchill, accompanying Edith, had the Prince's letters, which were 'of the most compromising character', she claimed to Alix. If Sporting Joe, who seemed to have more of a way with horses than hussies, went to court, the Prince's letters, they threatened, would be released to the press and he 'would never sit upon the throne of England'. The hot-headed Churchill had already boasted to friends that he held the Crown of England in his pocket.

From cables and telegrams at ports of call, the Prince had learned enough to rush Lord Charles Beresford – with messages to the contending parties – back to England via Brindisi. As HRH's second, he was to challenge Lord Randolph to a duel with the Prince with pistols somewhere in France, where violent settlements of honour escaped punishment.

Unaware of that possibility, the Queen would write to her son via Knollys, 'What a dreadful disgraceful business.... And how unpardonable ... to draw dear Alix into it! ... Poor Lord Aylesford should not have left her. I *knew* last summer this was going on.' The implication was clear. Bertie's invitations to his playboy intimates to a spree in India had facilitated such scandals to which weak women and their admirers were susceptible. From Brussels (having fled England), Blandford wrote to his brother Randolph that he was resigned to a divorce hearing. 'If A. leaves matters as they are between him and Edith' – that is, unsettled – 'I shall only wait until HRH comes back to appear on the scene and then if A. tries to lick me I shall do my damndest to defend myself and afterwards if I am all right, I shall lick HRH within an inch of his life for his conduct generally, and we will have the whole thing up in the Police Court!!'

Equally unwisely, Churchill answered the Prince in writing. Beresford duly hurried the response to the *Serapis* at Malta, having twice in his mission crossed the Continent north to south by train. The possibility of a duel between the Prince and the writer was absurd, Lord Randolph wrote insolently – which was, he suggested, why HRH felt bold enough to propose it. Advised of the scandal, Disraeli intervened, and through April and early May, with the assistance of the Earl of Hardwicke, a friend to both parties, he sought a quiet settlement before the *Serapis* docked at Portsmouth on 11 May. Family efforts were also under way to deflect any potential embarrassment by stage-managing the Prince's return as a celebration of his successes in India. As *The Times* observed wryly that morning, 'Invention is taxed to keep Royalty in the front of that stage of active and original life upon which all eyes are fixed.'

With the press in mind, Alexandra boarded the *Serapis* 'first and *alone*' (as she put it) before the ship anchored. With their children, and accompanied also by the Duke of Edinburgh and the Queen's cousin the Duke of Cambridge, Alix and the Prince mounted a special train to London, and proceeded to Marlborough House in an open carriage before throngs of cheering subjects alerted by the newspapers. Immediately after, the Waleses changed into opera dress and went to Covent Garden for a performance of Verdi's *Un ballo in maschera*, being seated before the second-act curtain. The audience expected the Royals, and whispers of 'They are coming now!' filled the theatre during the prolonged interval. People rose to shouts and cheers and bravos as the Prince arrived, and he bowed repeatedly from his box. Finally the curtain rose. Signor Auguste Vianesi lifted his baton, and the chorus, with diva Emma Albani as soloist, sang 'God Bless the Prince of Wales', followed by 'God Save the Queen'. The crowd was delirious. It was almost the post-typhoid thanksgiving all over again. The press might inveigh against the heir's scrapes, but people appreciated his style. He was acting like the special person they wanted to see in him. In the dawning of the culture of celebrity the Prince of Wales was beginning to learn that bravado often eclipsed indignity.

The next day, 12 May, Hardwicke wrote happily to Ponsonby to inform the Queen that Sporting Joe would neither sue Edith nor invite her back. 'The result is that no Public Scandal will take place. He will arrange his matters privately and will separate from his wife making proper Provision for her.... I went to Marlboro' House late to see the Prince of Wales ... & told him the result of my interview with Ld Aylesford.... Thank God it is over & I am most thankful.' Victoria pronounced herself 'much relieved' that the case – and the Prince – would be kept out of the courts.

Lady Aylesford, having relinquished her children, settled in France with Blandford, who had deserted his wife. The lovers were to have a son in 1881, but when Blandford inherited his dukedom he abandoned Edith and – now divorced – married as his second wife a rich American widow. Despite the Prince's attraction to Randolph's wife, the beautiful Jennie Jerome Churchill, Blandford's brother Lord Randolph remained a social outcast for eight years, the Prince refusing to enter any house where the couple were entertained. With his two sons ostracized, the embarrassed old Duke of Marlborough sold off some family art treasures at Blenheim to afford Disraeli's offer to be Lord Lieutenant of Ireland. Withdrawing from England with some new pride of place, the Duke left for quieter

Dublin. Sporting Joe purchased a ranch at Big Springs, Texas, where he died of alcoholism in the early 1880s.

But the Aylesford affair had dragged on. In the last days of 1876 the Prince of Wales agreed to accept an apology from Lord Randolph 'if couched in language dictated by Ld Chancellor, Hartington & Beaconsfield' (Ponsonby's words, on behalf of the Queen). The Prince acknowledged the written regrets but refused to accept them as sincere. 'However ungraciously done,' Ponsonby deplored to the Queen, 'it was *done* by Ld Randolph & he performed his part of the agreement. He is entitled to have it accepted.' When the Prince remained stubborn, Churchill went to Dublin. The Queen was to receive Lord Randolph and Jennie long before the Prince did. Only in March 1884 was there an armistice, when both men attended a dinner arranged by the MP Sir Henry James.

As the Prince tried to distance himself from scandal and re-establish his pre-India routine of public appearances, *Punch* lampooned the royal calendar for its triviality:

Illustrious Personage: Well, it really is pleasant to be at home again. All that ceremonial in foreign parts was terribly exhausting. I shall be very glad of a rest. *A propos*, is there anything to do tomorrow?

Private Secretary: Yes, Sir. Deputation at twelve, Council at two, Foundation Stone at four, and two Balls and the Opera in the evening.

Illustrious Personage: Hem! How about Tuesday?

Private Secretary: Review in the morning, Sir, at Aldershot, *Levée* in the afternoon at Buckingham Palace, a Flower Show, and a City Dinner.

Illustrious Personage: Is Wednesday free?

Private Secretary: Well, no, Sir. Launch of an Iron-clad at Portsmouth in the morning, Sir. Reception in town in the afternoon, Sir. Your Royal Highness talked about one of the theatres for the evening.

Illustrious Personage: Ah, to be sure – so I did. What have I to do on Thursday?

Private Secretary: Opening of a new wing at a Hospital, Sir, in the morning. Lunch with the Life Guards. Polo in the afternoon, and a Fancy Dress Ball in the Evening, Sir.

Illustrious Personage: How about Friday?

Private Secretary: Distribution of Prizes. Inauguration of a new College. A Court, Sir, and four Balls in the evening.

Illustrious Personage: Saturday filled up, I suppose?
Private Secretary: Yes, Sir. Rather a heavy day, your Royal Highness. Three Foundation Stones, a Review, a Concert, a Council Meeting, two Deputations, and Fireworks at [the Crystal Palace at] Sydenham. I think that you said, Sir, that your Royal Highness wished also to be present at the Royal Italian Opera.
Illustrious Personage (smiling): I am afraid my rest will have to be deferred for the rest of the season.

One of the actual appointments in the Prince's diary was a meeting with the Duke of Edinburgh (who also loved opera – and divas even more), and Arthur Sullivan, formally to establish the National Training School of Music. It would later be called the Royal College of Music, with Sullivan as its Principal, a post he occupied until 1881. Thirty-five and unmarried, Sullivan would soon be in the Prince's orbit and a habitué at Marlborough House. Through HRH, Sullivan acquired his mistress, Mrs Landon Ronalds. A wealthy, bosomy American soprano of thirty-seven, she lived at 7 Cadogan Place without her Bostonian husband. (A previous lover had been Jennie Churchill's wealthy father, Leonard Jerome of New York.) Mary Frances Ronalds soon went everywhere with Sullivan. She held Sunday evening musicales for the rich and famous, and at home or as guest was predictably called upon to sing Sullivan's 'The Lost Chord', which the Prince claimed he would travel the length of the kingdom to hear. At these occasions he sometimes played the piano and his brother Affie the violin. The curious symbols in Sullivan's appointment book after *his* visits to Cadogan Place suggest intimacies which, given the social hypocrisies of the time, the dissolution of Mary's pro forma marriage would have made impossible. Ronalds sent money and neither visited nor divorced his wife.

For years the Prince attended all Sullivan's light operas written with W. S. Gilbert, pressed for Sullivan's knighthood (it came in 1883), and enjoyed special small concerts arranged at the composer's home at 1 Queen's Mansions, Victoria Street, to promote his music. One of the Prince's favourite performers was the soubrette Jessie Bond, who sang in *Ruddigore, Pinafore, Mikado* and other operettas, and a letter exists from Sullivan asking her to 'entertain' the Prince on a Sunday night, and 'dress and undress in my bedroom'. But she entertained only with song, and evaded anything more. 'May I come to see you, Miss Bond?' he once offered. 'What for?' she enquired innocently – and for once HRH was speechless.

In his first social season after India, another entry in his appointment book was for a musical party at Lady Rothschild's. One of the guests was the American physician and author Oliver Wendell Holmes, who had once written verses marking the Prince's visit to Boston. It was, Holmes wrote, 'a very brilliant affair; Patti sang to us, and a tenor, and a violinist played for us.... In the same row of seats was the Prince of Wales.' In front of Dr Holmes was Princess Alexandra, 'in ruby velvet, with six rows of pearls encircling her throat, and two more strings falling quite low'. Several other 'great beauties' were present, but Holmes preferred 'the shades of departed beauties on the wall, by Sir Joshua [Reynolds] and Gainsborough'.

Among the more unusual appointments on the Prince's post-India calendar was a visit in July 1876 to the Central London Polytechnic in Regent Street, which exhibited the latest marvels of engineering. One was a three-ton diving-bell that descended at intervals into a great tank while guests sat within the apparatus, supplied with air from two eight-cylinder air pumps conveyed via leather hoses. Papers carried stories that one could 'obtain a more perfect oxygenation of the blood and a more complete expansion of the breathing system, resulting from inhalation of the high-pressure air'. The Prince may have hoped for some benefit to his tobacco-impeded respiration, rather than merely the anticipated frisson of going down in the bell under water. His experience of the water was to extend much further, however, as he had bought the yacht *Hildegarde*, a 205-ton schooner, and was on board on 7 August 1877 when it won the Queen's Cup at Cowes. The victory turned him into an enthusiastic yachtsman although no participant gave him any racing edge.

The Prince's pleasure at aristocratic sporting and social events was as fleeting a joy as were the excesses of ceremony. He still longed for a substantive role in government. Using his experience of South Asia and the Middle East as a basis, he began offering unsolicited political advice to his mother and the Prime Minister on the growing instability in Ottoman domains, especially in the Turkish Balkans. Gladstone and others among the Liberals had begun exploiting alleged atrocities against Christians as reason to deplore Tory support for Turkey, and to promote unholy Russia as the defender of Christian rights in the Balkans and Asia. To Victoria the Prince wrote on 2 October 1876 that Gladstone and his allies 'have created the excitement throughout the country, which is called public opinion' – and suggested this had further emboldened Russia. It was a definition worthy of Disraeli, and the Prince may very well have picked up the phrase in conversation with the Prime Minister. Well into 1877 he would be a 'Jingo' with Disraeli, writing to his mother, 'I suppose we shall now sit with our hands folded, and let the Russians do their worst, and I see nothing to prevent their taking Constantinople. I fear we shall cut a very ridiculous figure in the world, as we can bark but dare not bite, and we shall very soon find ourselves left out of the councils of Europe, and we shall have only ourselves to thank for it.' He signed the message 'Albert Edward' to emphasize his seriousness.

Over the matter of what came to be called the 'Eastern Agitation' he began to assert himself as future sovereign – not publicly, which would have been improper, but to the Queen and the Cabinet. When a Great Powers congress was being planned, he implored his mother 'to urge Lord Beaconsfield to go', rather than a surrogate, to deal with Bismarck. The Prime Minister, she rejoined, was elderly and ailing, and 'my great support and comfort'. Although she did not want to risk his health, Disraeli did go, and the Berlin conference was a personal triumph for him. Suddenly, to the Prince's surprise, Victoria agreed with her son's views. He was taken seriously, and that boosted his confidence. 'If we make use of big words such as "British interests" at the present moment,' he wrote to the Queen on 23 December 1877, 'unless we are ready to enforce them by force, we shall never be able to hold up our head again in the eyes of the world.' He knew from his travels in the Indian highlands of the 'Great Game' being played between British and Russian authorities for influence in central Asia, and he was friendlier than most of his countrymen towards the Ottomans, who had fussed over him since he was a young man. As a result he became very cool toward Gladstone, who had begun working up the electorate to see atrocities everywhere in the Turkish Balkans, and to view Russia as the friend of mistreated Christians, whose patron the Tsar had cynically become. After the wedding breakfast for Albert Grey, Gladstone noted in his diary, 'The P. of W. gentlemanlike but as now usual shirked saying a word.'

The Prince's political agenda, sometimes influenced by the ubiquitous Laurence Oliphant, included wooing the friendship of Midhat Pasha, the Governor-General at Damascus, whose favour Oliphant was currying to promote a colonization scheme to resettle persecuted (which often meant

Russian) Jews in Syrian Palestine. When in England, Midhat was hosted
by both the Prince and his friend the Duke of Sutherland, who were
counting on the shiekh to secure the necessary *firman* from the Sultan at
Constantinople. The campaign was prolonged as Midhat fell out of
favour, then was restored to conditional grace. For some reason – perhaps
political distance – it was Princess Helena rather than her brother who
signed a letter to Disraeli asking him to give Oliphant a hearing on the
subject, and in due course the Prince hosted a house party at Sandringham
so that influential politicians could meet Oliphant. But in early 1880,
with a General Election approaching and Gladstone raising anti-Turkish
feeling to unseat the Tories, the Palestinian scheme finally foundered.

Despite his political efforts, when the last of Samuel Beeton's swollen
verse satires on the Prince of Wales, *Edward VII*, appeared late in 1876, it
struck again at HRH's lack of occupation. 'What's to be done?' the verse
Edward complains. 'A man can't smoke for ever.' He doesn't 'read much',
he confesses. 'Except the *Field*, the *Sportsman*, new French novels.' The
Queen in the verses calls him an 'ingrate son', and demands that he stay
at her side, but he rejects spending 'My mornings with you at the
Mausoleum', and 'My nights in social converse with *his* bust'. Rather, he
explains,

> Fast is my line. I've taken patents out
> For reckless driving through each hedge and fence
> Of social life! I am the Great Fast Prince!
> For why? Great-uncle George was surely not
> A very tortoise in his mode of life.

While the Queen 'feels abroad' even in Surrey, he prefers refreshing
himself in France, 'across *La Manche*', unless something more interesting
comes along. Something does, as Beeton and his writers invent what
already seemed inevitable – a war between Russia and Turkey, with India
menaced by the Tsar's 'dark designs'. The Prince takes up the sword after
one of his retainers challenges,

> ... Let [us] show
> Our countrymen we are not merely rakes;
> That wild oats' sowing's not our only role....
> We may not be the goody-goody prigs
> Some folks would have us; ...

> For we are Englishmen, and have hot blood,
> And have many passions that will have their vent,
> E'en if it be in nonsense: but now comes
> The chance we longed for ...

The imagined crisis results in a conference at the Berlin suburb of Potsdam (prefiguring the actual one in Berlin in 1878), led jointly by Bismarck and Disraeli. The fictional congress is convened by the Crown Prince of Germany, brother-in-law of the hero. Encamped on the Indian Northwest Frontier with Russia, and led by the heretofore unmilitary Prince of Wales, the English, augmented by Indian levies, await the battle. In Beeton's lines the Prince confesses,

> It was high time that England had a war:
> We all of us were hasting to the bad.

Patriotism engulfs England; even the members of the Marlborough Club volunteer *en masse* for the Middle East. On the Northwest Frontier the Prince shortly confronts Frederick and his Prussians aiding the Tsar at the orders of 'Mismarck'. The Crown Prince is defeated and surrenders to a foe 'I thought the Prince of Pleasure'.

The price of victory is heavy for the Prince's cronies. Lord 'Smotherland' is wounded and ['Charlie'] 'Slaughterford' is killed. But Albert Edward has shown cool courage even beyond what he had demonstrated 'when shooting in the jungles of Ceylon'. From London comes news by telegram that Her Majesty has abdicated in favour of her son, and in India, as British soldiers hail the new Edward VII, the King praises his mother's unanticipated 'gracious act'. Echoing Shakespeare's *Henry IV*, the new King declares, in Prince Hal style,

> I now my loose behaviour throw right off,
> And pay the debt I never promised:
> My reformation, glittering o'er my faults,
> Shall show more goodly, ...
> And with my Queen beside me, I will seek
> England's first place among the powers to keep.

Padded with society gossip from London and Paris, with irrelevant anti-Semitism, and with reminders of the *Serapis* and the junket to India, *Edward VII* is nevertheless a remarkable *tour de force* of foreshadowing and fancy, skirting libel on almost every one of its ninety double-columned pages. For sale at sixpence there was also a thirty-page 'key' to the characters, in which the longest description was inevitably that of the Prince of Wales. Although he had 'no actual power', the key explains, 'The Prince is the sun round which revolve the stars in our social firmament', and 'keeps gaiety pulsing and money in circulation'. He had 'his faults', but was 'no meddler' and had 'no evil ambitions'. He was exactly right, the unsigned key explained, for 'our Constitutional Monarchy'. Most intriguing in the verse philippic itself, however, were the Prince's imagined dreams of military glory in a war nearly everyone saw coming between Russia and Turkey, and of a moral reformation for which in life he could not discipline himself. The unlikely abdication of his mother to end his wait for the throne expressed a longing which, but for Beeton, he could only keep to himself.

The Prince's itch to demonstrate manly courage beyond having tigers beaten toward him had to come vicariously. In the late 1870s he appointed Henry Frederick Stephenson, a naval captain with a record of daring exploration in the Arctic, as an equerry, from which Stephenson went on to further glory in the Middle East. Social access to adventurers like Laurence Oliphant and Richard Burton also added spice to London life. When the Prince's friend Lady Marian Alford gave a party to open her new house at Prince's Gate, she invited Burton, asking him to come costumed as a Bedouin sheikh. Burton brought with him his wife Isabel's young Syrian maid, Khamoor, in Arab dress. To Isabel and Khamoor he spoke Arabic, and to the other guests some broken English and French invented for the occasion. The Prince and his brother Affie knew of the masquerade and entered into it when, after dinner, Khamoor brought a tray of coffee balanced on her head, and, kneeling, served the princes. The disguises, which had served Burton well in Arabia, were now only a parlour trick, but the Prince was enchanted. He had conspired in deception with Burton.

The Prince's escapes across the *Manche* to Paris were now fewer because he was finding new consolation at home. Accessible in London as well as in Paris was a striking actress from Imperial days, Sarah Bernhardt, named directly in Beeton's satire and described as

> ... famed for dignity,
> And leanness so pronounced that she could drape

Herself, poor creature, quite abundantly
In half a yard of tape.

She had returned to the Prince's life and bed, and was unusual among his
women in that, like Alix, she was by no means voluptuous: her attraction
lay in the burning theatricality she exhibited even offstage. For her, he
would cross to Paris even after her London seasons became annual events,
and when *Fedora*, the suspenseful, lurid melodrama by Victorien Sardou
about Russian Nihilists, became one of her great successes, he was there.
In her dressing room he confided that he would have liked to be an actor,
but that accident of birth had made that impossible. Daringly, for its
London production she had him dressed for one performance as
Vladimir, Fedora's husband, whose corpse is brought home to her to
weep over. The Prince of Wales would make his wordless and unbilled
theatrical debut lying on a bier on the stage of the Vaudeville Theatre in
the Strand.

For amorous reasons he was often in France in 1878, his official excuse
that of his presidency of the British section of the International
Exhibition in Paris, to which he had lent his exotic Indian collections.
He was serious about his involvement, communicating almost daily with
Cunliffe-Owen of the British Commission, once sending him a letter
that covered fifteen sheets. At a banquet in Paris he reiterated his contention that an *entente cordiale* already existed between the two nations, and
that it was essential to European peace. His cultivation of the *entente*
extended to friendships with all political sides, although Lord Salisbury
as Foreign Secretary warned him politely about interference in Cabinet
affairs. (Later, Salisbury would praise him warmly for his good offices.)
The Paris Exhibition was to cost him one friendship, however. He had
used his influence to get his unreliable friend Charley Buller a job overseeing the Indian collection, and Buller had had to be fired for incompetence and – very likely drunken – insolence.

Alexandra had learned to accept her own role as royal consort outside
the sheets. When, at a reception, the Prince introduced the sultry Sarah
Bernhardt to Alix, the Princess was wearing a gardenia pinned with a
pearl brooch. She removed both and fastened them to the tragedienne's
gown. Always curious about celebrated actresses, the Queen (very late
in her life, in 1897) asked to receive Bernhardt, which she did when both
were at Nice. After performing a touching, half-hour monologue,

A " PAS DE TROIS."

Punch *salutes the Prince on his appointment as President of*
the British Commission of the Paris Exhibition. That it recognized
his additional opportunities for Parisian pleasures
is also obvious (Punch, *9 November 1878*)

Bernhardt was asked to write something in Victoria's guest book.
Kneeling on the floor, Sarah scrawled across a page, '*Le plus beau jour*
de ma vie'. By then she had long been out of the Prince's love life,
although he loyally continued to see her onstage and off, and kept on
his desk in Marlborough House her foot-high bronze self-portrait bust
she had sculpted in 1880 with its eerie bat's wings rising from an inkwell
base.

The most talked-about royal inamorata in the later 1870s was a blue-
eyed beauty of blooming figure and no known talent other than steely
ambition. Daughter of the compulsively philandering Revd W. C. Le

Breton, Dean of Jersey, and wife of Edward Langtry, an obscure gentleman whose income came from a ship-owning Belfast grandfather, Emilie (Lillie) Langtry was twenty-three in 1877. She discovered how striking she was when she arrived in London with an increasingly uninteresting husband and was pursued by painters, photographers and gentlemen admirers. To become a professional beauty and live by one's looks required posing for sepia prints of 'cabinet' photos, just over six inches by four inches, to be sold in corner shops, usually by tobacconists, for albums, large wallets men then used, sideboard shelves, and – if particularly revealing – for locked desk drawers. Some beauties outside society were even paid for their sittings. Her portrait was first sketched by Frank Miles, later a companion of Oscar Wilde, who noticed her at a party. Within weeks, Mrs Langtry gazed at rapt Londoners from penny-postcard stands, and was famous.

Alix was visiting her royal brother in Greece in May 1877, when at a society supper the Prince first met Mrs Langtry. He already knew her face. His call on her immediately after, in the middle of a racing week, required no explanation on his part. Although Alix soon returned, the Prince was seen riding, walking, and talking with Mrs Langtry in the fashionable places where gossip was generated. The Princess of Wales's afternoon carriage rides in Hyde Park, along Rotten Row, had become 'an institution', James Brough wrote, 'like the changing of the palace guard or the trooping of the colours'. Gentlemen bowed and women curtseyed as the wine-red barouche passed. When Mrs Langtry rode side-saddle on 'Redskin' in a black habit that displayed her figure as if she were sewn into it, often now accompanied by the Prince of Wales, men and women stood on park benches to watch *her*. When the Prince indicated that he could only attend a country house weekend when the Langtrys were also invited (and her bedroom obviously located conveniently to his), she became the most socially sought-after lady in England.

John Millais portrayed her as 'The Jersey Lily', her sobriquet thereafter. Frederic Leighton, James Whistler, George Frederic Watts, Edward Poynter, Val Prinsep and Edward Burne-Jones also painted her. (Many of the artists were associated with the new Grosvenor Gallery in New Bond Street, at which the Prince had been with Alix for the opening on 1 May 1877.) 'I never wanted all this publicity,' Lillie claimed much later. '... I was shocked and bewildered when it came. I remember my husband used to be terribly annoyed at it all. He used to lose his temper and blame me.'

What must have been the ultimate indignity was the column in the scan-dalmongering *Town Talk* that closed with a sexual innuendo that was impossible to escape. Since she was displayed 'in conjunction with representations of well-known harlots, ... the question arises, "Who is Mrs Langtry?" ... There was something not very pleasing to the loyal mind to see, in a dozen shop windows, Mrs Langtry side by side or else beneath the Prince of Wales.' Her husband had married a country girl who had become a sex goddess. Assisted by whisky, Edward Langtry bore his public humiliation while she made the most of her body.

While the Prince usually gave jewellery to women he had bedded in the way other men offered a half-crown or a sovereign for sexual services, the alluring Lillie expected much more. Her complaisant husband, rapidly accumulating debts, could not maintain her new style in furs and dresses. The Comptroller at Marlborough House paid her bills, and Langtry himself began living apart except when he was needed to play husband.

For a rendezvous beyond London, the Prince built for Lillie (through an intermediary) a house atop a cliff, and overlooking the beach, at fashionable seaside Bournemouth. It had a large bedroom for him, with his monogrammed brushes unconcealed on a bureau. Her maid and his servants took it as another day's work, and guests came and went without any secrecy. One supper was followed by a table-turning séance, at which young Prince Louis Napoleon, son of the late Emperor, rocked the table and was ejected. For the sake of appearances, when Lillie dined with the Prince at Marlborough House or Sandringham or aboard the *Osborne*, both her husband and Alix were present, and when the young princes Eddy and George sailed aboard the *Bacchante* on a training cruise to the West Indies, Lillie further charmed them with souvenirs for their watch-chains from Benson's, the exclusive jewellers in Cowes. 'I had to take off Grandmother's locket to make room for it,' Eddy confided to his father's mistress.

Heir to the heir, Eddy remained a dilemma for his parents. He was even more uneducable than his father had been as a boy. Formal school-ing, his tutor the Revd John Neale Dalton had advised, was beyond the capacity of Prince Albert Victor. Dalton recommended that the boy undergo naval training on the cadet ship *Britannia* at Portsmouth, and that the more studious George accompany his lethargic brother. By 1879, when the boys were to sail on the *Bacchante*, Dalton's prognosis for Eddy was bleak. He had failed every subject and 'the abnormally dormant condition of his mind' continued to prevent him from 'fix[ing] his attention to any given subject for more than a few minutes'. Backed by the First Lord of the Admiralty, W. H. Smith, Dalton suggested, after a Cabinet meeting on 19 May 1879 had approved the proposal, that the boys continue as cadets rather than go on to public school, but that they be separated and sail on separate ships to compel Eddy to be on his own.

The Prince of Wales was angry at the intrusion into his parental prerogatives, and vetoed the plan after complaining to Disraeli, who apologized for his Cabinet. Dalton resigned but withdrew his resignation only a week before the *Bacchante* sailed, and the parents saw the last of their sons for two years. Although the voyage did nothing to improve Eddy, his absence freed the Prince of Wales for more congenial pursuits, which included not merely amorous affairs but foreign affairs.

Although the Khedive of Egypt had attempted to forestall bankruptcy by sales of Suez shares, his finances were being monitored by British and French Ministers to protect the viability of the Canal. The Khedive's private extravagances, however, continued, and he attempted to evict his overseers and regain control. Writing to Disraeli, the Prince suggested that the 'difficult and troublesome' question affecting control of Suez could be solved if Britain and France could act 'in concert'. In a curious foreshadowing of 1956 he asked, 'Can we depose the Khedive?' Since the Sultan of Turkey, Abdul Hamid, had suzerainty over Egypt but exercised little of it, the Western powers went to him for nominal support, and replaced Ismail with his son, Prince Tewfik, whom the Prince of Wales had decorated with a Star of India in Cairo en route to Bombay in 1875. From London came a new official to supervise Egyptian finances: Sir Evelyn Baring of the banking family, afterwards Lord Cromer. The Prince felt that he had stirred the powers into action.

For his thirty-sixth birthday, *Punch* published some ironic verses about the Prince having everything about which poets dream: 'A peerless wife stands by thy side', went one line, while another claimed, 'Thy children are a Nation's pride'. Since 'Home [was] such perfect bliss', *Punch* could hardly 'wish thee more than this'. From Washington, Henry Adams wrote to an English friend that he hoped that 'the republican broom' that swept Napoleon III from France would eliminate 'the Prince and his whole crew'. He wanted 'a revolution' that would 'cut off the heads of all the people who ever went to Marlborough House. Nothing short of this will clean society. Positively I do not dare hint a doubt of Mrs Langtry's virtue, for fear of getting myself into trouble.' Hardly in tune with the accommodating English public which Adams never got to know when in London in the 1860s, he wished that the Prince 'were hung, or drowned, or anyway got rid of'.

There was no shortage of women in the Prince's life, and their marriages were often only a helpful technicality. The Duchess of Caracciolo had walked out on her husband on their wedding day to return briefly to her straying lover, Prince Josef Poniatowski, then equerry to Napoleon III. That spirit made the daring Blanche interesting, beyond her good looks. After she became pregnant in the last days of the Empire, the Prince had arranged a cliffside villa for her in Dieppe, overlooking the Channel, where he visited regularly, crossing in a friend's yacht. When the Duchess had her daughter, to whom he remained devoted, he stood as godfather while the infant was named Alberta Olga Caracciolo. It was as close as he would come to acknowledging a child, although there were, and would be more, mysterious royal godchildren. Villa Olga, called by some 'Villa Mystery', was no secret to the élite English colony, and Lee Jortin, the local English consul, was kept informed of HRH's visits. The house itself was a precedent for the Langtry residence, and the arrangement with the Duchess was to last much longer.

The Queen herself wanted to meet the glamorous Lillie. As she was married and undivorced she was acceptable at Court. At a Tuesday afternoon levée at Buckingham Palace – Victoria made a rare visit from Windsor for the purpose – one of the handsome coaches filling the Mall and the paths in St James's Park to the Palace for presentations was Lillie's. Her husband and escort wore initialled gold cufflinks presented by the Prince, who coolly stood in the reception group with his mother and Alix. The Queen wore her inevitable black gown, with a small diamond crown and the blue ribbon of the Garter. Lillie overheard the Lord Chamberlain advise, 'Mrs Langtry comes next, your Majesty,' and Victoria, at a loss for appropriate words, silently extended her plump hand to be kissed. Puzzled, Lillie proceeded on. Protocol prevented her from speaking to the Queen without being prompted to do so. In a memoir she wondered about the curious introduction, 'as the Lord Chamberlain had not yet received my card'.

Afterward the Queen complained to Bertie that as Mrs Langtry was so far down in the list, the tag-end of the presentations could not be left as usual to Alix as surrogate. Victoria had wanted to see for herself the lady who, next to the Queen, had become the most famous woman in England.

It was the first time that the Prince had flaunted a mistress, and the scandal press revelled in coy hints about the relationship, which was more domestic than a mere affair. When the enterprising Brixton journalist Adolphus Rosenberg, editor of *Town Talk*, published yet another Lillie story, 'The Langtry Divorce Case', and unwisely named the Prince as a co-respondent, the cuckolded Edward Langtry sued for criminal libel. Under oath he denied any divorce proceeding, or that his wife had been unfaithful, and on 25 October 1879 Mr Justice Hawkins at the Old Bailey sentenced the unfortunate Rosenberg to eighteen months in prison. Recognizing the rarity of Langtry's appearances in London, an American satirical paper, *Texas Siftings*, would observe geographically on another occasion, 'Mr Langtry has gone to Wales. That's right. Wales used to visit Mrs Langtry, hence the propriety of Mr Langtry visiting Wales. It is merely an exchange of family courtesies.' There was no testimony from the Prince or from Lillie. They had left the Red House in Bournemouth and were conveniently unavailable in Paris. A practised hand at trowelling foundation stones, the Prince had evaded any ceremonial association with the one visible at the Red House. It bore the date 1877 and 'E.L.L.' for Emilie Le Breton Langtry.

Just before Rosenberg was to be sentenced at the Old Bailey, he published a piece in *Punch* style, unrepentantly ('without spite or satire'), but without a hint of Mrs Langtry, on how the Prince of Wales spent a typical day. There was even some truth in it:

> At about half-past five in the morning he is awakened by a fanfare of trumpets outside his bedroom door … , and poor Alexandra says: 'Dear, it's a nuisance, but you must do your duty.' Then he arises, and having snatched a hasty repast from the remains of last night's supper (lentil soup, as a rule), he has to rush away to catch a train for some lucky country town that has codded him on to open an 'Asylum for Destitute Pigs,' or a 'Dogs' and Cats' Home,' or some other equally benevolent institution. Perhaps, on his journey, the train stops at fifteen or sixteen railway stations, and at each one he has to listen to the dreary twaddle of an address.… Having passed through this ordeal, he opens the Asylum, and having then done an ordinary man's

day's work, ... has to 'train' back to London only to rush off to the seaside to lay the foundation of a 'something' somewhere else. Here he has to go through the purgatory of a mock prayer-meeting, with a spice of mason's work, and a knowledge that he is 'the fun of the fair,' that he is the 'show'.... Then he has to lunch, and be toasted by Smith, Brown, Jones, and Robinson, who, because they keep the biggest shops in Muckville, are aldermen, and consequently entitled to bore our Prince with their ungrammatical effusions.

Then, *Town Talk* went on, he had a ship to christen, a bridge to open and an art gallery to give 'undeserved prestige'. All his travel and associated expenses, it claimed, were borne by the Prince 'ungrudgingly', although he could not afford it and his mother could. (Gladstone's Private Secretary, Edward Hamilton, in 1880 would estimate the Prince's deficit resulting from the 'retirement' of the Queen at an annual £10,000.) Despite the tiresome schedule imagined by *Town Talk*, the tireless Prince returns home,

> fresh as a lark, and, after snatching a hasty dinner, or perhaps a crust of bread and cheese, or a quarter of a pork pie and a glass of bitter at a railway refreshment bar, he has to go by train to meet some foreign potentate, whom he amuses until he is located in Buckingham Palace, and whom he has to get out of that place and take to Marlborough House, because his mother's gas bill and coal merchant's account must not be made too extensive, and his geniality and liberality have saved England from many a hard hit that might have appeared against Her Majesty in continental newspapers.

There still remains an exhibition to visit, a deputation of mayors to meet, a review to attend, his correspondence to go over with his Private Secretary, and to have a cup of tea and a biscuit. Then the Prince must dress for the opera or the theatre, for which his patronage redeems 'his mother's neglect of them'. Yet even that hardly suffices for the busy twenty-four hours, for

> It is not generally known ... that Albert Edward is an enthusiastic student of the Arabian Nights, and that, like Caliph Haroun al Raschid, he wanders abroad after his daily toil to see how his subjects are getting on, and to blow the effects of the Mayors' addresses off his mind. He adopts various disguises when on these missions and may

often be seen in an excellent make-up in different parts of the Metropolis, sometimes as a policeman in the Haymarket, at others as a life-guardsman in Petticoat Lane. Thus he sees phases of life among his subjects, and becomes intimately acquainted with the woes and grievances which his mamma so studiously avoids. Whether behind the scenes … or laughing gaily at a public race-meeting, he is always the same, a thorough hearty, jovial English gentleman, and though his high position connects his name with many scandals, he suffers that penalty of greatness with dignity.

That Lillie was not even hinted at was a sign that the Langtry relationship was waning. The Prince of Wales had too many ceremonial responsibilities where her presence was inappropriate, and she had too much ambition to be sequestered in Bournemouth. The Prince had no idea that she was also involved, when apart from him, with Arthur Jones, a childhood friend from Jersey who lacked the social cachet she wanted to maintain. Only in 1880 did he learn that yet another lover was secretly sharing her busy bed: Bertie's young cousin Louis of Battenberg. Too late to matter, she realized that the handsome, black-bearded, waxed-moustached Hessian Prince was too ambitious himself to make an inauspicious marriage.* And she could only marry again if divorced – the ultimate taboo in Victorian society. However, Lillie failed to recognize that, despite the openness of her liaison with the Prince of Wales, it could not last much longer.

Their break was signalled when, at a charity bazaar in the Albert Hall, she presided, as a society lady was expected to do, at a refreshment stall. To be served a cup of tea from her hands cost gentlemen five shillings. For an extra guinea – twenty-one more shillings – she would share the cup, taking the first sip, imparting an almost sexual thrill to her admirers. When the Prince and Princess of Wales came to the stall with their daughters, Lillie poured tea and, unasked, put her lips to the cup. Whatever she did in the intimacy of the Red House, the gesture was too presumptuous before Alix and the girls, and HRH reacted accordingly. He set the cup down untasted. 'I should like a clean one, please,' he said. Accepting another, the Prince took a perfunctory drink, set down some coins, and walked away.

---

* He was to marry a daughter of Princess Alice, Anglicize his name to Mountbatten, and become the great-grandfather of Elizabeth II's consort, Prince Philip, Duke of Edinburgh.

While preoccupied with Mrs Langtry it had still been necessary for him to produce Alix at public occasions, as when on 10 May 1879 the Prince and Princess of Wales were at the Royal Society for a demonstration of one of Alexander Graham Bell's telephone instruments. Publicly affectionate to Alix, he took her on the *Osborne* to Denmark in the autumn of 1879, forgoing his usual stay without her in Homburg, and the next year he hosted her brother, the King of the Hellenes, at Marlborough House. Sometimes with her, he had laid foundation stones, inaugurated exhibitions, visited hospitals and schools, and opened a museum. He attended the House of Lords nineteen times in 1879 alone, and even spoke once (for three minutes) in favour of a bill to legalize marriage with a deceased wife's sister, which was opposed by the clergy, and defeated. And with Alix he drove in a press-covered procession of carriages over Lambeth, Vauxhall, Chelsea, the Albert and Battersea bridges, pausing at each to declare the spans free of tolls in perpetuity.

Remaining publicly visible, in May 1880 he spoke at the Royal Academy dinner, and delighted a first-time guest, the new American consul in Glasgow, once-popular frontier writer Bret Harte, by asking to be introduced to him. ('He's more like an American than an Englishman,' Harte wrote excitedly to a friend in Boston.) And when Disraeli's Tories were defeated by the Liberals in April 1880, the Prince first urged his mother to send for Lord Hartington (who was 'the most moderate' alternative) rather than the more extreme Gladstone. When Gladstone insisted on returning to office, Harty Tarty loyally withdrew, leaving Bertie to write to Ponsonby, as conduit to the Queen, that Hartington was now 'anxious' to have Gladstone form a government, which would be 'more moderate ... than one Hartington would have to constitute'. (A realist, the Prince was courting the Liberals to gain some influence.)

The Queen had no way of resisting the pressure to recommend the party choice, but sent a note to Ponsonby, intended for her son, that he had '*no* right to meddle', and that Hartington was to be warned that the Queen would not allow any 'private and intimate [political] communication' between the new ministers and the Prince of Wales, 'or all confidence will be *impossible*'. Yet she wrote to 'Dearest Bertie' to ask his help in keeping 'thinly-veiled *Republicans*' out of 'this dreadful Radical Government'. The Prince invited the Gladstones to dinner at Marlborough House, a useful setting for informal political talk, and

Edward Hamilton, the Prime Minister's secretary, noted in his diary approvingly that the Prince of Wales 'always does the right thing'.

Victoria detested her son's friends, old or new, and when he asked in the same week to be able to stay at Windsor with his circle during the Ascot races (as she would be away), she made that impossible by insisting that she approve his list of guests. One, formerly an outspoken Republican, Sir Charles Dilke (who ten years earlier had attacked the Prince), was now even welcome at Marlborough House, and on occasion was a political informant. Despite his mother's hostility, the Prince would support Dilke later for a Cabinet post, and his friendships with the other once-hostile Radicals would make him useful as an intermediary to gain access to a political sector Victoria would not recognize.

Dabbling in politics and foreign affairs was the only way the future king could wait out his turn. It embittered him that he had no formal role, and that his youngest brother Leopold (to be Duke of Albany in 1881) did, having become a confidential secretary to his mother and possessor of a prized golden key to the Cabinet red boxes. Displaying it proudly to James Bodley, Dilke's Private Secretary, Leopold crowed, 'It is the Queen's Cabinet key which opens all the secret despatch boxes. Dizzy gave it to me, but my brother the Prince of Wales is not allowed to have one.' Later, *New York Times* London correspondent George W. Smalley wrote that he 'believe[d] it to be ... true that after the death of the Prince Consort, in 1861, the Queen desired the Prince of Wales to take up some portion of the duties of his father, and offered him a place as her private secretary. The Prince, for whatever reason, declined it.' It was not true, but Smalley must have acquired the story from the Prince, whom he knew, or from his circle. At twenty, Smalley guessed, the Prince's 'strong *joie de vivre*' prevailed over duty. 'Some years later,' he continued, 'a truer sense of his position and duties and opportunities came to him. He offered to accept, and besought the Queen's permission.... Her Majesty made answer that the post had been filled, and never from that time onward did she open to the Prince of Wales the door she then closed.'

This story of a plea for a second chance was no more true than the first, but the post had indeed been filled from within the family when Prince Leopold came of age. Only rarely did Albert Edward evince his jealousy, as when, during the imbroglio over the succession to Disraeli, he had switched to the Hartington line. At the Prince's instructions, his secretary wrote a message to Lord Granville intended to reach Victoria, 'The

Prince of Wales feels sure that if the Queen would only look upon Mr Gladstone as a friend instead of as the enemy of Her Majesty and the Royal Family, which Prince Leopold deliberately delights in persuading her he is, she will find him all she could wish.' At the time the Prince of Wales was urging on Gladstone baronetcies for four men with little claim to such honours, and Edward Hamilton noted in his diary on 11 April 1881, 'It is perhaps hardly fair to say so, but these recommendations have rather an ugly look about them.' A clergyman from Nuneaton had already alleged to the Prime Minister that a gentleman was offered a baronetcy by 'an emissary of the Prince of Wales ... on condition that he would pay the sum of £30,000 to the Prince's agent on receiving the title.' The Prince's debts were burgeoning, and his pleas for unworthy candidates genuine, but the charge that he was trying to sell influence remains unproven. Investors with £30,000 to risk would surely have realized that he had no such clout in Court or Cabinet.

The Prince of Wales was seldom called upon by the Queen other than on family business, as eldest son. (Leopold was twelve years Bertie's junior.) When his sister Alice succumbed to diphtheria in Hesse on 14 December 1878, the seventeenth anniversary of her father's death, the Prince of Wales represented the Queen at the funeral in Darmstadt. Yet even then, Leopold, despite the threat of haemophiliac relapses, accompanied him. Bertie did not blame his brother for usurping a role rightfully his: he knew that the Queen considered her heir unreliable and indiscreet. He had also tried to prevent the betrothal of his sister Louise to the Marquis of Lorne, heir to the Duke of Argyll, preferring a minor European Royal to an English subject. That intervention had failed, and Louise married the closet homosexual Lorne, who was offered by Victoria the governor-general's post in Canada. Accepting the situation, the Prince of Wales wrote an affectionate farewell letter to Louise before they sailed, forecasting that she and Lorne had 'a great future' before them. They did not, and lived mostly apart, and childless, after the Canadian years.

The major 'family' event in which the Queen leaned upon her heir was only 'family' in a premature and conditional sense. Victoria had not allowed the devastating loss of Alice, or the problematic marriage of Louise, to impede the marriage of her third son, Arthur, to a minor Prussian princess, or even to postpone her holiday to Lake Maggiore. But tragedy on an immense scale occurred when the Queen apparently conspired with former Empress Eugénie to link their families through the

Prince Imperial and the Queen's youngest daughter, Beatrice. Few, even among Victoria's intimates, realized how important Prince Louis Napoleon was to her. Of her own four sons, only Arthur, Duke of Connaught, a career officer in the Army and named after the Duke of Wellington, was not a disappointment. Bertie was unreliable, Affie was dissolute, Leopold was a chronic invalid. The Prince Imperial was almost the son she never had, and indeed almost a son-in-law. Victoria and the ex-Empress of France seemed discreetly interested in a match between 'Baby' and Louis, despite the religious barrier. After all, Alfred had married Marie of Russia in Orthodox ceremonies.

Louis Napoleon had trained in the British Army and in 1879, at twenty-three, sought to acquire a reputation in it that would give him some cachet in England. He lobbied to go to South Africa to serve in the Zulu wars. Disraeli was opposed on political grounds – it might offend the French Republican government. With the connivance of the Army chief, the Queen's cousin the Duke of Cambridge, the matter was arranged anyway by the two mothers. 'I am quite mystified about that little abortion, the Prince Imperial,' Disraeli wrote with exasperation to his Foreign Minister, Lord Salisbury, on 28 February 1879. It was too late. Although the Prince went technically only as an observer, his unit was ambushed and he was killed by Zulu assegais. 'But what can you do', Disraeli said when he heard the news on the afternoon of 19 June, 'when you have to deal with two obstinate women?'

Louis Napoleon's remains arrived in England three weeks after the catastrophe. Although the Queen could not by custom go to the funeral itself she went to Chislehurst on 17 July. In the rain she took a carriage with Beatrice to pay her respects in St Mary's church, at the side of the magnificent casket into which the hideously ravaged body had been conveyed. All the Queen's sons were pallbearers. The obsequies were conducted in their presence, and that of the Princess of Wales and Princess Beatrice, by the Roman Catholic Bishop of Southwark. Such royal regard for Catholicism was unprecedented. Beatrice remained kneeling so long that a priest gently asked her to rise. The Queen had also been present when the body was removed from Eugénie's residence, Camden House, to the church several days earlier, as had the Prince of Wales, after which he had written to his mother, 'One has at any rate the satisfaction of feeling that everything that could be done to pay all honour and respect to the poor young Prince who met with such a horrible and untimely death was done. The arrangements seemed to me in every respect admirable.' There were a few things accomplished by the Prince of Wales which even his mother felt were admirable. But they were little more than ceremonial.

Occasional exasperation aside, Bertie genuinely liked his frail youngest brother, who was often in his company. Leopold, who loved the theatre, was even given prized access to Sarah Bernhardt in her dressing room at the Gaiety when she starred in *Froufrou* and *La dame aux camélias*, and was privileged to have an hour with Lillie Langtry – 'who was looking as lovely as ever', he wrote in his diary. More significantly – she must have accepted him as a channel to his brother – Lillie told him sadly of the death of her own brother, mauled by a tiger in India, and she 'recounted the whole Shrewsbury & Battenberg affairs to me, & I gave her some advice'.

The young Lord Shrewsbury,* a callow boy of nineteen, had been entrusted to Lillie by his worldly mother, Theresa, one of the leading London hostesses, to be introduced to the facts of life. How thorough Mrs Langtry's instruction was remains unknown. Unfortunately a note she had sent to the Prince of Wales requesting that he put off an afternoon call did not reach him in time. In a *Candida*-like scene he found her with young Charles. According to Wilfrid Scawen Blunt, who got the story from the encyclopaedic Skittles, HRH was 'very miffed'.

Leopold was one of the first to learn, in July 1881, of Lillie's assigning her unwelcome pregnancy to Louis Battenberg – which may have relieved the Prince of Wales on two counts. He was not identified as the father (the child was probably not his, anyway), and he would have an excuse to loosen the Langtry bonds, which had become increasingly inconvenient. Yet she had to be taken care of, and her public respectability preserved. Abortion was illegal as well as hazardous. Prince Louis was also told of her condition, as was Arthur Jones, who hoped the child was his. Battenberg was warned by his parents in Hesse that marriage to a divorced commoner – and there was as yet no divorce – would put an end to his ambitions, and arranged for a quiet financial settlement. Louis slipped out of England on 18 October 1880 on a long cruise on the appropriately named HMS *Inconstant*. There was barely time for Mrs Langtry to divest herself of her London property before her husband, out

---

* Charles Henry John, 20th Earl of Shrewsbury (1860–1921).

of the way in America, and near bankruptcy, returned. As long as she remained in the public eye she had to conceal an inevitably thickening waistline through corset laces. Her town residence at 17 Norfolk Street was sold, with its contents, but she kept the house in Bournemouth. When she could no longer appear safely she returned temporarily to the care of her mother in a rented cottage in Jersey. On 6 November 1880, the *New York Times* reported cryptically, 'Mr and Mrs Langtry have given up their London residence, and for the present Mrs Langtry remains in Jersey. Is beauty deposed, or has beauty abdicated?'

The Prince of Wales – the details remain concealed – seems to have arranged for a further haven in France with one of his friends, possibly the princesse de Sagan, who had a Paris home and three châteaux. He happened to be in Paris, returning from the wedding of his insufferable nephew, Vicky's son Willie, in Berlin, when Lillie's daughter was born on 8 March 1881. She was named Jeanne-Marie, perhaps after Jeanne-Marguerite de Sagan, and would be told (it was a common fiction) that her mother was actually her aunt. Lillie was to see little of the Prince thereafter. Although he remained supportive, he had moved on to new priapic interests. Curiously, he was still transfixed by Sarah Bernhardt, and arranged for Ferdinand de Rothschild to host a midnight supper party for the actress on 1 July 1881, at his Piccadilly mansion, after one of her performances, so that the duc d'Aumale, the elderly fourth son of the ill-fated King Louis-Philippe, could meet her. Often, now, the Prince used the good offices of the Rothschilds, or his new friends the Sassoons, to accomplish things for him that he could no longer do directly. The openness of the fading Langtry affair had damaged him. One of the indicators of his changing direction, at least for the moment, was that when he bought a new racing yacht despite his depleted finances, he named it *Aline*, after a daughter of baron Gustave de Rothschild of Paris. It suggested both a new group of friends and a new source of borrowed money.

While Proust's snobbish prince de Guermantes in *À la Recherche* will not even receive a Rothschild, and would rather let a wing of his prized château burn than ask for water pumps from a nearby Rothschild house, Albert Edward spurned inherited prejudices and enjoyed himself at Rothschild gatherings. He attended the marriage of the Earl of Rosebery with Hannah Rothschild in March 1878 (along with the Duke of Cambridge), and on 14 January 1881, despite a snowstorm, he attended the Central Synagogue in Great Portland Street for the wedding of

Leopold de Rothschild with the elegant and shy Marie Perugia of Trieste, a sister of the wife of Arthur Sassoon, another of the Prince's Jewish friends. The Prince even stood opposite the Ark with the wedding party, and signed the register as witness along with baron Alphonse de Rothschild. At the wedding breakfast at the home of Albert Sassoon, brother-in-law of the bride, at 2 Albert Gate, the Prince offered the toast 'to the health of the bride and bridegroom'. And after the wedding cake was cut and sent round, and the former Prime Minister, Lord Beaconsfield, toasted the Prince of Wales, HRH returned his thanks, recalling his long acquaintance with the Rothschilds and his personal regard for them. He understood that in the new world resisted by his mother there were royal families other than their own.

After the funeral of the Earl of Beaconsfield on 28 April 1881, where Alfred de Rothschild had assisted in closing Disraeli's coffin, Prince Leopold, to Bertie's chagrin, represented his mother. However, all three of Victoria's sons then in England – the Prince of Wales and Prince Arthur, as well as Leopold – led the mourners. Then Bertie went, without Alix, to the wedding of Crown Prince Rudolf with Princess Stephanie of Belgium – and stayed in a Vienna hotel to evade difficulties from the persistently anti-Semitic Hapsburgs. Despite them, he intended to accept the hospitality of the Austrian branch of the Rothschilds. Before he returned to Marlborough House on 23 May, he spent a week *en garçon* in Paris. Without Lillie Langtry awaiting him in England, he was ready again for the mixture as before.

In London he could not help but encounter Lillie socially, for he could not acknowledge publicly that their intimacy had ended. He had wanted to be introduced to Oscar Wilde, who happened to be a passionate if platonic admirer of the Jersey Lily, and when asked why, the Prince modestly fashioned an Oscarish epigram: 'I do not know Mr Wilde, and not to know Mr Wilde is not to be known.' On 4 June 1881 he met Wilde at a thought-reading séance, at the house in Tite Street shared by Wilde and Frank Miles. Among the company was Lillie Langtry.

On 9 November 1881 the Prince of Wales was forty. The editor of *Town Talk*, unrepentant after eighteen months in prison for a Langtry libel which he knew was fact, wished the Prince 'very many happy returns of the day'. With unconcealed irony, *Town Talk* hoped that his days as 'a gay young man of pleasure' were behind him, and took 'for granted that the Prince [now] takes an interest in technical education and the opening of new docks'. Adolphus Rosenberg also hoped that HRH would discard the 'noble gentlemen known to be the Prince's closest friends', and take counsel 'with the wise men of the nation'. Let him show, the column concluded, 'that he has some of the grand and lofty ideas that distinguished his noble father, and that he is inspired by those feelings which in rulers help to make a country great and its people prosperous'.

Little that the Prince was seen as doing in his forty-first year augured such a metamorphosis, and it was obvious that if his mother, the Queen, could have moved her youngest sons, Arthur and Leopold, up in the succession, she would have. The year closed with the Prince of Wales's attendance of a matinee at the Haymarket on 20 December in which Mrs Langtry appeared as Kate Hardcastle in Goldsmith's *She Stoops to Conquer*. Stooping to the commercial stage to exploit her notoriety, Lillie was making a new career. Even Gladstone would seek out the tempting Mrs Langtry, visiting her three times while endeavouring to 'rescue' her from sin. Risking his reputation, the Prime Minister still slipped out on night walks to intercept prostitutes, offering them Bibles and money in their rooms, and relieving his excited state in his usual fashion on returning. (Often he put a tiny symbol of a whip in his diary afterwards.) He encouraged Lillie, she later recalled, to employ a two-envelope subterfuge to keep his secretaries from opening her letters to him, should she want to arrange further moral counsel. 'I hardly know what estimate to form of her,' he would write enigmatically in his diary. 'Her manners are very pleasing & she has a working spirit in her.'

'It was her début,' the Prince wrote blandly to his younger son, George, after her premiere, 'and a great success. As she is so very fond of acting, she has decided to go on the stage and will, after Christmas, join Mr and Mrs Bancroft's company.' It was in character for Lillie Langtry to begin at the top. In some ways the Prince was also beginning again. Liberated from Lillie and more circumspect about his private life, he aspired to be kingly. But that required at least a semblance of kingly occupation.

XII

The Occupation of the Idle Man

1882–1886

THINKING THAT THERE would be 'some appropriateness' in the gesture, Thomas Hardy posted an inscribed copy of his Napoleonic wars novel *The Trumpet Major* to the Prince of Wales. Since HRH was neither a Wellington nor a Napoleon, and not likely to be, the fact that it would prove to be one of Hardy's lesser works was as close as the symbolism would get. The Prince was far more interested in an ongoing war, hoping that he might play a conspicuous role in it. European greed for territory surfaced at its most cynical in Africa. Colonial rivalries arose among otherwise friendly nations, and nowhere more than in Egypt, where the post-Ismail instability had made strained partners of Britain and France. Through the century, Egypt had been a colonial dependency of Turkey, of Napoleonic France, and now, it seemed, of England.

French and British interests had been colliding in the Mediterranean after Disraeli's acquisition of Cyprus from Turkey in 1878. During the brief period in power of French statesman Léon Gambetta, he and the Prince of Wales became close. The Prince easily communicated a love for France, and – since they agreed on many things – Gambetta saw the makings of a great statesman in the future king. It was, he told a friend, 'no waste of time' to talk over affairs with the Prince, 'even over a merry supper at the Café Anglais'. (They even discussed the potential of a Channel tunnel.) If all princes were like him, Gambetta confided, there would be no Republicanism in Europe.

Republicanism was already fading in Britain despite the attractions of Socialism, as evidenced by Oscar Wilde's explaining to a lecture audience that he was 'a thorough republican' because no other form of government was so responsive to Art. 'Of course,' he backtracked, 'I couldn't talk democratic principles to my friend the Prince of Wales. That you understand is simply a matter of social tact.' It was also a matter of the pervasive snobbery that undermined English Republicanism and seemed to make the Prince of Wales essential.

Unfortunately for the *entente cordiale*, the down-to-earth Gambetta was unseated as Prime Minister early in 1882, just as the rise of the militant Egyptian nationalist Arabi Pasha was creating new tensions between France and Britain over Egypt and the Sudan. Africa had replaced Asia as the Prince's new interest, and his imperialist views strained his relations with Gladstone, who wanted to withdraw from empire-building. With the Queen and the Cabinet on opposite sides, the Prince and the Queen found themselves in rare agreement. Influence in the world, they believed, came from possessions and the ability to exploit them. To Gladstone, only moral and spiritual power counted, and foreign possessions were the plague of budgets. A later entry in Victoria's journal reflected her impatience with the unambitious Government that had replaced her adored Disraeli. 'It is to me inconceivable', she fumed, 'that a handful of men sitting in a room in London, the greater part knowing little about Egypt, should pretend to say whether there is danger or not.'

On 14 August 1882, an embodiment of the colonial dilemma called on the Queen at Osborne House. Cetewayo, king of the Zulus, whose warriors had ambushed young Louis Napoleon, had been captured after the defeat of his primitively equipped army, and brought to England to be impressed by British might. Once his docility was assured, Gladstone wanted to restore him as chieftain in unruly Zululand. Wearing what Victoria described as 'a hideous black frock coat and trousers' over a colourful native tunic, Cetewayo arrived with two native generals and spoke with the Queen through a Colonial Office interpreter. 'I said,' she recorded, 'through Mr [Henrique] Shepstone, that I was glad to see him here, and that I recognised in him a great warrior, who had fought against us, but rejoiced we were now friends.' Cetewayo also visited Gladstone at Downing Street, and called at Marlborough House on the Prince of Wales, who was away. 'After [Cetewayo] had been made known to the young princes and princesses,' Gladstone's secretary, Edward Hamilton, noted in his diary, 'he asked where was the Princess of Wales. He declined to believe that the lovely young woman he saw before him was the mother of such tall children.'

By that time, Egypt had replaced southern Africa as flashpoint, and Cetewayo could be an exotic celebrity. In Egypt, exploiting discontent over the Khedive's heavy foreign debts and high taxes to lead a coup, Ahmed Arabi had ceased payments to European bondholders, mainly French and English bankers. In Alexandria, Europeans were killed in riots, and Arabi mounted cannons at harbour approaches to intimidate foreign intervention. However hurt, France hesitated to become involved in what was seen as a nationalist convulsion. Egypt was legally a subject territory of the Sultan of Turkey, but with British interests to protect – and Christians 'murdered with impunity', the Queen reminded the devout Gladstone – the Government determined, reluctantly, to eliminate Arabi. Although the European powers failed to provide an umbrella of legitimacy, Parliament voted credits to finance intervention, despite Cabinet worries of a rise of a penny in the pound to the income tax.

The prospect of a quick and exotic war proved unexpectedly popular. Very likely echoing old Gladstone, Edward Hamilton deplored the 'bad taste' of gentlemen in minor government posts who sought leave in order to volunteer. The Prince of Wales himself offered his services – a dilemma for the Government. Craving a real role, and seeing it as emerging only from foreign affairs, in which he had hands-on expertise, HRH was serious about Egypt, which he had already visited four times (including on his way to and from India). Although he had just been made, at his insistence, Colonel-in-Chief of the Brigade of Household Cavalry, the possibility that the portly and unmilitary heir to the throne, now forty-one, might risk himself in a war horrified the Queen.

The Prime Minister had other causes for concern about Bertie. Hamilton noted in his diary on 27 July 1882, 'The Prince of Wales has volunteered to go out. Ponsonby telegraphed [for the Queen] this morning to Mr G. to know what his views were. Mr G. naturally and properly threw cold water upon the proposal.... He said it was contrary to precedent ... and that, while the Prince's patriotic feeling would be much appreciated by the country, the objections far outweighed the advantages.'

The Prince had already enlisted the predictable familial support of the Duke of Cambridge, still stubbornly and ineffectively in charge of the Army, and also claimed that of the commanding general in Egypt, Sir

Garnet Wolseley, but this time Gladstone and the Queen were in rare agreement. Frustrated, the Prince declared that he would go anyway, with all his equerries – as if he were fielding his private little army. If that gesture were refused, he threatened to resign his commission as a field marshal and go as a volunteer. Wolseley and his staff, the Queen telegraphed Gladstone, 'earnestly hope H.R.H. will not go'. Yet Wolseley had already permitted the Duke of Teck, Cambridge's useless German brother-in-law, to be attached to his staff. 'It really savours', Hamilton complained, 'of turning a very serious business into a joke.'

Ponsonby communicated Victoria's veto in his most courtly language, observing to the Prince that the Queen hoped that the 'gallant offer' would become generally known. The next day (31 July) Lord Granville repeated the consolatory adjective in representing the Cabinet's views to the Prince of Wales. More subtle was the Foreign Minister's qualifying *almost*:

> Her Majesty, I may almost say, fully agreed with Your Royal Highness's desires to be of use, warmly appreciated the gallant wish to see service, and was proud that the Prince of Wales should not shrink from sharing the dangers and privations of her troops.
>
> But on the other hand, the imperative demands of public duty compelled Her Majesty to point out the grave difficulties, and inconvenience, of such a proceeding; and ... the Queen finally and conclusively decided that it was necessary to ask Your Royal Highness to abandon the idea.

That evening the disappointed Prince hosted a farewell dinner at the Marlborough Club for twenty-three officers of the Household Cavalry. He had hoped to sail to glory with them. Instead, the royal family was represented in Egypt by his brother the Duke of Connaught. At thirty-two a legitimate if very young major-general, Prince Arthur would be on the field at Tel-el-Kebir on 13 September, when – in forty minutes of butchery – the motley and ill-equipped army of Arabi Pasha was smashed. The British suffered eighty casualties, the Egyptians 10,000. The Queen telegraphed her pride to Wolseley that Arthur was 'worthy of his own dear father' and of the 'great godfather' whose name he bore, the Duke of Wellington. Shut out of glory, Bertie was unmentioned.

When the troops returned to parades and awards in Hyde Park, the Prince of Wales was off on more suitable undertakings. The first

Napoleon had observed that women were the occupation of idle men and the relaxation of the warrior. *Punch* pictured him (26 August 1882) in yachtsman's cap and jacket, and clenching a huge cigar, crossing the Channel to take 'a well-earned holiday'. HRH retreated to fashionable spas like Homburg, where the three or four streets off the baths and the tennis courts – gambling had been banned since 1869 – were rendezvous sites, as were the nearby woods. 'When you had once seen His Royal Highness,' American correspondent George Smalley wrote, 'leaning against the railings of a villa ... and talking to a lady leaning out of the first-floor window, and this interview lasting a quarter of an hour, you felt that the conditions of life and the relations of royalty to other ranks of life had taken on a quite new shape in Homburg.' Among the other changes were the new lawn tennis courts. The Prince had taken up the game as part of an exercise and weight-loss regime. Homburg relied on the Prince's stays for its cachet, and Cannes, where HRH also holidayed regularly, added lawn tennis to its attractions. Unsurprisingly, as tennis took physical effort, he quickly lost interest. While the sport gained in prestige, the undisciplined Prince gained weight.

Although he insisted on his dignity as 'Sir' or 'Your Royal Highness', even when registered under a transparent lesser title, denizens of Homburg were at their ease with him, and enjoyed overhearing such badinage as passed between him and his good friend the Marquis of Hartington, who drank none of the salubrious but foul-smelling local waters:

> 'Hartington, you ought not to be drinking all that champagne.'
> 'No, Sir; I know I oughtn't.'
> 'Then why do you do it?'
> 'Well, Sir, I have made up my mind that I had rather be ill now and then, than always taking care of myself.'
> 'Oh, you think that now, but when the gout comes what do you think then?'
> 'Sir, if you will ask me then I will tell you. I do not anticipate.'

Everyone laughed, and the Prince turned his roving eye toward newcomers among the ladies. One in the earlier 1880s was a pretty Ohioan, a Miss Jane Chamberlain from Cleveland, whom Alix referred to irritably as 'Chamberpots'. Whatever the Princess's exasperation, he saw to it that Jennie Chamberlain was a guest in drawing rooms and at dinner tables at which Americans of any social quality were rare. In her country, where one's antecedents meant little, distinction was directly related to dollars. Her grandfather, Selah Chamberlain, had been chief stockholder in the Cleveland, Lorain and Wheeling Railroad, a major carrier of iron and steel. As in many families with new money and awakened social aspirations, Chamberlain's son William Selah, on inheriting a third of his father's ten millions when a single million was a fortune, relocated to London. There, Jennie, only eighteen, and her sister Josephine, could shop for titled husbands. A flirtation with the Prince of Wales would only add to her desirability. Seeing only the worst in such types, Henry James would write in his notebooks about his interest in writing another 'international' tale in the manner of his *Daisy Miller* about 'An American girl, very pretty but of a very light substance, easily depraved, [who] marries a young Englishman and lives in the smart, dissipated set, the P[rince] of W[ales]'s, etc, in London. She is frivolous *outre mesure.*'

'Mr G.', the Prime Minister's secretary reported in his diary on 30 June 1884, 'met the notable American lady – Miss Chamberlain – at the [Robert Charles de Grey] Vyners yesterday.* He was struck by Gladstone's naiveté. No one is so easily taken in as he is.' However young and unsophisticated, the lady was no innocent abroad. On 25 July Edward Hamilton observed the royal infatuation for himself. 'After dinner went to a party at Mrs [Samuel Charles] Allsopp's,** where the Prince of Wales had been dining. As usual, he occupied himself entirely with Miss Chamberlain. Tonight is the concluding one of the season, and I am not sorry it has come to an end.'

Hamilton's exasperation with pushy Americans was long-standing. One who remained more discreetly in the Prince's orbit for years was Mary Morton Hartpence Sands, the young second wife of New York socialite and millionaire Mahlon Sands. Her privately circulated portrait photograph was in the Prince's possession as early as November 1874, when she was twenty-one and new in London. She would become a regular at Regatta Week at Cowes, and Racing Week at Epsom, and by the early 1880s was compared in loveliness with Jennie Churchill,

---

* Mrs Vyner, known as the Queen of the English colony on the Riviera, also had a villa at Cannes.
** Allsopp became Lord Hindlip in 1887.

Lillie Langtry, Patsy Cornwallis-West, and Hélène Standish. The Prince asserted that he liked American women 'because they are original and bring a little fresh air into Society. They are livelier, better educated and less hampered by etiquette.' Mrs Mahlon Sands, as she was known, became a close friend. How close is unknown. The Prince had few platonic female friends, one of them Jennie Churchill, to whom he had been attentive but without apparent success. Mary Sands may have been another, although her husband, Mahlon Sands, was elderly and interested only in yachting and rounds of country-house visits from their usual base at Claridge's Hotel.

Long before, with seeming inverted snobbery, Henry Adams had carped at the Prince's interest in American women, who were pretty, wealthy, sometimes married, and lively additions to his society. Pointing in curmudgeonly fashion to unfounded gossip about them, Adams had written to his English friend Charles Gaskell, 'I could wish that the Prince of Wales would patronize a rather more respectable set of society. He is imitating Napoleon III whose court was overrun by Americans but who never had a respectable American associate.' The charge was close to the mark when lodged against the late emperor, but few of the Prince's American friends fitted the description.

Mary Sands often occupied the Rothschilds' box at Ascot, perhaps a recognition of her husband's bank account. Rothschild guests were often interchangeable with the Prince's invitees. As 'Uncle Sam Ward', the American expatriate banker who seemed to know everyone who mattered, wrote to his friend Sidney Webster in June 1883, 'The Royal enclosure was like a ball room with the roof off. Crowds of pretty women and royalty arrived in scarlet state. The Prince was everywhere.... He was busy with his betting book, busy with the Old Ladies, and a little more so with the young ones.... What with old acquaintances I did not recognize and who rushed up to thank me for hospitalities I had forgotten, and with new ones male and female, I passed four very exhausting hours on my feet. Nor was the fatigue diminished by the cordial shake of the Prince of Wales' hand as, not having the King's evil,* the royal touch did not revive me.'

The Prince took it as his seignorial right to flirt with any woman, even

---

* From the time of Edward the Confessor to the reign of Queen Anne, the royal laying-on of hands was considered a cure for scrofula – 'the King's evil'.

some so removed from feudal privilege as Americans, who were flattered by the admiration of the First Gentleman of England. He was, *Town Talk* chaffed, 'a connoisseur of female beauty. His opinion on the subject, like Ruskin's on a picture, is beyond question, cavil, or dispute. The cultivation of this branch of the Fine Arts has led to the Prince's being judged by inartistic mortals, who cannot conceive a study of the most delightful of Nature's products, inspired by purely artistic ends. Hence the scandals of which some people are never tired of inventing about the Prince.' Earlier it had observed, 'Women especially condemn him, and the same women who condemn him would welcome his attentions most gladly.' For his own countrymen, attentions paid to their wives might (only rarely did it happen) lead to some preferment unobtainable by such open means as contributing to party funds.

According to *Town Talk*, hardly authoritative in this case, the Prince dined at the home of an ambitious gentleman who had a beautiful wife, and who proceeded to fall soundly asleep after dinner. The Prince took advantage of the opportunity 'to show marked attentions to the wife of his host'. Exploiting the distractions of his master and mistress, a servant attempted to pilfer a bottle of fine wine – but the host, who had only feigned a post-prandial nap, exploded angrily, 'You infernal scoundrel! Do you suppose I go to sleep for the benefit of everybody?' Apocryphal as the story very likely was, it was an index to HRH's notoriety. There were many attractive English matrons (abetted by complaisant husbands), who thought that the caresses of a portly, bearded, balding prince of the blood, who looked older than his forty-odd years and smelled of strong cigars and Dewar's whisky, were – whatever the dubious benefits to an uncaring spouse – worth a bit of discreet adultery. After all, the Prince of Wales would be king.

In 1883–4 Zola's *Nana* was being serialized in *Town Talk*, which – since the actress-chasing Royal was identified as the 'Prince of Scots' – furnished readers openly with another facet of the Prince's womanizing reputation. Should the Prince of Wales ever go in for authorship, the *Town Talk*'s editor suggested audaciously, 'I hope he will give us his theatrical experiences. *Behind the Scenes. Glimpses of the Green Room*, would not be a bad title.' Had HRH done so, Lillie Langtry would have merited a chapter or more. In the United States, where she had taken her acting charms and her celebrity on tour, the outspoken press linked her fame to her former dalliance with the Prince of Wales. A story long current in

England described Lillie, at a house party where most guests had drunk more than enough, as putting ice down the back of the surprised Prince's neck. In the US a cartoon of the incident would appear in a magazine. More sombre was an American cartoon showing Lillie walking demurely across a stage, while the gross shadow she casts on the curtain is unmistakably that of the Prince of Wales, sceptre in hand.

Another issue of the taunting *Town Talk*, after quoting press innuendo about the Prince as 'susceptible to feminine charms', challenged, ostensibly in his defence, 'Point me out one woman who can say, "This man has wronged me."' None ever did. It was a safe, if daring, contention, for there were ladies in the Prince's life with children who may have been his. In a rare contemporary novel that mentioned the Prince, Anthony Trollope's *Marion Fay* (1882), Lady Amaldina and her lover, Lord Llwddythlw, talk of marriage and children, and note that the Prince of Wales 'had declared that he had hoped to be asked to be godfather long ago'. Being godfather sometimes signified more, as perhaps with another professional beauty beloved of photographers, Mary ('Patsy') Cornwallis-West, of Ruthin Castle, Wales, and 49 Eaton Place, London. Daughter of an Irish marquis and wife of William Cornwallis-West, honorary colonel of the First Volunteer Battalion, Royal Welsh Fusiliers, she was charged by *Town Talk* with co-operating with photo portraitists to such an extent that she had a studio and darkroom in her home near Belgrave Square, and made thousands yearly in commissions on sales. The Colonel sued for libel. Although Cornwallis-West won his slander suit it did not save himself or his wife from rumours of complicity with the Prince of Wales. When the small daughter of a labourer on the estate of the Duke of Westminster told her father that she had seen the Prince of Wales 'lying on top of' Mrs Cornwallis-West in the woods, she was struck 'a violent blow and told she'd be killed if she repeated the story'.

The Prince was godfather to Patsy's son George, born in 1874. 'The Prince of Wales often came,' George Cornwallis-West recalled, 'and was invariably kind to me and asked to see me. Never a Christmas passed without his sending me some little gift in the shape of a card or a toy.' Later the Prince would watch over his godson's military career and intervene to promote it.

Society beauties came and went, and sometimes returned, to the Prince's amorous life. Another was mezzo-soprano and pianist Mabel

Batten. She possessed the plump curves in fashion in the 1880s, made much of in her portraits by Edward Poynter and John Singer Sargent. An added interest to HRH was that she had been born in Barrackpore and had the reputation of being 'fast' in the amoral Anglo-Indian colony in Simla, where the Prince may have met her on his tour. (She had been married there at nineteen in 1875.) Soon after, she had affairs with Indian Viceroy Lord Lytton (she was the wife of his Private Secretary) and with scandal-mongering poet Wilfrid Blunt. Later the Prince would become godfather to her eldest grandchild, and he accepted, in 1901, the dedication to him of a song she had composed. Even when Mabel turned to lesbian partners in middle age (one of her lovers was *Well of Loneliness* novelist Radclyffe Hall) she would continue to display proudly her signed photo of HRH.

Having private fun about the Prince's proclivities, the Earl of Rosebery – who sometimes placed unprintable annotations in his books – circulated an essay among presumably discreet friends, 'Copulation – Ancient and Modern', which purported to be a joint lecture by Ferdinand de Rothschild (a lonely and neurotic widower) and the Prince of Wales, delivered at the Imperial Institute.

One of the ironies of the Prince's involvements with women, and their subsequent need on occasion for a discreet doctor, was that he importuned the Government to grant a knighthood to the physician who had served him when such problems arose since the days of the pathetic Susan Vane-Tempest. Gladstone's Private Secretary Edward Hamilton noted knowledgeably and unhappily in his diary (2 November 1882), 'In deference to the Prince of Wales, Oscar Clayton has been submitted for knighthood. It is to be hoped that no disagreeable stories will come out about him.'

After Gambetta, the Prince's long love-affair with France temporarily cooled. North Africa was not the sole reason. Anti-royalist agitation had arisen, and the Chamber of Deputies decreed the expulsion of all Bourbons and Bonapartes. With his friends gone from Paris, the Prince ostentatiously went instead to Berlin twice in 1883, and even tried to make friends with his surly nephew Willy, for whom he brought a Highland costume in Royal Stuart tartan. Willy had himself photographed in it, and even distributed prints to his friends – but scrawled on each an implicitly hostile line in English, 'I bide my time.' His Anglophobia, born out of frustration and spite, and encouraged by

Bismarck, was already pathological. Writing conspiratorially to Tsar Alexander III in 1884 about a family visit of his uncle to the Crown Princess, Willy's mother, he claimed,

> The visit of the Prince of Wales has yielded ... extraordinary fruit, which will continue to multiply under the hands of my mother and the Queen of England. But these English have accidentally forgotten that *I* exist! And I swear to You, my dear cousin, that anything I can do for You and Your country I will do, and I swear that I will keep my word! But only it will take a long time and will have to be done very slowly.

A year later, just before another visit from his uncle ('this unexpected apparition'), he would write to the Tsar that 'your brother-in-law' (their wives were sisters) had a 'false and intriguing nature' and might be expected 'to do a little political plotting behind the scenes with the ladies'. Some of the conspiring that Willy imagined had to do with the Bible-quoting General Charles ('Chinese'*) Gordon's expedition to the Sudan, where a militant mystic calling himself the Mahdi, or prophet, had raised a new nationalist rebellion. Gladstone would have preferred to see the British out of Egypt, and considered Gordon at least half-mad, but found himself forced by public opinion to send an army to rescue the troops beleaguered in Khartoum. 'May the Mahdi chuck them all into the Nile!' Prince Willy exploded to the Tsar.

As Lord Wolseley prepared his relief expedition, the Prince of Wales again pleaded for active service. On his recommendation, Wolseley had added the fearless Lord Charles Beresford to his staff as something of a sop to the Prince's disappointment. 'Indeed I wish it were possible that you, Sir, would take part,' Wolseley wrote diplomatically (on 28 August 1884) to the Prince. 'So many officers bearing famous names', Philip Magnus wrote, 'accompanied Lord Wolseley that Gladstone's disgruntled Radical followers denounced the expedition as a social stunt.' Recognizing his inability to control the campaign, Wolseley confessed to the Prince from Egypt that the venture was 'not one after my own heart as the General responsible ... , although I should have gloried in it if I held a subordinate command'. He imagined 'little [newspaper] boys

---

* For his exploits in the capture of Peking in 1860 and in command of a Chinese force during the Taiping Rebellion in 1863–4.

running along Pall Mall with great printed placards announcing the DEATH AND DEFEAT OF LORD WOLSELEY.'

Beresford distinguished himself as commander of the Nile naval brigade at Abu Klea, but little else went according to plan. The Prince of Wales, receiving Wolseley's letter, replied on 22 January 1885, 'Most sincerely do I trust that you will get safely to Khartoum … and find Gordon safe and sound.' But understanding that Gordon was an unpredictable eccentric, he added, 'But what will you do with him when he is released? And what will you do after occupying Khartoum? … I sincerely hope that we are not going to hurry away and leave the Sudan in the state you have found it. Not being a member of HM's Govt., I can give no opinion on the subject.'

He was at Cannes with the princesse de Sagan on 5 February 1885 for the annual 'Battle of Flowers', hardly an auspicious location or occasion in the circumstances, when news reached London that after a siege of eleven months, Khartoum had fallen to the Mahdi. Gordon was dead; the relief expedition had arrived two days after the catastrophe. The Queen fired off a furious telegram to Gladstone about too little and too late, and deliberately sent it uncoded so that anyone along the line could read it – a curious form of public rebuke. In music halls, performers sang a song in which the pious party initials for the Prime Minister, 'GOM' for Grand Old Man, were reversed into 'MOG' – for Murderer of Gordon. All the Prince could do was to return from Cannes for a memorial service at St Paul's, and to preside at a fund-raising dinner to initiate a foundation for the Gordon Boys' Homes. Before Henry Morton Stanley set out for the Sudan to search for Gordon's lieutenant, Emin Pasha, the Prince asked him to Sandringham. Later he encouraged Stanley by letter. In return, Stanley, on discovering a lake not yet named by Europeans, christened it the Albert Edward Nyanza.

The Gordon embarrassment strained already poor relations between the Queen and Gladstone. On both Imperial affairs and the question of home rule for Ireland, the two were at unresolvable odds. With the GOM's Liberals fracturing on what to do about Ireland, his stepping down had become inevitable, and several of his colleagues in a Government friendly now with the Prince asked him to intercede with Victoria to give him, on retirement, the coveted Order of the Garter. The Prince suggested that as she was happiest in the remoteness of Balmoral, he would approach her then. In September 1884 she went to Scotland,

and in November the Prince visited and found her, he told Lord Granville, 'unresponsive'. When Gladstone did relinquish his ministry she offered him an earldom. He called it 'generous' – and refused it.

Among the Prince's frustrations in the early 1880s was the failure of his eldest son to show any signs of being other than a public embarrassment. When Eddy and George had completed their two years' cruise on the *Bacchante*, the Prince took them to Downing Street to meet the Prime Minister. Edward Hamilton, who received them with Gladstone, diplomatically described them (20 August 1882) as 'much improved', and thought Eddy the 'most taking' (attractive) but Prince George 'the cleverer of the two'. Although George may have been the cleverer, he did not anticipate becoming king, and wanted a career in the Royal Navy. His elder brother needed the traditional exposure to university life, and a year later, after some urgent and ineffective cramming, he was sent to Cambridge. Though few newspapers were unkind about the hapless heir to the heir, *Punch* published a series of cartoons in November 1883 showing Prince Albert Victor sitting unhappily to dine with dons even more bored with him than he was with them ('a lively dinner party'), looking glassy-eyed at Chapel, playing cautiously at hockey ('oh don't hurt him!'), eating jam from a jar for breakfast, throwing stones at boats in the Cam, sleeping very soundly in a huge bed. He proved even more useless than his father had been as an apprentice Army officer. On his twenty-first birthday Eddy evinced no signs of future kingliness, and Victoria heard bluntly from the Duke of Cambridge, a ready defender of privilege, that Prince Eddy loved uniforms, but was 'an inveterate and incurable dawdler, never ready, never there'.

Loyally, Gladstone penned a congratulatory letter to Eddy on reaching his majority, and his father was so pleased at Eddy's reply (any response whatever was beyond parental expectation) that he asked the Prime Minister's leave to release it to the press. 'On reading it over this afternoon,' Edward Hamilton confided to his diary on 14 January 1885, 'I found [that] part of it admitted to no possible grammatical construction; so I took it to Marlborough House and got the Prince of Wales to agree to my suggested alterations and then sent copies of it round to the papers.' Prince Albert Victor's letter as he had not written it appeared in *The Times* the next morning.

Only a heartbeat or two from the throne, Eddy was, the Queen worried, too 'languid', yet she hoped that he might grow into responsibility. Even

Bertie showed signs of maturity at forty-four. He had not only accomplished the trowelling of foundation stones and the ceremonial standing-in for her, but had conducted himself respectably on a Royal Commission. He had performed creditably if informally in foreign and domestic political negotiations, and as head of the family as senior male he had handled well the pathetic aftermath of the sudden death of his youngest brother. A haemophiliac, Leopold had lived on the edge. Victoria had made him Duke of Albany in 1881, when he was twenty-eight. At thirty, despite his physical fragility, he determined to marry. Princess Helen of Waldeck and Pyrmont, a German statelet of no consequence west of Kassel, was twenty and had no prospects, although an elder sister, Emma, had wed King Willem III of the Netherlands (who was sixty-four to her twenty-two). Leopold and Helen married at Windsor in April 1882, the Prince walking with a stick after his most recent episode of bleeding.

Despite its appetite for gossip, the press printed nothing about the Duke of Albany's chronic disability, although the medical fraternity had learned of it in *The Lancet*, which was available to any reader with access to a good library. Somehow, Leopold continued his secretarial work for the Queen, hoping that when Princess Louise's husband, Lord Lorne, completed his stint as Governor-General of Canada, he and Helen could replace them. The Government had already recommended someone else, but Leopold made sufficient fuss for *Reynolds's Newspaper* to pick up the story and describe him cruelly (and falsely) as a feeble-minded invalid who would not even be able to find Canada on a map. An authentic intellectual, Leopold was the only one of Prince Albert's four sons who inherited his abilities.

Early in 1884, Leopold went to Cannes alone to recuperate from several falls. Helen, with a baby daughter, was again expecting, and ordered not to travel. The Prince of Wales was promoting to the Queen the idea of offering Leopold the governorship of the Australian province of Victoria some time in 1885. At his hotel Leopold slipped on the tiled lobby floor, struck his knee on a stair, and haemorrhaged. The next morning, 25 March, he died – and the Prince of Wales, away placing his bets at the races at Aintree, was telegraphed. The Queen immediately sent her aides Sir John Cowell and Alick Yorke to Cannes, and the Prince followed after arranging the return and obsequies. They brought the body to Cherbourg by train and then by sea to Portsmouth. Interment was at the Chapel Royal, Windsor.

With Leopold's unexpected death leaving a gap in the Queen's secretariat, the Prince of Wales renewed his campaign to be entrusted with state papers. Gladstone intervened on the Prince's behalf after a complaint to Edward Hamilton that the heir, already forty-four, was still 'kept in the dark'. Checking with Francis Knollys, Hamilton learned that the Prince had earlier been conveyed sensitive Cabinet information by Disraeli without the knowledge of the Queen, who had specifically advised him to send only such dispatches 'as were not very confidential'. But the Queen, on Gladstone's entreaty to be permitted to 'tell His Royal Highness anything of importance that takes place in the Cabinet', initialled it firmly with 'not approved', the *not* heavily underlined – twice. 'Mr Gladstone must have been misinformed about Lord Beaconsfield sending regular reports to HRH,' she insisted, 'as HM is convinced this was not done.' The Prince could not be trusted with 'secrets'. Eventually she agreed to inform him selectively – the selections her own – about Cabinet matters.

Despite the Prince's raffish reputation, Gladstone as Prime Minister had yearned to have him to deal with rather than the exasperating Victoria. The Deanery at Windsor had fallen vacant the year before, and the Queen had made known her desire to appoint her own chaplain, Randall Davidson, to the prestigious post. He was only thirty-five, and to Edward Hamilton she was selfishly consulting 'her own convenience'. The Deanery was, he sighed to Gladstone – at odds as usual with Victoria – 'the most charming of all ecclesiastical berths'.

'Yes,' said the exasperated GOM, 'if the Prince of Wales were King, but not with the present Sovereign.'

While the Prince held no serious religious beliefs, he accepted religion as a medium of social stability, and broke with the Liberals in 1883 on the Affirmation Bill, which was meant to eliminate the last religious oaths requirement in Parliament. It had kept atheists like Charles Bradlaugh from taking a seat to which he had been overwhelmingly elected several times. The Prince had no reason to view Bradlaugh charitably. An outspoken Republican even after other Radicals had recanted, he had published a diatribe, *The Impeachment of the House of Brunswick*, which mocked the heir apparent as a military incompetent good only at shooting pigeons, and ridiculed his qualifications to reign. To assume his withheld seat in 1886 Bradlaugh took the standard oath, rendered meaningless by his swearing it. The Prince's resistance to change seemed to reflect less his personal pique than conservative values that might diminish public concerns about his private life. It was in his interest to appear actively and usefully involved in public affairs.

With Lillie Langtry now in the past, by January 1884 the Prince's rehabilitated reputation was such that Edward Hamilton thought the public mood would permit Parliament to repair the royal finances. The quiet re-mortgaging of Sandringham with Rothschild money had carried the Prince through additional years of excesses, but Hamilton felt that it was now 'impossible that HRH can be otherwise than heavily insolvent'. A sum to pay off his liabilities and increase his income might be voted while good feeling about him lasted. 'The Prince is popular, the British public know him, his zeal in discharging his duties and making himself useful is recognized.' A few weeks later Hamilton raised the subject with Gladstone as they walked together toward the Chapel Royal for morning prayers. Grudgingly penurious with public funds, the Prime Minister grumbled that no such bill could be brought to a vote without a preliminary 'commission of inquiry'. The potential for embarrassment, he implied, remained considerable.

Although the Prince would never be thought of as an intellectual like Leopold, and read little but the newspapers, he was genuinely interested in the visual arts and seriously involved with English musical life, especially the opera. Through his efforts and those of his brothers Alfred and Leopold, the school of music they had sponsored in South Kensington became the Royal College of Music in 1883, with the Prince chairing the first session of its Council at Marlborough House. Edward Hamilton called the meeting 'businesslike and satisfactory'. When Sullivan's forty-first birthday was celebrated at a dinner party, and that evening's performance of *Iolanthe* at the Savoy Theatre was relayed sketchily to the guests at their tables by Alexander Graham Bell's 'Electrophone', the Prince was present. Afterwards HRH lobbied for knighthoods for three stalwarts of the College, Arthur Sullivan, musicologist George Grove, and composer George MacFarren. And he secured Jenny Lind, past her concert days, as a teacher of voice. Also, in an echo of his father's strategies, the Prince promoted the International Fisheries Exhibition, a model for annual industrial and commercial exhibitions to follow.

The Prince was not as immune to the plight of the poor as his spendthrift ways suggested. Throughout 1883 the Radical press had been deploring the evils of housing for the working classes. A searing pamphlet

OUR ROYAL COLLEGE OF MUSIC AND INTERNATIONAL FISHERIES COMBINATION CARTOON.

As impresario of exhibitions which seemed to have no relationship
to one another, HRH is portrayed by Punch *(19 May 1883)*
as Arion, son of Poseidon, the sea god, and a master
of the lyre, 'playing the scales to the fishes'

anonymously published by a Congregationalist minister, *The Bitter Cry of Outcast London*, reminded the middle class that slum conditions for the poor led to irreligion and immorality. Frank Harris (who later traded on his acquaintance with the Prince) then published a parallel exposé in the *Fortnightly Review*, 'The Housing of the Poor in the Towns.' Charles Dilke, in his first year as head of the Local Government Board, pressed for strict application of existing legislation to inspect and regulate properties. Two months later, in February 1884, the Government convened a Royal Commission to inquire into the living conditions of the working classes. A broad spectrum of society was drawn from for the investigation, including a trade unionist and a spokesman for agricultural labourers. For dramatic effect the Commission also included Lord Salisbury of the Opposition, Disraeli's former Home Secretary Richard Cross, Cardinal Manning, and the Prince of Wales. The Prince also tried to get social reformer Octavia Hill appointed but Gladstone felt that putting a woman on a Royal Commission went too far.

Always looking for a lark but this time with serious intent, Lord Carrington suggested that he and the Prince and Dr George Buchanan, LCB Chief Medical Officer of Health, survey what the Prince would call 'the worst and poorest' slums in Clerkenwell and St Pancras. Early on 18 February they met at Carrington's mansion in Whitehall, changed into workmen's clothes – the Prince covered his with a slouch hat and off-the-rack ulster – and called for a four-wheeler to go the East End. A police cab stood apart as quiet security. The Prince was soon astonished. (He had not read Dickens.) Going from alley to alley (while worried constables tried to dissuade them and had to be summarily dismissed), the now unescorted party discovered entire families each living in a single unfurnished room. With the property owner accompanying them, they found a gaunt, shivering woman on a heap of rags with three nearly naked children too dazed by cold and hunger to make any response. The landlord, Carrington reported, then asked her where her fourth child was, and she said, 'I don't know, it went down into the Court[yard] some days ago, and I haven't seen it since.'

'What can I do with her?' appealed the landlord. 'She can't pay any rent and she won't go.' According to Carrington, the Prince 'was so horrified that he wanted to give her a five pound note. Had he done this, I don't think we could have got out of the Court alive, as the news would have spread like wildfire.' Carrington had difficulty hailing a cab to extricate them, but they got off to a rendezvous set up by Buchanan with one of his junior assistants who had not been privy to the Prince's identity. Assuming the success of the mission, and that they were do-gooding gentlemen, he slapped HRH on the back with a pleased 'What do you think of that, Old Buck!' The Prince, said Carrington, 'kept his temper and behaved very well. It was a droll sight! We visited some very bad places … but we got him back safe and sound to Marlborough House in time for luncheon.'

Four days later, on 22 February 1884, the Prince made the most serious speech he would ever deliver in the House of Lords, describing what he had seen and urging housing reform. 'The condition of the poor, or rather of their dwellings', he said, 'was perfectly disgraceful.' He urged passage of 'measures of a drastic and thorough character'. The sudden death of his brother Leopold was to draw him away, and after he returned to London he soon left again for the wedding of his ambitious cousin Prince Louis of Battenberg to the late Princess Alice's daughter, Victoria of Hesse. 'I deeply regret being away from the Commission,' he wrote to Carrington, 'and am completely losing the thread of the inquiry; but I fear it cannot be helped.' Making amends later, he cancelled plans for an autumn stay at Homburg, remaining until business was adjourned on 5 December, and attending seventeen further sessions. Then, to be filled in on what he had missed, he invited a Radical member of the Commission, Henry Broadhurst, MP, to Sandringham over the weekend of 12–15 December. The working-class Broadhurst, on principle rejecting proper dinner attire for his stay, felt relieved that he was permitted to have dinner in his rooms. A Bill prepared by Dilke became law in July 1885 but had to be superseded by a new Act with more teeth in 1890. Although the Prince was serious about social amelioration, he would be given few opportunities to demonstrate it.

A more notorious public question emerged in 1885 when W. T. Stead, the crusading editor of the *Pall Mall Gazette*, inveighed against child prostitution – another outcome of pervasive poverty – under the heading 'Modern Babylon'. His aim was to get protective legislation into the Criminal Law Amendment Act before Parliament. In a series labelled 'The Maiden Tribute' in May and June he described the abduction of children by brothel-keepers and the sale of young girls by their parents. Stead proved his point by purchasing a thirteen-year-old from her mother and describing the transaction in print. Further, he exposed the ignorance of physiology and sex among the poor entrapped girls, and revealed that he had arranged for the child he had bought to be cared for by the Salvation Army. Issues of the *Pall Mall Gazette* sold out, partly for their notoriety and partly for what was taken as near-pornography. The clergy were divided between support and suppression. The Prince of Wales stopped delivery of the *PMG* to Marlborough House. The subject was too indelicate.

Attempting to be more politically active despite the reining in by his mother, the Prince scheduled a visit, with Alexandra, to Ireland for April 1885. (Victoria had spent only a few weeks in Ireland since her accession in 1837.) The announcement in London prompted the irreconcilable Fenians in America to denounce him as a representative of 'British tyranny', and the United Irishmen there arrogantly offered a $10,000 reward – it was safe to do so from New York or Boston – for his body, alive or dead. Threats against the Prince of Wales from Fenians were not new. In 1874, Clan na Gael firebrand John McCafferty in Baltimore devised a plan to rescue insurrectionists deported to Australia. He and a raiding party would kidnap the Prince and hold him as a hostage on a sailing vessel, its location unknown to the authorities, until the Government released all Irish political prisoners. McCafferty even drew up a memorandum on the Prince's favourite amusements (women excluded) to keep him occupied while in custody, and requested $5,000 from American funds which the Clan had collected to pay for the operation. The plan was vetoed as impractical, and other implausible solutions adopted.

The Queen, who frowned on the Irish trip as too hazardous, told the Home Secretary, Sir William Harcourt, that the new Fenian threat was 'monstrous', and asked what could be done. Nothing, he said, except to discount it and give it no publicity. Yet all auguries for the visit seemed adverse. On 16 March, the Dublin City Council voted, by 41 to 17, to take no official part in the Prince's reception. The Nationalist paper *United Ireland* published a special supplement featuring scornful comments about the Prince, among them an attack by the influential Archbishop of Cashel.

The royal party, including Prince Eddy, embarked anyway, assured of a rousing reception from Protestant loyalists. (Eddy had also accompanied the Prince to Germany in March for the eighty-eighth birthday celebrations of the doddering German emperor, William I.) On 7 April they arrived at Kingstown in the *Osborne* and drove in the afternoon from Dublin Castle, seat of the viceregal Government, through the city to an agricultural show. The streets were crowded with people eager to see their heir apparent, and no trouble surfaced then or later in Dublin, as the entourage went through a crowded schedule that included receiving from the new Royal University of Ireland honorary degrees of Doctor of Laws for the Prince and Doctor of Music for Alexandra. To the south of Dublin the crowds became ugly. The Prince's patience was tried, but his considerable tact and grace held. It was clear that he believed that even Home

Rule, however insufficient for the Nationalists, was incompatible with the integrity of Great Britain. There were, Francis Knollys wrote to the Irish Secretary in London, 'disgraceful allusions to HRH in the recent speeches of Messrs [William] O'Brien, [Richard] Deasy, [John] O'Connor and [Timothy] Harrigan. Nothing could have been more outrageous than the manner in which Mr O'Connor rounded on the mob on the quay at Cork.' Along the railway route at Mallow, black flags painted with skulls and crossbones were displayed; in Cork the streets were draped in black and symbolic coffins set along the route. Resolutely, the Prince went to the races at Punchestown, attended balls and held levées, and proceeded north to noisily loyal crowds in Londonderry and Belfast.

When the party had been about to embark on the Irish visit, the press had warned of the hazards the Prince might encounter. Most dangers, *Town Talk* claimed, could be guarded against by troops and detectives. Yet there were even more subtle perils, it smirked, 'against which soldiers and policemen alike can do nothing.... The Prince runs the danger of being ensnared, of losing his heart, of falling a victim to Hibernian charms.... The Princess, however, is with him, and we feel sure that she will prove the greatest safeguard against this danger.' That the charge was absurd made little difference: it merely reflected his reputation.

Afterward, Henry Campbell-Bannerman, the Irish Secretary, wrote imaginatively that the positive impact of the visit was 'unmistakable', and that the feeling in the House of Commons was 'one of admiration and gratitude for a great public service'. A fulsomely unrealistic letter from Gladstone also greeted the Prince. Agreeing on the service rendered, the Prime Minister (the principal advocate for Home Rule, a policy which was splitting the Liberals) conceded ambiguously that 'the perfect harmony and brilliancy of the reception' had broken down 'at one or two points of the Royal progress'. The Prince wrote in return, almost as if he believed it, that the 'disapproval of our presence in given places' was far outweighed by 'the enthusiasm displayed by the loyalists'. He announced himself 'ready to pay another visit to Ireland, ... I hope at a not too distant date'. But he would never return as Prince of Wales.

Another mixed blessing for the Prince was the rise of Randolph Churchill to Cabinet prominence under the brief Tory administration of Lord Salisbury, which began with the fall of the divided Liberals in June 1885. For the Privy Council meeting on the composition of the Cabinet, the Queen actually invited her son to Windsor for advice. He knew many of the candidates for office. In her diary for 24 June 1885 Victoria wrote, 'Bertie kindly came to be with me during the Council, and lunched with us ... [and] kindly spent the whole afternoon at Windsor, which was the greatest help to me.' Under pressure, the Prince had made his peace with the brilliant but unstable younger brother of Lord Blandford, who became Secretary for India, and Bertie enjoyed being consulted on Cabinet appointments – which happened again when, seven months later, Gladstone returned briefly to Downing Street for a stormy eight months. The elderly and incompetent Duke of Cambridge, still protected by the Queen's refusal to replace him as Army chief, as usual wanted to dominate civilian authority at the War Office, but the Prince, putting national interest above family loyalty, prevailed upon Gladstone to name Campbell-Bannerman as Minister. The Prince also dissuaded the Queen from insisting on Lord Lorne, Princess Louise's failed husband, as Under-Secretary for the Colonies.

Gladstone's next (and not unexpected) defeat in the Commons on Home Rule in June 1886 ushered in what seemed another revolving-door Salisbury Government, but it remained in office until August 1892. Salisbury, too, exploited the Prince's many foreign and domestic contacts in forming his Cabinet. As *quid pro quo* he authorized Lord Iddesleigh (the former Stafford Northcote) to let the Prince see secret Foreign Office dispatches, a practice quietly begun by the Earl of Rosebery under Gladstone. Earlier in 1886 a gold key to the red boxes was discovered at the Foreign Office, where it had lain since Prince Albert's death in 1861. Rosebery gave the key to the Prince of Wales, but it did not afford him full access into state papers. That had to wait for another six years and another appeal to the Queen. But for the first time, whatever the party in power, the Prince had achieved some of the political influence he had so long sought.

To persuade Lord Londonderry to become Irish viceroy, Salisbury invoked what he described to the Prince of Wales as 'Your Royal Highness' powerful assistance and advocacy'. The Prince also sponsored Earl Cadogan as Lord Privy Seal, backed the hot-headed Randolph Churchill as Chancellor of the Exchequer, and proposed Charles Beresford, back from the sea as an Irish MP, for a seat in the Cabinet but settled for his appointment as Fourth Lord of the Admiralty. 'I know how anxious he is to be of use and have work,' the Prince explained to

Salisbury in a tone that suggested his own frustrations. But Lord Randolph, despite Jennie's closeness to the Prince, was becoming more difficult to support. Unstable and unpredictable, he was also now affected by the mental deterioration (probably tertiary syphilis) that would eventually kill him. While a guest at Windsor Castle just before Christmas 1886, Churchill arrogantly sent a letter of resignation to Salisbury on Windsor-crested writing paper. In vain (and unhappily, as she also doted on Jennie) the Queen warned her son, 'Pray don't correspond with him, for he is really not to be trusted and is very indiscreet.' Beresford's appointment – Lord Charles was another hot-head – was to prove equally unsuccessful but would take longer to implode. Again a woman would be involved, one that the Prince as yet hardly knew: the domineering Lady Brooke.

Favourites of the Prince often achieved social success after being tried between the sheets. A showgirl, Rosie Boote, left the Prince's bed to become Marchioness of Headfort, and young society ladies of whom the Prince was briefly enamoured would exploit their cachet to marry into the Marlborough House circle. A royal anomaly, the discreet and loyal Blanche Caracciolo remained in Dieppe, lacing her slender waist in the manner of Princess Alix and raising the almond-eyed Alberta Olga to model, as a teenager, for Sickert, Whistler, Boldini and Helleu. Venturing to Brighton, Alberta (who later preferred the more exotic Olga) was also drawn by Jacques-Emile Blanche in 1887. She pasted his striking sketch of a charming girl with waist-length hair in her scrapbook. In her mother the Duchess's home in Dieppe, Blanche recalled, were 'colour prints of racecourses, hunting subjects, cats, portraits of Queen Victoria and [of] the Prince of Wales in various uniforms, all signed by him. When the august godparent of Olga came incognito we were supposed not to know, although plain-clothes policemen paraded our quarter in relays day and night.'

Gladstone had still been in office on 4 May 1886 when, with unusual morning frost still on the ground at eleven, Victoria left Windsor to open the Colonial and Indian Exhibition at South Kensington. With Bertie at her side she proceeded from Paddington Station, passing excited crowds little used to seeing the reclusive Queen. Planned during the pre-Gladstone months, the Exhibition symbolized everything the Prime Minister disliked about colonial involvement. There was an Indian Hall, a facsimile bazaar, and exhibits from all the red-tinted swatches of the globe, a glimpse for the public of Imperial England across the seas. The Prince of Wales had personally sampled much of the reality. For the Queen it was a tactile introduction to the Empire she would never see, a journey into her Imperial fantasies. She was delighted, although the walk for an elderly and lame lady was 'long and fatiguing'.

For such occasions the Prince was becoming indispensable. 'Bertie kindly helped me up and down the steps, whenever we came to any,' she wrote in her journal. He was also her surrogate. After the singing of a choral ode by Tennyson at the Albert Hall, set by Arthur Sullivan in a collaboration commissioned by the Prince of Wales, he read an address to the Queen. She replied briefly, after which Bertie kissed her hand, and presented her with a catalogue of the Exhibition and a symbolic golden key to it. Speeches, prayers and hymns followed, closing with 'Rule Britannia', sung with fervour by an overflow audience not in sympathy with Gladstone's doctrine of diminishing Empire. It was the first of many ceremonials leading up to the Jubilee year of 1887, the fiftieth anniversary of the Queen's accession, for which the Prince of Wales would increasingly become impresario – his principal public role in a reign in which otherwise he had only a frustrating (if increasingly significant) place in the shadows.

XIII

Impresario

1887–1891

EARLY ON 23 February 1887, a mild earthquake rattled the Riviera. It was the morning of Ash Wednesday, the beginning of the Lenten season of fasting and penitence. Revellers, only recently asleep after the merrymaking of Shrove Tuesday ended long after midnight, rushed from their beds into streets littered with carnival debris. In Cannes for the festivities with some of his French friends, the Prince of Wales awoke as the floor in his hotel shook. 'If everybody had behaved like the Prince,' *The Times* reported, 'the panic would not have been so great. Apprised by his suite of the fright caused by the earthquake, he declined to go down into the garden and, having tranquillized everybody [in his party], [he] remained in bed.'

Although the Queen planned to begin her Golden Jubilee progresses with a visit to Birmingham a month later, on 23 March, in effect the celebratory year had begun with the calendar when, at Osborne, she opened Bertie's New Year present to her – a Jubilee inkstand. The lid was a crown, on the inside of which was her royal face, which looked into a pool of ink. In her journal she described the gift as 'very pretty and useful'. While most Jubilee souvenirs ranged from the useless to the absurd, there were also some, like china tea mugs and teapots, from which her broad face also benignly smiled.

His amorous life in limbo, the Prince had spent January mainly at home with his family, but he had wanted to delay the opening of Jubilee festivities as long as possible in the spring, realizing that the burden of being impresario would be his. As a preliminary, however, he invited

Thomas Huxley, the scientist and popularizer of science, to speak at the Mansion House, ostensibly under the auspices of the Lord Mayor, whose venue it was, on the Prince's pet Jubilee project for South Kensington. The Prince's Albertine scenario for the complex already in place was to celebrate the Jubilee and promote science, industry and empire in an 'Imperial Institute'. He still had no substantive royal role, and to his continuing chagrin, Cabinet papers had to be scrutinized by the Queen, despite her failing eyes, before even a censored summary was permitted to go to him. Every government since Disraeli's had tried to relax her rigidity, the successes achieved slowly and grudgingly.

Since the Prince's information network remained his friends and his guests, he invited former Prime Minister Gladstone, his wife and his Private Secretary to Sandringham for the last weekend of January, Edward Hamilton arriving without dinner garb because his servant had been late to St Pancras Station. Joining the guests, the Prince of Wales shared the same carriage from London, and when knowledgeable crowds gathered at intermediate stations en route, 'the Prince', Hamilton noted in his diary, 'took the demonstrations very well and good-humouredly. The excitement to get a glimpse of Mr G seems to be as great as ever.' Long a toiler for the GOM, Hamilton took it for granted that the curious and the loyal were out to gape at the elderly Gladstone. When they arrived at Sandringham, 'one of the requirements of the house' was 'to be weighed and to enter one's weight in a book'. The Prince was exempted as host, but he was bulking larger than ever. His tailors, as always, performed sartorial prodigies to mask his mass under double-breasted jackets and coats. For the Princess there was a Choice Book (a confession album) to be filled out, page by page, with 'pretty jottings and jokes'.

Bowling and billiards followed Saturday dinner – no cards or wagering with the pious Gladstones present – and on Sunday a 'short practical sermon from the Bishop of St Albans'. Clergy who did not keep their sermons brief were not invited again. After luncheon, the citified bachelor Hamilton wrote, came 'the accustomed round – to see the dogs without end of all kinds and sizes, the [tame] bears, goats, birds, horses, cows and flowers. Everything is certainly in the most perfect order, on a Royal scale, and marked with singularly good taste – without any obtrusive ostentation.' What impressed him most reflected the Prince's membership of the Parliamentary committee that had investigated working-class housing, for his local practices had anticipated its recommendations. 'There is not a single cottage on the estate which has not been rebuilt or newly erected by the Prince since the estate has belonged to him.' Yet despite his paternalism, the workmen, HRH remarked ruefully, had voted in the last election for Joseph Arch, the founder of the National Agricultural Labourer's Union, who was then MP for North-west Norfolk. Hamilton explained it as 'fellow-feeling for one of their own class'.

Wherever one went in England early in 1887 the signs of Jubilee fund-raising were omnipresent, from coppers collected by schoolchildren to golden sovereigns to celebrate the Queen in bricks-and-mortar somewhere in her Empire. *Punch* used the opportunity to remind readers that the Prince of Wales needed support for his lifestyle far more than did his mother, who actually had done very little but hoard her income. Long before, as bureaucrats began considering how to mark the Jubilee, *Town Talk* (10 October 1885) had expended a full page on a satirical 'Grand Programme of Arrangements' that began with references to Victoria's pinched insulation from reality. To begin with, it proposed grandly, 'The Queen will come to London and stop there a whole week.' While there, 'Her Majesty will spend five shillings with two London tradesmen,' and a delegation of London merchants would then 'present an address to Her Majesty to commemorate this generosity'. The procession would include 'one million starving working men', and the royal entertainment would include a comic song, 'Mind and be Home when the Clock Strikes Nine', to be sung by the Prince of Wales. A cartoon showed a smartly tailored Prince competing with two citizens soliciting Jubilee contributions, one with outstretched hand, the other with a large slotted box. Between them the top-hatted, cigarette-smoking Prince holds an upturned hat for coins and asks,

> Am I alone to be out in the cold, gentle Sirs, as Her Majesty's Jubilee nears?
> Everyone now is a-touting for everything, Church Houses, Institutes, Hospitals, Towers.
> Has no one a good word for me and my gardens, my fun and my fireworks, my fountains and flowers?

The Queen remained destitute of good words for him. Before the Prince left for Germany to represent her at the ninetieth birthday of Emperor Wilhelm I, now seriously failing, she issued strict guidelines for family members making ceremonial appearances for her in the Jubilee year. Always jealous of her status and privileges, she wanted it understood that Royals were not undertaking such duties in their own right. Ponsonby was instructed that at Jubilee ceremonies, and 'always' thereafter, her children were to insert 'my dear Mother' into their remarks to validate the authority under which they appeared – 'it should never be omitted when they represent her'. That included her heir.

On the ceremonial trip to Germany, the Prince would be accompanied by *his* heir, the dim Albert Victor, to expose him to the roles he was expected to fill. Photographs of the period show Eddy somewhat glassy-eyed, as if he were not quite in tune with the space he inhabited. Eddy had been quietly withdrawn from Cambridge as unfit, but in June 1888 he was ceremoniously awarded an honorary Doctorate of Law, which *Punch* in a cartoon treated as the huge joke it was. He had already been put into ostensible service in his father's own 10th Hussars, which only meant wearing the uniform.

As they went to Berlin, the Queen (as 'Countess of Kent') went south with a huge entourage to Cannes and Aix-les-Bains, to ready herself in health, she claimed, for the rigours of the Jubilee. One of those strains would be the invalid presence of her son-in-law, the German Crown Prince. Her news in mid-April was that he had what no one would say explicitly was cancer of the throat, and that excising the growth would only add pain to the inevitable. Frederick's heir, Prince Willy, scorning the liberalism of his father, looked forward to reigning sooner than expected, and represented the other major German problem. As Willy had already demonstrated, he was Anglophobic and impossible. His Uncle Bertie thought him quite mad. Yet he wanted a role in the ceremonies beyond his position.

Such problems were the Prince of Wales's responsibility. Lord Salisbury, the Prime Minister, appealed again to the Queen to recognize the Prince's status and permit him to have a legitimate Cabinet key. A new opportunity had arisen because a change of keys was in progress. Until then she had allowed him only to see some 'despatches of a highly confidential nature'. Now, despite her dithering about a new key for the Prince's own use, she was willing to have him in the sensitive role of Jubilee judge of protocol. He happily issued instructions on royal salutes, orders of precedence, modes of address, placement in processions and at dinners, and appropriateness of uniforms and insignia of Orders.

At Windsor Castle on 4 May a deputation of colonial premiers and governors from eighty countries and colonies, led by the premier of Newfoundland, offered 'humble, earnest and united congratulations'. It was the first major Jubilee event for which the Prince of Wales officiated as impresario. On the ninth, a levée at Buckingham Palace was opened for the first time, at Victoria's command, to divorced ladies who were legally blameless for their condition – a liberalization of the strict Court etiquette in effect during the first fifty years of her reign, and a recognition of social change. The Queen remained only an hour, sitting down several times because of fatigue, and Princess Alix stood in for her. At Buckingham Palace on the 11th, a Jubilee ode by the prolific Poet Laureate, Lord Tennyson, commissioned by the Prince and set to music by Charles Villiers Stanford, was performed privately for the Queen in advance of its public presentation. The orchestra and singers vastly outnumbered the invited audience, as had often been the case when mad King Ludwig of Bavaria ordered Wagner's operas to be performed almost for himself alone. Although the Queen was delighted, the press would be less so at its public premiere, referring to 'inanities', and to 'thunders moaning in the distance'.

Jubilee ceremonies continued almost daily, with presentations of illuminated addresses on scrolls, and introductions of foreign and domestic dignitaries. At the Albert Hall early in June, after a fanfare on silver trumpets, the loyalty of the Freemasons of the United Grand Lodge of England was accepted for the Queen by the Prince of Wales. The address, in a royal-blue velvet casket lined with white satin, wished her 'a long and happy continuance of your reign over a loyal and devoted people', a line typical of the many salutes to which the Prince responded with dignity for this often-absent mother.

The great day itself was Monday 20 June, the fiftieth anniversary of her accession at eighteen in 1837. A special train took her from Windsor to Paddington Station, from which she drove in an open landau through cheering crowds to Buckingham Palace. At the Garden Entrance, all the invited royals assembled – she was related by blood or marriage to many of them, from Portugal to Russia. At a luncheon she was escorted by the blind King of Saxony (at his side the Grand Duchess of Mecklenburg-Strelitz), but the Prince of Wales presided. The next day was even more crowded, with yet another progress, in a gilt landau drawn by six cream-coloured horses, down Piccadilly, past Trafalgar Square, along the new

Northumberland Avenue to the Embankment, and then to Westminster Abbey, scene of her coronation. The Queen wore a black and white bonnet of starched lace. 'Dear Fritz', the now nearly mute German Crown Prince, dressed in white and silver with a German eagle atop his helmet, rode painfully but impassively before her carriage, and 'George Cambridge' – her cousin – next to it. Preceding them cantered a guard of honour of twelve Indian officers, followed by 'my 3 sons, 5 sons-in-law, 9 grandsons, and grandsons-in-law'. After the royal landau came the carriages with 'my 3 other daughters' (Beatrice accompanied her), '3 daughters-in-law, granddaughters, one granddaughter-in-law, and some of the suite'. The crowds were huge. In his diary, Bernard Shaw wrote in frustration, 'Saw the coachmen's hats.'

At dinner later in Buckingham Palace Victoria appeared in a dress 'with the rose, thistle, and shamrock embroidered in silver on it', and at the start King Christian of Denmark, Bertie's father-in-law, offered the toast. 'And after *God Save the Queen* had been played,' she wrote, 'Bertie proposed the healths of the Sovereigns and Royal guests now assembled here, doing so in my name.' The formalities had nearly been disrupted by her royal Belgian cousin and by her eldest grandson, Prince Willy, who complained to his mother's lady-in-waiting, Hedwig von Brühl, of being treated by Victoria 'with exquisite coolness, with bare courtesy', even to the placing of his wife, Princess Augusta, a future empress of Germany, 'behind the black Queen of Hawaii'. Clearly Uncle Bertie must have plotted such *lèse-majesté*.

At the state banquet following the Abbey ceremony, the Prince of Wales had diplomatically escorted the large, dusky Queen Kapiolani, while her sister-in-law, the future Queen Liliuokalani,* was taken in by the Prince's brother, the Duke of Edinburgh. Assigned to the King of the Belgians for the supper procession, Liliuokalani had been left standing by the arrogant Leopold II, who in his fiefdom of the Congo was working hundreds of thousands of blacks in conditions of near-slavery. Courtiers hurriedly reassigned her to the Duke of Saxony, who, even though he could not see her, also refused to escort a 'coloured' person. The Queen and Prince had to rush in Affie.

On the 22nd the ceremonies continued, with 30,000 children gathered

---

* She was to succeed her brother in 1891 and become the last sovereign of an independent Hawaii.

in Hyde Park, each to receive 'an earthenware pot with my portrait on it'. (It was actually a mug manufactured by Messrs Doulton, with which the children received a meat pie, a piece of cake, a bun and an orange.) The Prince and Princess of Wales escorted a little girl to the Queen's carriage, who presented Victoria with a bouquet trailing ribbons which read, 'God bless our Queen, not Queen alone, but Mother, Queen and Friend.' Then the Prince introduced the Committee for the event, including Lords Rothschild, Hartington and Derby. Times had changed sufficiently for her to list Natty Rothschild first in her diary. 'The children sang *God Save the Queen* somewhat out of tune,' she added, 'and then we drove on to Paddington Station.' She preferred being in London as little as possible. Bertie could entertain the army of Jubilee guests remaining there.

On the 29th she returned to Buckingham Palace in further processions, for a garden party at five, largely for foreign guests. 'People were spread all over the garden, and there were a number of tents, and a large one for me, in front of which were placed the Indian escort.' (Her love-affair with India was vicarious but insistent.) 'I walked right round the lawn in front of the Palace with Bertie, and I bowed right and left, talking to as many as I could, but I was dreadfully done up by it.' She walked with a stick, for the public did not know that in private she used a wheel-chair. One knee was stiff and lame, and her legs swelled with edema when she stood for any length of time. The next day was reserved for 'Indian Princes and Deputations.... Sir Partab Singh, who is an A.D.C. to Bertie, stood behind me.'

The great midsummer Jubilee event was a naval review off Spithead, timed for the Queen's return to the Isle of Wight. For her grandson Willy, for whom his nation's Navy was an obsession, it was the major event of the Jubilee, but the Queen had urged the Prince of Wales to keep the difficult Willy 'sweet' while in England, and beyond the pageantry, his Uncle Bertie took him to a review of the Prince's own regiment, the 10th Royal Hussars, at Hounslow. This crack regiment had a novelty weapon, the invention of an American residing in England, Hiram Maxim. Three years earlier, Maxim had urged the firm of Vickers to manufacture his machine gun, but stuffy Army authorities would not buy it, and Colonel Liddell of the Hussars paid for one out of his own pocket and had it mounted on a two-wheeled horse-drawn carriage. The astute Prince William was charmed, and when he invited the colonels of the four regiments he had inspected to Berlin as his guests, Uncle Bertie arranged that they take him as a gift an identical Maxim gun on what Willy had called a 'galloping carriage'. Seventeen years later, updated versions of the Prince of Wales's gift would decimate British divisions in Flanders.

Now a committed yachtsman, HRH was central to the event, but his major Jubilee interest lay in a curiously Albertine conception that seems to have emerged from his visit to India. In 1886 he had opened the Colonial and India Exhibition and had even induced Lord Tennyson and Sir Arthur Sullivan to produce a choral ode for the event. The Exhibition's popular and financial success had led him to suggest commemorating the Jubilee in a bricks-and-mortar fashion, using as seed money the profits of the 'Colinderies' – as the exhibition had become known. He envisioned an Imperial Institute in South Kensington ('Albertopolis') to promote knowledge about the lands of the Empire, and to become a setting for allied scientific and technological research. On 12 January 1887 he had presided over a meeting at St James's Palace at which he sketched out his plans, and began soliciting subscriptions in his own hand, particularly targeting wealthy Indian maharajahs.

On 4 July of that year the Queen, escorted by the Prince of Wales, had laid the foundation stone of the proposed building, but subscriptions lagged. In exasperation he wrote to his friend Charles Carrington – then a provincial governor in Australia – 'What a pity that the Imperial Institute does not find favour among those you are now governing; but we must have patience, and I trust that when New South Wales hears that the edifice is now built, they will not hang back but give a handsome donation.' Yet the public and home and abroad were to hang back, and the Prince lacked his father's single-mindedness and persistence. To the Prince Consort, practical philanthropies and scientific institutions were central to his being. To his son, they were only peripheral to a life of more variety and spice.

One example in the Jubilee year was his purchase for his racing stable at Sandringham, at the recommendation of his trainer John Porter, of the mare Perdita II. A racing stud would become a consuming and expensive interest, but he was acquiring friends, such as the Sassoons, and Baron Hirsch, with money to spare and passion for the turf. (Breeding took time, but by the 1890s he was producing winning thoroughbreds.) Yachting, racing and impresario responsibilities left him less time for women. In October 1887, when Aline, the daughter of baron Gustave de Rothschild of Paris, whose name he had taken for his yacht, was married to Edward Sassoon, Sir Albert Sassoon's son and heir, the Prince of Wales sent a silver basin and ewer depicting Hercules succumbing amorously to a nymph. What they implied about the Prince's yearnings can only be guessed at.

When the Prince returned from a visit to a Mediterranean squadron commanded by his brother Alfred, it was to unveil, in the Queen's presence, a statue of her erected at Balmoral, its cost raised by subscriptions from her Scottish staff. It was, Victoria wrote effusively in her journal, 'a most pleasant visit.... He had not stayed alone with me, excepting for a couple of days in May in '68, at Balmoral, since he married! He is so kind and affectionate that it is a pleasure to be a little quietly together.' That harmony could not last, largely because the Prince's loyalties to old and unreliable friends often harmed him. The unstable but charming Lord Randolph Churchill had travelled to Russia with Jennie, taking with him a letter of introduction from the Princess of Wales to her sister, the Russian Empress. Churchill used the letter to convey the impression that the Prince of Wales, who had encouraged his wife to write it, was behind the journey, and indeed Lord Randolph did write long and informative letters to the Prince, which he had sent via the British embassy. The Marquis of Salisbury felt impelled to write to Moscow (and to the Queen) 'that Lord R. Churchill does not represent the opinions of either the Government or the country'. Agreeing, the Queen urged her son, '*Pray don't* correspond with him, for he really is *not* to be trusted and is very indiscreet.'

At home as 1888 dawned, the Prince was going through another crisis in his finances, and lobbying for a bail-out by Salisbury's Government. A crisis of a different kind intervened when his brother-in-law Fritz, Crown Prince of Germany, imminently to become emperor as his father was dying, underwent an emergency tracheotomy. On 10 February, on his mother's behalf, the Prince rushed to San Remo on the Italian Riviera to see Friedrich (whose illness Victoria had refused to believe was malignant until the very end). In Berlin, Friedrich's enemies, from Bismarck to the eager Prince Willy, knew the truth, for the scheming *éminence grise* at the Foreign Office, Friedrich von Holstein, had a spy in San Remo, Crown Princess Vicky's maid-in-waiting Hedwig von Brühl. A month later Wilhelm I was dead, and the failing, mute Friedrich III was en route by train to Germany to claim his crown.

A few days earlier the new Kaiser's throat cancer had been acknowledged, and back in England the Prince of Wales, who was unhappy about the 'great hubbub in the press', could do little but wait to represent his mother once more, either at a coronation or a funeral. Early in April, Friedrich III took a turn for the worse, and Victoria determined to go to Charlottenburg herself, where the new Crown Prince, Willy, impatiently awaiting his own accession, told the castle commandant, 'The moment you hear of the Kaiser's death, man the entire castle and let no one go out, without exception.'

Victoria arrived on 24 April, met with the bedridden Friedrich (who scrawled notes on a pad); with her distraught daughter, the embattled

A SILVER WREATH FOR A SILVER WEDDING.

The Prince and Princess of Wales look happily married
(Punch, *10 March 1888*)

Kaiserin; and with the real ruler of Germany, Prince Bismarck, now seventy-three and tenacious as ever. A month later the dying Kaiser, thin and pale and supported by a cane, appeared silently at the wedding of his second son, Henry, to Princess Irene of Hesse. No one had expected to see him in public again. Afterwards the Prince of Wales, again in Germany for the Queen, conferred at Charlottenburg with Count Herbert von Bismarck, the Chancellor's son, who declared bluntly that a sovereign who could not talk should not be permitted to reign. 'If I had not taken into consideration that good relations between Germany and England were essential,' he told his mother on returning, 'I should have thrown him out.'

Returning to England, the Prince lived in limbo, awaiting the inevitable. A telegram on 14 June from the Queen's eccentric throat specialist, Sir Morell Mackenzie, from Berlin, warned, 'The Emperor is sinking.' The Prince of Wales telegraphed to his mother that he was ready to start for Germany, then delayed irresolutely when no further change was reported later in the day. The next morning, after a reign of ninety-nine days, Friedrich was dead. He was fifty-six. 'Greatly relieved to hear that dear Alix would go with Bertie to Berlin, as I begged her to,' Victoria wrote painfully in her journal. '... The misfortune is awful. My poor child's whole future gone, ruined.'

The Prince and Princess of Wales stayed, prudently, at the British Embassy. The new Kaiser had invited no foreign heads of government, and rushed the lying-in-state and burial. At the funeral on the 18th, his uncle walked behind the hearse to the left of his nephew Wilhelm II, who was sovereign at twenty-nine while the Prince of Wales, old at forty-six, still waited his turn. 'Try, my dear George,' he wrote to his younger son on 16 June, 'never to forget Uncle Fritz. He was one of the finest and noblest characters ever known; if he had a fault he was *too* good for this world.' (It would have been pointless writing anything to Eddy.) To the Queen he added, two days later, 'I felt, on leaving the Church, that I had parted from the noblest and best man I had ever known, except my ever-to-be-lamented Father.'

The Prince of Wales had to plead with Willy for accommodations for the ex-Kaiserin that were not demeaning. She was being evicted unceremoniously from Charlottenburg. Following up the futile pressure, the Queen wrote earnestly to her grandson that after all, the royal widow 'is *your* mother'. The Prince of Wales would have the aggravating burden of his arrogant, paranoid nephew to bear thereafter. The Kaiser's own entourage was also to exchange confidential messages about how difficult he was, and he would become more so. The increasing tension between uncle and nephew was an acknowledgement of the Prince's expanding political role behind the scenes, at a time when new tensions were also building in his private life.

In the later months of 1888 Lord Salisbury had to continue negotiations over replenishing the Prince's finances while also engaged in painful deliberations with Count Paul von Hatzfeldt, the German ambassador. On 13 October Hatzfeldt had reported to Salisbury the Prince's conversations with Herbert von Bismarck about 'the differences' (so the Prime Minister described it) 'which had arisen between the Emperor of Germany and the Prince of Wales'. According to Bismarck the Prince was interfering in German foreign affairs, by suggesting indiscreetly that, had Friedrich lived, he would have made – in the interests of peaceful accommodation – concessions to the French in Alsace and to the Danes in North Schleswig, and restored the Duke of Cumberland's confiscated German properties, seized from his father (Victoria's cousin) when ejected as king of Hanover. Hatzfeldt also complained that the Prince treated the new German sovereign 'as an uncle treats a nephew, instead of recognizing that he was an Emperor, who, though young, had still been of age for some time'. Further, Bismarck implied that the outraged young Kaiser would not visit any foreign capital while Prince Albert Edward was present. 'I warned him,' Salisbury explained to the Queen about Hatzfeldt, 'to prevent any proposal to visit England at present, as it would not be accepted.'

Victoria considered Willy as 'really too *vulgar* and too absurd ... almost *to be believed*. We have always been very intimate with our grandson and nephew, and to pretend that he is to be treated *in private* as well as in public as "his Imperial Majesty" is *perfect madness!*' She would not 'swallow this affront'. It evidenced 'a very unhealthy and unnatural state of mind; and he *must* be made to feel that his grandmother and uncle will not stand such insolence. The Prince of Wales must *not* submit to such treatment.'

Salisbury shared the exchange with the Prince, and also a letter from the Queen insisting to the Kaiser that her 'poor brokenhearted daughter' Vicky be permitted to visit England – although reprisals, the Prince warned, might await her on return. 'You all seem frightened of them,' the tough-minded Queen telegraphed from Balmoral on 24 October, 'which is not the way to make them better. Tell the Prince of Wales this, and that his persecuted and calumniated sister has for months been looking forward to this time of quietness. Please let no one mention this again. It would be fatal and must not be.'

Hastening to Scotland by overnight train, the Prince spent two days in discussions with his mother on the German question, which would loom ever larger despite efforts to contain the burgeoning distrust. Willy's birth injury resulting in a withered arm, and the Prussian warrior culture for aristocratic males, had combined pathologically to create a monarch tragically wrong for his times. Uncle and nephew represented the future and the past.

The Prince was again impresario when the yacht *Victoria and Albert*, with Vicky aboard, arrived from Germany. He led the Queen, her stick in hand, up the gang-plank into the ship to escort his petite sister, nearly obscured in deep widow's mourning, to the dock and to the train to Windsor. Count Hatzfeldt was present, looking, Victoria wrote, 'greatly distressed'. The situation at home was beyond his control. Two days later the former empress would be only forty-eight, but her life was effectively over.

In the interval between the funeral of Friedrich III and his widow's retreat to England, the Princess of Wales and her daughters went to Copenhagen while the Prince went to Homburg, then on to Vienna to be available when Wilhelm II was scheduled for a state visit. He dined with Emperor Franz Joseph and his heir, Crown Prince Rudolf, and awaited a meeting with them and the Kaiser, hoping it would heal their rifts. At the ready – he was even photographed in it – the Prince had his uniform as honorary colonel of the Blücher Hussars. Instead, he received a message from Sir Augustus Paget, the British ambassador, that his presence in Vienna during the Kaiser's stay would be unacceptable to the Kaiser.

To avoid an ugly situation, HRH made a point of going to the races and attending a dinner in honour of the Russian Tsar's birthday, before entraining for Croatia to observe the autumn exercises of the Austrian Army. Leaked to the press, however, were deliberately embarrassing reports that the Kaiser had threatened to cancel his visit if his uncle remained. Before leaving Vienna, the Prince on 12 September dictated to his senior equerry, Major-General Arthur Ellis, a letter to the Kaiser deploring any 'mischief' made by third parties, and asking about *'the meaning of all this'*. But he knew that his own indiscretions, however accurate in fact, continued to exacerbate his nephew's sensitivities. In Hungary he would fulminate to one of his titled hosts, who repeated the remark eagerly, 'William the Great needs to learn that he is living at the end of the nineteenth century and not in the Middle Ages.'

Again by Danube steamer the Prince continued to Budapest and then to Bucharest, where he stayed with the King and Queen of Romania and felt, he wrote to his mother, 'thoroughly at home'. But he also told her of the Vienna imbroglio, noting, 'I felt sure how pained, surprised and indignant you would be.' Returning, he hunted bear (with no success) with Crown Prince Rudolf, and in Styria he pursued chamois, killing four and wounding two – 'the prettiest sport I have seen for a long time', he wrote to his son George. In France he went shooting with Alphonse de Rothschild, visited two Parisian theatres, a circus, and Louis Pasteur's laboratory. Nocturnal interludes were not reported.

Punch (on 21 November) explained his frenetic travelling in 'The Visible Prince' – which suggested, also, an invisible Prince. 'All you have to do is to wear this,' an unidentified someone explains, 'and express a wish to follow H.R.H.' The narrator finds himself receiving an old opera hat in the coffee room of his club from a member he had not seen before. 'Do you mean to say', he asks, 'that if I put this on it will carry me anywhere?' The stranger nods affirmatively.

I put the old opera-hat on my head, and wishing myself near the Illustrious Personage in question, suddenly found myself in Bulgaria. … There was the Illustrious Personage … taking a hurried shot at a bird. He fired successfully, and then looked at his watch. Then he shook hands with someone in attendance, and was gone. I had mechanically removed my hat on finding myself in his presence, and at once found that, uncovered, I was helpless – could move neither hand nor foot.… I put on my hat [nevertheless], and uttered a wish. In a moment I was in Hungary, inspecting a cavalry regiment. The Colonel of the regiment was complimenting the men on their smart appearance. Wearing my hat (for I had already found that my *chapeau* rendered me invisible), I approached nearer, and discovered that the Commanding Officer who was so complimentary was no less a person than the heir to an Illustrious Throne.

By pulling his hat on and off, *Punch*'s narrator follows the Prince of Wales, visiting 'Athens, Berlin, Homburg, Monte Carlo, and Copenhagen. Although I had the advantage of my travelling opera-hat which conveyed me from place to place without effort, I felt that I was wearing myself out, while the illustrious Personage ... seemed to me never to experience fatigue. He was always courteous, always cheerful, always looking at his watch.' After Paris and further wanderings, including the Queen's hide-away on the Isle of Wight, the writer wishes he were back in his own club, and returns the magical hat. 'Thank you,' he says to the stranger, 'but as pleasant as travelling may be, I honestly believe there is only one man in the world who is equal to the strain.' And across from him he notices 'the Illustrious Personage, who ... had just taken out his watch and was looking at it'.

Lord Salisbury met the Prince at Marlborough House on his return, granted half-an-hour before HRH went off for three days to the races at Newmarket. Afterwards the Prime Minister advised the Queen that the Kaiser's denials of any insult to his uncle had to be accepted unless one had the evidence in writing; but the aggravations continued into 1889, the Prince writing to Vicky that he was 'sick' of 'the whole affair'. The Queen wanted an apology, but the Kaiser would only explain to the British ambassador in Berlin, 'My mother and I have the same charac-ters. I have inherited hers. That good stubborn English blood which will not give way is in both our veins.' The Queen unbent enough to invite Willy to Cowes in August for a naval review, to which he sailed in his imperial yacht *Hohenzollern*. Wearing his new British uniform as an hon-orary admiral of the fleet, he was accompanied by his uncle and his cousins Eddy and George.

Like Eddy and Eddy's father, the Kaiser had a passion for uniforms. The monthly *Fun* published a cartoon showing a motherly Queen separ-ating the squabbling (and gaudily costumed) Prince and Emperor with the admonition, 'Now, Albert Edward, here is William come to see us; be a good boy and show him all the pretty things.'

Willy aside, 1889 had begun placidly for the Prince. For July, he and Alix planned a grand wedding for Princess Louise, twenty-two, and the forty-year-old Scottish landowning Earl of Fife; July; and in anticipation, Parliament finally settled the vexing Royal Grant question by increasing the Prince's annual provision by £36,000 from which to provide for his children. Approved also was a capital grant of £60,000 to reduce his debts. It was far from what he wanted because Gladstone, now in Opposition, felt that the Queen should allow her heir a further £50,000 from her own vast resources 'in consideration of the extent to which she allows him to discharge her social duties for her'. But parliamentary oratory meant nothing to the Queen.

Campaigning for the grants, the Prince ingratiated himself with any-one who might command a favourable vote or still a hostile voice, Frank Harris recalling seeing HRH chatting with Socialist agitator H.M. Hyndman. Even the Irish Nationalist Charles Stewart Parnell agreed not to oppose the grants, and at the table at which Gladstone had offered him some concession Lady Gregory suggested placing an inscription, 'At this round-table Parnell was squared.'

From the Queen's standpoint nothing changed. When the Sultan of Zanzibar came, she left most of his entertaining to her son, permitting the Sultan only a luncheon at Windsor, to which the Prince riskily assigned Eddy as escort. When Nasr-ed-Din, the Shah of Persia, again visited, HRH once more had to bear the entertainment, delegating some of it to wealthy and well-placed friends, including the Rothschilds and Sir Albert Sassoon. In May, Natty Rothschild had been named Lord-Lieutenant of Buckinghamshire, about which Charles Carrington carped to the Prince, even though he and Bertie and Lord Rothschild had once been schoolmates at Cambridge. 'It would have been strange ten years ago,' the Prince explained, 'but times change. He is a good fellow and man of business, and he and his family own half the County!'

The month before, on the island of Molokai in Hawaii (then known in Britain as the Sandwich Islands), Father Joseph Damien, a Belgian priest, had died of leprosy in the hospital-colony he had founded to care for its victims. Sympathizing with his sacrifice, Frank Harris suggested to the Prince's friend Mrs Vyner at a luncheon that a memorial fund be established to seek a cure for leprosy. She persuaded him to see the Prince, who might stand as sponsor. Harris first saw Francis Knollys, then the Prince of Wales. 'I'll back you up in every way,' he assured Harris. 'We'll have the meetings here.'

The National Leprosy Fund was established on 18 June 1889 at Marlborough House by an invited committee of the wealthy and élite. Some £20,000 was subscribed, according to Harris, in the first half-hour. A foundation was also initiated for a leprosy hospital in Calcutta, which the Prince approved being named after Albert Victor (who needed something positive associated with his name). Months later, on 13 January 1890, the Prince of Wales presided at a dinner in London to keep the Leprosy Fund's momentum going.

After evading further assignments as impresario, he left on 13 August for Homburg, Copenhagen, Venice and Athens. His retreat to France had come earlier in the year, for the annual Carnival-week Battle of Flowers in Cannes, where, costumed in scarlet, he was the Devil, complete with horns. In Paris he frequented the *Moulin Rouge* pleasure palace in Montmartre, which opened in 1889 and where the sauciest can-can dancer, the bisexual blonde Louise Weber, known as *La Goulue* (glutton), had licence to jeer familiarly, '*Ullo, Wales! Est-ce que tu vas payer mon champagne?*' Henri de Toulouse-Lautrec was to paint her memorably in *La Goulue entering the Moulin Rouge*.

At *Le Chat Noir*, where the doorkeeper was decked out like a Swiss Guard in the Vatican, complete to halberd and sword, the Prince was once greeted loudly by the proprietor, Rodolphe Salis, with 'And how is that mother of yours?' His Royal Highness laughed with the crowd. At the *Cabaret de l'Enfer* (Hell), one entered the red-and-black interior through a gaping Devil's mouth, to be greeted by naked women adorned with cardboard flames and waiters dressed as skeletons. Next door at the *Cabaret du Ciel* (Heaven), barefoot angels in scanty white nightdresses served its patrons 'ambrosia of the gods' – one-franc bock – and conducted burlesque religious rites.

Among the Parisian women who intrigued him was a lithe beauty known as a '*Horizontale*': Liane de Pougy, a one-time performer at the *Folies Bergère*. '*Monseigneur*,' she wrote to him (her English and Spanish were both excellent), 'I am about to make my Paris debut. I would be consecratedly yours if you would come and applaud me.' Charmed by her brazenness, he took along some friends from the Jockey Club, and was bewitched by her scanty costume, which left little to the imagination. As a *courtisane* she quickly commanded high fees, but the Prince, who helped make her a celebrity, could expect a discount.

That the Prince's obesity was beginning to impede his sexual performance in Paris, where little else impeded lust, was evidenced at the House of All Nations, an exclusive Left Bank bordello patronized by European royalty with exotic tastes. When future newspaper publisher Walter Annenberg, later ambassador to Britain, toured the premises in 1926 as a young man on school holiday, the former brothel was a museum. 'They took you around the bedrooms like Tussaud's wax works and told you about the clients,' he recalled. One bedroom was equipped with a hoist allegedly installed for the Prince of Wales, with stirrups and special supports for the object of his desire. 'He stepped in there as if he were going into a stall.'

As the Prince boasted about *belle époque* Paris, where people in the pleasure business (*La Goulue* and a few others excepted) respected his transparent anonymity, 'Everybody recognizes me and nobody knows me.' He could entertain friends at Maxim's, where someone else, flattered by his presence, often paid the bill, or he might slip out to the *Café Anglais*, where, on the second floor, was the *Grand Seize*, a private dining room in white, gold and red reserved for royalty (in Republican France), with a sofa discreetly set in an alcove, and a door which could be locked from the inside.

At the Comédie-Française the Prince could visit the curvaceous Jeanne Granier, described by playwright Jules Renard as possessing 'a bosom swollen with talent'. When she performed at the Théâtre des Capucines, according to Cornelia Otis Skinner, 'she captivated the Prince of Wales, who went backstage to present her with the flower from his buttonhole. Later he presented her with a collection of rare blue china; Granier undoubtedly presented the Prince with a fair exchange, and her reputation was made.' The Prince, however, had found it prudent to turn down the presidency of the British section of the hugely popular International Exhibition of 1889 in Paris, to which 33 million (including HRH) came, and for which the Eiffel Tower was erected. As a Royal, he explained, he could not take part in the celebration of the centenary of the excesses of the French Revolution.

The Prince of Wales's return to Paris was marked, curiously, by a full-page advertisement in *The World* of 9 October for Bushmills Whisky,* in which, escorting the turbaned Persian Shah through the Exhibition, the pair pass a display case and are shown a sampling of the pride of Belfast. The top-hatted Prince explains, 'This, your Majesty, is the celebrated Bushmills Whisky which you tasted in England and liked so much. I feel sure it will get the Gold Medal.' Since the Queen had already appeared, without her permission, on advertisements for Pears Soap, the precedent

---

* The present-day equivalent of Bushmills is manufactured in County Antrim, and spelt 'whiskey'.

left the Prince without legal remedy. Yet identifying him with a popular libation, here given some snob appeal, was excellent (if unsought) public relations.

On 5 September, one of the American ladies the Prince had conspicuously admired was married in London, at ultra-fashionable St George's, Hanover Square. Although he was not present, he sent a brooch in the shape of a horseshoe, studded with diamonds and pearls, to the bride, Jennie (later Jeannie) Chamberlain, and a diamond-and-ruby cravat pin to the groom, Captain Herbert Naylor Leyland, son of an art-collecting London millionaire. (A portrait of Jennie by Edward Hughes, showing a slender young woman in broad-brimmed feathered hat, a basket of flowers under her arm, would be reproduced in the annual *Book of Beauty*.) With studied malice, the *New York World* reported that Miss Chamberlain had been a frequent guest at Sandringham, 'the home of the fat heir to the English throne.... It was once said of her that, disliking the marked attentions of the Prince of Wales, she decided to administer a sharp rebuke, and hit upon a most exasperating title for the fat Prince. It was cabled to New York that at one of the receptions where the Prince was, she deliberately addressed him as 'Jumbo' [after the famous elephant in the London Zoo that had been purchased for America by Phineas Barnum]. This story was ... denied, Miss Chamberlain's friends declaring that she could rid herself of a nuisance without resorting to an unladylike affront.' That all of it was a malicious Republican invention would become obvious when Jennie's elder son was born the next year, and christened Albert Edward.

The Prince was still abroad in October 1889 when one of the more notorious excesses of the century in London – but not his kind of excess – broke into the newspapers. He must have known of the Cleveland Street scandal within days of its exposure, as at its centre was Lord Arthur ('Podge') Somerset, the thirty-eight-year-old son of the Duke of Beaufort and Superintendent of the Stables and extra equerry at Sandringham. On 21 August, a week after the Prince had left for Homburg, the bushy-whiskered Somerset confessed to his friend Reginald Brett that he was in deep trouble and was himself leaving for Homburg. Later the 2nd Viscount Esher and a confidant of the Prince, Brett was the former Private Secretary to Lord Hartington and a dilettantish writer close to the royal circle. In the closet himself, the bisexual Brett understood that morals charges were involved.

Somerset pleaded that he had to raise another £1,000 for his solicitor, Arthur Newton, and was dreading that the Prince, staying at the Villa Imperiale, would hear vicious rumours about him. If this were the case, Podge might have avoided dining with him, or even being seen there. 'A lovely place full of English people who were much surprised to see me', he told Brett. 'I am living here [in rooms] over HRH with whom I lunched yesterday.... I never tasted anything so nasty as the waters but I hope they do me good.... This is a highly moral place and all the ladies of pleasure are turned out!!'

He had apparently gone to Homburg to plead for the Prince's help but was then, for good reason, afraid to confess, and had rashly slipped back to England. On the 27th a warrant was issued for Lord Arthur's arrest, which he avoided by fleeing to Dieppe. From there he telegraphed to the Prince of Wales, who had demanded a meeting on a subject neither had to name. Somerset pleaded that he could not risk it. The Prince had his own sources of information, and an ear for scandal, yet he insisted to an intimate, 'I won't believe it any more than I would if they had accused the Archbishop of Canterbury.' On second thoughts, he allowed warily that Somerset must be 'an unfortunate lunatic'.

On the run, Podge wrote to friends on imposing Marlborough House notepaper, seeking money to buy off informers. Early in October he received another message from the Prince, who wanted to see him and probably knew by then that it was the police's intention to arrest Somerset unless he resigned his appointments and left the country. (It was an unspoken solution for homosexual offences by upper-class men.) Briefly he slipped back to Sandringham and then went openly to the Marlborough Club to recruit help, even going to see Sir Francis Knollys, but not the Prince, on 19 October. Two days later Podge was safely in Rouen. Still, the Prince's own household remained implicated because Eddy was a close friend of Lord Arthur – and 19 Cleveland Street, west of Tottenham Court Road, was a homosexual brothel.

'Your interview with Somerset must have been a very painful one,' the Prince wrote to Knollys while cautiously delaying his own return. 'I had a very kind but sad letter from [Podge's father] the poor Duke – and cannot say *how* deeply I feel for him and the Duchess.... Since the dreadful affair – names of other people who we know will have been mentioned.... It is really *too* shocking! One, a married man whose hospitality I have frequently accepted. If these people are in the same boat as poor Podge – are they to be allowed to go about as before – whilst he has fled the country?' The phraseology suggests that the Prince did not – perhaps yet – connect the scandal with his elder son. But by 10 December 1889, when Podge had learned that the Prince would not help secure for him a job (with horses) in Hungary or Turkey – he had now fled as far as Constantinople – he was less reticent with Brett. Lord Arthur had even offered his prize horse at Sandringham to the Prince, he told Regy, but HRH had turned the tainted gift down. 'My dear old Redge,' Podge confided, 'I can understand the P. of W. being much annoyed at his son's name being coupled with the thing but that was the case [even] before I left – in fact in June or July.'

Concerning Prince Eddy, he explained, 'It had no more to do with me than the fact that we (that is Prince & I) must both perform bodily functions which we cannot do for each other. In the same way we were both accused of going to this place but not together.... Nothing will make me divulge anything I know even if I were arrested.' Yet he had just done so, although the discreet Brett would reveal nothing. No one among the aristocratic Cleveland Street clientele would be tried. A few lower-class telegraph boys would be charged with sodomy, and Newton, the solicitor, pleaded guilty to having attempted to obtain false evidence to vindicate a client, and was sentenced to six weeks' imprisonment. From Downing Street, the wily and knowledgeable Lord Salisbury quietly quashed further litigation, and on family money Podge lived out the remaining thirty-six years of his life in exile in Hyères, on the Riviera.

Having published what it could within the libel laws, and under pressure from persons of influence, the press dropped the matter. Prince Eddy had been quietly under review by the Deputy Public Prosecutor, Hamilton Cuffe. Home Secretary Henry Matthews, acting for the Prime Minister, warned the Director of Public Prosecutions against any 'fishing enquiries about other charges and other persons' beyond Lord Arthur Somerset. Somerset's own solicitor had already cautioned Cuffe that if the case were pursued further 'a very distinguished person will be involved (P. A.V.)',* but evidence was lacking as the Cleveland Street appointment book had mysteriously disappeared. 'I cannot see what good I could do Prince Eddy if I went into Court,' Somerset had written to Brett. 'I might do harm because if I was asked if I had ever heard anything against him

* Prince Albert Victor.

... the questions would be very awkward. I have never mentioned the boy's name except to Probyn, Montagu and Knollys when they were acting for me and I thought they ought to know.'

Eddy escaped charges, although his name was also connected in rumour with the 'Jack the Ripper' killings, as the possible assailant. It was highly unlikely. The grisly Whitechapel murders of apparent prostitutes seem too strenuous an activity for the languid Prince Albert Victor. He would give his family more grief, but not in the courts of law. To keep him distant from scandal, his father sent him almost immediately on a trip to India. The American press, less circumspect about Cleveland Street, published a rumour that to get Prince Eddy out of the way, he might meet with a fortunate accident during his tour (*New York Times*) or, if that failed, that he might be recalled under circumstances 'peculiarly painful to himself and his family' (*New York Herald*). On his return the Queen would infelicitously name her grandson Duke of Clarence and Avondale, adding a doubled title to a double name. To the public he remained 'Collars and Cuffs'.

To remedy the Prince of Wales's own failings as a young man, his parents had sought instant matrimony. Now it was the hapless Eddy's turn. Victoria agreed, and set to finding him a bride. How much the Queen knew is uncertain; the Prince of Wales's actions confirm that he knew everything and said nothing.

Having avoided public scandal in the case of his son and heir, the Prince failed to limit the damage for himself in the following year. His post-Jubilee prestige was still high. As the Queen's impresario he was the symbolic first passenger on the new Underground line* in November 1890. He was host to the unpredictable Kaiser at Spithead for yacht races, and squired Queen Elizabeth of Romania, better known for her poems and plays as 'Carmen Silva', although the Prince very likely had not read a word of them. The press reported a plethora of events in which, foreshadowing the monarchy's future, he was a mere royal ornament. But he could not resist the lure of cards and stakes – and women. Early that September, for the Doncaster Races, the Prince was guest of Mr and Mrs Arthur Wilson at Tranby Croft in Yorkshire. St Leger Week was the great sporting event in the North. Christopher Sykes, with

* The City and South London Line, now part of the Northern Line, at Stockwell Station on 4 November 1890. It was the first royal journey by tube railway.

A TRIPLE ALLIANCE.

*Kaiser Wilhelm II and his uncle exchange toasts of
friendship between nations. It meant nothing. They disliked each
other passionately* (Punch, *11 July 1891*)

whom the Prince had always stayed, was now bankrupt from an excess
of royal entertaining. The butt of Bertie's practical jokes in more affluent
days, in his own country home, Sykes had endured having brandy
poured on his head and his hand singed by the Prince's glowing cigar,
always responding with the obsequious, long-suffering, 'As your Royal
Highness pleases!' Now he was, as a neighbour, only the guest of the
Prince's new hosts.

The Wilson brothers' shipping line was a great national asset, a fact the
Prince, while promoting the social aspirations of the Wilsons, recognized. The visit was also an opportunity for the philandering Prince to

further a new liaison. He expected his current fancy always to be a guest at the country houses where he stayed, and the Wilsons duly invited Lord and Lady Brooke. Other guests included General Owen Williams (who had accompanied the Prince to India), Lord Edward Somerset and his cousin Captain Arthur Somerset (neither tainted by Cleveland Street), Reuben Sassoon the banker, Sub-Lieutenant Berkeley Levett (nephew of the Earl of Denbigh), and several friends of the Prince, including a lastminute addition at his request, Sir William Gordon-Cumming, a lieutenant-colonel in the Scots Guards who had served in the Zulu wars.

The important catch was Lord Brooke, for he had agreed to be there in order to make his wife available for the Prince. This was nothing new for Brooke. Her most assiduous lover had been the Prince's close friend Lord Charles Beresford, who, like Williams, had accompanied the Prince to India. Frances ('Daisy') Brooke, radiantly beautiful even in her teens, had been unsuccessfully targeted by the Queen as a bride for Prince Leopold. Victoria remained a friend of her mother, Lady Rosslyn, and in 1886 the Prince and Princess of Wales had stayed at Easton Lodge, at Dunmow in Essex, with Lord and Lady Brooke while the Beresford affair was going on. Lord Charles, however, had made the mistake late in 1888 of also bedding his own wife. She became pregnant, and the demanding Daisy Brooke was furious at Beresford's infidelity. She wrote a reckless, scorching letter to Lord Charles in January 1889, reproaching him and reminding him (if true) that one of her children was his.

The letter arrived at 100 Eaton Square when Beresford was away in Germany. Claiming later that her husband had instructed her to open all his mail in his absence, Mina Beresford – Lady Charles – read it with alarm, testifying later that Lady Brooke 'conjured him to leave me and return to her; that I had in fact no right to have a child by my own husband'. (She was now seven months' pregnant.) On her return to London, Daisy Brooke received a letter from George Lewis, the omniscient advocate one went to when social or marital disaster threatened. The most feared lawyer in London, he knew the seamy underside of upper-class life and used his canninness to keep most cases out of court. Lewis warned Daisy Brooke to cease harassing Lady Charles's husband – or, his message implied, her letter would be made available to the press.

Lady Brooke determined to retrieve her letter. Her witchery had unmanned others – why not the staid George Lewis? On second thoughts, she decided instead to appeal first to His Royal Highness, who might have more success with Lewis. She arranged an interview at Marlborough House, also arranging herself to appeal to the Prince's susceptibilities. At twenty-eight, she was slender, blooming and dazzling. 'He was charmingly courteous to me,' she wrote later, 'and at length told me he hoped his friendship would make up in part, at least, for my sailor-lover's loss. He was more than kind ... and suddenly I saw him looking at me in a way all women understand. I knew I had won, so I asked him to tea.'

Lewis had long advised the Prince on confidential matters, and had been a guest at Marlborough House himself. Enraptured by Daisy, but considering his intervention only an act of chivalry, the Prince rashly slipped out that night alone and knocked on George Lewis's door at 2 a.m. Once admitted, he asked to see the notorious letter. Overawed by the hour, the man and the demand, Lewis agreed, but said that it was in the files of Lewis and Lewis, Solicitors, in Holborn. (When the Prince did see it he was shocked, and requested its return – which could not legally be done.) In the morning Daisy's new champion called on Lady Charles at Eaton Square and asked her on the basis of their long friend-ship to order George Lewis to destroy the letter, which, if exposed, could injure all parties concerned. She refused, and the Prince left in anger, implying that he could mandate her social death. After further considera-tion, he paid Mina another call, and found her still unwilling. The letter was, she argued, her only protection against Lady Brooke's schemes to re-entrap Beresford. Daisy, the Prince promised, would never bother Lord Charles again. Once the Prince left, Mina Beresford wrote to Lord Salisbury describing the visit. She was certain, she said, that HRH had fallen under Lady Brooke's spell.

Neither Lady Charles's assessment nor the Prince's expectations were misplaced. He was soon offered more than tea with Daisy Brooke, and further dalliances seemed assured at her villa on the Riviera. Hostesses like the eager Mrs Wilson began competing to invite the Brookes in order to snare the Prince of Wales. (Mina Beresford was dropped from such invitation lists, and Beresford was helpless and furious, once encounter-ing the Prince and threatening to strike him.) The Prince gave Lady Brooke the gold ring inscribed 'V & A' that was his parents' confirmation gift, and began calling her 'my own darling Daisy wife'. At the time of the Tranby Croft visit they had, when apart, been writing to each other in a Latin code tied to a common dictionary, in the way that businesses telegraphed in a simple cipher. One telegram in 1889 from the Prince read, 'Mellitorum Hotel de Provence Cannes Ventilo Venicula Verbena.' The three words following the address made no syntactical sense together. *Mellitorum*, the only word unlikely to be found in an ordinary dictionary, was his salutation to Daisy. It meant *Honeysweet*.

On 8 September 1890 at Tranby Croft, after dinner, the Wilsons' daughter, Mrs Ethel Lycett Green, sang sweetly, and as part of the post-prandial entertainment, guests offered recitations. Although it was already eleven, the Prince, bored and impatient, suggested that they play baccarat. The courts had ruled baccarat illegal on grounds that it was a game of chance rather than skill, but the Prince of Wales was social dictator wherever he went, and had brought his own baccarat counters. Dutifully, the Wilsons improvised a baccarat table in their library by putting together smaller whist tables covered by a colourful cloth. HRH took the bank and Sassoon took charge of the counters. As drinks were served, the required four packs of cards were shuffled together and the game began, with most of the guests looking on. Lycett Green went to bed.

An experienced player who often wagered up to £25 per coup, Gordon-Cumming suggested that they place their stakes on a sheet of white paper on which he kept personal score, as the counters were difficult to distinguish against the tapestry cloth. After a few hands, the Wilsons' son, Arthur (known as 'Jack'), thought he saw Gordon-Cumming slyly increasing his stake once the cards were declared in his favour, multiplying his winnings. 'My God, Berkeley,' he whispered to Levett, 'this is too hot! This man next to me is cheating.' Levett refused to believe it, but there was quiet discussion the next day after Gordon-Cumming retired with his winnings, and another game was arranged for that evening to trap him. Those close at hand thought he had again cheated. After most guests retired, General Williams was consulted. He agreed that the Prince Wales would have to be told, and Gordon-Cumming confronted. In exchange for a promise of secrecy, he was to be pledged to give up cards.

Gordon-Cumming quickly denied foul play and entreated His Royal Highness not to believe the charges. 'There are five accusers against you,' said the Prince. The accusers had already prepared a confession for Gordon-Cumming to sign: 'In consideration of the promise made by the

gentlemen whose names are subscribed to preserve silence with reference
to an accusation which has been made with regard to my conduct at baccarat … I will on my part solemnly undertake never to play cards again
as long as I live.' He signed, with the Prince of Wales signing as witness.

Such delicious scandal proved hard to keep quiet. The Prince did his
part by refusing even to answer an appeal from Gordon-Cumming not
to alter 'your manner or love to me when we meet, as meet we must, if I
am to continue to live as I have hitherto lived in the world'. Shortly he
telegraphed the Prince 'that the whole story is the subject of comment in
the Turf Club and elsewhere.… The promise of secrecy made has been
broken by those concerned.' He asked that HRH meet with him but the
Prince would only acknowledge receipt of the telegram. Many blamed
Lady Brooke, alleging that she had heard the story from the Prince, but
Gordon-Cumming sued only his five accusers for slander.

As counsel for the defendants, George Lewis instructed Sir Charles
Russell, once Gladstone's Attorney-General, who was handling their
brief, 'We are desirous that the Prince of Wales's name should not be
introduced unduly into the case.' Inevitably, it was. He had been a guest
of the Wilsons at the time, a participant, and a signer of the breached
document. The trial opened on 1 June 1891. The Lord Chief Justice, Lord

The Tranby Croft trial as perceived by the satirical weekly Moonshine,
13 June 1891, showing Lord Coleridge's complicity in treating the Prince lightly

Coleridge, a close friend of Russell, presided. Sir Edward Clarke, one of the top advocates in England, represented the plaintiff.

The case had already been tried for months in the press, Lewis himself publishing an opinion in the *Pall Mall Gazette*. The affair was, Henry James wrote to Robert Louis Stevenson in Samoa, 'a curious, complicated, ugly *fin de siècle* drama of the "great" world – with the extraordinary stamp of vulgarity on it that is on everything the Prince of Wales has to do with'. Distraught because of the bad publicity for the Prince whatever the outcome, the Queen wrote protectively to Vicky, who was back in Germany, 'I must correct an error which you seem to have made in thinking Bertie wishes to shield this horrid Gordon-Cumming. On the contrary he is very anxious that he should be punished. The incredible and shameful thing is that others dragged him into it and urged him to sign this paper which of course he never should have done. He is in a dreadful state about it for he has been dreadfully attacked.'

As anticipated, the Prince was called as a witness and may have worried as much about the exposure of his relationship with Daisy Brooke as about the baccarat scandal. Clarke was displeased that in the courtroom the Prince had been seated in a red morocco chair on Lord Coleridge's left, emphasizing the special consideration granted him, but the lawyer adroitly used the fact to damage the defence. His long sideburns waggling, Clarke reminded the jury that HRH was a field marshal and presumably familiar with the rule that when an officer's conduct was impugned, it was a military duty to report that to his commanding officer and have an investigation initiated. That had not been done. Called as witness on the second day of the trial, the Prince was offered the opportunity to remain seated, but stepped into the box, kissed the Bible, and, in an uncertain voice – 'a little hoarse and rough', according to the *Daily Chronicle* – denied that he had seen any improprieties himself but had made his judgment on the advice of the others. 'I acquiesced,' he admitted.

'You were greatly distressed at the occurrence?' he was asked. 'Most certainly', he said, again hoarsely.

Both examination and cross-examination were conducted with extraordinary reticence, and shed no light on the case, but as the Prince turned to sit down, a small and hardly noticeable gentleman in the back of the jury box exercised his right to question a witness. He was Goddard Clarke, a businessman from Camberwell. 'Excuse me, your Royal

Highness,' he began. 'I have a question or two to ask you.' The court-room fell silent. 'Are this jury to understand', he went on in a cockney accent, 'that you, as banker on these two occasions, saw nothing of the alleged malpractices of the plaintiff?'

'No,' said the Prince, this time more confidently; 'it is not usual for a banker to see anything in dealing cards, especially when you are playing among friends in their house. You do not for a moment suspect anything of the sort.'

'What was your Royal Highness's opinion at the time', the little juryman continued, 'as to the charges made against Sir William Gordon-Cumming?'

The Prince shrugged – 'made a French gesture with his arm and shoulder' – and explained, 'They seemed so strongly supported – unanimously so – by those who brought them forward, that I felt no other course was open to me but to believe what I was told.'

The juryman sat down, and the audience, tension relieved, laughed, pleased with the plucky interrogator who had matched wits with the Prince.

During the weekend pause in the proceedings, Bertie wrote to his sister Vicky about the 'unnecessary and abominable trial'. The plaintiff, he predicted, had no chance of a favourable verdict 'as the confidence of the defendants is so conclusive, but the British jury are composed of a peculiar class of society and do not shine in intelligence and refinement of feeling. The Lord Chief Justice is very fair and calm.' But as Sir Edward Clarke summed up the plaintiff's case to the jury, he exploded a bombshell. 'If you find that Sir William Gordon-Cumming was *not* guilty of that which is charged against him, and if, as I trust he may, he goes forth from this Court justified by your verdict, I am bound to say that I think it is impossible that Sir William Gordon-Cumming's name be removed from the Army List, and that the names of Field-Marshal the Prince of Wales and of Major-General Owen Williams should remain there.'

Clarke's breathtaking implication was that if the slander could not be proved, the Prince of Wales was unfit by his actions to be a field marshal and also unfit to be king, and if so, should withdraw from the succession in favour of his eldest son and heir. Unperturbed, as the only thing he took seriously was embarrassment, His Royal Highness had never even appeared for the seventh and last day of the trial, Tuesday 9 June. Instead, he had decamped to Ascot. The afternoon *Star* charged that the racing meet at Ascot was too trivial an affair to occupy the Prince's attention while a jury considered the question of honour. Yet Lord Coleridge dismissed the question of honour. Nine-tenths of the solution, he contended to the jury, was to protect the Prince of Wales from dishonour. Loyalty to the monarch had long led people to sacrifice their honour, and Gordon-Cumming may have signed the document to save the Prince of Wales from disgrace. But would a completely innocent man append his name to a document confirming his dishonour 'for fear it should be known that the Prince of Wales had done something of which many

THE GREAT CARD SCANDAL.
THE QUEEN OF HEARTS GIVES THE JACK OF CLUBS "WHAT FOR."

Fun, 25 February 1891, shows the Queen's displeasure at the Tranby Croft scandal

people would disapprove? … You must judge of these acts and of all [Gordon-Cumming] has done exactly as you would judge the acts of any person either in the middle or the lower class of society. And now I send you to your duty.'

The jury found for the defendants. Mrs Wilson seized a telegraph form and dispatched the joyful news to Ascot. The defendants, escorted by George Lewis – who in two years' time was to be knighted – were hissed by spectators as they left the Court. At the races, the Prince and Princess of Wales were greeted by jeers of 'Oh, Baccarat!' and 'Have you brought your counters?' Despite the rude reception, the *Pall Mall Gazette* reported, the Prince, in his dark grey frock coat, 'appeared sufficiently well pleased with himself'. Yet he was heard to remark to a friend that George Lewis had predicted that Russell's painful summing-up for the defendants 'will give the Radicals 100,000 votes at the general election'.

Even *The Times* wished that the Prince 'had signed a similar declaration' to that of the embattled Gordon-Cumming abjuring gambling at cards, and the Queen pressed her son on the matter. The verdict had been widely deplored and the Crown left, for the moment, in disrepute. Victoria insisted that her son write a letter to the Archbishop of Canterbury, to be made public, deploring gambling. It was an empty gesture recognized as ludicrous by newspaper readers who knew the Prince of Wales had been betting on horses at Ascot as the jury was rendering its decision. Lord Salisbury advised that a public letter would be 'injudicious', but under his mother's pressure the Prince of Wales wrote one anyway. Released to the press, it expressed his 'horror of gambling', which may have been interpreted as his horror of being discovered at it. Cartoonists were delighted. In the satirical monthly *Fun* for February 1891 a cartoon of two playing cards filled an entire page. One showed an angry Queen waggling her finger under the caption 'NO CARDS'. The other, a Jack, pictured a tearful Prince of Wales, wearing a 'baccarat' sash, beneath the caption 'NEVER NO MORE'. *Puck* featured a grotesquely large and glowering Victoria brandishing a thick-handled feather-duster in one hand while holding up, for a pygmy Prince of Wales to see, a list of his recent offences, including 'keeping low company', 'advertising actresses', 'hard drinking', 'in debt to everybody', 'loose morals', 'inveterate gambling propensities', and 'too, too, too fond of baccarat!' On his coat is a placard reading, '*Ich deal*', a pun on the Royal motto *Ich dien* – I serve.

L'Enfant Terrible *(Puck, June 1891)*

In the early 1920s, Max Beerbohm was to publish a cartoon that summed up the Queen's likely reaction as it could not be pictured in 1891. In it the large, balding Bertie is shown standing in the corner at the order of his grim, glowering mother, who sits formidably in the foreground. It is captioned, 'The rare, rather awful visits of Albert Edward, Prince of Wales, to Windsor Castle'.

With the Prince also continuing to be a subject of scandal because of his public amours – Daisy was known as the 'babbling Brooke' – Alexandra, who had shown herself loyally at Ascot, spent much of her time away from her husband. She had long played her public role of consort, but beneath that there was no marriage left. The sole exception remained the children – and even there the Prince concerned himself very little indeed about his three daughters. The couple's joint conundrum was the matrimonial prospects of Prince Eddy, a future king in any predictable order of things. He had escaped censure in the Cleveland Street affair, about which she may have known more than it appeared. He had numerous orders, honours and titles, all of them empty. He appeared vacuous because he was exactly that. He could barely read, had inherited deafness from his mother, and had a drooping, vacant face that some women – and perhaps some men – found attractive. Little of his actual life was known to Alexandra, who hoped that a woman of character might prop him up. The Queen had ideas of marrying him to one of Princess Alice's daughters, Alix of Hesse, but she was wisely not interested. It showed 'great strength of character', her grandmother acknowledged to Vicky, for the girl was refusing 'the greatest position there is'.*

Prospective wives could not have been entirely unaware of Prince Eddy's reputation. Sharing his life would have been neither easy nor easeful, even for a future queen. He drank heavily and chain-smoked strong Turkish cigarettes; he had been treated for gonorrhea and possibly for syphilis; he had gout, although he was only twenty-seven. His manly enthusiasms extended from the hunt to the boudoir and the homosexual brothel. Nevertheless, Victoria searched assiduously for brides, with Vicky canvassing the German possibilities, including other cousins. Perhaps because she was exotic and unsuitable, Eddy became interested in Hélène Louise, the daughter of the comte de Paris, a devout Roman Catholic. Although Victoria warned that she was constitutionally ineligible, Eddy proposed and was accepted, but her father, a pretender to the non-existent French throne, considered conversion too high a price to pay and ordered his daughter home. Eddy quickly transferred his affections to Lady Sybil St Clair Erskine, whose rank, the Queen declared, would not do. By January 1891 an English-born cousin was put on show at Sandringham. Princess May – her name was Mary – was the daughter of Princess Mary Adelaide, Duchess of Teck and the Queen's first cousin, who was the sister of the Duke of Cambridge. May was fair, stately, and nearly twenty-four. She had given up hope of finding a suitable husband. Eddy was not the picture of her dreams, but his prospects made up for his many deficiencies.

Her parents were wild over the possibility. 'Fat Mary' – May's mother – was the most popular Royal in the kingdom. The Queen found her buoyancy and jollity oppressive, and Mary had seldom been a royal guest.

---

* Instead, Alix married the future Tsar, and was murdered by the Communists after the revolution in 1918.

From a current photograph Victoria declared the Princess to be acceptable, and summoned her to Balmoral in May with her brother Adolphus. The eccentric Duke and his Duchess were not invited, and Victoria conducted an unhindered inspection. That Princess May passed muster was made clear by a letter of 19 August 1891, from Sir Francis Knollys to his counterpart at Windsor, Sir Henry Ponsonby, to the effect that Albert Victor's parents had suggested, assuming the Queen's approval, that he marry May the following spring, after further seasoning-by-travel to the Continent and the colonies. To the Prime Minister's Private Secretary, Knollys had already admitted (8 August 1891) that the Queen's '*views on certain social* subjects are so strong, that the Prince of Wales does not like to tell his real reason for sending Prince Eddy away, which is intended as a *punishment*, and as a means of keeping him out of harm's way'.

'I think the preliminaries are pretty well settled,' Knollys explained to Ponsonby, 'but do you suppose Princess May will make any resistance? I do not anticipate any real resistance on Prince Eddy's part if he is properly managed.'

Eddy had already been away, under close supervision, enduring as long a trip to India as officials had been able to arrange for him while the Cleveland Street affair was fading, for lack of information, from a press far less intrusive than it would become in the next century. On returning, he was meaninglessly promoted to lieutenant-colonel in his regiment, and sent off anew. He came back looking thin and yellow beneath his doe-like eyes and waxed, turned-up cavalry moustache. As the Prince of Wales began planning his uncomfortable impresario role at the wedding of his heir, he explained to the Queen, 'The real reason why we thought visits to certain Colonies were desirable was because the voyages would be longer.' The Queen understood. A timely betrothal was 'for the good of the country'. The future of the monarchy, Victoria understood – if it survived Bertie – lay in a young woman who would have to be more guardian than wife. She also had to look like a queen.

The Princess of Wales was away in Denmark in October and Russia in November. She intimated no plans to return. The Prince had intended to mark his fiftieth birthday alone at Sandringham. While he pondered how to restore the domestic status quo, May arrived at Balmoral for Victoria's further inspection just after noon on 5 November 1891. (Her parents were again not invited.) On 8 November, the day before the Prince of Wales's birthday, Prince George fell ill. When his condition

A JUBILEE GREETING!

Mr. Punch *(for self and everybody)*. "HEARTY CONGRATULATIONS, SIR!—KNOWN YOU FIFTY YEARS,
AND LIKE YOU BETTER THAN EVER!!"

*Mr Punch greets the Prince on his fiftieth birthday as the public
continued to discount his private failings (*Punch, *14 November 1891)*

worsened, he was moved to Marlborough House for more expert medical
oversight. Alix had planned to remain indefinitely in the Crimea with her
two unmarried daughters, but once George was diagnosed with typhoid
fever she hurried back, arriving in London on 22 November, and was
briefly reconciled with her husband over George's sickbed. He was pronounced out of danger on 3 December, just in time for the announcement of impending nuptials for his elder brother.

After carriage rides in the hills, amateur theatricals indoors in weather
even Victoria (who liked Scottish chill) found 'wet & cheerless', and
desperate visits to Princess Beatrice with her brother 'Dolly' to smoke

cigarettes out of range of the Queen, May understood that she had passed her final examination. On 3 December the Prince of Wales confirmed to his mother that Eddy had been instructed to propose. Visiting Windsor soon after, he gushed to the Queen, 'I have some good news to tell you; I am engaged to May Teck.' Victoria said she was delighted.

Before Christmas all of England knew. In a speech at the annual Civil Service Dinner the Prince of Wales declared, 'I am quite proud to think that my son marries one who was born in this country, and has the feelings of an Englishwoman.' *Punch* on 19 December 1891 published a full-page drawing, 'Home and Beauty', showing a bemedalled Eddy in uniform with May at his side, clinging to his arm. The Queen allotted them post-nuptial apartments in St James's Palace, and on a trip they made to Windsor she conducted the happy couple into the Mausoleum at Frogmore for the ritual posthumous blessing of the Prince Consort.

A splashy wedding was becoming essential, not only to ensure the succession, but to distract the public. In London, *Truth* had published a satirical piece based on the Kaiser's last tempestuous visit, inventing Willy's views (that were very likely accurate) of Tranby Croft, and of Bertie's women and their complaisant husbands. An anonymous pamphlet about the Prince of Wales and Lady Brooke, unsubtly titled *Lady River* (and actually authored by Mrs Gerald Paget) was captivating purchasers with its spicy innuendo. According to *Truth*, all a London hostess had to do was to announce a drawing-room reading from *Lady River* to fill her guest list. Despite the promise of a royal wedding, it was a glum Christmas at Sandringham. Rather than be under his own roof, the Prince of Wales prudently absented himself.

In its post-Christmas issue, *Punch* ran a cartoon that, despite the Prince's troubles, offered him some consolation. He had just received a letter from Lord Charles Beresford condemning the social ostracism of his wife, and refusing to accept explanations that the Prince had never intended to cause her any inconvenience. 'Sir,' wrote his one-time boon companion, now commander of the *Undaunted*, 'I cannot accept your Royal Highness's letter as in any way an answer to my demand, Your Royal Highness's behaviour to my wife having been a matter of common talk in the two years that I have been away from England on duty.' Since Beresford had served in the Cabinet before returning to sea, the Prince turned the letter over to Lord Salisbury, who knew all, but despite the rebuke to the Prince, intended to keep out of the affair.

The Christmas issue of *Truth*, never respectful of the Royals, included an illustration juxtaposing the young Queen in 1841 as the epitome of virtue and family life with the Prince of Wales in 1891 as the devotee of card-playing and wagering on horses. HRH looked better in *Punch*, where, in an imaginative cartoon, he caroused with Falstaff and jovial Mr Punch at the venerable Boar's Head Tavern in Eastcheap. The three discuss how the ways of princes had changed, and how public-spirited was the life of Prince Albert Edward compared with that once led by Prince Hal. Although Falstaff agrees, he slips into calling Bertie 'Hal' (as Disraeli had privately done), and Mr Punch concedes that a great prince requires diversions. The Prince confides that decades of laying foundation stones and other empty activities as royal impresario have wearied him. Sympathizing, Falstaff toasts the Prince of Wales, calling him 'most Royal imp of fame', as well as 'sweet boy' and 'my King'. In such contradictory fashion the king-in-waiting ushered out 1891.

XIV

King-in-Waiting

1892–1897

To join in the celebration of Prince Eddy's twenty-eighth birthday on 8 January 1892, Princess May and her parents arrived at Sandringham four days in advance. May hardly knew her future husband, yet their wedding was set for 27 February, seven weeks away. A rare occurrence – although few realized how rare it had become – was that the Prince and Princess of Wales were together under the same roof. Under a spousal truce, guests filled Sandringham after the new year. Influenza had struck London, and some visitors were in the early stages of illness or just recovering. Both May and Eddy had colds, but the bridegroom-to-be went off shooting with friends anyway, returning on the afternoon of 7 January, the day before his birthday, so ill that he went directly to bed. The next morning he was barely able to totter downstairs to examine his gifts, and May found herself more nurse than guest. A screen was set up in Eddy's bedroom over which visitors could peer, but only May and Alix were permitted at the bedside by Dr Laking.

When Eddy's fever rose on the 9th and it was obvious that at best he had influenza, Laking sent for Dr W. H. Broadbent, who had treated Prince George. Eddy was said to be suffering from an inflammation of the lungs. Physicians were shy of using the frightening word *pneumonia*, and no one was going to suggest a venereal connection. By the 12th he was 'rather worse' although on the 11th he had been 'going on rather satisfactorily.' On the 13th he was delirious, raving and shouting the names of people who were not there, and never had been. 'Who's that?' he asked over and over again, seeing no one. Early on the morning of the 14th he alternately raved and slept, and a clergyman was called. Princess Helena, his aunt, kept the Queen posted. As Eddy sank, his mother turned to Dr Laking to ask hopelessly, 'Can you do nothing more to save him?' Laking shook his head.

Helena brought to the Queen the news that the heir presumptive to the Crown (after his father) had died. 'Poor, poor parents,' Victoria wrote in her journal; 'poor May to have her whole bright future … merely a dream! Poor me, in my old age, to see this promising young life cut short!' Like others in the family and in the Government, she knew that the loss was far less than a tragedy, but emotions at such times overwhelm reality. Cautioned not to attend the funeral in the January chill, Victoria put Windsor at the disposal of the bereaved parents, and remained at Osborne. It was, she wrote, 'a horrible dream'.

'Gladly would I have given my life for his,' Bertie lamented to her, 'as I put no value on mine.' At St George's Chapel on 20 January, as Alix occupied the balcony from which Victoria, in perpetual mourning, had watched the Princess's wedding in 1863, May placed a bridal wreath of orange blossom on the coffin. The press recalled Hamlet's lines about Ophelia's bridal flowers strewing, instead, her grave, and Tennyson rushed into print a poem of consolation beginning, 'The bridal garland falls upon the bier.'

The romantic pathos of the death captured the nation as the life of the flaccid and unpromising Prince could never have. Shops and theatres were shut across the nation, and ministers sermonized the following Sunday about a dead prince who would never be king, rather than about a suspected denizen of Cleveland Street. Newspapers, too, preferred not to observe how hopelessly wrong Eddy would have been for the lot to which the accident of birth had destined him, and there was an outburst of public sorrow. To old Gladstone, soon to be in Downing Street once more but away in Biarritz chasing the sun, the Prince described Alix and himself as 'heart-broken'. It was, he wrote to his friend of Oxford days, Mrs Lorina Liddell (mother of the Alice of *Alice in Wonderland*), 'one of those calamities that one can never really get over'. Blind to what a potential calamity Eddy was, the Princess of Wales receded into her grief, preserving in Victorian fashion Eddy's bedroom as it was and draping a Union Jack over the deathbed. For years she ordered a daily fire for his grate. At Sandringham, Alfred Gilbert, sculptor of *Eros* in Piccadilly Circus, planned a tomb for St George's Chapel at the family's commission that would show a fallen warrior, sword in hand and martial cloak open to reveal his uniform. In bronze, Eddy would remain 'Collars and Cuffs'.

Princess May was immediately the subject of intense national speculation. Why should she not marry the Duke of Clarence's brother, and remain in possession of her destiny? George was twenty-six and unmarried. 'May was never in love with Prince Eddy,' Victoria would concede, contributing to the speculation, but she put no pressure on the 'crushed flower', or upon George. At Sandringham the situation was different. Both bereaved parents made it known to her that they continued to regard her as a daughter, and Alix asked May to call her *Mama*, as before. No one had to be reminded that twenty-six years before, Alix's own sister had married Alexander, the heir to the Russian throne, after his brother Nicholas, to whom she had been betrothed, had died. And she now wore the crown. There was other covert pressure on Prince George. Although he turned aside a request from the Queen that he call himself Albert when he came to the throne himself, she agreed to his father's request that he be created Duke of York. She urged him, also, to leave the Navy and prepare for the role he had never anticipated.

Prince George thought he had an informal arrangement with a cousin, Marie, the seventeen-year-old daughter of the Duke of Edinburgh, his uncle, but Marie's mother, a Tsar's daughter, loftily rejected the suit. George also had young women of another sort at Southsea and St John's Wood, both inappropriate for his prospects. The public knew nothing of any of them, and hoped that there was still a chance for May.

A grand new wing which the Prince of Wales could not afford was being added to Sandringham, and a new yacht, the *Britannia*, also beyond his income, was being built for him on the Clyde. Uninterested in supervising the construction of either one, he was impatient, as every spring, to be away. With Alix, he had already made the required trip to Denmark, for the golden wedding festivities of his parents-in-law, the King and Queen. 'Poor Bertie', the Queen wrote to the widowed Vicky that June, '– his is not a nature made to bear sorrow, or a life without amusement and excitement – he gets irritable.'

Far more painful, privately, for the Prince than the loss of the expendable Eddy was the serious illness of a long-time friend, Sir Arthur Sullivan, who was wracked by excruciating kidney stones and surviving on morphine. The Prince sent his doctor to Sullivan at Monte Carlo, who advised that the composer, only forty-nine, would not survive risky surgery. Without it, Sullivan somehow pulled through, convalescing at Sandringham and composing *Haddon Hall*, produced without W. S. Gilbert, from whom he was estranged, at the Savoy Theatre on 24 September. It was not a success.

The Prince took his usual weeks at spas and on the Riviera after mourning for Eddy had officially abated. Lady Brooke had a villa at Beaulieu, just to the west of Monte Carlo, where he could indulge his infatuation. At Bad Nauheim he made his uneasy peace with Wilhelm II, who saw it as the price for an invitation to England to race his yacht at Cowes. At Nauheim, too, that July, the Prince met 'Mark Twain'. The humourist had boasted in a facetious magazine piece a few years earlier that although he had not met the Queen personally, he had once seen the Prince of Wales from an omnibus going in the opposite direction. Probably the most distinguished living American author, and famous for his scoffing at royalty, Sam Clemens seemed to seek introductions to the mighty to compensate for his upstart status. One of his daughters joked, 'Soon Papa won't have anyone to meet but God.'

He and the Prince did not hit it off. Although HRH did not read much, he must have known of the book published in England only two years before as *A Yankee at the Court of King Arthur*, an irreverent spoof which some English critics had attacked as offensive to monarchy.* What the Prince did not know, and Clemens did not venture to tell him, was that an earlier Mark Twain novel, *The Prince and the Pauper* (1882), an indictment of the class system described by an English reviewer as 'a ponderous fantasia on English history', began in first draft with young Prince Albert Edward changing places with a boy in an early Victorian slum setting. Some months later (November 1877) Twain moved his plot back in time, writing in his notebook, 'Edward VI & a little pauper exchange places a day or so before Henry VIII's death. The prince wanders in rags & hardships & the pauper suffers the (to him) horrible miseries of princedom, up to the moment of the crowning, in Westminster Abbey, when proof is brought & the mistake rectified.' The Prince of Wales could have told Clemens, from his own childhood, about some 'horrible miseries of princedom'.

* Royal sensitivities to the encroachments of democracy were such that in March 1893 both the Queen and Prince of Wales were hostile to the raising of the Legation in Washington to the status of Embassy. Neither wanted a diplomat with the rank of ambassador representing them in any nation which had no monarch as head of state.

At Bad Homburg the Prince of Wales awaited his son, now Duke of York, who had just left the Navy to be groomed as future king. Without ambition, the new Duke also lacked confidence. Bertie planned soon to meet with May's parents. Marking time at the Kursaal until George arrived, the Prince noticed the thirty-seven-year-old popular novelist Marie Corelli (formerly Minnie Mackay), whom he invited to sit at his left at dinner, which established her local reputation. 'You must not stand on ceremony with me,' he told her. Soon came a note from the Prince's equerry asking her to lunch at the Ritter's Park Hotel. As she arrived the Prince drew forward a black-bearded young man and said, 'Miss Corelli, my son George, who is well acquainted with your books.'

Since Miss Corelli had a public, the Prince of Wales was eager to explain his awkward position as heir. He did not want to go to the races at Baden, he claimed, but only his presence would help the dull season. He did not want to race his new yacht at Cowes, as two seamen on the *Britannia* had drowned in an accident, but the owner of the *Vigilant* threatened to take the Challenge Cup back to America, which could not be tolerated. The lot of a Wales was difficult indeed. During one of their strolls on the wooded paths near the Kursaal the novelist gave the Prince a copy of her best-selling *A Romance of Two Worlds* in the Hindi translation – which for HRH was as good as in any other language.

Miss Corelli was to see him again, and included a scene in her *The Sorrows of Satan* (1895) in which the narrator is received at a levée at St James's Palace. En route in their carriage in Court dress, his friend Lucio Rimanez scoffs, 'His Royal Highness the Prince of Wales is not exactly the Creator of the Universe…. There is as much fuss about him as if he were –, in fact, more. The Creator doesn't get half as much attention bestowed upon him as Albert Edward. We never attire ourselves in any special way for entering the presence of God; we don't put so much as a clean mind on.'

'But then,' says the narrator, 'God is *non est*, and Albert Edward is *est.*'

A change of governments loomed in London in August 1892, as Gladstone, in his early eighties, deaf and failing in sight, was again to be Prime Minister. While the Queen had no choice but to name him – as earlier, all his rivals withdrew when he announced his intentions – she hoped for a more amenable Cabinet, in particular to have the Foreign Ministry in safe hands. The Prince urged her to press for the Earl of Rosebery, now practically in the Rothschild cousinhood as he had married Mayer's only child, Hannah. (Bertie had signed the register.) But Hannah had recently died and Rosebery wanted nothing to do with politics. Asking him would 'not do for me', the Queen explained to Bertie. He should do it. Writing from his yacht, *Aline*, at Cowes, the Prince drafted a persuasive, statesmanlike letter asking Rosebery to reconsider, and to preside for at least six months. Writing as 'Albert Edward', he added,

> There are many grave questions at the moment affecting our interests in India, Egypt, and Morocco; and it requires a very watchful eye to prevent Russia and France from harming us, and a thorough knowledge of the subject which nobody possesses more than you do. Let me, therefore, implore of you to accept office (if Mr Gladstone will give you a free hand in foreign affairs, and not bind you to agree with him in *all* his home measures) for the Queen's sake and for that of our great Empire!
>
> Forgive me for bothering you, my dear Rosebery; but I should not write so strongly if I did not feel the grave importance of your accepting office in the present serious political crisis.

With reluctance, Rosebery accepted, and the Prince, emboldened by his success, raised with the new Government the question of his thwarted access to Cabinet decisions. Diffident about high office despite his distinguished record, Rosebery was privately suspected of harbouring a dark side to his life belied by his idyllic marriage and family life. His now-chronic insomnia, attributed to the death of his beloved Hannah, may have also been due to worry about exposure of his relationship, never proved, with Viscount Drumlanrig, his Private Secretary and the eldest son of the irascible, eccentric 8th Marquess of Queensberry (who was also the father of Oscar Wilde's last lover, Lord Alfred Douglas). At Bad Homburg in August 1893, Queensberry confronted Rosebery with a horsewhip. He considered the Earl a 'cur and Jew friend' and a 'Snob Queer', and accused him of homosexual improprieties with Drumlanrig. The Prince of Wales, and then the local police, intervened, and the incident was hushed up. In October 1894 Drumlanrig shot himself in what was publicly described as a hunting accident, but may have followed an attempt to blackmail him. Rosebery desperately wanted to retire into private life. The Prince of Wales saw him as his best ally in the Cabinet, and – despite Rosebery's private anxieties – wanted him at the top of it.

Now optimistic about the Prince's long-denied access to the Cabinet red boxes, Edward Hamilton, still Gladstone's Private Secretary, noted, 'As latterly the Queen seems more disposed to take counsel with the Prince, I should think his wishes may very probably be met.' They were not. The Queen queried Gladstone whether his predecessor had briefed the Prince, and was informed that Salisbury had not done so in any systematic fashion. Very well, said Victoria. Brief the Prince only on 'any important decision'. He would still have no Cabinet key. Gladstone's memorandum on the ministerial meeting of 7 November 1892 read, disappointingly for Bertie, 'The Prince of Wales to have information as to Cabinets on the same footing as heretofore.'

Formally he remained without status, and powerless, making ironic a comment by the grey-goateed, coppery Sebele, heir to the throne of British-protected Bechuanaland (now Botswana) in South Africa. Sechele, the *Kgosi*, had by 1892 ruled for six decades, and his son wrote, wryly,

> I, Sebele, am the same age as the Prince of Wales.... I am the eldest son of Sechele, the Chief of the Bakwena; Albert Edward, the Prince of Wales, is the eldest son of the Queen of England. My father still rules and I do not govern; it is the same with His Royal Highness – he does not rule in England. So I say I resemble the Prince of Wales.

With his future predetermined, Albert Edward returned to the frustrating present, in which he divided his time between the required supervision of ceremony and family, and the pursuit of pleasure. It was no longer much of a chase. Daisy Brooke was eager to be the focus of his life, which meant the focus of all the social life in England that really counted. Usually with her complaisant and invisible husband, she was at balls at Marlborough House and wherever the Prince was invited. She sailed with him at Cowes, almost under the disapproving eye of the Queen, who was often nearby at Osborne. She was at the races with him at Ascot, Doncaster, Epsom, and Newmarket. When in Paris at his favourite hotel, the Bristol, he arranged rooms close by for her at the Hotel Vendôme. When she shopped at such elegant couturiers as Worth's and Doucet's, the Prince would accompany her; when they dined in public they patronized the élite establishments. The press might print gossip about them, but separately, sometimes on either side of a semi-colon, to link them without obvious scandal. When he stayed at Easton

Lodge, her country home in Essex, never without a large party of other guests, Lord Brooke was in the background, the Prince's ostensibly pleased host. And for Brooke, in compensation, there was always the possibility of dalliance with another lady in their set. As Mrs Gerald Paget, the author of the scurrilous *Lady River*, put it about her côterie and time, 'As cultivated courtesans, we practised upon other men the arts which had been taught us by our husbands.' Layers of petticoats and tightly laced stays never inhibited lovers, as affairs among the luxuriously clothed were seldom furtive and impulsive, but leisurely and pre-arranged. Ladies' maids who tidied up any disarray were discreet, or dismissed without references – occupational death.

Although one of the Brookes' neighbours in Essex was another romantic novelist, Elinor Glyn, who wrote lightly in memoirs of how guests at Easton Lodge adroitly amused themselves, it was Marie Corelli in *The Sorrows of Satan* who described in fiction the accepted view of the upper-class house party of the early 1890s. In a letter meant to be read between the lines, the novel's Lucio Rimanez declines, from Paris, an invitation to Willowsmere Court:

> You will have enough to do in the entertainment of your distinguished guests, for I suppose there is no amusement they have not tried and found more or less unsatisfactory, and I am sorry I can suggest nothing particularly new for you to do. Her Grace the Duchess of Rapidryder is very fond of being tossed in a strong table-cloth between four able-bodied gentlemen of good birth and discretion, before going to bed o'nights – she cannot very well appear on a music-hall stage you know, owing to her exalted rank, – and this is a child-like, pretty and harmless method of managing to show her legs, which, she rightly considers, are too shapely to be hidden. Lady Bouncer, whose name I see in your list, always likes to cheat at cards, – I would aid and abet her in her aim if I were you, as she can only clear her dressmaker's bill by her winnings.... The Honourable Miss Fitz-Gander, who has a great reputation for virtue, is anxious, for pressing and particular reasons, to marry Lord Noodles, – if you can move on matters between them into a definite engagement of marriage ... , you will be doing her a good turn and saving society a scandal. To amuse the men I suggest plenty of shooting, gambling and unlimited smoking. To entertain the Prince, do little, – for he is clever enough to entertain himself privately

with the folly and humbug of those he sees around him.... He is a keen observer, – and must derive infinite gratification from his constant study of men and manners, which is sufficiently deep and searching to fit him for the occupation of even the throne of England.... And there is nothing he will appreciate in his reception as a lack of toadyism, a sincere demeanour, an unostentatious hospitality, a simplicity of speech, and a total absence of affectation.... Of all the Royalties at present flourishing on this paltry planet, I have the greatest respect for the Prince of Wales.

While Lillie Langtry had been an exotic creature, foreign to the Princess of Wales's set, Alix looked differently upon Lady Brooke. An aristocrat, she was soon by her husband's inheritance to become Countess of Warwick. If the public was unaware of her liaison with the Prince before Tranby Croft, it knew thereafter; and Alix, like others, assumed that the 'babbling Brooke' was a betrayer of Bertie's confidences. When the 5th Earl succeeded to Warwick Castle, overlooking the Avon, Daisy remodelled a wing to give the Prince of Wales his own suite next to her own bedroom and dressing room. When she gave a ball in his honour, whether at the Castle or at Easton Lodge, she ordered special trains from London. As *The World*, edited by the fearless Henry Labouchere, had written wryly on 10 June 1885, 'It would be affectation to ignore that the presence of the Prince of Wales is the goal on which the eyes of the professional entertainers ... is fixed. But that beatific vision is reserved only for those who ... have passed through a period of probationary ordeals, and have risen, by slowly graduated ascents, to an altitude that is truly sublime.' Daisy had bypassed the intermediate steps.

In a memoir in old age she claimed that her husband and the Prince were the best of friends: 'They shared a great liking for sport, which drew them close together.' This was a fiction. On public occasions the cuckolded Brooke had to be visible, but she consulted the Prince of Wales about the guest list, and her husband was relegated to a distant bedroom. His chief distinction, beyond gossip, was to become Mayor of Warwick in 1894.

Although the Princess of Wales preferred not to offer even the most token, pro forma, acknowledgement of Daisy Warwick, Alix was obliged to play the royal role into which she had married. In June 1893 she was observed in an 'omnibus-box' at the opera with her husband, and several peeresses including Lady Lonsdale and Lady Brooke. At a concert at Alfred Rothschild's mansion, where the Prince offered a toast to Adelina Patti, and the Princess was at his side, Lady Brooke was resplendent in white and silver. It was an especially bleak time for Alix, as she had doted on the hapless Eddy, and just a year after his death she lost the only love she cared about, Oliver Montagu. The commander of the Royal Horse Guards and an equerry to the Prince of Wales, the forty-eight-year-old Montagu had served Alix like a *cavalier servante* of old, with loyalty and a love just short of its physical aspect. He never married: all his emotions were expended in her service. She wept for three days. According to Reginald Brett, writing to a friend, 'For many years her life can only have been interesting through its relation to him.... So she will probably turn away with her broken wing and gravitate more to her relations in Russia and Denmark.'

Although she was to do exactly that, her escape from oppressive loneliness, while the Prince carried on with Daisy, had to await the betrothal of Prince George to May of Teck in the early months of 1893, and a grand royal wedding. The anticipated formal proposal of marriage occurred on 3 May 1893. On 6 July, in the Chapel Royal, St James's Palace, the regal May became the third lady in the land, the pre-eminent two looking on with gratification. That May herself was pleased with her rescue from the fate into which either marriage to Prince Eddy – or his death – might have plunged her, was clear from Lady Geraldine Somerset's snide description of the procession: 'Instead of coming in the exquisite, ideal way the Princess of Wales did at her wedding with her eyes cast down – too prettily – May looked right and left and slightly bowed to her acquaintances! A great mistake.' Quoting from *The Tempest* the press cited 'a contract of true love'.

While Alix escaped to Copenhagen, the newlyweds honeymooned at Sandringham House, then moved to spacious York Cottage on the estate, given to them by the Prince of Wales. Sandringham House itself was a curious place for the bride to be, as her mother-in-law continued to keep Eddy's deathbed room unaltered. Presumably the door remained closed. In 1896, when the Waleses' daughter Maud married her Danish cousin Prince Charles (second son of the King), who in 1905 would become King Haakon of newly independent Norway, the Prince of Wales gave them for their use in England his Appleton Farm, also on the sprawling Sandringham estate.

In the face of his obvious abandonment by Alix, it was important for the Prince of Wales not only to carry on his expected functions, but also to counteract criticism of his personal life, and to be perceived as increasingly kingly. Despite appearances to the contrary, his mother could not reign for ever. Her journals note her progressive immobility – 'rheumatism in my legs', as she described it; and her eyesight was deteriorating as cataracts clouded her vision. The Prince accepted an appointment to serve on the Commission to Investigate Relief for the Aged Poor, and would attend thirty-five of its forty-eight sessions, cancelling his annual spring holiday in France to do so. One Radical Liberal member, James Stuart, assumed that he had been prompted to ask particular questions when his turn came, 'but I soon found out they were on his own initiative, and that he had a very considerable grasp of the subjects he dealt with'. Still, the Commission failed to resolve whether old-age pensions should be state-funded or contributory, and the Prince would not sign the controversial result. In 1908, as king, he assented to an Old-Age Pensions Bill.

The Commission on Housing, on which he had also sat, had come up with recommendations that had proved inadequate, as they failed to require landlords to maintain their properties in habitable condition, trusting to private-sector competition for tenants. More drastic measures would be needed, and the Prince of Wales in a speech on Lord Mayor's Day in November 1895 conceded, 'We are all Socialists now-a-days.' Again moving with the times, he sat in the Lords in February 1893 when Gladstone spoke for two hours, until his voice became feeble, in introducing his Home Rule Bill, which had no chance of passage. Both the Queen and the Prince were hostile to it, but the Prince knew, nevertheless, that Home Rule was for the best, and telegraphed to his mother in Osborne that the speech was 'impressive'.

Between trips to France to visit Daisy Warwick, the Prince, accompanied by his cousin 'Fat Mary', the Duchess of Teck, appeared on 20 April at the second night of Oscar Wilde's *A Woman of No Importance*, at the Haymarket, a witty melodrama about lovers' deceptions. The play was to have a long run, but Wilde, in white waistcoat with a bunch of lilies at his buttonhole, was booed for the line, 'England lies like a leper in purple.' After the curtain the Prince told Wilde with delight, 'Do not alter a single line.'

'Sire,' said Oscar, 'your wish is my command.' But he quietly cut the controversial 'leper' line, though he would remark, 'What a splendid country, where princes understand poets.' Yet in the same season, acting as an arbiter of morals, HRH objected to the musical comedy *The Gaiety Girl*, by Harry Greenbank and Sidney Jones, because a parson was burlesqued. Lord Carrington, another long-time moralist, was sent to see the play, and the manager, to recommend that the clergyman be 'turned into a Squire or a Doctor'. Despite the hypocrisy of the censorship, the show ran for 413 performances. In the next year, the Prince went with his brother Arthur (now a general) to the Avenue Theatre to see Bernard Shaw's satire on love and war, *Arms and the Man*. Although the play was set in the Balkans during the 1885 war between Serbia and Bulgaria, the Royals were convinced that the sly inversions on courage in battle (Major Saranoff becomes a hero because his horse runs away with him; Captain Bluntschli carries chocolates rather than bullets in his cartridge belt) were aspersions on the British Army. As they left after the curtain, the Prince of Wales could be heard muttering to the Duke of Connaught about the playwright, 'The man must be mad!' However, there was nothing to censor. When Wilde's *Salome* was deemed unplayable in London because of its alleged blasphemy, among other offences, and Sir Edgar Mackennal defiantly exhibited his bronze nude of Salome holding the sword with which she decapitates John the Baptist, the Prince purchased one of the twenty-guinea copies.

Before slipping back to dissipations in France, the guardian of national morals presided for the Queen at the opening, on 9 May 1893, of the Imperial Institute in South Kensington, where, perhaps not incongruously, the royal wedding presents were to be exhibited, and the curious would wait patiently for hours in a lengthy double queue. *The Star*, an afternoon paper of Liberal-to-Radical persuasion, covered the ceremonies by having its three anonymous reporters posted along the procession, the last of them inside. The ailing Sir Arthur Sullivan conducted the orchestra. After a flourish of trumpets, the third *Star* man, Bernard Shaw, reported wryly, the Royals began their progress, led by 'Persons with sticks ... walking backwards'. Among the dignitaries were 'the heroic George of Cambridge' and his sister, 'the buxom [Mary of] Teck'. The Queen, in black, is helped up the steps to the dais

by her two sons, Wales and Edinburgh. Everyone is affected: the *Star* man weeps with loyalty. Then the Prince of Wales reads the address, clearly but without much artistic turn for the platform. He needs a course of practice in Hyde Park under [Socialist politician] John Burns to drive his style home. When he has done, the Queen shows him the proper way to do it. There is not an actress on the English stage who could have done it better – tone, style, are all of the best. The *Star* man's artistic instincts get the better of him; he feels that it is a pity that so able an artist should be wasted on a throne. After the addresses, Sir Arthur Sullivan strikes up his new march, not so very new either. … The gold key is now presented and the Queen, after inspecting it dubiously, declines the responsibility of working the apparatus with it. The Prince, after a brief apprenticeship, gets it into the keyhole, and after a final explanation, produces with it – first a ring-ting on the table, then a burst of change-ringing from the bells outside and at last a salute from the Park artillery.... Finally the Queen, using her walking-stick a little, is helped down the steps by the Prince, President of the Institute and the Duke of Edinburgh … and the *Star* man vanishes from the hall.

With Alexandra now often away, or isolating herself from the Prince's life, he could be flaunted by Daisy Warwick, who displayed her catch during racing weeks, at a three-day Christmas party at Warwick Castle, in London restaurants and theatres, even on Sunday mornings in church at Euston. When he was ceremonially busy and away from her, or when he found it socially necessary to be on a long country-house weekend with his cold and increasingly deaf spouse, he wrote letters as never before, unconcerned that Alix was nearby. His prose could not have stirred Daisy's passions, but she had acquired him for exhibition. 'Now my loved one,' he uxoriously concluded a note from Chatsworth, where he was accompanied by Alix, 'I bring these lines to a close as I must dress and breakfast. God bless you, my own adored little Daisy wife.' He signed it 'Your only Love'.

The unrecognized beginning of the end for the liaison came in February 1895 when, at a costume ball at Warwick Castle, her guests were instructed to dress as denizens of Marie Antoinette's Versailles. With sublime arrogance, Daisy had costumed herself as the Queen. The four hundred guests swamped jewellers, costumiers and hairdressers in London and Paris, and filled a special train to Warwickshire. Newspapers covered the event avidly, but one Socialist weekly, *The Clarion*, attacked the waste of resources on a 'few hours' silly masquerade' while so many citizens lived in grinding poverty. Impulsively, the Countess took a train to London, found a cab to Fleet Street, and announced herself indignantly to Robert Blatchford, the *Clarion's* editor. He was unfair to her, Daisy charged: her ball had provided work for half the county and hundreds elsewhere. 'Will you sit down', he asked, 'while I explain to you how mistaken you are about the real effect of luxury?'

Blatchford furnished a quick lesson in the differences between productive and unproductive labour, and persuaded her that her ball had not added to the national good. She understood very little of what he had said, but something had percolated through her anger. 'During the journey home,' she wrote later, 'I thought and thought about all I had been hearing and learning. I knew that my outlook on life could never be the same as before this incident.' Very likely her epiphany took longer than that, but when the Prince had remarked not long after that everyone was now more or less a Socialist, he did not yet know that the definition would include his darling Daisy wife.

To the larger public the Prince was doing all he could do as king-in-waiting. As *Punch* described an invented artist 'drawing H.R.H. the Prince of Wales',

He draws him at foundation stones, a trowel in his hand
(The point of silver trowels I could ne'er understand);
He draws him opening railways, or turning sods of grass,
And he draws him as a Colonel, in helmet and cuirasse.
We see him dressed for London, a-riding in the Row –
I wonder if he ever finds his London pleasures slow;
And we see him down at Sandringham, his country-home in Norfolk,
Where the Royal pair are much beloved, especially by poor folk.
And oft at public dinners, in Garter and in Star,
We see his Royal Highness enjoying his cigar.
I wish they wouldn't vary quite so much his Royal figure,
For they sometimes make him leaner, and sometimes make him bigger.
Be that as it may, I feel that, while my life endures,
I know by heart my Prince's face, my future King's contours.

In France in the winter of 1894, before the height of the London season (when he was expected to show himself with Alexandra), the Prince was in Paris, and then on the Riviera, with Daisy or the ever loyal Jeanne-

Marguerite de Sagan. It was from there that one of his American friends placed a telephone call to Paris. At the Scala, where chanteuse Yvette Guilbert was singing, the Manager, M. Marchand, learned that someone was enquiring whether Mlle Guilbert could perform – and soon – for a private party in Cannes. She would be paid whatever she wanted. Irritated, she asked, 'Who on earth is this ignoramus who can't understand that an artist who is actually playing in Paris can't possibly leave Paris?'

'The ignoramus is my client, Mrs Ogden Goelet, an American!' said the voice on the telephone. 'I don't know her!' snapped Yvette. 'Really, Monsieur, I have the right to refuse to travel if I choose.'

Marchand whispered, 'Quote a figure that would put an end to the conversation.' She said, laughingly into the telephone, 'Fifteen thousand francs'. (Sarah Bernhardt was earning two thousand francs a performance.) Without a pause, the fee was accepted, and the next day Mrs Goulet's representative visited her and explained that his client, a wealthy American, had a villa at Nice and was accustomed to receiving the Prince of Wales. (Her husband, Manhattan and Newport multi-millionaire Ogden Goelet, had a heart ailment and spent much of his time on his yacht at Cowes or Cannes. Some years later as a moneyed widow, she was to become the mistress of cosmopolitan New York lawyer and *littérateur* Walter Van Rensselaer Berry, who was also the lover of Edith Wharton.) When the glamorous Elsie Goelet had asked HRH whom he would like to have invited to sing, he had proposed Mlle Guilbert. In a few days she was in Cannes. She arrived at the Goelet villa at ten. Dinner was not over, and Yvette and two young entertainers from the Comédie-Française were shown into a small drawing room, where Mrs Goelet welcomed them and advised that because of the presence of royalty – the future king of England – Mlle Guilbert should sing only her 'least risqué songs'.

As the dinner guests filed into the drawing room, the Prince of Wales first, she noticed that 'his eyes were attempting to discover which of us was Yvette Guilbert.... He went straight up to a young woman in a red dress with big roses in her hair, but she replied that Yvette Guilbert was the tall girl in white satin with black gloves. I noted the surprise on his face.' He looked at her closely before walking over. '*Quelle distinction, Mademoiselle,*' he said. '*Cela vaut une célébrité.*'

While she waited for her cue she heard two women 'exchanging the usual scandal about the marquise de Gallifet.... After pulling her to pieces they turned on the princesse de Sagan. At last my turn came to sing.' The Prince carried his chair closer. After a few songs he took her arm and said, softly, 'Dear Mlle Guilbert, why don't you let me hear your songs of Montmartre?' He wanted 'the spirit of the Chat Noir'. Yvette explained that she had been instructed to sing only songs '*pour jeunes filles*'. He laughed, and, leaning against the piano, asked for her 'most delightfully Parisian items'. She complied, and he declared when she finished that it had been an 'unforgettable' evening. 'What can I do for you, Mademoiselle?'

'Give me your patronage', she said, 'when I come next season to London for the first time in my life, your Highness.'

For her opening at the Savoy, he asked Sir Arthur Sullivan to give a reception in her honour, to which the ladies of the Court would be invited. At Sullivan's dinner, she was seated between the Prince and the Austrian ambassador, Count Albert Mensdorff, who whispered to Yvette, 'He doesn't care for art; he hobnobs with moneyed people', – a covert reference to the Prince of Wales's Jewish friends. Then, as he added an aspersion about the Prince's familiarity with *La Goulue*, and his 'going about with rich Americans', HRH turned in the ambassador's direction as if he had heard, and the Austrian calmly explained, 'I was telling Mlle Guilbert how much your Highness loves France, her artists, her wines, and how popular your Highness is.' The Prince smiled. Mensdorff was a charming but untrustworthy Coburg cousin. Mlle Guilbert recalled being 'scandalized'.

Another, though more remote, critic and gossip was historian Henry Adams, who returned to Washington society the next year – 'after the season', he wrote to his old friend Charles Milnes Gaskell in London. Adams suggested that he recognized the long-distance impact of the Prince, who rolled his r's in the Continental fashion, 'I hear now and then, in the corner of a drawing-room,' he claimed sourly, 'the grassey-ing* of the Prince of Wales's *r*, which is the innocent mark of American social aspirations. When we were young, it was the English stammer, but now young Englishmen no longer stammer, because, I imagine, George the Third is forgotten, and his descendants have other tricks. Really elegant women – in New York – must all roll their r's like a Marseilles baker.'

---

* From the French *grasseyer*, to roll one's r's.

Following Mlle Guilbert's London success, HRH, with Baron Maurice de Hirsch, was back in France to be at the running of Hirsch's Matchbox, a 6–4 favourite at the Grand Prix. Matchbox, like two promising colts the Prince owned, had been sired by the same prize thoroughbred, St Simon. Enthusiastically, HRH bet £600 on Hirsch's horse, which lost by a head. It was the most he was recorded as ever placing at a race. If the baron somehow made good the loss – it was a sum the owner of numerous European railways would hardly have noticed – there is no evidence of it. The Prince's 'Jewish Court' did things subtly.

Hirsch's friendship with the Prince of Wales had become close in 1890. The Baron had a sumptuous home on the rue de l'Elysée and another on the Riviera, and added a London residence when his royal patron included him in his set. The Prince had been so deeply in debt that Lord Lytton, then ambassador in Paris, heard that he was negotiating for a £40,000 loan in Paris, and that when the terms were too steep and it fell through, the Rothschilds had supplied the francs. Lytton discounted the story – the Rothschilds were too cautious for that – and suggested that Hirsch had advanced the money. Whether or not Hirsch had furnished the francs at the time, he did soon after, and on his death in 1896 the debt vanished, one of his many philanthropies. The *Westminster Gazette* published with the 'utmost confidence' a denial that HRH had inherited a million pounds from Hirsch – which was at least literally accurate. In the year of the Prince's accession, the French ambassador in London, Paul Cambon, informed his Foreign Minister that Hirsch had advanced the Prince at least 15 million francs, then worth an immense £600,000, on the nominal surety of his sister, the Dowager Empress of Germany. (Vicky had died four days earlier, on 4 August 1901.) Apparently recognizing the baron's intentions, the debt had been quietly waived by his widow.

With the first wedding anniversary of Prince George and Princess May imminent, both the Prince and Princess of Wales materialized in London together to host a lavish Marlborough House reception on the afternoon of 5 July 1894 – 'say 2000 [guests]!' Gladstone noted in his diary. Every ambassador was there, and a royal tent on the lawn drew the most élite of the guests. Two weeks earlier, the efficient May had given birth to a prince who would be called David after the patron saint of Wales, but who, more than forty years later, would be briefly Edward VIII.

The next royal wedding of note was to link a prince who so resembled

George of York that he was taken for his double, and George's cousin, Alexandra of Hesse, daughter of the Prince of Wales's late sister, Alice. The Tsarevitch was already Nicholas II by the date of the wedding, 26 November 1894. His father, Alexander III, had died, at forty-nine, a week earlier. Mourning was suspended for the marriage, which the Prince of Wales and Duke of York attended before leaving quickly as the Russian Court donned black again. There were no occasions for diplomatic triumphs, but the Earl of Rosebery, who had succeeded the faltering Gladstone as Prime Minister that March, extolled the Prince's mission to St Petersburg in language suggesting that he was cultivating relations with the future king. 'I am anxious to be among the first to welcome your Royal Highness home,' he wrote fulsomely, 'and to express my deep sense of the good and patriotic work that you have accomplished since you left England. Never has your Royal Highness stood so high in the national esteem as today, for never have you had such an opportunity. That at last has come and has enabled you to justify the highest anticipations, and to render a signal service to your country as well as to Russia and the peace of the world.' The most significant duties the Prince had performed in 1894 had been to preside at Speech Day at Harrow early in June and again at the opening, on 30 June, of the neo-medieval Tower Bridge across the Thames.

Despite the Queen's leaning more and more on her heir, her unwillingness to formalize any role for him would take absurd turns. In her later years, despite her well-known antipathy to warmth, she had begun to take a winter holiday on the Riviera. Her absence abroad required someone nominally to undertake the Guardianship of the Realm. Rosebery proposed the Prince. He was 'convinced', he assured her, 'that on such a call of duty his Royal Highness would readily forgo his [own] tour abroad'. With fast trains and the telegraph and telephone (the latter which Victoria would not use), no crisis would be far removed from her. The Queen gave in, but instructed her secretary, Colonel Arthur Bigge, to write to the Prime Minister that she did not want to propose it to the Prince herself. She preferred 'not suggesting to H.R.H. what she thinks will be inconvenient, and what he might find difficult to decline coming direct from her. And the Queen does not want to prevent his going abroad.' She would prefer, she made it clear, a committee consisting of her son Arthur (Duke of Connaught), her cousin George (Duke of Cambridge), and the Lord Chief Justice.

Between the lines, the Prime Minister read her hope that HRH might decline, as the designation might keep him from certain friends in France. The Prince jumped at the offer, however, as it was a breakthrough into Crown responsibility. 'For that purpose,' Rosebery assured the Queen after meeting with the Prince of Wales on 13 February, 'the Prince will greatly curtail, if not altogether forgo, his trip abroad.' He was not, however, entirely to forswear seeing his harem, which stretched from Dieppe to Nice. On one visit in 1895 or 1896 – the year is unclear but the event is not – he was having breakfast on the terrace of the Café de Paris in Monte Carlo. A teenage waiter named Henri Charpentier – later the famous chef – waited at his table. 'Among the diners', he recalled, '... was a beautiful French girl named Suzette. I cannot recall her last name. It does not matter. His Highness ordered crêpes – a French pancake. I mixed the sauce and added a brandy blend of my own. As I did, the flame of the chafing dish accidentally set the simmering cordials afire. I was embarrassed, but I did not show it. I poured the fiery sauce on the crêpes, as if the flames were set on purpose. The Prince tasted, then he smiled, and said: "Henri, what have you done with these crêpes? They are superb!"'

Thrilled, Charpentier 'offered to name them in his honour. But he declined. "Henri," he said, "We must always remember that the ladies come first. We will call this glorious thing crêpes Suzette." And so they have remained to this day.'

For the Prince it was a disappointment that the Rosebery Government fell in June 1895 after sixteen months and was replaced by Salisbury's Conservatives. The Queen, who liked Rosebery but not his predecessor Gladstone, had gone out of her way to make her feelings about the GOM known, refusing the Prince's entreaties to close Gladstone's career with honours he might accept. At the marriage of the Wales's daughter Princess Maud in July 1896, Victoria snubbed the aged Gladstones, and somehow they were also not invited (or failed to recall their invitation) to the wedding breakfast. When the Prince discovered the omission he asked the couple separately to Marlborough House. 'They were extraordinarily kind,' Gladstone wrote in his diary on 27 July. 'The Prince kissed C[atherine]'s hand. I cannot avoid thinking that they do much toward us from a sense of the Queen's deficiencies.'

What little political influence the Prince thought he had under Gladstone and Rosebery evaporated in 1895 under Salisbury. HRH had little time to brood about it, for his exasperating German nephew, Wilhelm II, arrived at Cowes on 4 August, his splendid yacht *Hohen-zollern* escorted by the German Admiralty's newest warships. Aboard the *Wörth* two days later the Kaiser, in British waters during what was to be a social visit, tactlessly toasted the twenty-fifth anniversary of the defeat of Napoleon III's French. (He had begun the year, to his uncle's outrage, by congratulating Boer President Paul Kruger on quashing the illegal Jameson Raid* and 'defending the independence' of the Transvaal without having to call on 'friendly Powers' – meaning Germany.) On the 8th, while dining with the Prince of Wales and alluding to British nego-tiations with the French about defining the unmarked border between India and Indochina, Willy joked that the dispute might lead to war. 'So you'll soon be off to India again, and we'll see at last what you're good for as a soldier!' And he thumped his uncle on the back. The Prince swal-lowed his anger.

The Kaiser was then currying favour with Tsar Nicholas, trying to set up a political alignment which might overawe the English and French. German militarists feared they would ally despite long mutual antipathy, in the Prince of Wales's long-desired *entente cordiale*. For the Prince in his middle fifties, overshadowed by the two young sovereigns – both his nephews – while he still waited in the wings, it was a frustrating period. On the 20th the Prince left for Germany – Homburg, where he did not expect to encounter Willy. One of his solutions to put the belligerent Kaiser down was to replace the retiring Sir Edward Malet at the Berlin Embassy with a top soldier, Field Marshal Lord Wolseley. But the Prince, deviously, had more than that in mind. He had persuaded his Uncle George, the seventy-six-year-old commander of the Army, to retire in November, and wanted to keep the desk at the Horse Guards open for Arthur, Duke of Connaught. Salisbury, as Prime Minister, was his own Foreign Secretary, and convinced his Cabinet to offer Wolseley his choice of the Horse Guards or Berlin. For a professional soldier there was no option. When a career diplomat, Sir Frank Lascelles, was appointed to Berlin, the Prince of Wales again recognized his own lack of clout.

---

* Leander Starr Jameson, in apparent collusion with Cecil Rhodes and Colonial Secretary Joseph Chamberlain, attempted a rising by British settlers in Johannesburg as a provocation, then enter the Transvaal in 'support' of their countrymen. It was a fiasco: the raiders were captured; and the British Government, while admitting no official wrongdoing, was embarrassed.

Still, Americans thought he had some influence, and when the Venezuelan crisis caused belligerent feelings on both sides of the Atlantic he was called upon. A dispute over the frontier between British Guiana and Venezuela had led to a British ultimatum and blustering diplomatic intervention from Washington, which embarrassed the Foreign Office. From New York, as both sides threatened force, the proprietor of the *New York World*, Joseph Pulitzer, telegraphed the Prince of Wales for his views, and the Prince, long a warm friend of the United States, drafted a reply which he sent to Lord Salisbury for an opinion on its propriety. 'I earnestly trust and cannot but believe', he planned to cable, '[that the] present crisis will be arranged in a manner satisfactory to both countries, and will be succeeded by [the] same warm feeling of friendship which has existed between them for so many years.'

Salisbury advised against sending it. Perceiving the triviality of the dispute, the Prince cabled it anyway on 23 December 1895, and Pulitzer happily and symbolically published it on Christmas Eve. The problem was referred to a boundary commission and settled pacifically, to Venezuela's inconsequential advantage.

Not for lack of trying, all the Prince garnered from Victoria and Salisbury were ceremonial tokens. On 14 May 1896 and each year thereafter, he replaced the Queen at the trooping of the colour at the Horse Guards Parade – the closest he could get to the seat of military authority. His only success came on the turf, on 3 June, when one of his thirteen horses, Persimmon, a 5–1 bet, won the Derby by a head over Leopold de Rothschild's St Frusquin, the favourite. (Presumably the Rothschild horse was not held back a stride to permit a royal win.) It was a very popular victory. He led Persimmon himself into the winner's enclosure to the most enthusiastic ovation of his life. *Punch* even published an ode to the 'princely sportsman'. The Royal Stand at Ascot had been redecorated, and the Prince was to host a large luncheon (served by the Lord Steward at Windsor Castle) in the dining room behind the stand on each day of the races. Whether she realized it or not, the Queen was paying for her heir's indulgences. At his annual dinner at Marlborough House for members of the Jockey Club on the evening following the triumph of Persimmon, he was momentarily the happiest man in the kingdom. He was to earn £28,734 in stake money in 1896, almost enough to pay the expenses of maintaining his stud. To her lady-in-waiting Marie Mallet, the Queen, then at Balmoral, expressed no satisfaction, confiding

A DERBY FAVOURITE.

Although the Prince of Wales never rode a mount in race competition,
*his Persimmon did win the Derby (*Punch, *6 June 1896)*

– although she had telegraphed congratulations to her son – '*Il faut payer pour être Prince.*'* She understood how costly it was to underwrite a stable in competition with a Rothschild.

   Although Lady Warwick would not be seen with him at the Derby if he appeared with Alix, she continued her attempts to direct his life, and arranged for him to meet W. T. Stead, once of 'Maiden Tribute' notoriety. According to her memoirs he agreed to see Stead in order to please her, although Stead worried that the Prince 'would think I was like brimstone and treacle and would regard me with a kind of holy horror'. The meeting had to be delayed because she had suffered a concussion in

* 'It is expensive to be a Prince.'

a fall while hunting. A new date was set, and Daisy assured Stead that he could bring up any subject, from South Africa to the Queen. At thirty-five, she was as beautiful as ever, and turning increasingly Radical in social remedies. Stead was easily persuaded that he would not be embarrassed.

On the appointed day, a cold afternoon in December, the Prince arrived at Daisy's town house near Hyde Park Corner for lunch with Stead. Recognizing his influence in the press, HRH began by praising the concept of old-age pensions, outlined in a series of articles in *The Times*, and perhaps pointed out to him by Lady Warwick. Stead in turn praised one of the Prince's favourite people, Cecil Rhodes, then under suspicion because of the embarrassing Jameson Raid. Rhodes was, the Prince agreed, 'a very remarkable man'. As they discussed politics and foreign affairs, their hostess excused herself to rest her head and to permit the men to have some privacy over their coffee and cigars. Stead left in hope that in some future press campaign he could secure the Prince's support.

While HRH appeared to be far less rigid than his mother, recognizing the changing social climate he would face as king, he drew a line at royal prerogatives, which he regarded as inflexible if royalty was to mean anything. Consuelo Vanderbilt (who became a very young Duchess of Marlborough as titled Englishmen sought out American heiresses to assist in the upkeep of their lifestyles) recalled visiting Sandringham that autumn for four days of shooting and dining. The women 'never looked lovelier – perhaps because the rooms were [still] lit by candles', and in the warm conviviality one lady, forgetting that the Prince's 'stout but stately presence' meant that a certain decorum prevailed, addressed him as 'my good man'. With 'a somewhat frigid intonation' he growled, 'My dear Mrs B——, please remember that I am not your good man.' Even his closest friends, such as the amusing Portuguese ambassador, the marquis de Soveral (a bachelor and therefore valuable at dinner parties), had to use appropriate ceremony.

As the Prince anticipated, he was given the authority to prepare a Diamond Jubilee to celebrate the Queen's sixtieth anniversary on the throne in 1897. Diamonds were more the symbol of a seventy-fifth anniversary, but even Prince Albert Edward, impatient to be sovereign, recognized that this was very likely to be the last grand-scale remembrance for his mother in her lifetime. Though tough and stubborn, she was failing. On 22 January 1897 he called a meeting at Marlborough House that included every major dignitary from the President of the Royal Society and the Lord Mayor to Cardinal Vaughan and the Chief Rabbi. It was the Prince's idea that all moneys raised would go to support 'the Metropolitan Hospitals and Convalescent Institutions'. Unlike the Golden Jubilee, crowned heads would not be invited. The expense of their upkeep would be enormous, and the Queen overly taxed by their presence. Also every effort was to be made to keep her nephew Willy away, and Sir Francis Knollys wrote to Victoria's Private Secretary to express the Prince of Wales's insistence on the matter, for the Kaiser 'would arrive also with an enormous suite, and would try to arrange things himself and endless trouble would arise'. Victoria advised Sir Arthur Bigge to 'tell the Prince of Wales that there is *not* the slightest fear of the Queen's giving way about the Emperor William's coming here in June. It would *never* do.'

While the details of the Jubilee ceremony and the minute-by-minute schedule were being worked out for him by Regy Brett, with everything culminating on the afternoon of 22 June, the Prince impatiently began learning (with many spills) how to ride a bicycle – the fad of the mid-1890s. For someone of his bulk, and in his fifty-sixth year, it was a hazardous undertaking, and his nickname among his intimates, which he resented, reflected it. (Once, at Sandringham, admonishing Sir Frederick Johnstone, one of his Tranby Croft cronies, he warned, 'Freddy, you're very drunk!' Johnstone, too inebriated for caution, and aware of HRH's forty-eight-inch waist, mimicked the Prince's rolling of his r's and mumbled, 'Tum-Tum, you're ve*rrr*y fat!' The Prince ordered Sir Frederick's servant to pack his bags.) Finding cycling a great source of mid-90s humour, *Punch* proposed that if HRH could master the apparatus, a change of his title should be 'seriously contemplated' – to 'Prince of Wheels'.

Chronically ill with nephritis, Arthur Sullivan wrote to the Prince on 1 April from St Jean de Villefranche – between visits to spas for phantom cures – to ask to be commissioned to 'reach the *hearts of the people*' at St Paul's with a hymn on the order of his 'Onward, Christian Soldiers'. It would, he said, crown the efforts he had made on behalf of English music. 'My career, Sir,' he appealed, 'is nearer its end than its commencement.' The 'glorious occasion' would impel him to a grand effort. He had seen the Queen at Cimiez during her own search for winter sun on the

Riviera, and she had agreed on a Jubilee hymn, but the effort foundered when he discovered that he was to set an effusion by the new Poet Laureate. Instead, the Jubilee would utilize his already composed and forgettable ballet, *Victoria and Merrie England*, remembered now only for the inner contradictions of its title. It was produced on 25 May to an audience notable for its collection of Royals. Sullivan was rewarded on 5 July with a conversation with the Queen, and a Jubilee Medal.

The celebration would spill over into several days on either side of the 22nd. The Windsor phase began on 20 June, when the Queen, with her seven surviving children, attended a service at St George's Chapel, and then visited Albert's tomb, with its neo-medieval sarcophagus of a recumbent Prince. For 22 June a Bank Holiday was decreed. Wooden stands were erected everywhere in the line of progress to and from St Paul's, nearly obscuring Whitehall, the National Gallery, Charing Cross Station, St Martin-in-the-Fields, and smart hotels in the Strand. The population of London had tripled, to nearly four million, in the sixty years since coronation crowds had jammed the streets, and it seemed that all of them were out that morning to get what many assumed might be their last glimpse of the Queen.

At seven the sky was dull and grey, but troops in dress scarlet and topped by tall bearskins, coming and going, kept the atmosphere agitated, as did the peddlers who hawked Jubilee pennants, flags, programmes, balloons, mugs, pictures, place mats, noisemakers and fireworks. At 11.15 the state landau drawn by eight horses departed Buckingham Palace with the Princess of Wales and Princess Helena ('Lenchen') sitting opposite the Queen, and the Prince of Wales and the old Duke of Cambridge, each on horseback, on either side. Prince Arthur, Duke of Connaught, now a field marshal and chief of arrangements for the procession, followed. Since Vicky's rank as Empress Dowager precluded her from sitting opposite her mother with her back to the horses, the Queen sat alone while her widowed eldest daughter proceeded in a separate carriage. By protocol Alfred, now a sovereign on inheriting the duchy of Coburg and Gotha, also had to ride separately.

The pace was slow. Yet that afforded time for the sun to emerge, lighting up the street ornaments and the finery, the flowers and the loyal banners. The orderliness of the crowds matched the regularity of the royal progress. There were more police marching than patrolling, more soldiers (40,000) stepping smartly than standing guard. There was an earnestness about the enthusiasm, appropriate to the veneration of a grandmotherly sovereign, and as many tears as cheers. At the entrance to St Paul's, her carriage paused before the masses of spectators, drawn-up colonial troops in colourful uniforms, bishops in their copes, and royal princes. A *Te Deum* was sung, a special Jubilee prayer intoned, and a benediction, followed by a lusty singing of the 'Old Hundredth'. Lugubrious new Jubilee lyrics for the hymn closed with:

> Grant her Thy peace, long may she reign.
> And when at length Thy call shall come,
> If so Thy will be, free from pain.
> Take her to Thine eternal home.

The Queen wept, wiped her cataract-clouded eyes, and the procession began its return phase, over London Bridge and back across Westminster Bridge toward Buckingham Palace.

Other Jubilee events continued into July. 'Eternal Father, Strong to Save' was often sung, and the Prince of Wales was once heard to mutter, impatiently, 'It's all very well about the Eternal Father; but what about my eternal mother?'

On the 2nd, colonial troops representing the disparate domains of her Empire were brought to Windsor. Two generals, Lord Roberts and Lord Methuen, walked alongside her carriage and assisted Victoria's fading sight by identifying each contingent. On the 7th, she received, for a final time, the fifteen colonial premiers, swearing them in as Privy Councillors and awarding them Jubilee Medals. Kept from public view was Daisy Warwick, who determined, nevertheless, to have her day. On her behalf the premiers were also invited by the Prince to Warwick Castle, but only three came. Ostentatiously, the Duchess of Devonshire (mistress to Harty Tarty long before he married her in 1892) hosted a fancy-dress ball as her part in the Jubilee summer. She greeted guests attired as Zenobia, Queen of Palmyra, while the Duke was costumed as Charles V, wearing a golden fleece borrowed from the Prince of Wales. HRH donned his gaudy apron and insignia as Grand Master of the Freemasons.

Despite the elaborate arrangements to keep the wheelchair-bound Queen little more than a visible eminence at each event, the occasions became more and more taxing. She was seventy-eight and exhausted by the excesses of the Jubilee. At her reception at Buckingham Palace for Members of the House of Commons and their families, Regy Brett wrote, the august legislators had seemed 'like a crowd being let onto the ground after a football match'.

The Prince presided at the opening of the Tate Gallery, and at the great naval review on the Solent where 173 warships in battle-grey steamed past while beflagged yachts carrying the Cabinet, members of the House of Lords, Admiralty bureaucrats and Royals criss-crossed through the smoke of cannoned salutes. Dozens of loyal addresses, many illuminated on parchment scrolls, were delivered instead to the Prince of Wales, acting in her name. Although the burly, now grey-bearded, Prince was soon to be king, some spokesmen, deprived of the dowdy presence of the old Queen, considered their audiences had second-class status, but at St James's Palace on one date alone – 21 July – he spent the entire day receiving (separately) forty-one presenting bodies, including the Royal Astronomical Society, the Royal College of Physicians, the Society of Architects, the Coroners' Society, several university delegations, a dozen religious groups including the YMCA, and town and city councils from Glasgow to the south of England. Few were disappointed, as he could be lively and ingratiating whereas the old Queen was solemn and immobile. As *Punch* remarked in the caption to a cartoon labelled 'H.R.H. Dr. Wales, F.R.C.P., the Popular Physician', showing him in a doctor's surgery, 'than whom no one better knows how to feel the pulse of the people'.

Not all organizations could be disposed of with the Prince as deputy. Some Protestant Dissenting bodies – ranging from Presbyterians and Baptists to the Society of Friends – possessed the legal 'right of personal approach to the Sovereign'. Many claimed it, as did the nation's most prestigious body of scientists, the Royal Society. All those whose rights were validated were bunched together on 15 July to meet Victoria and offer their addresses. Each was limited to a deputation of twenty. The long day closed her involvement in the Jubilee. For everything else that remained, the Prince of Wales stood in for the Queen.

When Jubilee duties wound down in August, the Prince planned a holiday in Marienbad 'for a course of the waters', and to visit Bayreuth with Arthur Sullivan for *Parsifal* and the *Ring* cycle. The press agreed that he had made the Jubilee summer a success, and after a visit by King Khoulalonkorn of Siam that required HRH's intervention about what Order to pin on the King that would not insult him, the Prince duly departed. Also winding down was his attachment to Lady Warwick. She

H.R.H. DR. WALES, F.R.C.P., THE POPULAR PHYSICIAN.

*Punch on the popularity of the future king following
the Diamond Jubilee of 1897, and the expected imminence
of his accession (*Punch, *7 August 1897)*

was publicly involved more and more with Radical causes that made him anxious. She even published articles about them, one of particular eccentricity in the Christmas 1897 issue of *Land Magazine*, proposing domestic colonies of 'unmarrying women' farmers. But she also did help to launch the long-proposed Jubilee venture of a Prince of Wales's Hospital Fund. Daisy Warwick had a relentless energy that the Prince was beginning to find overwhelming. He had wanted a womanly woman on perpetual ornamental call and she had found that role insufficient. Daisy had even returned to her husband his conjugal rights and, after an interval of thirteen years, she was again pregnant.

Before Christmas the Prince had written to Dr James Reid, the

Queen's physician, to invite him to Sandringham in January. Discovering it through a lady-in-waiting, the Queen was indignant and ordered him to decline, 'as I fear mischief, attempts at interference, more stories and gossip.... I will not tolerate any more stories, and exaggerations and more inventions.' As Reid knew, she was alluding angrily to the attempts of her children, especially the Prince of Wales, to curtail the influence of her handsome, black-bearded servant Abdul Karim, 'the Munshi', or clerk. Karim had insinuated himself from obscure young Indian attendant in 1889 to respendently attired, turbaned royal favourite almost on a par with the late, gruff, John Brown, who had died, to the family's relicf, in 1883.

The Munshi had his own grace-and-favour residences at each of her three homes, and on occasion taught the Queen enough Hindi to use in writing her diary. His appearances at her mandate in the *Court Circular*, and his increasing arrogance, infuriated her children, and the Prince had tried to get Reid to explain to the Queen that her public attentions to the ambitious Munshi embarrassed the throne because people gossiped about her as 'insane' over him. Audaciously, Reid had even used the words 'not sane', and she was outraged. Victoria may once again have been drawn to an exotically handsome young male she found pleasurable to have about or have been attracted by his symbolizing the exotic India she would never experience except, vicariously, in the Durbar Room she had added to Osborne House to display her artefacts from the subcontinent.* It had taken the efforts of many in the Court to keep her from giving Karim, now spoiled and fat, a Jubilee honour, and the *Graphic*, on 16 October 1897, had pictured her receiving one of her lessons from the Munshi under a caption ('The Queen's Life in the Highlands') sardonically suggesting Brown. Although Karim's influence was to decline, his queenly perquisites would not, and the Prince of Wales, who had also tried to curtail the influence of Brown, would not be forgiven. As king he would send Karim packing, but as prince he was helpless.

At Christmas, the Waleses were together at Sandringham distributing

---

* Her first Indian favourite had been the turbaned young Sikh Maharajah Duleep Singh whom she met in 1854 when he was sixteen. She owned his family's Koh-i-noor diamond. Portly in later years, he had been small, lithe and handsome, and had become a Christian at Victoria's urging. He would disappoint her by his relentless womanizing in England but she, nevertheless, displayed a statue of him as a young man in her Durbar Room. Singh had died in 1893.

gifts to members of their household while standing athwart a glittering tree in the ballroom. Not many Christmases before, the Prince of Wales could not even show himself in his own home. On New Year's Eve they observed the ritual of 'first footing', in which the great house was emptied just before midnight and the master and mistress of the manor opened the door at the first stroke of midnight to welcome the first to re-enter. It was supposed to bring good luck.

XV

Prince No More

1898–1901

IN JULY 1898, Victoria Sackville-West received a request from the Prince of Wales for him and Alix to visit stately, sprawling Knole House, south of Sevenoaks. Since the sixteenth century, Knole had been the seat of the Sackville family and the Earls of Dorset. He also wanted to include the Countess of Warwick and (the lady of the manor recalled), 'his new friend, the Hon. Mrs. G. Keppel. But I told him I preferred to ask some of the County Ladies.... He acquiesced and was nice about it.' That he had intended to bring with him not only his royal spouse, but his discarded mistress as well as his new inamorata, awed Victoria. Rather than contemplate how HRH could manage it, she evaded the indelicacy, and the Prince arrived only with Alix and their usual platoon of escorts.*

'I went to receive them at the wicket with Vita,' she wrote. Little Vita was only five, and had no idea why the Knole staff were so agitated. 'I felt desperately shy, and Vita nearly burst into tears.' (In part that shyness may have come from her memory that on the Riviera, years before, she had evaded the Prince's amorous pursuit.) The party, augmented by the overwhelming royal entourage, adjourned to the garden for a tree-

---

* The Prince of Wales apparently had one standard of acceptable behaviour for himself and a higher one for others, including his closest cronies. When the philandering Duke of Sutherland (the third duke had been Marquis of Stafford until, at thirty-three, he succeeded his father in 1861) was carrying on an affair with Mrs Mary Caroline Blair, the Prince commiserated with Sutherland's wife, Anne, 'Stafford seems to have lost all sense of propriety & decency by taking his Mistress to his Wife's and Children's home.' After Anne – created Countess of Cromartie by the Queen after being Mistress of the Robes 1870–4 – died in 1888, Sutherland married Mrs Blair.

planting ceremony by which the heir's visit would be remembered, and the inevitable photographs; and the considerate Princess of Wales held little Vita's hand.

By July 1898, HRH's amorous arrangements, if such they still were, had sorted themselves out. His public image, he seems to have considered, required the presence of a quasi-official mistress. That no priapic need was involved seems clear from the pregnancy of Daisy Warwick by her own husband, an unthinkable occurrence in earlier years. His new *amante* would also have a child, Sonia, by her own husband in 1900. The amply endowed Alice Keppel was more akin to jewellery to be worn on the royal arm than pliant femininity to be caressed between the sheets. In her cosseting of him she was almost the mother he never had. And she was an excellent bridge partner. (After the Tranby Croft scandal, baccarat was out; bridge was the nineties' fad at cards.) Obesity and more unseen disabilities had rendered the Prince's relationship with the passionate Daisy platonic. Skittles later claimed to Wilfrid Blunt that HRH had been impotent since 1895, but appearances were a form of reality. Philandering substantiated his manliness.

In January 1898, far advanced in pregnancy and discreetly out of public view, Daisy Warwick had written to the Prince delicately that it was time for mutual renunciation of their attachment, which she claimed had been platonic for some years. (The lines were meant to be shown to Alix.) They had maintained, Daisy suggested, a dignified and noble relationship, but it was time to part. (That her child was soon due was left unsaid.) She also wrote separately to the Princess, expressing hope that unpleasant and malicious gossip had not poisoned Alexandra against someone who wanted to remain a friend of both Royals. This pragmatic withdrawal was intended to rehabilitate Daisy at Court, and she knew her audience. The Prince showed his letter to Alix, and responded:

My own lovely little Daisy,
   It is difficult for me to describe how touched I was by your beautiful letter.... I gave it to the Princess to read. She was moved to tears, and said she felt *very* sorry for you and that 'out of evil good would come'. She kept the letter to read it again and return it to me at teatime, and begged me to thank you for the letter she received from you this morning, which she showed me. She begged me to tell you that you had no enemies that she was aware of who were friends of hers....

I know, my Darling, that she will now meet you with pleasure, so that your position is, thank God! better now than it ever was since we have been such friends, and I do not despair, in time, that you and she may become quite good friends.

The Princess, he contended, had been 'an angel of goodness throughout all this, but then she is a Lady, and could never do anything that was mean or small'. Daisy's interests, and his own, he agreed, now lay 'apart', for she had claimed her conversion to Socialism as the excuse, beyond her child, for their separation. Nevertheless, the Prince insisted diplomatically, 'we must still have so many objects in common'. In her delicate condition she was still 'my poor little love', and in a follow-up letter, in which he assured her that no one else would open her mail to him, he signed himself, perhaps out of habit, 'Your only love'. But by then there was another.

While inspecting the Norfolk Yeomanry that January, one of his many boring ceremonial duties, the Prince noticed the wife of Lieutenant-Colonel George Keppel, a handsome, moustached officer in the regiment and a younger brother of the 7th Earl of Albemarle. Alice Keppel, daughter of Admiral Sir William Edmonstone (and great-grandmother of Camilla Parker Bowles), was twenty-nine to the Prince's fifty-six. She was tall, buxom, blue-eyed, and wore her luxuriant chestnut hair piled high atop her head. A few days later he saw her again, at a race meeting at Sandown, crossing the paddock with a friend, John Leslie. HRH, honorary colonel of her husband's Norfolks, asked to be introduced to her. Mrs Keppel had a soft, throaty voice, and a lively manner, and was so advanced that she smoked cigarettes elegantly in a long holder. He sent Leslie off, and spent the rest of the day with Alice.

When the Prince hinted strongly that he wanted to see more of her, Mrs Keppel understood. She had other lovers, including his fashionable friend Lord Alington (once only Humphrey Sturt) and the immensely wealthy and still-unmarried Lord Stavordale, soon to succeed as the 6th Earl of Ilchester. But she was ready to serve the Crown. The heir apparently saw her next, by arrangement, at a large dinner party at the home of Georgiana, Lady Howe, a daughter of the Duke of Marlborough. There, according to the future Lady Sackville, he spent much of the evening chatting with Alice on the top landing, 'which rather shocked people, especially when they sat for a short time on two steps'. He discovered then that she liked to play bridge. On 27 February 1898 he was at her home in Belgravia for dinner. After that his green brougham (his least ostentatious carriage) was seen in Wilton Crescent most afternoons, once George Keppel had dutifully left for his club – until HRH determined that her new status required a more elegant address.

The Keppels moved to 30 Portman Square, a narrow six-storey house of eighteenth-century vintage but refitted with electricity and separate bedrooms and bathrooms for husband and wife. The relocated family of three employed seven servants, a modest number since it included the child Violet's governess and nanny; but the Keppels lived largely on his inadequate Army pay and a stipend from the Earl of Albemarle, who happened to be a largely honorific aide-de-camp to the Prince. Soon the additional funds which Mrs Keppel required to maintain herself at the height of fashion were discreetly furnished by one of the Prince's informal Court, the open-pocketed financier who had replaced the late Baron Hirsch as adviser. Sir Ernest Cassel would offer fiscal counsel, quietly settle Alice's dressmaker's and milliner's bills, and handle her own mysteriously acquired investments. (The wealthy and charitable Sir Ernest, who resembled the more portly Prince, was known to the envious as 'Windsor Cassel'.)

Alice Keppel cultivated rewarding relationships with bankers. Her daughter, Violet, born three years into Alice's marriage in 1894, was apparently fathered by the handsome, rich William Beckett, senior partner in the Yorkshire family banking firm of Beckett & Company of Leeds, and MP for Whitby. George Keppel forgave his wife. Her newest admirer, Violet remembered, was 'a fat, bald gentleman who smelt of cigars and eau-de-Portugal, whose fingers were covered with rings, and to whom one curtsied endlessly'. She called him 'Grandpapa'. Vita Sackville-West, an occasional playmate, recalled arriving of an afternoon to see a 'discreet little one-horse brougham' waiting in Portman Square when she arrived. Rolfe, the butler, would guide her into a corner of the hallway as she entered, explaining, 'One minute, Miss; a gentleman is coming downstairs.' The stout visitor would descend heavily, collect his hat, gloves and cane, and disappear into a haze of cigar smoke and cologne as Rolfe bowed him out.

The Prince wrote to Alice cautiously as 'Dear Mrs George', and she was even more circumspect. She left no diary, no memoir, and no revealing letters, and gave no injudicious interviews. When Vita Sackville-West published her sardonic, best-selling novel *The Edwardians* (1930), fictionalizing a country-house visit of HRH and Mrs Keppel under the usual properly improper circumstances, her Lady Roehampton is scandalized by the failure of the groom of the chambers to change the revealing blotting-paper in Mrs Romola Cheyne's bedroom:

> It makes one's blood run cold, doesn't it, to think of the hands one's letters might fall into? I suppose it's a letter to ...' And here she uttered a name so august that in deference to the respect and loyalty of the printer it must remain unrevealed.... 'Look!'

It was totally unlike Alice Keppel to have left anything compromising. She never felt compromised, whether she gave what the Prince called 'Mrs George dinners' or accompanied him sedately in society while the Princess remained at Sandringham or disappeared to Denmark. By the time that Daisy Warwick had her baby in March (christened Maynard as she had been Frances Maynard), and had found a new lover five years younger than her thirty-six years,* HRH had established a new routine with the agreeable Mrs Keppel. Possibly it had some physical side, as 'Mrs George' was generous with her favours, but the Prince, obese, athero-sclerotic and possibly diabetic, may by then also have been impotent, as the fading years of the Lady Warwick relationship suggest.** Whatever the nature of the new liaison, Edward Hamilton would concede, 'The presence of Mrs G. always ensures [HRH's] being in a good humour. She is a most useful and valuable institution.'

When Sonia Keppel was born in 1900, sired, most likely, by her lawful father, her mother's past months of pregnancy and withdrawal from society had little obvious effect on the Prince. His brougham continued to appear, if less regularly for a time, at her door. Happily, he had also cultivated a parallel intimacy with another lady at whose home his

---

* Joseph Laycock, an Army captain, was to go off to the Boer War and return to find a much younger woman, Kitty Downshire, whom he was to marry in 1902 after the Marquess of Downshire had divorced her for adultery. Lady Warwick immersed herself further in Socialist causes.

** Medical opinions are that a compelling case for impotence can be made on the basis of the Prince's atherosclerotic heart disease, the eventual cause of his death. His life-style, especially his overeating, obesity and heavy smoking, were contributory factors. Atherosclerosis can be a systemic disease, causing impaired function of many organs, including the genito-urinary tract. His obesity further suggests adult onset diabetes mellitus, also associated with impotence.

carriage also waited when he was not visiting 'Mrs George'. Also invited to dine with HRH at the home of Colonel George Keppel and his wife on 27 February 1898 had been Agnes and Fanny Keyser, the attractive but unmarried daughters of a wealthy Berkshire stockbroker, Frederick Charles Keyser (who, in pursuing business and social success, had abandoned Judaism for the Established Church). He had bought for his daughters, now aged forty-five and forty-seven, the leasehold of a mansion at 17 Grosvenor Crescent, near Hyde Park Corner, where they entertained lavishly. In return for invitations to them, the Keppels had invited the Keyser ladies to Wilton Crescent.

At Mrs Keppel's right sat the Prince of Wales, clearly besotted by his hostess. But Agnes Keyser, who was not only charming but had an hourglass figure, also had something else that interested His Royal Highness: an elegant home nearby that might be convenient. Soon Miss Keyser received a telephone call from a gentleman representing the Prince, who wondered whether HRH might drop over for tea on an afternoon the following week with Mrs Keppel. Agnes may have been surprised that she was being so readily exploited by the Prince, but even that was a compliment. The lovers arrived separately, and Miss Keyser was expected after tea, she understood, to leave them at least briefly to themselves. While the visits would be repeated, the Prince also developed a separate friendship with the formidable Agnes, who would invite him for dinners without 'Mrs George', remonstrating with him for smoking and gourmandizing, and offering him healthier fare like Irish stew and rice pudding. He visited Grosvenor Crescent often, enjoying her pampering and ignoring her advice.

Real devotion grew between them, but that there were any amorous overtures from either side seems unlikely. Nothing he did was ever completely unknown, and Lady Gregory would soon refer spitefully and curiously in her diary to 'Miss Keyser, the rich Jewess with whom the Prince constantly sups'. She obviously wondered whether supping was all that transpired.

As usual, he spent some time on the Riviera in March, his excuse that he was to lay the foundation stone for a new jetty at Cannes. There were always ceremonial duties to perform or evade. Since the Queen now sought the sun in early spring, he joined her briefly, arriving indiscreetly late to receive President François-Félix Faure at Cimiez. The portly Faure, who died ten months later of a heart attack atop his mistress, assured them that the sordid affair over Captain Dreyfus was 'greatly exaggerated', and 'misunderstood abroad', but they were unconvinced. In April the Prince was called on, in the Queen's absence, to preside, for the first time, over the Privy Council (conveniently at Marlborough House), to authorize and sign a declaration of neutrality in the war between the United States and Spain precipitated by the explosion of the battleship *Maine* in Havana harbour. In June he was at the launch of the HMS *Albion* at the Thames Iron Works when a large platform next to a Japanese cruiser also under construction gave way as the crowd on it was watching the launch. The improvised stand collapsed just as the guests on the royal dais were cheering the slide of the *Albion* down the ways. Hundreds floundered in the water and sixty died while the Royals, out of sight of the tragedy, were giving three hearty cheers. It was unlucky publicity, but there was nothing the Prince could do about it.

Among his appearances in the spring of 1898 was one appreciated by the public but deprecated by the Queen. Gladstone had died at eighty-nine on 19 May, and the Government authorized a Westminster Abbey funeral, the first grand obsequies for a commoner since the death of Wellington. The Prince of Wales asked to be a pallbearer, and also wanted his son, the Duke of York, to participate. Whether his motive was his genuine liking for the crusty GOM or his certainty that his mother would be quietly furious, he saw to it that Regy Brett handled the arrangements, and responded strongly to a telegram from his mother asking what precedent he had followed, and whose advice he had taken. He telegraphed back to Balmoral that there was no precedent and that he had taken no one's advice. She refused to eulogize Gladstone, telegraphing his widow only that he was 'one of the most distinguished statesmen of my reign'. To Salisbury, the Queen declared frankly on dispatching her grudging sympathy message, 'I am sorry for Mrs Gladstone, and as for him, I never liked him, and I will say nothing about him.' That the Prince of Wales kissed the widow's hand afterwards displeased her mightily. All he told the angry Queen by telegram on May 28 was, 'Funeral just over, a most impressive and touching sight, very simple and dignified.' He signed it 'Bertie'.

Fulfilling his bargain with Daisy Warwick, he arranged for her to be often in his company (with the Earl), and she was also among the guests at Waddesdon Manor, the palatial Buckinghamshire estate of Baron Ferdinand de Rothschild, when the Prince fell down the stairs at ten one morning and fractured his kneecap. (The spiral staircase in the tower tapered off hazardously, and had, then, no rail.) In her diary on 24 July the Queen called the accident 'most lamentable', a rather mild response. *The Times* reported that he had been treated with 'the X-rays', but the new technique had only determined the nature of the break. His immobility kept him from travelling to Copenhagen when the Queen of Denmark died on 29 September. (Alix had been there nursing her since early August.) Victoria, her courtier Victor Mallet wrote on 31 July, 'is to visit the Prince of Wales on board the *Osborne* this afternoon. Sir James [Reid, her physician] gives a most cheerful report of the invalid and says he has never seen him look better; his cheerfulness is remarkable. He sleeps on deck where a comfortable tent has been constructed and is looking forward to plenty of society of a congenial character but the fact remains he must not be allowed to move for at least two months and that it may be six or eight before he walks easily.' Several weeks later Daisy Warwick wrote to Stead, 'This week I am going to Cowes to spend a few days with the invalid.' Mrs Keppel prudently entrained with Violet to visit relatives in Scotland.

Forced into a healthy if sedentary regime, the Prince thrived. From Marlborough House, by special arrangement, he listened to what could be heard of an opera from Covent Garden via 'Electrophone'. He may even have read a book. Jennie Churchill's elder son, Winston, a young subaltern who had served on the Northwest Frontier, had written letters home, identified only as 'From a Young Officer', that were published in the *Daily Telegraph*. A born self-publicist, he was expanding them into a book, *The Malakand Field Force*. To build support for reassignment to the next trouble spot, the Sudan, he wrote to his mother's old friend, who was honorary colonel (among his other honorary colonelcies) of the 11th Bengal Lancers, Churchill's regiment. He had read the letters in the *Telegraph*, the Prince had replied, signing himself 'A. E.', and he looked forward to the book '–as you have a great facility in writing – which is a great advantage. I only hope you will be prudent in your remarks – & shun all acrid criticisms which would be resented by the authorities!'

Late that April, HRH had written again to praise Winston 'on the success of your book.... Everybody is reading it.' (he was to send a copy to his sister Vicky, and also refer to the book in a speech.) He had read it himself, the Prince claimed, 'with the greatest possible interest', although at that time, just returned from France, the Prince had probably only turned a few pages. 'Having now seen active service,' he closed in avuncular fashion, 'you will wish to see more....' He predicted a VC for Winston if he remained in the Army and did not resign prematurely to seek a seat in Parliament: 'You have plenty of time before you, and should certainly stick to the Army before adding M.P. to your name.'

On 15 October 1898, Victor Mallet declared that the royal patient 'has taken a new lease of life; the complete rest and discipline of an invalid existence has made him look younger and better than he has done for years and he has borne the trial with the greatest patience and good temper; it seems to have drawn him closer to the Queen and to his children and altogether seems a blessing in disguise. He walks with ease and will not have a stiff knee; he wears a sort of splint with springs that support the leg and you would hardly tell he had anything the matter with his leg.'

In December, by which time he was able to walk readily, the Prince had a shocking reminder of his accident at Waddesdon. His host then, Ferdy de Rothschild, only two years his senior, was dead. Writing to novelist Paul Bourget, Henry James recalled his own last visit to Waddesdon, and in a hint of the controversy over Captain Dreyfus, whose trumped-up trial for treason had brought anti-Semitism in France into the open, James added, 'What strikes me more than anything else, in connection with [Ferdinand's] death, is the marked difference between English and French nerves by the fact that the Crown Prince (by whom I mean of course the P. of W.) assisted yesterday, with every demonstration of sympathy, at [Rothschild's] severely simple Jewish obsequies.' Two very different funerals had shown the future king's mettle better, perhaps, than his continuing preoccupation with trophy beauties.

Alix kept her wifely distance from the Prince as his relationship with Alice Keppel gained momentum during the last months of 1898. When he was with Mrs Keppel in London and on the Riviera, or looking after the interests of earlier women in his life, the Princess was at Sandringham or on the royal yacht in the Mediterranean – not the *Britannia*, which the Prince had sold, ostensibly to economize, but on her mother-in-law's ageing *Osborne*. When the Tsar and Tsarina visited, Alix was at hand as aunt to Nicholas and, through her husband, also aunt to the Tsarina, another Alexandra. At Balmoral the Royals all gathered for photographs by William Downey, taken (the Queen wrote in her diary) 'by the new cinematograph process, which makes moving pictures by winding off a reel of film'. Assisting Bertie there in entertaining the Tsar was Prince Arthur, and, the indolent Nicholas wrote ruefully to his mother, Alix's sister, 'From the very first day, my uncles took charge of me. They seem to think it necessary to take me out shooting all day long. The weather is awful, rain and wind every day and on top of that no luck at all – I haven't killed a stag yet.' He gained a respite from the Scottish weather when the Prince hurried off by train to Newmarket to watch Persimmon run in the Jockey Club Stakes.

In London early in the new year, with many of his friends away, the Prince proposed to dine, at short notice, with Lady Dorothy Nevill, once an intimate of Disraeli (her youngest son, Ralph, the Nevill family knew, was almost certainly Dizzy's child). Now seventy-two, the eccentric Lady Dorothy was a collector of celebrities at her home in Charles Street, Mayfair, and HRH asked her to invite several people who interested him, including Cora Urquhart Potter, the popular actress who performed as Mrs Brown Potter, and was about to open as Olive Arnison in Henry Arthur Jones's *Carnac Sahib*. At Lady Haliburton's, where Augusta Gregory was visiting, Lady Dorothy arrived, very late for tea but 'very smart – having entertained the Prince at lunch'. Her hostess wondered what she served His Royal Highness. 'Oh, there was difficulty,' gushed Lady Dorothy; '– those wretched servants! I ordered what he was sure to like, boiled beef, & chickens, & bacon & beans, & marrow bones – but I told them to bring up the beef & chickens together – & they thought they knew best & brought the beef first – & he said, "No, I am going to have chicken" – and he had to wait till it came. Then he always likes bacon & beans, that I always have for him, tho' of course there are only flageolets to be had now, but he likes them on separate dishes – & that wretched cook squashed them all on to the same dish.' But he had remained, enjoying himself despite what Agnes Keyser might have thought of the gargantuan meal, until 4.30.

From Cannes, where he then holidayed with Mrs Keppel, the Prince worked out in correspondence with Gladys, Countess de Grey (whom he had seen at a dinner party), and Lillie Langtry, a strategy to have Lillie's daughter, Jeanne-Marie, presented at Court so that she could go out respectably into society. Lady de Grey would present to the Queen the daughter-in-law of one of Lillie's brothers, who would then introduce her 'cousin-by-marriage'. Jeanne-Marie would be safely launched. As with Daisy Warwick, the Prince looked after his former intimates.

At Cannes, too, the Prince (who had experimented with bicycling, and even with the newly invented motor car) now took up golf, determined not to be behind the times. Again the past intervened, as he materialized at the annual Battle of Flowers, among cartloads of anemones, cyclamen, carnations, daisies, hyacinths and orange blossom, where Victor Mallet, in the Queen's party at Cimiez, saw him. Perhaps an innocent, Mallet noted in his diary about the conspicuously absent Alexandra, 'her restlessness is alarming and her one idea is to be constantly travelling; she looks ill, so do her daughters, and I hear she dreads the possibility of reigning'. What she was dreading was reigning under marital embarrassments to which the future king seemed oblivious. She did not anticipate that the formidable Mrs Keppel would arrange matters – by her social standards – appropriately. Alice Keppel knew how to keep a triangle at least partly invisible. Yet when opening night of the opera season arrived on 8 May 1899, the Prince, as the press observed pointedly, was there without Alix. She knew, however, when she had to return to the bosom of her family. At Windsor on 24 May, the Queen would mark her eightieth birthday. 'May God still mercifully preserve me', she wrote in her diary, the pages of which she could hardly see, 'to work for the good of my country!'

For the Waleses, the new social season was abbreviated. They could be apart without press gossip, however, when the annual routine of the Prince's taking his cure at a spa while the Princess spent two months in Denmark again came round. Alone once more in London, on 10 September the Prince dined with Sir Edward Hamilton at the smart Carlton Hotel. 'I don't think he has ever before dined in the public room at a Restaurant in this country,' Hamilton wrote. 'It is an innovation; and I am not sure that it is quite a dignified one.' It was a curious, blinkered diary entry, for the Prince had used private dining rooms in hotels and restaurants hundreds of times to dally with the ladies, many of them not ladies at all; and in Paris he was a familiar figure in both fashionable and far-from-dignified Montmartre clubs and cafés.

The war in South Africa that the Jameson Raid had foreshadowed broke out a month later. Twenty years before, the British had annexed the Transvaal, settled long before by Dutch farmers – Boers – who had overwhelmed and all but enslaved the local tribes. Although the Union Jack flew, as gold and diamonds were being discovered and mined the defiant Boers labelled the British in the Johannesburg Rand (to whom

they refused to grant political rights) *Uitlanders*, and in December 1880
again proclaimed a republic. Under pressure from threatened 'Rand-
lords', and recognizing that their monetary system was based upon gold,
the British reinforced their garrison in Cape Colony. When Paul Kruger,
the Boer President, issued an ultimatum warning the British not to send
troops, war became inevitable. London papers derided the Transvaal as 'a
trumpery little state' run by 'impudent burghers'. Eager for a quick military solution, Lord Lansdowne, the Secretary for War, boasted to an
equally ebullient Joseph Chamberlain, the Secretary for the Colonies,
'My soldiers are in ecstasies.'

Eventually it was to take nearly half a million troops fighting in hostile
terrain and hampered by stretched communications to subdue 88,000
obdurate Boers in a vicious, scorched-earth war. In England, confident
newspaper readers first considered it a tea-time affair; and gentlemen,
until then preoccupied with Race Week at Newmarket (where the Prince
of Wales inevitably was at the time), besieged Whitehall with requests to
serve. One supplicant was a subaltern, George Cornwallis-West (very
likely the Prince's son), who had learned that Lieutenant-General Baron
Methuen of Corsham was being sent to South Africa to command the 1st
Division and wanted an aide-de-camp for his old regiment who could
ride well. Cornwallis-West applied to the Prince, who responded, 'I had
the opportunity of speaking to Lord Methuen at the station yesterday
when I took leave of Sir Redvers Buller [another general going to South
Africa], and strongly urged him to take you on his staff, so I hope it may
be satisfactorily settled. I envy you going out on active service with so fine
a battalion, and wish you good luck and a safe return home.'

Soon young Cornwallis-West was on his way, marching in the fog at
five in the morning from Chelsea Barracks on King's Road to Waterloo
Station as part of the first 47,000 men to leave in chartered civilian liners.
In Boer country he fought with his brigade until two attacks of sunstroke
left him desperately ill and he was invalided home. Before another relapse
returned him to the hospital, he was sent for by the Prince, and at
Marlborough House recounted to HRH his 'short but exciting' war.
Earlier that year, before the Transvaal, he had been sent for by the Prince,
for very different reasons, to visit aboard the royal yacht at Cowes.
Cornwallis-West had been 'about a good deal together' with the widowed
Jennie Churchill, forty-five and still radiantly beautiful. (Lord Randolph
had died in 1895.) HRH took him aside to emphasize 'the inadvisability

of my marrying a woman so much my senior'. George listened dutifully and married Jennie anyway, in July 1900. Her son Winston was only two weeks younger than her new husband.

After service in India and the Sudan, young Churchill had left the Army to be a war correspondent in South Africa. A month after hostilities began he was taken prisoner when the Boers ambushed a munitions train, and from prison camp in Pretoria he used his enforced leisure to lobby for some possible political advantage with the future king. HRH had learned about Churchill's capture in the papers, and had telegraphed Jennie to 'pray he may be safe and sound'. Not knowing that, Churchill began his letter to the Prince dramatically. 'I venture to think', he opened, 'that perhaps your Royal Highness will be interested to receive a letter from me and from this address and although of course the censorship excludes me from writing v[er]y freely – as freely as I have sometimes done – I daresay that you will not consider that an overwhelming disadvantage.' He regretted losing his opportunity, previously arranged with the firm of Longmans, to write a book about the events in which he could no longer participate, but, he acknowledged, 'War means risk and danger.' He hoped that the Prince had read his second book, the two-volume *The River War*, about the Sudan expedition that had ended in the victory at Omdurman.

Having already interfered in British–Boer relations and exacerbated his unpopularity in England, the Kaiser made his long-postponed visit to his irritated royal grandmother five weeks after the war began. That the visit had come off at all was the result of colonial settlements with Germany in the South Pacific far from Africa, and a temporary truce between the prickly Kaiser and his proud uncle. At an interview with Wilhelm, Sir Frank Lascelles, the ambassador, reported to the Prince, 'He ... said that he knew the Prince of Wales was his Uncle and his Mother's Brother and looked upon him as a silly boy, but that His Royal Highness seemed to forget that the silly boy had become German Emperor, and had the interests of the Empire to consider even before those of his family relations.' Despite such vainglory, the Foreign Office and the Colonial Office wanted the visit to happen, to suggest to the Boers that they could not count on German support, and the Kaiser had done his symbolic placating of the British after his encouragement of Paul Kruger by telegraphing congratulations to the Queen following General Kitchener's victory over the Sudanese at Atbara.

In Germany, where the Boer cause was popular and commercial rivalry with the British increasing, public opinion was hostile to any rapprochement, and the news of early British reverses was greeted with undisguised happiness. Still, the Kaiser sailed on the *Hohenzollern* to visit his grandmother and show off his grand yacht. While visiting the Queen he had learned on 20 November that British troops had finally defeated the Khalifa and his Dervish army in the Sudan. *That* war, at least, seemed over, and the Kaiser, standing before the medieval Round Tower at Windsor Castle, which more than any other place reinforced his intermittent infatuation with England, exclaimed grandly to his staff, 'From this Tower the world is ruled!'

At Sandringham, Alexandra found him repellent but was reluctantly hospitable to his entourage, which included the Foreign Minister, Count Bulow. With the Kaiser, Bulow talked politics with the Prince. A compromise had been worked out in advance whereby the Kaiser's naval aide-de-camp, Admiral von Senden, a touchy Junker who complained to Wilhelm that the Prince had offended him the year before, would not accompany the others. Von Senden was unwelcome at Sandringham. The Kaiser refused to go to England without him, but the admiral was left on the *Hohenzollern*.

Whatever reconciliation occurred in England vanished as soon as the Germans returned to Berlin. Their ethnic affinity with the Boers and their ambitious efforts to build a belated overseas empire remained at odds with British interests. Besides, things were going very badly for the complacent but poorly prepared British in South Africa. The war had become an expensive and unexpected embarrassment. Chartered passenger liners that had ferried troops to the Cape began returning with unanticipated numbers of casualties. During 'Black Week' in late December, Lord Methuen was defeated at Magersfontein, General Sir William Gatacre at Stormberg, and Sir Redvers Buller (popularly rechristened 'Sir Reverse') at Colenso. Two days before Christmas, the sixty-seven-year-old Lord Roberts of Kandahar, VC, whose only son Frederick had died of wounds suffered at Colenso, was hurriedly sent to take charge of the faltering war. Now in his late fifties, the Prince of Wales could only get close to the war by getting close to the participants. 'Arthur, Uncle George, and I', the Prince telegraphed to the Queen, 'have just taken leave of Lord Roberts at [Waterloo] railway station, a dense and unmanageable crowd, with danger of being squashed.' Prince Arthur wanted to serve, but as a field marshal he would have outranked Roberts. Uncle George Cambridge, who had left the Army so unfit, could only watch them struggle against an enemy vastly inferior in numbers but spirited and effective on its own soil.

One of the few bright moments in December had been young Winston's escape from the Boers. From the safety of Pretoria he wrote again to the Prince of Wales – lengthily, and with a view to expanding such descriptions of his bravado into yet another book. 'It is to be hoped', the Prince replied (19 January 1900), 'that you will not risk falling again into the hands of the Boers!' Events had filled him with 'considerable anxiety', and he saw the relief of Ladysmith as 'the whole difference' in reversing the cycle of defeats. He had indeed received Winston's book *The River War* but had 'not yet found time to read it seriously, wh[ich] I hope to do.'

At her Grosvenor Crescent house, Agnes Keyser was busying herself converting much of it into a hospital for officers evacuated home. As the war worsened she had asked the Prince, 'What part can we play?' When he suggested a small hospital for wounded officers, she protested that she had no nursing experience. What she did have, he pointed out, was the wherewithal to pay nurses and the social prestige to attract physicians who might offer their services. By 'Black Week' she was readying twelve beds and an operating room for visiting surgeons, and had recruited six experienced nurses. At each visit the Prince watched the conversion proceed in what Miss Keyser called, after the smart Parisian hotel, he fancied, 'Bristol fashion'. She and her nurses wore uniforms of starched white linen but Agnes herself had no medical credentials. 'What am I to call myself, Sir?' she asked him. Since religious orders had done some of the earliest organized nursing, and 'Sister' designated the head of a ward, he said, promptly, 'You should be called Sister Agnes.'

In the closing days of 1899, 'Sister Agnes's Hospital' announced itself ready to receive patients. Hospital ships from Durban took the wounded to England, and by mid-January, horse-drawn ambulances were conveying officers from Waterloo Station to Grosvenor Crescent. One of the ships was the *Maine*, named after the cruiser sunk in Havana harbour, and the brainchild of Jennie Churchill. She had raised American dollars for it, got the Queen's authorization to fly both British and American flags, hosted a final fund-raising party for it at Claridge's and arranged to have Princess Alix see the ship (with Lady Randolph Churchill herself aboard) off to sea.

From Marlborough House the Prince went often to Grosvenor Crescent on bleak winter evenings to look in and listen to stern if affectionate admonitions about his heavy smoking, which meant no more from Sister Agnes than they had from plain Agnes. The Prince helped by encouraging his wealthy friends to contribute to a trust to maintain the facility, and amid the publicity the denizens of Mayfair and Belgravia wondered about his continuing relationship to Sister Agnes. 'Miss Keyser', Lady Gregory gossiped on 2 February, '... has by his suggestion given up dinner parties & offered the first floor of her house for wounded officers, to be kept free of charge.'

Like Germany, France also gained a not-so-secret satisfaction in Boer victories and British casualties. Many in the French ruling classes, and most of the military, took offence at sympathy for the dismissed and imprisoned Captain Dreyfus, and still seethed over the Fashoda incident in the Sudan in 1898, where Kitchener had expelled a French expedition bent on claiming territory for the tricolore. Both the Queen and the Prince of Wales cancelled winter trips to France. For the Prince, it meant less time with Mrs Keppel, who had been offered the use of the former villa of the late Napoleon III at Biarritz, now owned by Sir Ernest Cassel. As a result, Agnes Keyser saw much more of HRH.

Despite failing sight and a weakening heart that caused her to doze away much of each day, the Queen insisted on being wheeled out to watch troops parade before her at Windsor before they embarked for South Africa. On 2 February the Mayor of besieged Mafeking telegraphed to her the devotion and resolve of the garrison. On the 16th, news came of the relief of besieged Kimberley, and her grandson Willy telegraphed to her, slyly hinting at British greed as motive: 'How happy Mr Rhodes will be!' Eight days earlier, the Prince of Wales had forwarded to his mother a letter from the Kaiser downplaying British defeats as much like a setback in a sporting match. Willy had suggested, 'Even the best football club, if it is beaten notwithstanding the most gallant defence, accepts finally its defeat with equanimity. Last year, in the great cricket match of England *v.* Australia, the former took the victory of the latter quietly, with chivalrous acknowledgment of her opponent.'

'I told him', the Prince wrote to his mother, 'that I could not liken our conflict with the Boers to our defeat last year by the Australians in the cricket matches ... as we were fighting for the very existence of our

Empire, which he knew full well, and that we must use every effort to prove victorious for the sake of our supremacy in South Africa.'

Assuming powers (or, at the least, influence) which the Prince did not have, the Kaiser also tried to frighten him, and through him, Lord Salisbury, by revealing an attempt by Russia to exploit British weakness. That March, the wily Willy told his uncle that Count Michael Muraviev, the Tsar's Foreign Minister, had invited Germany 'to take part in a Collective Action with France and Russia against England for the enforcing of Peace and the help of the Boers'. Although this was true, because of French enmity toward Germany the poorly kept secret proposal was to fail. What remained significant was that the Kaiser was beginning to think of the Prince of Wales as imminent king.

English embarrassments were not restricted to remote places. The founder of the Salvation Army, General William Booth, had published a book a decade earlier equating a phrase commonly used about Africa with conditions at home – *Darkest England*. With candour reminiscent of earlier service on a committee examining slum housing, HRH made a speech on 3 March at the opening of a London County Council housing estate in Bethnal Green confessing his own sins. He was embarrassed, he told an audience largely of working men, that he was an owner of slum property in Lambeth. Their condition was a disgrace to a Christian country, he confessed – but he was unable to improve his properties because they were let on long leases.

Despite his intellectual limitations, the Prince exuded sincerity and, often, gravity. At a gathering in Queen's Hall the month before, he had awarded 900 London County Council scholars their certificates. According to Beatrice Webb, a Socialist and no admirer of his, HRH 'acted like a well-oiled automaton, saying exactly the words he was expected to say, noticing the right persons on the platform, maintaining his own dignity while setting others at ease, and otherwise acting with perfectly polished discretion. But observing him closely you could see that underneath ... there lay the child and the animal, a simple kindly unmoral temperament which makes him a good fellow.... There is something comic in the great British nation with its infinite variety of talents, having this undistinguished and limited-minded German bourgeois to be its social sovereign.' She regretted not having, in his place, someone of 'real distinction' who might 'further our civilization by creating a real aristocracy of character and intellect'. And she deplored his recommended Jubilee commemoration, 'in this morning's papers' (6 February), of 'the freeing of the hospitals from debt, the sort of proposal one would expect from the rank and file of "scripture readers" or a committee of village grocers intent on goodwill on earth and saving the rates'. The difference between them was that she was a utopian dreamer and he a bourgeois pragmatist. And even in that role, the Prince was aiming too high.

Rather than holidaying on the Riviera, the Queen, at her son Arthur's suggestion, made a state visit to Ireland, where she had not been seen in forty years. (The Duke of Connaught now commanded the Army in Ireland.) Although largely confined to a wheelchair or an open carriage, she chose symbolism over invalidism, and, amid deafening crowds, even made a trial run in the form of a royal progress through London. Crippled and hardly able to peer past her cataracts, she went from Windsor to Woolwich Arsenal, visiting along the way a military hospital, a naval school for boys, and a home for crippled children. Excluded from her entourage, and spurning Paris and the new International Exhibition (even though he was chairman of the British Section), the Prince of Wales accompanied Alix to Copenhagen. Travelling via Belgium rather than France, he planned to remain for the sake of appearances until he could quietly escape to the bosom of Alice Keppel. At the railway station in Brussels on 4 April 1900, the day that the Queen disembarked in Dublin, the Royals caught the 5.30 train, from which, looking out of the window of their carriage as it began moving, they saw a gunman fire at them at close range from the footboard. Perhaps the jolt of the train upset the questionable marksmanship of the would-be assassin. Two bullets passed between the heads of Prince and Princess. Before Jean-Baptiste Sipido, the sixteen-year-old apprentice tinsmith, could fire again, he was knocked to the ground by people on the platform.

After some commotion, and the arrest of Sipido, the Prince telegraphed openly to Mrs Keppel to reach her before the morning newspaper did, 'As we were leaving Brussels a man jumped on the step of our carriage and fired a pistol at us through the open window. I don't think there was a bullet in it.' He asked the authorities to go easy on the youth, who he assumed was mentally retarded, and he continued on to Copenhagen. From Denmark he wrote to his sister Louise – whose message was among 'shoals of letters and telegrams' that entailed 'a considerable labour in answering them' – that his assailant 'fortunately proved to be a very bad shot' from 'two yards distance'. But he asked railway officials to dig out the bullet that had lodged in a panel so that he could have a souvenir of the incident.

Sipido's parents were to petition the Queen to ask clemency for their son, who had been exploited, allegedly, by older men. Anti-British sentiment over the Boer War proved more than sufficient. At a trial in October, Sipido confessed that the plot had been hatched by him with two others over drinks in an anarchist café, and that he was only sorry he had missed, for the Prince of Wales was responsible for the deaths of thousands of Boers in South Africa. They jury found him not guilty, and from Balmoral the Queen wrote to Bertie of her shock over Sipido's 'escape'. To the Prince's disgust, Sipido had not only been let go, but had disappeared into France. His nephew Willy wrote to sympathize over Belgian indifference, 'Either their laws are ridiculous, or the jury are a set of d——d, bl——y scoundrels; which is the case, I am unable to decide.' The Prince could sense little sincerity on the Kaiser's part, other than a German desire for orderliness. While he was in Copenhagen, a paper in French had been delivered to him which purported to outline German overtures to Russia and France to join in a coalition against Britain and be rewarded by colonial gains in Egypt and India.

When the inaugural ceremonies for the French Exposition took place on 14 April, the British Section was unrepresented by the Prince. Anglophobia had become so common that near-obscene caricatures of the Queen and Prince of Wales were on sale at newspaper kiosks. Even the British ambassador was absent, having been recalled in an unsubtle protest at French *froideur*. 'Dearest Bertie,' Victoria appealed from Ireland, 'I wish to express to you my earnest hope that you will not go to Paris.... We are all most anxious that your precious life should not be jeopardised.' Since his mother was to be away for three weeks, the Prince planned in any case to be available in England.

Punch loyally published a cartoon by Linley Sambourne, its chief artist, showing the Prince, an aged fifty-eight, leaving his railway carriage to be welcomed at Charing Cross Station by a bowing Mr Punch with a 'Glad to see you back, Sir, safe and sound!' On 20 April, crowds cheered him as he drove home in his carriage to Marlborough House. That evening he composed a statement thanking the nation for the outpouring of affection after the failed assassination. It was published in most newspapers. It continued to rankle, however, that there had been no message

"GOD BLESS THE PRINCE OF WALES!"

Mr Punch welcomes home an unscathed Prince of Wales
*after the failed assassination attempt in Brussels (*Punch, *18 April 1900)*

from Parliament, even though when Prince Alfred had escaped assassination at the hands of Irish Radicals in Australia in 1870, Westminster had been quick to record its thankfulness. He asked Sir Francis Knollys to question the Prime Minister about it – in effect a rebuke for Lord Salisbury. Lamely, Salisbury explained that on 6 April the Cabinet had discussed doing something, and had sought out precedents, but that the House of Lords had adjourned that day, and its recall would have been necessary. Besides, 'It was not then known that the pistol contained a bullet, which the extreme youth of the culprit rendered doubtful.' HRH was reacting prematurely as a king. The Prime Minister was unready for that.

The Queen, returned from Ireland on 26 April. 'I own I am very tired,' she wrote. She would be eighty-one in May, a month which would be better remembered for the lifting of the Siege of Mafeking on the 19th, a few days before her birthday. (The eruption of enthusiasm all over Britain for the small but symbolic victory would not be matched until Armistice Day in 1918.) The Prince's impatience with the Prime Minister had been aggravated by a number of factors he could not name. He realized that he would soon inherit Salisbury at Downing Street, and expected greater sensitivity from him. At seventy-one, Salisbury had been a politician at the highest levels too long to ignore appropriate courtesies, but he had long answered to no one.

The week after Mafeking, the impresario in the Prince was again in view as he hosted a dinner at the Carlton Hotel to mark the completion of the vast *Dictionary of National Biography*. Leslie Stephen had been editor of the first twenty-seven volumes, after which Sidney Lee, who was to become the Prince's biographer, oversaw the completion of the original 63-volume series, one of the great collective intellectual efforts of the time. 'The dinner was sumptuous – any quantity of dishes and wine,' Stephen, then sixty-seven (and a pipe-smoker in private), wrote to a friend, 'and what especially bothered me, a pause in the middle to smoke cigarettes.... I thought it barbarous. I ate as little as I could, though I foolishly allowed myself to drink a little champagne.... We went out to smoke, and Lee presented me to H.R.H. He looked good-tempered and said that he remembered dear Jim [Stephen], who coached his son one long vacation. He also asked me whether I smoked. That was our whole conversation.' Among the guests were the eminent historians Lord Acton, James Bryce and William Lecky, all contributors, and the scholarly Mandell Creighton, Bishop of London, another *DNB* contributor and President of the Church Historical Society. The Prince, however amiable, was very likely hard-pressed to make conversation with any of them. One who stood out was Canon Alfred Ainger, a biographer who had written the entries on Charles and Mary Lamb. 'Who is the little parson?' HRH had asked. 'He is not a writer.' Someone explained that Ainger was 'a very great authority on Lamb'. Putting down his knife and fork the Prince asked in wonderment, 'On *lamb*?' 'Presently,' Stephen wrote, 'the Prince left, and I fled, and got upon the top of a bus, which brought me home, wondering at the whole affair.'

The Prince found time weighing heavily on him. Alice Keppel's pregnancy had kept her from the fashionable dinners that the Prince enjoyed, and long country-house, cards-playing weekends that without her no longer interested him. He had not been shut out of her life, but was prudently spending more time under the asexual solace of Agnes Keyser. Mrs Keppel later claimed to her daughters to have spent Mafeking Night among the celebrants, sitting atop one of Landseer's lions in crowded Trafalgar Square. Since she had given birth to Sonia a fortnight after Mafeking, the tale is difficult to accept. But well before the arrival of Alice's second daughter, the Prince's carriage had disappeared from Portman Square.

He had other, less happy, distractions. His eldest sister, Vicky, to whom he was far more close that he was to their three younger sisters in England, was dying painfully of spinal cancer. In July his brother Alfred, Duke of Coburg, died of throat cancer. The Prince went to Osborne to console his mother, and found that she knew without having been furnished the medical details about how gravely ill Vicky was. He rushed off to Coburg for Affie's funeral, returned briefly, then went to Homburg as he had originally planned to do, but left several times to visit Vicky, who was being shunned by Willy for her English loyalties, at Friedrichshof, near Cronberg.

Whatever satisfaction came to the Prince was on the turf. On 30 March with Ambush II, he had won the Grand National, worth then only £1,975, most of which he gave to the jockey, trainer and head stable-boy. Altogether in 1900 he would win the Two Thousand Guineas, the Newmarket Stakes, the Eclipse Stakes, the St Leger and the Derby: purses totalling nearly £30,000. Perhaps because of the unavailability of Alice Keppel during much of the year he was publicly busier than ever. Philip Magnus's biography counts eighty-six ceremonial appearances, thirty-one meetings, nine sittings of the House of Lords, thirty-seven race meetings, forty-five shooting dates and forty-eight operas and plays attended. Much of it was make-work he no longer sought out. He was still biding his time.

The war in South Africa showed few signs of turning around. Despite some successes, it was proving increasingly costly and the papers were full of casualty lists. Through sources like Winston Churchill he was informed beyond what officialdom offered him. Visits to hospitals, and receiving at Marlborough House officers invalided home, told him much more about the war, and suggested gross incompetence at the highest levels. Much as the Queen was failing, she knew, too, and tried to realize her dream for her son Arthur – the command of the Army – by having him make a reputation in South Africa. She met at Balmoral with Bertie and Arthur to plot strategy, and was disappointed in their reaction. They saw no future for the family in the Horse Guards, and she wrote without optimism to Lord Salisbury expressing her desire to see Arthur 'at the head of the Army during my lifetime'.

From young Churchill the Prince heard that his hopes that the ambitious son of his old friends might continue a career in the Army would be unrealized. His escape from the Boers had made Churchill a national hero, and he wanted to exploit that momentum to gain a seat in Parliament. Writing to the Prince of Wales on 17 October, Churchill first criticized what he considered to be an unpatriotic attack on the Army by a well-born participant home from the war, and then added, 'I have to thank your Royal Highness for the kind remarks about my candidature at Oldham which you made privately in your recent letter to my mother. I trust Sir that I may always preserve your personal approval in my political life.' Churchill won his seat.

The clockwork calendar by which Victoria functioned was breaking down in the waning months of 1900. Her autumn visit to Balmoral was the shortest in decades; she returned to Windsor briefly, and, now nearly blind, received invalided troops from South Africa whose insignia she could not see, their identities described by a wounded, one-legged Australian chaplain. The Prince arrived to talk with her 'for some time' (she recorded, using one of her granddaughters as scribe), probably among other things about the dying Vicky, who would be sixty on 21 November. Her condition, the Queen knew, was 'heartbreaking'. For Victoria, too, time was running out. On the evening of 17 November Dr Reid came to the Prince's rooms in the Castle to discuss Victoria's deterioration, and on 2 December, with the Prince back in London, Reid felt impelled to describe the gravity of the Queen's weakening at length to her heir. Reid claimed, ambiguously, that she had 'materially improved', but that she was 'enfeebled' and going 'down-hill' in a 'progressive' fashion. Her travelling abroad again to seek the sun would now be an inadvisable risk.

'I truly understand and appreciate everything you have written,' the Prince replied. The Queen has much extraordinary vitality and pluck.... I hope that the present shock and the indisposition from which she has suffered may keep away ... but I wish you could induce the Queen to see our friend Laking.' Sir Francis Laking was the Prince's physician. Reid had no confidence in him, but diplomatically sent for him, and they concurred that it was safe for the Queen to go to Osborne House, where she spent her Christmases. (Neither physician had ever seen their charge in bed, but rather in a chair, and Reid had looked after the Queen for twenty years. Whatever medicines he had authorized for her to be taken during the night had been administered by her maids and dressers, and he had never examined her unclothed.) The Prince approved of Osborne, although he always associated it with his unhappy childhood,* feeling that her accustomed surroundings would 'occupy her mind and take her, I hope, out of herself'. But the Prince did not go there to see the situation for himself, fulfilling instead his litany of engagements in London, which included accompanying Leopold de Rothschild and other City notables to the annual Smithfield Club Cattle Show. The *Illustrated London News* shows the dignitaries, all top-hatted and frock-coated, and brandishing canes, observing unusually docile bulls held in check by their keepers. At Christmas he remained at Sandringham with Alexandra.

Visiting Sandringham, Princess Louise reported to Reid on New Year's Day, 1901, that the Prince 'bids me to say what a comfort your letters and telegrams are to him, and he has such confidence in your judgment'. As the Queen declined, a vacuum of legality and ceremony was apparent, but the Prince of Wales could formally fill only some of it. Victoria's secretariat had long coped with her withdrawal discreetly, but some matters could only await the inevitable, among them the 6,600 Army commissions she could no longer sign.

The war was now turning favourably, largely through overwhelming numbers and superior firepower, as Lord Roberts returned home to replace Lord Wolseley at the War Office. (Sir Horatio Kitchener was to take over in South Africa.) On 3 January 'Bobs' arrived in London to be greeted by the Prince, who drove with him past cheering crowds to Buckingham Palace. Roberts then went to Osborne to pay his respects to the Queen, who, from a chair, conferred on him the expected earldom. Assuming he was unneeded, on 7 January the Prince entrained for Chatsworth, ostensibly for shooting with the Duke of Devonshire.

---

* As king he would never use Osborne.

Mrs Keppel would be there. News of the Queen, which followed him about, continued to record her deterioration, and when he returned to a routine of commuting between London and Sandringham, Dr Reid (who had now examined Victoria in bed, as she could not be moved) reported the Queen's sudden 'dazed condition'. Reid did not say so, but Victoria had apparently suffered a series of small strokes.

The first rumours that she was failing appeared in the London papers on 17 January, although the *Court Circular* reported – possibly a fiction – that she had 'driven out' the day before. When Reid, with Sir Arthur Bigge, drew up a statement for the next *Circular* to prepare people for the worst, and telegraphed the text to Marlborough House, the Prince replied that he wanted as yet 'no statement whatever' to be made. Yet Victoria's memory now flickered, and she had to be told who was at her bedside. On 18 January, a Friday, Reid telegraphed the Kaiser, who had asked to be informed, about 'disquieting symptoms'. Willy prepared to leave for England. That evening the Queen asked Reid, 'Is the Prince of Wales here?' Reid explained that he could be summoned from London. 'I do not advise it at present,' she said dismissively, unaware of her actual condition.

From Marlborough House the same evening, Dr Laking sent Reid an obtuse telegram declaring that since he considered everything 'quite satisfactory', the Prince could go to Sandringham for the weekend. Bigge, however, did not want him that far away from a fast train, and telephoned to the Prince that alarming reports were appearing in the press, and that some official statement had to be released. The result, on Saturday morning, was a bulletin from Osborne published under the caption, 'The Health of the Queen', which played down her actual condition and reported only that the Queen 'has not lately been in her usual health'. Early that morning Bigge again called Knollys at Marlborough House to warn that the Prince might be needed 'at a moment's notice'. Yet an obstacle to his presence surfaced. Princess Helena (formally Princess Christian, in acknowledgement of her husband) appeared close to hysteria, and was refusing to accept the fact of her mother's imminent death. Helena was telegraphing her brother to contradict Reid's pessimism, and upbraiding him for urging Bertie to come. With curious indirection, the Prince was nevertheless on his way.

He seemed to need the emotional support of Sister Agnes, and had invited himself for her plain fare at Grosvenor Crescent that Friday evening. While her hospital functioned in adjacent rooms, they talked of the likely death of the Queen, the Prince confiding that he felt quite unworthy to succeed her. She poured glasses of brandy for both of them, and assured him that he was up to whatever would come his way. That was presumably why he had sought her out. Shortly, he called for his carriage, returned to Marlborough House (Alix was in the country and would travel separately), and the next morning, a Saturday, he departed for Portsmouth, arriving across the Solent at five.

At Osborne he told the attending physicians that it might be best if the Queen did not know yet that he was there. A few hours later Victoria said to her doctors with surprising lucidity, 'I think the Prince of Wales should be told I have been very ill, as I am sure he would feel it.' Reid explained that he was already in the house. 'He is most concerned and is anxious to come as soon as Your Majesty would like to see him. Would Your Majesty like him to come now?'

'Certainly,' she said, 'but he needn't stay.'

The Prince came in, saw his mother, and emerged, making no comment to Reid, who then went in alone. 'I should like to live a little longer', she told Reid, perhaps as a result of her conversation with her son, 'as I have still a few things to settle. I have arranged most things, but there are still some left, and I want to live a little longer.'

Her momentary clarity of mind made the Prince of Wales feel that he had been sent on a fool's errand – or at least his sisters, the Princesses, claimed he had implied as much to them. As a result, when he heard that the Kaiser was coming, accompanied by Prince Arthur (who had been visiting in Berlin when the news came), he felt that a deathbed visit from his excitable nephew was premature. He dreaded the inevitable inappropriate scene. The Prince proposed to rush back to London to restrain Willy from going to Osborne, fibbing if necessary that no one but her doctors could see Victoria.

The Kaiser's telegram to the Prince of Wales, apparently deliberately uncoded, announced that his party would arrive in London at 6.15 p.m. on Sunday, 20 January. Since telegraph clerks received payments from newspapers for purveying confidential information, the news raced through the city. Thousands understood that the Queen was sinking. And she was. Her lucidity had again faded. By Sunday evening she was slipping in and out of consciousness, a frail figure in white on a great canopied bed. Her somnolence was so deep that Randall Davidson, the Dean of Windsor, who had been at Osborne House earlier in the day and had left, was again sent for. And again the Queen rallied, awakening in the early hours of the morning and asking Reid, 'Am I better at all?' He told her that she was, and she asked for her white pomeranian, Tutti, which was placed on the bed but was too restless to remain. By then Victoria had slipped again into deep sleep.

Londoners who glimpsed the Prince in the early evening darkness, on his way to Charing Cross Station, would have seen an incongruous figure. He had returned to Marlborough House to change into the colourful and inappropriate dress of the Prussian First Dragoon Guards, ostensibly – although he loved uniforms – as a courtesy to the Kaiser, a motive more appropriate to the *Charlottenberg Bahnhof* than to Charing Cross. This costume change suggests anxiety and confusion. There had been telephoned messages to him in London about the Queen's slipping again into unconsciousness, and Reid wanted the Prince back as soon as possible.

The Royals spent the night at Marlborough House but took a special train early Monday morning to Portsmouth, the Prince of Wales no longer attired as a German. He, the Duke of York, the Duke of Connaught, and the Kaiser arrived (Reid wrote in his diary) 'in the forenoon, and I took them all in separately to look at the Queen from the foot of the bed, but I did not then think it advisable for any of them to speak to her or to rouse her'. By evening the tracheal rales foreshadowing the end had begun. Reid took the Prince in to see the Queen and to speak to her. After he left, Reid and Mrs Tuck, the Queen's dresser, went to the bedside, and Victoria, Reid wrote, 'took my hand and repeatedly kissed it. She evidently in her semi-conscious state did not realise the Prince had gone, and thought it was *his* hand she was kissing.' Mrs Tuck understood, and asked if she still wanted the Prince of Wales, and she said 'Yes'. He returned, and the Queen murmured, 'Kiss my face.'

A member of the Royal Household mused to the Prince, 'I wonder if she will be happy in heaven?' HRH thought about it and confided, perhaps to lighten the atmosphere, 'I don't know. She will have to walk *behind* the angels – and she won't like that!'

Soon after, Reid took Princess Alix in, but her mother-in-law was again losing consciousness and did not recognize her. Through the night, doctors plied the Queen with oxygen to assist her breathing. In the morning of the 22nd, the Princesses Helena, Louise and Beatrice took turns in telling Victoria who was at the bedside, but omitted the Kaiser, who was standing there with the others. Reid whispered to the Prince of Wales, 'Wouldn't it be well to tell her that her grandson the Emperor is here too?' The Prince turned closely to the doctor, out of Willy's hearing, and said, 'No, it would excite her too much.' Toward noon, when the family was sent out so that attendants could perform their duties, Reid told the Kaiser that he would take him in alone, and Willy asked suspiciously, 'Did you notice this morning that everybody's name in the room was mentioned to her except mine?'

'Yes,' Reid confessed, having no idea of the intense family animosities involved, 'and that is one reason why *I* specially wish to take you there.' Reid then went to the Prince of Wales and asked permission to do so, and the Prince could do nothing but agree, saying, 'Certainly, and tell him the Prince of Wales wishes it.' Reid asked the attendants to leave the Kaiser alone with the Queen, and afterwards Victoria, again briefly awake, told Reid, 'The Emperor is very kind.'

When the family was again summoned at three, the Dean of Windsor and the vicar of nearby Whippingham church entered with them and began intoning prayers. Irritated at their haste to rush the Queen off, the Prince of Wales asked that the clergymen return at a more definitive time. That came quickly. At four the same afternoon, about an hour later, the Queen began sinking rapidly. As the family watched around the bed, the clergymen returned. Reid raised Victoria's head, supporting it under the pillow to ease her breathing. On her other side, Willy rushed to assist with his unwithered right arm, and the two remained there uncomfortably, not shifting positions, for two-and-a-half hours. Over the murmured prayers, with the end imminent, the children and grandchildren who now crowded the bedroom began calling out their own names to the dying Queen, perhaps hoping to send something of themselves with her into the beyond. At 6.30 the pinched face relaxed. Ten minutes later the final bulletin of Victoria's reign was issued over the signature of the Minister-in-Residence at Osborne House, Arthur Balfour. It was a single sentence: 'The Queen died peacefully at 6.30.'

Later that evening the family gathered around the canopied bed for a final farewell to the wasted figure in white. The next morning, Albert Edward, no longer Prince of Wales, crossed the Solent to attend a Privy Council at St James's Palace, at which he was to be formally proclaimed King. (Knollys had informed the Council that on accession, His Majesty would cease using the double name he detested.)

APPRECIATION.' 1901.

The last time that Kaiser Wilhelm II earned anything but
opprobrium in England was on the death of his grandmother. The new
*sovereign bids him farewell (*Punch*, February 1901)*

On 1 February, while a gale whipped across the strait from Cowes to Portsmouth, the Queen's small coffin, covered by a white and gold pall, was placed in the *Alberta*, which moved slowly through an avenue of warships, en route via London to the state funeral at Windsor. Standing on the bridge of a trailing cruiser, the new sovereign noticed the yacht's Royal Standard flying at half-mast. He enquired about it.

'The Queen is dead, Sir,' explained an officer.

'The King of England lives,' said Edward VII – and the flag fluttered in the brisk wind to its full height.

Afterword

1901–1910

'WE GROVEL BEFORE fat Edward' – E[dward] the Caresser, as he is privately named,' Henry James wrote to Oliver Wendell Holmes, Jr, in Massachusetts. '... But I mourn the safe and motherly old middle-class queen, who held the nation warm under the fold of her big, hideous Scotch-plaid shawl and whose duration had been so extraordinarily convenient and beneficient.' He was even more gloomy in a letter to Clara and Clare Benedict, also across the Atlantic. The Queen's death, he prophesied from his perspective of exclusive London drawing rooms, 'will let loose incalculable forces for possible ill. I am very pessimistic. The new King's accession', he continued, was 'the worst omen for the dignity of things', and he expected 'vulgarity and frivolity'. Even Edward's own trusted aide, Lord Esher, told his son Maurice that the new King 'has one great fault for me, which is his commonplace personality. I cannot find in him any trace of original thought or feeling. So unlike the Queen, who was unique.'

Lecturing in Canada as a Boer War celebrity, even Winston Churchill wrote sarcastically to his mother on hearing the news of Victoria's death, 'A great and solemn event: but I am curious about the King. Will it entirely revolutionise his way of life? Will he sell his horses and scatter his Jews or will Reuben Sassoon be enshrined among the crown jewels and other regalia? Will he become desperately serious? Will he continue to be friendly to you? Will the Keppel be appointed 1st Lady of the Bedchamber? ... I am glad he has got his innings at last, and am most interested to watch how he plays it. ...' Yet as early as the funeral procession for the late queen, Lady Gregory, not one of the King's admirers, confided to her diary that he had 'risen to the occasion & looked like Henry VIII'. And *Punch*, shedding decades of criticism, pictured 'Mr Punch' assuring the sovereign, 'Your Coronation awaits your Majesty's pleasure, but you are already crowned in the hearts of your people.'

'The scene at Marlborough House during the first weeks of King Edward's reign', Esher wrote, 'was in sharp contrast to everything to which we were accustomed. He himself was accessible, friendly, almost familiar, frank, suggestive, receptive, discarding ceremony, with no loss of dignity, decisive but neither obstinate nor imperious.... The impression he gave me was that of a man who, after years of pent-up action, had suddenly been freed from restraint and revelled in his liberty.'

Whatever his past, the new King came to the throne with the dignity of his years in waiting and popular belief that as sovereign, however much only a symbol, he would be visible and approachable and knowledgeable about the role so long denied him. His past lifestyle augured a new openness to ideas and manners as a new century opened, and although his coronation had to be delayed because of an attack of appendicitis that could have happened to him at any age, observers were surprised (although not in print) by one dimension of this openness. At the solemn ceremonies in Westminster Abbey, Sarah Bernhardt, Lillie Langtry, Daisy Warwick, Alice Keppel, and Olga Alberta Caracciolo, now the Baroness de Meyer, sat in Court dress in what was gossiped about as 'the King's loose box'.* And no one really cared.

The King never let his liaisons, past or present, affect his sense of the public interest. When the Countess of Warwick began to support critics of the war in South Africa and brazenly supported a pro-Boer parliamentary candidate in Essex, she received a visit from Lord Esher, now a power behind the throne. 'He told me, with charming courtesy and frankness', she recalled, 'that he thought it would be as well for all concerned if my close association with great affairs were to cease, as it was giving rise to hostile comment, which distressed Queen Alexandra.' Edward was never associated with the distancing of Daisy although it was obviously his doing. The Boer War was only the last of the events which

* Loose box: a stall in which horses are not restrained (*OED*). Olga, now married to the society photographer Adolphe de Meyer, bore a Saxon title arranged for her by her 'godfather', who would often take tea with her in her home overlooking Windsor Park.

had isolated Britain from the Continent, and the King, always interested in diplomacy, made it his priority to reverse the policy of going it alone. He seemed always in transit to foreign capitals as, literally, uncle to Europe, to seek peaceable relationships in a Continent beset by the building of larger battleships and longer-range cannons.

At home the King sent the Munshi packing, removed his mother's memorabilia of John Brown, and ordered the rehabilitation of Buckingham Palace, virtually unused by the late Queen. There was upheaval, too, at cluttered Windsor, and Osborne was to be relinquished as a royal residence. To the surprise of most, given his slender reputation as reader and scholar, he established the Order of Merit, inspired by the French Academy, to honour outstanding achievements in science, literature and military service, limited – to underline its élitism – to twenty-four members. Among the first twelve were Lord Lister, pioneer of antiseptic surgery, Florence Nightingale, Thomas Hardy and Edward Elgar. His long-desired *entente cordiale* with France was formalized in 1904, thawing relations after a decade or more of hostility, and he established closer ties with Russia, ruled by his nephew, although at the expense of chillier relations with Germany, ruled by another nephew seemingly set upon military and commercial competition and convinced his country was being encircled. The King did not shift the axis of pre-1914 Europe but encouraged the realignment and helped make it happen.

Despite his years and his circumference, Edward VII seemed constantly in motion. He adopted the new motor car, acquiring a fleet of his own, painted in claret with blue-leather upholstery and the royal arms on the doors – as on the carriages he now seldom used. He still visited spas, and the Riviera (often with Alice Keppel), with the regularity of his visits to the races. He again won the Derby, with his horse Minoru, in 1909, but had less success winning over Parliament, where the Commons was becoming increasingly Liberal and the largely Conservative Lords were remaining steadfast about defending hereditary privileges to block unpalatable legislation. As sovereign, Edward could lawfully emasculate the Lords by creating hundreds of new Liberal peers, but in his last year that implied threat faded, as he realized that the few prerogatives remaining to the sovereign might be at risk. His domestic impact was only metaphorical. For decades during the purdah to which his mother had clung since the death of Prince Albert, the monarchy was only visible during brief ceremonial bursts. He revitalized its accessibility and enhanced its symbolism.

The King's last years were weighed down by the effects of years of indiscipline in eating, smoking and drinking. Obesity, heart disease and asthma slowed him, yet were always dismissed as something less. He still played bridge and was cosseted by the formidable Alice Keppel at country house weekends, and he went to the opera and more public assemblages with Alexandra when she was not crusing in the Mediterranean or visiting her extended family. Effectively, Edward VII had two Queens, one public and one private.

On 2 May 1910, wheezing with asthma, he returned to London by automobile from chilly, windswept Sandringham and had dinner that Monday evening with the loyal Agnes Keyser at Grosvenor Crescent. The next day, Alexandra was urged by telegram to return home from Greece, and she was back in London by the evening of 5 May. A medical bulletin signed by Sir Francis Laking had already announced uninformatively that the King had bronchitis, which was causing 'some anxiety'. In the tradition of such bulletins, only the last word was accurate. The public recognized the signal, and Alix understood when the King did not meet her train – a visible gesture toward their marriage which he always made.

On the morning of 6 May, Edward insisted – despite a series of small unreported heart seizures – on getting out of bed, telling his doctors, 'I will not give in.' In truth it was easier for him to breathe sitting up, and he did. Wearing his frock coat, and upright in an armchair, he received Sir Ernest Cassel, stubbornly lighting (to defy the inevitable) a large cigar he could not smoke. Soon after, he collapsed, and a team of doctors looked in and declared that nothing could be done for him.

He was still hunched, semi-conscious, in his chair, refusing to be assisted to his bed, when he learned late in the afternoon that his horse, Witch of the Air, had won the Two-Year-Old Plate at Kempton Park by half-a length. 'I am very glad,' he said, and lapsed into a coma.

In his last hours, Mrs Keppel sent the Queen a letter which Edward had written to her in 1901, when he was about to undergo surgery for appendicitis. If he were dying, he wrote, he would want the opportunity to 'say farewell' to her, and he was 'convinced that all those who have any affection for me will carry out the wishes which I have expressed in these lines'. Alexandra sent for her, and she was driven to Buckingham Palace. The Queen had little choice. She shook hands with Alice stiffly, saying,

'I am sure you have always had a good influence on him,' and turned away. The King, now comatose, did not recognize 'Mrs George'. For the first time anyone could remember, Alice lost control of herself. 'I never did any harm,' she cried; 'there was nothing wrong between us! What is to become of me!' She was led from the room. The imperturbable Esher noted in his diary, 'Altogether it was a painful and rather theatrical exhibition and ought never to have happened.'

At 11.30 it was apparent that the end was close. The King was lifted out of his armchair and placed on his bed, where he died at 11.45. Edward VII had been King for little more than nine years, Prince of Wales for fifty-nine. Like the Queen, Mrs Keppel began using letter-paper bordered in black.

Sources

General

Many sources are identified in or can be inferred from the text itself. Where information is duplicated in numerous biographies and other studies of Edward VII, I have not singled out a particular volume. Basic published sources of documentation are Sidney Lee, *King Edward VII* (New York, 1925, 1927); Hector Bolitho, *Queen Victoria the Widow and Her Son* (London, 1934); Philip Magnus, *King Edward the Seventh* (London, 1964); Kinley E. Roby, *The King, the Press, and the People. A Study of Edward VII* (London, 1975); Gordon Brook-Shepherd, *Uncle of Europe. The Social and Diplomatic Side of Edward VII* (New York, 1976); Christopher Hibbert, *Edward VII: A Portrait* (London, 1976); Giles St Aubyn, *Edward VII, Prince and King* (New York, 1979); and George Plumptre, *Edward VII* (London, 1995). The basic sources I have drawn from for Queen Victoria are the nine volumes of her letters, the first series (London, 1907), ed. A. C. Benson and Lord Esher (Reginald Brett), the second (1926) and third (1932), ed. G. E. Buckle.

On succeeding to the throne, Edward VII ordered that most letters by his mother about her family in the Royal Archives be destroyed. He was largely successful but some documentation was missed and other materials deliberately preserved. (The King also had almost everything related to John Brown and the Munshi destroyed.) In his will he directed, also, that all his private correspondence in the Royal Archives be incinerated, especially that with Alexandra and Victoria, and – with few exceptions – all papers that had remained at Marlborough House since his marriage in 1863 were indeed burned. At the same time, Princess Beatrice, the Queen's youngest child and Victoria's designated literary executrix, destroyed (after re-transcribing, with vast omissions and alterations) her mother's diaries. One must deal cautiously with what replaced the originals, as the Queen almost certainly had harsher words for her children than in the substitute texts. On the other hand, King Edward's diary survives at Windsor and is quoted by biographers and editors; however it is scrappy and usually laconic. After her death in 1925, Alexandra's own personal papers were destroyed by Lord Knollys's sister, Charlotte, a confidante and a Woman of the Bedchamber, presumably on the former Queen's instructions, as Alexandra left no will. Fortunately, many of the relatively few letters that Albert Edward wrote were preserved by their recipients, although even some of these were destroyed, including his letters to Disraeli, which the loyal Lord Esher retrieved from Disraeli's executor, Lord Rothschild. Thus, with a dearth of personal papers, the biographer must rely on alternative sources.

Preface

Henry James's letter to Oliver Wendell Holmes, Jr, is quoted in Leon Edel, *Henry James. The Master: 1901–1916* (New York, 1972). Jane Austen's letter about George IV is quoted in Saul David, *Prince of Pleasure. The Prince of Wales and the Making of the Regency* (London, 1998). The Prince's hosting a private dinner at which there were Anglicans, Roman Catholics and Jews is referred to by Countess Battersea (Constance Rothschild) in her *Reminiscences* (London, 1922). She notes also that Dr Magee, Bishop of Peterborough and later Archbishop of York, who was also there (as was Disraeli), referred to it in his own memoirs. The editorial in *The Indianapolis Journal* regretting the Prince of Wales's recovery is quoted from a reference to it in the Portsmouth [NH] *Daily Chronicle*, 2 January 1872. The music-hall song ('On the day King Edward gets his crown on') is from Peter Keating, *The Haunted Study. A Social History of the English Novel 1875–1914* (London, 1989).

1 The Future King

The flogging of the Prince by his father is described in a story in the *New York Tribune* in May 1853, translated from a dispatch in a 'North German paper' from its London correspondent. George V is quoted about fear of his father in Kenneth Rose, *George V* (London, 1983). There is an enormous medical and psychological literature on dyslexia. I have consulted, in particular, Russell A. Barkley, *Attention-Deficit Disorder* (New York and London, 1990); Harold N. Levinson, *A Solution to the Riddle of Dyslexia* (New York and Heidelberg, 1980); and Daphne M. Hurford, *To Read or Not to Read: Answers to All Your Questions About Dyslexia* (New York, 1998).

The story from the *Birmingham Journal*, 'The Boy that "Licked" the Prince of Wales', was reprinted in the Portland [ME] *Eastern Argus* on 30 May 1856. Bertie as 'Winter' in a children's tableau is recalled by a photo of the scene (1854) in the

Windsor Archives. Dr Becker's photo of nine boys dragooned as playmates for the Prince at Buckingham Palace, also in the archives, can be dated as 24 June 1854 from the Prince's boyhood diary at Windsor Castle. 'The Education of a Prince. Extracts from the Diaries of Frederick Waymouth Gibbs', was published in *The Cornhill.* A few quotations from the original also appear in Magnus.

2 The World Outside

The Prince's boyhood diaries at Windsor detail how he accompanied his parents on visits related to the Crimean War. Disraeli's comments are from vol. 6 of his *Letters*, ed. M. G. Wiebe (Toronto, 1997). The career and reproductions of the works of Hippolyte Belangé are from Jules Adeline, *Hippolyte Bellangé et son oeuvre* (Paris, 1880). The painting of the preparations for the hunt at St Germain, presented to Victoria and Albert by Napoleon III, is now in the Royal Library, Windsor Castle. Many details of the French Emperor's visit to England and the reciprocal visit to France are from the Queen's diaries.

The allegations that the Prince brought an expensive gift for the Pope and that he was under papistical influence, was made by John Campbell, DD, in *The British Standard*, in a series of weekly admonitions to the Prince Consort, especially in the issue of 16 March 1860. That no gift was authorized, even if the Pope were to present one, is made clear in letters between Prince Albert and Col. Bruce, Bertie's Governor, in RA VIC/Z 444/57 and 444/64.

The praise in *The Times* of British university life over the German appears in the issue of 10 June 1855. Elizabeth Gaskell's comments about seeing Bertie at Oxford are in her letter of 5 April 1860 to Charles Eliot Norton, in *Letters of Mrs Gaskell* (Cambridge, MA, 1967), ed. J. A. V. Chapple and Arthur Pollard. Albert's exchanges with his son at Oxford are quoted by Lee. Benjamin Moran's diary entries are from *The Journal of Benjamin Moran, I* (Chicago, 1948), ed. S. A. Wallace and F. E. Gillespie. Elizabeth II's comment about Prince Charles's ears as a child, paralleling Victoria's aspersions, is from Richard Kay and Geoffrey Levy, 'The Making of a Very Modern Prince', *Daily Mail 'Weekend'*, 13 June 1998.

3 The New World: Canada

Basic contemporary sources are Henry James Morgan, *The Tour of H.R.H. The Prince of Wales through British America and the United States. By a British Canadian* (Montreal, 1860); Kinahan Cornwallis, *Royalty in the New World: or the Prince of Wales in America* (New York, 1860); Robert Cellem, *Visit of His Royal Highness the Prince of Wales to the North American Provinces and United States in the Year 1860* (Toronto, 1861); Pierre Joseph Olivier Chauveau, the anonymous author of *Relation du voyage de son altesse royale le prince de Galles en Amerique, reproduite du Journal de l'instruction publique du Bas-Canada*

(Montreal, 1860); and reports in the *Ottawa Citizen*, the *Montreal Gazette*, and the *New York Herald*. Unless otherwise noted, sources for this chapter are from these volumes or from the general biographical literature described above.

Data about the Duke of Newcastle when not from the sources above is from F. Darrell Munsell, *The Unfortunate Duke. Henry Pelham, Fifth Duke of Newcastle, 1811–1864* (Columbia, MO, 1985). Canadian photographs of the visit (about 600 were presented to the Prince in 1861 in a silver-bound maple box containing three folios) are described in Ralph Greenhill and Andrew Birrell, *Canadian Photography: 1839–1920* (Toronto, 1979). Additional data about the Orangemen imbroglio can be found in Joseph Pope, *Memoirs of the Right Honourable Sir John Alexander Macdonald, G.C.B., First Prime Minister of the Dominion of Canada*, I (Ottawa, 1894), and on Georges-Etienne Cartier in Alastair Sweeney, *George-Etienne Cartier* (Toronto, 1976). Further information about the knightings of Sir Henry Smith and Sir Narcise Belleau was supplied by Professor M. G. Wiebe of Kingston and Professor Michel Pharand of Ottawa. For the Prince at Niagara Falls, an unusual first-hand account is that of Salamon de Rothschild, a visitor from Paris, in *A Casual View of America. The Home Letters of Salamon de Rothschild 1859–1861* (Stanford, CA, 1961), ed. and trans. by Sigmund Diamond.

4 Celebrity: The Prince in the United States

Cornwallis, Cellem and Morgan (see Chapter 3) are basic sources for the United States portion of the trip, as is the *New York Herald*, for which Cornwallis wrote. Supplementing these are many other contemporary and later accounts. A lengthy report of the Prince's departure from Windsor, Ontario, and arrival in Detroit is in the *Portsmouth* [NH] *Journal*, 29 September 1860. Young Thomas Edison's battle in Port Huron, with other boys, resisting the pranks by boys from Sarnia, Ontario, to upset the Prince's visit is reported in Paul Israel, *Edison. A Life of Invention* (New York, 1997). For the Prince's stay at Dwight, Illinois, the primary source, using contemporary reports and photos, is Clement Steichen, *The Prince of Wales and the Making of a Prairie Village: Dwight, Illinois, 1853–1860* (Pontiac, IL, 1987). For the Prince at the St Louis Agricultural Fair, American novelist Winston Churchill adds a fictional young lady, Virginia Carvel, to whom the Prince is attracted, in *The Crisis* (New York, 1901).

The Prince's visit to Washington was well covered by the *New York Times* as well as the *New York Herald*, beginning with their issues of 4 October 1860. President Buchanan's invitation to the Prince (via Queen Victoria) and his report on the visit are both in the Queen's *Letters*, Series 1. John Updike's scatological imagining of the White House visit is in his play *Buchanan Dying* (New York, 1974). A London view of the trip, especially of Washington and New York, is by William Hardman in *A Mid-Victorian Pepys*, ed. S. M. Ellis (New

York, 1923). Harriet Lane's schoolmistress friend Mrs Smith is described by Benjamin Moran in a diary entry of 6 July 1861. An anonymous but frequently reprinted poem, 'Before the Grave of Washington', about the Prince's visit to Mount Vernon, appears in the *Portsmouth* [NH] *Journal of Literature and Politics*, 8 December 1860. Detailed accounts of the Prince's visit to Philadelphia, beginning on election eve, are in the *Philadelphia Press* and the *New York Times*.

For the Prince Consort's narrow escape from death on a visit to Coburg while Bertie was in the US, see S. Weintraub, *Albert. Uncrowned King* (London, 1997).

A satiric verse-summary of the public frenzy over the Prince's travels, including the purloining of souvenirs, from his gloves to his cravat to strips of bedsheets, and with emphasis on New York City, is found in R. J. de Cordova, *The Prince's Visit: A Humorous Description of the Tour of His Royal Highness, the Prince of Wales, through the United States of America, in 1860* (New York, 1861). Salamon de Rothschild's account of the New York ball is in his *A Casual View* . . . (see notes to Chapter 3); George Templeton Strong's diary entries about the ball are in *The Diary of George Templeton Strong. The Civil War 1860–1865* (New York, 1952), ed. Allan Nevins and Milton Halsey Thomas. The episode of the Prince's oversized gloves at the ball is told (anonymously) by Julian Osgood Field, based upon his mother's memory of the event, in *Uncensored Recollections* (Philadelphia, 1924). Mathew B. Brady's picture-taking opportunities in New York are described in Roy Meredith, *Mr Lincoln's Camera Man* (New York, 1946). The Prince's visit to Trinity church is described humorously by George Templeton Strong, and straightforwardly by John Adams Dix in his *Memoirs*, I (New York, 1883), compiled by Morgan Dix.

The most thorough accounts of the Boston–Cambridge days are found in the *Boston Daily Evening Transcript* and the *Boston Journal*, beginning with the issues of 15 October 1860. Additional details appear in the *Proceedings of the Massachusetts Historical Society* for 1860–2 in the section for October 1860. Dr O.W. Holmes's ode to the Prince, sung by schoolchildren, appeared in the Portsmouth [NH] *Morning Chronicle* on 19 October 1860. Among the detailed descriptions of the 'Renfrew Ball' in Boston, and its venue, are those of Marjorie Drake Ross, *The Book of Boston – The Victorian Period, 1837–1901* (New York, 1964), and Lucius Beebe, *Boston and the Boston Legend* (New York, 1935). A report of the Prince's party acquiring Boston-made boots, from the *Shoe and Leather Reporter*, appears in the Portsmouth [NH] *Morning Chronicle*, 20 October 1860. Longfellow's urging Hannah Davie to see *her* prince in Boston, 15 October 1860, is from *The Letters of Henry Wadsworth Longfellow*, V (Cambridge, MA, 1982), ed. Andrew Hilen. New York cameraman Jeremiah Gurney's pursuit of the Prince to Boston is described in a sale of his eleven photographic plates by Bristow & Garland, antiquarian booksellers, Fordingbridge, Hampshire, in Occasional List 3–98 (1998). O.W. Holmes's lecture, 'The Weaning of Young America', in part covering the larger meaning of the Prince's visit, was quoted from substantially in the *Boston Daily Evening Transcript*, 4 November 1863.

5 Higher (and Lower) Education

Emily Eden is quoted about the storm-slowed voyage home in Munsell's life of Newcastle (see Chapter 3). The Queen's similar concerns are voiced in her *Letters*. Benjamin Moran's anxieties are reflected in his diary entry for 13 November 1860. One of his tutors at Oxford, Goldwin Smith, describes Bertie there in his *Reminiscences* (New York, 1911), ed. Arnold Haultain. The Prince's run-in with Farmer Hedges would seem apocryphal if it had not been reported immediately and in detail in *The Times*, 26 March 1860.

Charles Kingsley's experience in Cambridge as a tutor is described by Brenda Colloms in *Charles Kingsley. The Lion of Eversley* (London, 1975). Documents in the Royal Archives concerning the Cambridge residency include Henry Phillpott's letter to Sir Charles Phipps (PP Vic 3693, 3 March 1860) and Phipps's in return (PP Vic 3693, 8 March 1860), and Phillpott's to the property owner, Lady King (25 January 1861), Col. Bruce's to Prince Albert (19 January 1861, RA Z446), and Bertie's to his father (Z461, 25 January 1861). The Prince's letter to his mother about the visit of young Arthur is Add. Mss. A/3 (13 May 1861). Col. Bruce's letter to Lady King about the abrupt departure from Madingley, with detailed arrangements spelled out, is also an RA document (588/C 155, 20 December 1861).

Many details about the Prince's private life in Cambridge emerge from the letters now in the Rothschild Family Archive, of Nathaniel Rothschild to his parents Lionel and Charlotte, which continue until the Prince Consort's death, when Bertie leaves Madingley. These include RFam C/3/6, C/3/8, C/3/9, C/3/10, C/3/12, C/3/58, C/3/63, C/3/67, C/3/74, C/3/79, C/3/80, C/3/86, C/3/93, C/3/102, C/3/120, C/3/123, C/3/125 and C/3/128. Madingley Hall is still accessible, with some rooms now offices of the University of Cambridge Board of Extra-mural Studies, and upstairs rooms used by the Prince and his father kept much as they were in 1861.

Arthur Munby's diaries recording encounters with the Prince at Cambridge are *Munby. Man of Two Worlds. The Life and Diaries of Arthur J. Munby 1828–1910* (Boston, 1972), ed. Derek Hudson. Gladstone's comment about the Prince's 'misleading comrades' (21 December 1861) is from *The Gladstone Diaries*, VI (Oxford, 1980), ed. H. G. C. Matthew. For details of Albert's death and Bertie's presence at the end, see Weintraub, *Albert. Uncrowned King*.

6 Bachelorhood

Although it appears from hints in letters and journals that the Prince and his mother had a long, agonized continuing dialogue from the time of Albert's death over what name he would take as king, the Prince rejecting Albert, the first entry on the subject in the Queen's journal is dated two years later – 13 January 1864. However, Victoria's diaries were censored and rewritten, and the originals destroyed (after her death) by her executrix, Princess Beatrice, to protect the princess's siblings, who were often excoriated in the Queen's entries. The first leak in the American press I have found was published in mid-April 1863. The Prince would sign letters 'A. E.' or 'Albert Edward' but never use 'Albert' alone. Still, references to him as Prince Edward became common although he carefully avoided that on his own.

The Prince's exclusion from any political role at Victoria's insistence is examined in detail, from Royal archival documents, in Simon Heffer, *Power and Place. The Political Consequences of King Edward VII.* He sees few results from the Prince's 'career of [attempted] political interventionism'. Victoria's comment to Mrs Disraeli about catching Bertie smoking appears, without source, in the *Little, Brown Book of Anecdotes* (Boston, 1985), ed. Clifton Fadiman. The Queen's exchanges via Knollys and Phipps negating any role for the Prince appear in St Aubyn, in Plumptre, in Magnus, and in Brian Connell, *Regina v. Palmerston* (London, 1962), as well as in her letters and journals. Dickens's comments on the Queen and Prince are from *The Letters of Charles Dickens, 10, 1862–1864* (Oxford, 1998), ed. Graham Storey and Margaret Brown. Henry Adams's acerbic comments are from the *Letters of Henry Adams*, I (Cambridge, MA, 1982), ed. J.C. Levenson et al. Moran's comments on the lack of a twenty-first-birthday book for the Prince, and on the Prince's holding levées, are from his diary. Laurence Oliphant's relationship with the Prince is described in Anne Taylor, *Laurence Oliphant 1829–1888* (Oxford, 1982). The Prince's description of climbing a pyramid at Gizeh unassisted is from his diary.

Natty Rothschild's comment about the Prince and his 'first-rate' horse is to be found in RFam C/3/29, 16 January 1863, in the Rothschild Archives. The Parisian kitchenmaid tale is told by Princess Marie Louise in *My Memories of Six Reigns* (London, 1956).

The arranged courtship is drawn from Georgina Battiscombe, *Queen Alexandra* (London, 1969); Richard Hough, *Edward and Alexandra: Their Private and Public Lives* (New York, 1993); Graham and Heather Fisher, *Anatomy of a Royal Marriage* (London, 1974); biographies of Victoria and Edward VII; and the public press. The hand-tinted photo-portrait miniature of the Prince in tailcoat sent to Alix, with the original envelope, was offered for sale in the Clive Farahar & Sophie Dupré catalogue 15 (Calne, Wilts) as item 725. George Henry Lewes's letter to his son Charles Lee on the likely mobs at the time of the marriage is from *The George Eliot Letters*, IV (Oxford, 1955), ed. Gordon S. Haight. Hardman on the Prince's pre-marriage public shyness is from *A Mid-Victorian Pepys*. Telegrams on the wedding arrangements are in the Julian Browning catalogue 19 (1998). Sceptical readers can find the classified advertisement about

Cockspur Street in *The Times* on Saturday, 28 February 1863, p. 1, col. 6. Munby's comments on the wedding procession are from his diary. Robert Browning on the event is from *Browning to His American Friends* (New York, 1965), ed. Gertrude Reese Hudson. John Wodehouse's diary entries are from *The Journal of John Wodehouse First Earl of Kimberley for 1862–1902* (London, 1997), ed. Angus Hawkins and John Powell. Lyrics by A. G. Prys-Jones to Brinley Richards's 'God Bless the Prince of Wales' are from *The National Songs of Wales* (London, rev. edn, 1959), ed. E.T. Davies et al. Gladstone's reaction to the wedding is from his diaries; Disraeli's is from his letters; Moran's from vol. 1 of his diary.

7 Falling out of Love

Dickens's letter to Carjat is from vol. 10 (see above); Disraeli's to Mrs Brydges-Willyams is from S. Weintraub, *Disraeli* (London, 1993). The sexual lifestyle of the Prince's country-house set is described wittily by Anita Leslie in *The Marlborough House Set* (New York, 1973). She also discusses the Sagan intimacy. The Prince's relationships hereafter with the Rothschild family, unless otherwise cited, are documented from the family archives by Niall Ferguson in *The World's Banker. The History of the House of Rothschild* (London, 1998). Ferguson also quotes Earl Spencer's vicious remark about the 'accidental beauty' of a Rothschild daughter. The Queen's letters to her daughter Vicky in Germany appear in a six-volume series begun with *Your Dear Letter* (London, 1971), ed. Roger Fulford, and completed by a sixth volume, *Beloved and Darling Child* (Far Thrupp, Gloucestershire, 1990), ed. Agatha Ramm. Bertie's letters to the Queen which survived incineration are in her *Letters*, series 2 and 3. In an 1864 letter she responds to his apparently oft-stated desire to be Edward that she wished to 'repeat' that it was his father's desire that he bear 'both' names. (As early as 15 February 1864 the far-off Portsmouth [NH] *Morning Chronicle* was reporting, 'The name by which the Prince of Wales will ascend the throne will be King Edward the Seventh.') His letters to his sister Louise were collected in *Darling Loosy: Letters to Princess Louise 1856–1935* (London, 1991), ed. Elizabeth Longford. For John Wodehouse's journals, see the notes to Chapter 6. George Meredith's letter to William Hardman on Alix's pregnancy, 4 July 1863, is in *The Collected Letters of George Meredith* (Oxford, 1965), ed. C. L. Cline.

The most useful work for this book of many on the exotic world of the nineteenth-century spa was E. S. Turner, *Taking the Cure* (London, 1967). Emile Zola's *Nana* (Paris, 1880) is quoted from the Modern Library translation by Ernest Boyd. The most useful biography of Hortense Schneider is by Elizabeth Forbes, 'Hortense Schneider', *Opera*, 23 (December 1981). Bertie's escapades in France, ignored by the more staid newspapers across the Channel, are reported in England only in the gossip sheets. Many publications on the denizens of Proust's raffish world, such as George Painter, *Marcel Proust. A Biography*, 2 vols (New York, 1959); and Jean-Yves Tadié, *Marcel Proust. Biographie* (Paris, 1996), deal with the Frenchwomen (and men) in the Prince's life. A portrait of Finette by Nadar (Gaspard Tournachon) is in the collections of the J. Paul Getty Museum, Los Angeles. A brief biography of her (mentioning no other identifying name) is in M. Willson Discher, *Wrinkles and Champagne* (London, 1938).

8 The Sport of Kings

The Prince's relationship with Lord Houghton is described in James Pope-Hennessy, *Monckton Milnes. The Flight of Youth* (London, 1951). Anthony Trollope's letter to Houghton, 8 March 1868, is in *The Letters of Anthony Trollope* (Stanford, 1983), ed. N. John Hall. The Duke of Hamilton's method of keeping the Prince from smoking at dinner is recalled by his son, Lord Frederic Hamilton, in *The Days Before Yesterday* (London, 1902). Thomas Barker's painting, *A Big Shoot at Sandringham* (1867), is in the Royal Collections. That 'the Boy' was still in use as a term for champagne is evident from a rhyme in *Punch* in 1882 about 'magnums of "the Boy"'. His visit to baron Mayer de Rothschild at Mentmore is described in a letter from Natty Rothschild to his mother, Charlotte, 6 March 1868, in Rothschild Archive RFam C/3/50; the Prince's concert on his wedding anniversary, 10 March 1868, is described in RFam C/3/51. Princess Alexandra's nine-row choker of pearls is visible in a contemporary photograph offered by Maggs Bros, Ltd, in 1999 in their Catalogue 1275 as item 3. The Prince's encounter with the cigarette maker Marcovitch is described by G. C. Williamson in *Memoirs in Miniature* (London, 1933). Delane's description of a sparkling dinner at Marlborough House (while the Princess lay ill upstairs) is in Arthur Dasent, *John Delane* (London, 1908).

The Mordaunt case is described in London law documents under Divorce Appeals, 1874; the Prince's letters to Lady Mordaunt were published in London newspapers but never entered into evidence; most of the sleazy testimony was published in the press. Lady Elizabeth Hamilton's *The Warwickshire Scandal* (Norwich, 1999) contends that Harriett Mordaunt feigned madness to escape ignominy. Justin McCarthy's exposé of the Prince, perhaps the most devastating to appear in print in his lifetime, appeared in *Galaxy*, a New York monthly, in vol. 9 (March 1870). His relationship with Skittles over many years, based largely on Wilfrid Scawen Blunt's diaries and reminiscences (he was an intimate of the lady), is described in Henry Blyth, *Skittles. The last Victorian Courtesan. The Life and Times of Catherine Walters* (London, 1970); and in Elizabeth Longford, *A Pilgrimage of Passion. The Life of Wilfrid Scawen Blunt* (New York, 1980). (As king, Edward VII arranged that his letters to Skittles were burned.) The Prince's involvement with La Barucci (Giulia Beneni) is described from the surviving documents by St Aubyn and Plumptre. Anthony Allfrey also writes about La Barucci in *Edward VII and His Jewish Court* (London, 1991), declaring that it was the duc de Gramont who introduced her to the Prince as described. St Aubyn and Plumptre also write of the Lady Susan Vane-Tempest pregnancy, which is referred to as well in Munsell's *The Unfortunate Duke* (see Chapter 3) and in Virginia Surtees's biography of the ill-starred Newcastles.

The Prince in costume at the Waverley Ball as Lord of the Isles was photographed by A. J. Mellhuish (National Portrait Gallery); Alix's oval portrait as Mary Queen of Scots (photographer unknown) is in the Scottish National Portrait Gallery, Edinburgh. Joseph Chamberlain's mocking election challenge involving the unpopular Prince of Wales is quoted by Peter T. Marsh in *Joseph Chamberlain. Entrepreneur in Politics* (London, 1994).

The Revd Francis Kilvert's reaction to the Prince's life-threatening illness is quoted from *Kilvert's Diary* (London, 1971), ed. William Plomer. The press covered the Prince's illness voluminously, *Reynolds's Newspaper* characterizing the reportage as 'the great epidemic of typhoid loyalty'. Mark Twain's aspersions about it appear in his *Notebooks & Journals*, II (Berkeley, 1979), ed. Robert Pack Browning, Michael B. Frank and Lin Salamo.

9 Relapse

Alexandra's signed copy of the effusive *The Prince and the Prayer* is in Special Collections, Paterno Library, Pennsylvania State University. Lady Susan Vane-Tempest's appeals to the Prince are in Plumptre. The loving cabinet photo of the Prince and Princess, August 1872, is pictured in the Clive Farahar and Sophie Dupré catalogue 15 as item 109 (Calne, Wilts). *The Coming K——* is in *Beeton's Christmas Annual, 13th Season*, London, 1872. Although its anonymous authors were Samuel Orchart Beeton, Evelyn Jerrold and Aglen Dowty, it has also been ascribed to other versifiers. Hannah Cullwick's ungrammatical reminiscence of the Prince at Charing Cross is quoted in Munby's diary (she was Munby's mistress). Courtenay Boyle wrote to Earl Spencer about the masked ball at which the Prince appeared as a Cardinal: see *The Red Earl. The Papers of the Fifth Earl Spencer*, I (Northampton, 1981), ed. Peter Gordon. At another masked ball the Prince went as Charles I – according to Maude Howe Elliott's *Uncle Sam Ward and His Circle* (New York, 1938). Bernal Osborne's quip to the Prince about playing for half-crowns rather than crowns is from Lady Battersea's *Reminiscences* (see above).

The Prince's grand entry at Ascot on 12 June 1873 is humorously described by Mark Twain in his Notebook 12, *Mark Twain's Notebooks and Journals*, I (Berkeley, 1975), ed. Frederick Anderson, Michael B. Frank and Kenneth M. Sanderson. The text of the Prince's cable exchange with President Ulysses S. Grant on the new telegraphic link with India is in *The Papers of Ulysses S. Grant*,

20 (Carbondale and Edwardsville, IL, 1995). His involvement with Adah Isaacs Menken is described in Allen Lesser, *Enchanting Rebel. The Secret of Adah Isaacs Menken* (New York, 1947), and Alan Lloyd, *The Great Prize Fight* (New York, 1977). The Prince's visit to Birmingham in 1874, at which Joe Chamberlain made fulsome amends, is described in Peter Marsh's *Joseph Chamberlain*. It was widely covered by the press and the subject of a cartoon in *Punch* (14 November 1874). For the Prince's Proustian cronies, see earlier chapters. Marie Bashkirtseff's diary entries for 31 March and 1 April 1875 are in *I am the Most Interesting Book of all: The Diary of Marie Bashkirtseff* (San Francisco, 1997), trans. by Phyllis Howard Kernberger and Katherine Kernberger. For the preparations for the voyage to India, see the notes to Chapter 10.

Jon Duan: A Twofold Journey with Manifold Purposes was Beeton's Christmas satire for 1874, authored anonymously by Samuel O. Beeton, A. A. Dowty, and Evelyn D. Jerrold. *The Siliad, or, The Siege of the Seats* was the Beeton Christmas satire for 1873, written anonymously by Beeton and Dowty with George Rose Emerson. The Prince's interest in prize-fighting referred to in the Beeton *Coming K——* is described also in Julian Osgood Field's *Uncensored Recollections*.

10 Embodying the Raj

The basic source for the India journey, although diplomatic and circumspect, is the volume compiled by the reporter for *The Times* who accompanied the Prince, W. H. Russell, *The Prince of Wales's Tour* (London, 1876). For the earlier phases of the progress one can also consult Julia A. Stone, *Illustrated India: Its Princes and Its People ... to which is added An Authentic Account of the Visit to India of His Royal Highness the Prince of Wales* (Hartford, CT, 1877). The newspaper and periodical press covered the journey assiduously and in detail, from the continuously hostile *Reynolds's News* to the cheeky *Punch*. The Prince's letters home, and those of his companions and staff, surface in various biographies of both the Prince and Alexandra. His complaints to Disraeli about being kept in the dark about the Titles Bill, and about the Suez shares purchases, are quoted in Bolitho's *Victoria, the Widow and Her Son*. The Queen's letters to Vicky about Bertie's junket, which she disapproved of from the beginning but found impossible to abort, are in the volume of their letters, *Darling Child. Private Correspondence of Queen Victoria and the German Crown Princess 1871–1878* (London, 1976), ed. Roger Fulford. The illustrated catalogue of his gifts received on the tour, and items purchased (mostly enamelled vessels and elaborately decorated weapons), was published in two volumes, respectively, for Marlborough House display pieces (1898) and those at Sandringham (1910). Lord Lytton's letter to George Hamilton is quoted in Plumptre.

11 The Mixture as Before

The Prince's heated exchanges with Lord Randolph Churchill and his brother over the Aylesford affair are printed by his grandson in *Winston S. Churchill. Companion,* 1 (Boston, 1967), ed. Randolph Churchill, Anita Leslie in *The Marlborough Set,* St Aubyn and Plumptre. Others free of 'authorized' constraints, such *Edward and Alexandra* (see above), also deal with the Aylesford affair. An obituary of the Earl of Aylesford appeared in the *New York Times* on 15 January 1885, when he was a resident of Big Spring, Texas. Details of the return voyage from India are given in W. H. Russell, *The Prince of Wales's Tour* (see above). The satiric spoof on India, anonymous but almost certainly by Beeton, is *The Return of the Heir: An Episode in the History of the Family of Runsquick* (London, 1876). Beeton's Christmas annual for the year was *Edward the Seventh, a play on the past and present times with a view to the future* (London, 1876), again, probably, by the trio of Beeton, Emerson and Dowty. The anonymous *The Key to Edward the Seventh, being an elucidation of the dark allusions in that Libellous Lampoon, with Brief and Authentic Biographies of the various distinguished personages therein mentioned* (London, 1876) is ascribed to 'One Behind the Scenes' and published by a different publisher (Gobaud, 40 Bedford Street, Covent Garden / Will Williams, Falcon Court, Fleet Street), but Beeton very probably had a hand in both.

Lillie Langtry's relationship to the Prince is widely dealt with, most definitively in Laura Beatty, *Lillie Langtry* (London, 1999), but also informatively, although less reliably, in Ernest Dudley, *The Gilded Lily. The Life and Loves of the Fabulous Lillie Langtry* (London, 1977) and James Brough, *The Prince and the Lily* (New York, 1974). An original cabinet photograph of Lillie as described was pictured as item 98 in a 1999 Maggs Bros catalogue. Henry Adams's vituperative letter to Sir Robert Cunliffe about the Prince and Lillie, 12 November 1882, is in the *Letters of Henry Adams* (see above). His quip about Oscar Wilde, and his encountering Wilde and Langtry at a 'thought-reading séance' are in Richard Ellmann, *Oscar Wilde* (New York, 1988). Also utilized for Bertie's and Leopold's relationship with Lillie was Charlotte Zeepvat, *Prince Leopold* (Thrupp, 1998). The Prince's relationship with Blanche Caracciolo is explained in Jacques-Emile Blanche's *Portraits of a Lifetime* (New York, 1938); Alberta Olga Caracciolo also sat for him. The Duchess and her daughter may have been guests at Sandringham at least once, according to H. E. Wortham, *Delightful Profession* (London, 1931). Biographies of Baron and Baroness (Olga) de Meyer also deal with the relationship, as does Anita Leslie in *The Marlborough House Set* (see above), and Edna Woolman Chase and Ilka Chase in *Always in Vogue* (New York, 1954).

The Prince's long friendship with Arthur Sullivan (and Fanny Ronalds) is dealt with in Arthur Jacobs, *Arthur Sullivan. A Victorian Musician* (Aldershot,

1992), and in Leslie Baily, *The Gilbert & Sullivan Book* (New York, 1957), which prints the letter from Sir Arthur asking Jessie Bond to entertain HRH. Miss Bond's dialogue with the Prince rejecting his offer to come and see her is quoted by Hesketh Pearson in *Gilbert and Sullivan* (London, 1935).

His employment of Capt. Stephenson as equerry is the subject of a series of letters in *A Royal Correspondence. Letters of King Edward VII and King George V to Admiral Sir Henry F. Stephenson*, ed. John Stephenson (London, 1938). HRH's relationships with the Jewish community in England as detailed in the press are reproduced with illustrations from the articles and reports in *Victorian Jews through English Eyes*, ed. Anne and Roger Cowen (Oxford, 1986), in *Edward VII and His Jewish Court* (see above) and in *The World's Banker* (see above). Fergusson in *World's Banker* cites a £160,000 Rothschild mortgage on Sandringham 'which was discreetly hushed up'. The Prince's alleged sale of jewellery to Joseph Joel Duveen is recounted by S. N. Behrman in *Duveen* (New York, 1951). Oliver Wendell Holmes's sitting with the Prince and Alix at a Rothschild musical dinner party is described in Holmes's *One Hundred Days in Europe* (Boston, 1887). His going along with Richard Burton's exotic masquerade is documented in Byron Farwell, *Burton* (New York, 1963). His attendance at a table-turning where Prince Louis Napoleon overturned the table is recalled by Lillie Langtry in *The Days I Knew* (London, 1934). The descent in a diving-bell is described in Williamson's *Memoirs in Miniature*. The meeting with Bret Harte is written about by Harte to Samuel Barlow, 5 May 1880, in *Selected Letters of Bret Harte* (Norman, OK, 1997).

Sarah Bernhardt's sculpted self-portrait inkwell with batwings was placed prominently behind the desk in HRH's study at Marlborough House in his lifetime. She writes about the Prince in *Ma Double Vie*, trans. by Victoria Tietze Larson as *My Double Life* (Albany, NY, 1999). His apparently harmless crush on the shrewd young Miss Chamberlain (her name misspelt in various ways in the London scandal press and private letters) is reported at length in such papers as *Town Talk*, and in Edward Hamilton's diary, and across the Atlantic in many American papers, including the *New York Times*, 'A Young American Beauty', 5 October 1883. Henry James's suggestion to himself that he should write about the Prince of Wales's attraction to a young American beauty appears in his notebook entry for 20 June 1887, in *The Complete Notebooks of Henry James* (Oxford, 1987), ed. Leon Edel and Lyall H. Powers. The Prince's alleged involvement with other women is touched on, short of libel, in the scandal press. Mrs Sands is referred to also in Henry James's and Henry Adams's letters. His employment of Mrs Vyner as hostess and go-between is noted by Edward Hamilton, and by Frank Harris in *My Life and Loves*.

HRH's correspondence with his mother on political matters, when not in the second and third series of her *Letters*, is in *Victoria, the Widow* ... (see above). For Leopold's access to his mother's Cabinet red boxes, see Zeepvat, above. That

Disraeli made Cabinet decisions available to the Prince of Wales is explained in a memorandum from Edward Hamilton to Gladstone, 12 May 1885, where he writes of the Prime Minister's 'jotting down on a piece of note paper, informally and unsigned, any decision of importance taken at a Cabinet and placing it under cover to the Prince'. (Gladstone Papers, British Library, MS 44769) Gladstone's concern that the Prince 'as now usual' avoided words with him is in vol. IX of the *Diaries*, 9 June 1877. Carrington's report on the Prince's anonymous foray into the East End slums is quoted in *Edward and Alexandra* and reported at length in Magnus.

12 *The Occupation of the Idle Man*

Hardy's offering of his novel to the Prince is described in his letter to Francis Knollys, 14 December 1881, in *Letters*, I (London, 1978), ed. Richardy Purdy and Michael Millgate. George Smalley's description of Homburg as it was when the Prince amused himself there is in his *Anglo-American Memories* (London, 1910). Lady Amaldina's lover refers to the Prince as a godfather in Trollope's *Marion Fay* (London, 1882). Wilde's reluctance to 'talk democratic principles' to the Prince of Wales is quoted in Ellmann's *Oscar Wilde*. Mabel Batten's relationship to the Prince is noted in Wilfrid Blunt's diaries and in Diana Souhami, *The Trials of Radclyffe Hall* (London, 1998). Additional details on the Duchess Caracciolo and her daughter Alberta Olga (afterward de Meyer) are in *Portraits of a Lifetime*, where the author (Blanche) refers to the protective activities of Lee Jortin, the English consul; and in Philippe Jullian's lengthy preface to *De Meyer* (New York, 1976), ed. Robert Brandau, where photos by Adolph de Meyer of Olga in later life appear. George Cornwallis-West's description of his relationship with the Prince of Wales as godchild is in *Edwardian Hey-Days* (London, 1930).

The Royal Enclosure at Ascot is colourfully described by Sam Ward to Sidney Webster in June 1883 in *Uncle Sam Ward and His Circle*. Gladstone's various encounters with the Prince are noted in vols VIII–XI of the *Diaries*. The Prince's continued frustrations in obtaining a key to the red boxes is described in Bolitho, *Victoria, the Widow ...* and in Robert Rhodes James, *Rosebery* (London, 1963). Rosebery's parody-lecture he attributed to the Prince of Wales and Ferdinand de Rothschild, 'Copulation – Ancient and Modern', is referred to in Rhodes-James. Biographies of Rosebery are discreet about his alleged relationship with Lord Drumlanrig, but it is exposed in Ellmann's *Oscar Wilde*. John McCafferty's wild plot to kidnap the Prince of Wales is referred to in Thomas Keneally, *The Great Shame and the Triumph of the Irish in the English-Speaking World* (New York, 1999). The Prince's many difficulties with the German (Prussian) court, with its spies and informers, and with the growing megalomania and Anglophobia of Prince Willy, afterwards Wilhelm II, are documented in this chapter and later chapters in *The Holstein Papers*, of which vols

I and II are Count Holstein's diaries (Cambridge, 1957), ed. Norman Rich and H. M. Fisher.

The Prince of Wales's burgeoning re-interest in French pleasures, cited further below, is noted in *Uncensored Recollections* (see above), which returns to the princesse de Sagan, in the many books on the *Belle Epoque*, which place the Prince in Montmartre and on the Riviera such as June Rose, *Suzanne Valadon. The Mistress of Montmartre* (New York, 1998), and Cornelia Otis Skinner, *Elegant Wits and Grand Horizontals* (Cambridge, 1962).

13 Impresario

Golden Jubilee events are dealt with at length in biographies of the Queen, in the press, in her letters and journals, in the diaries of Gladstone, Hamilton and others identified in the text. HRH's continuing interest in Jennie Chamberlain of Cleveland, which becomes almost avuncular, is noted in the *New York Times* from 1883 into her marriage in 1889, and recalled in the *New York Times Illustrated Magazine* for 7 August 1898. Her family background and her life in London are detailed in *The Chamberlain Association of America. Report of Annual Meetings ...* (Portland, ME, 1911).

The Father Damien scheme is written about by Sidney Lee in the first volume of his life, and at length by Frank Harris is his *My Life and Loves*. HRH's financial connections with Baron Hirsch are described in *Edward VII and His Jewish Court*. Lady Gregory's political comment about Parnell's alleged bribery to vote for the Prince's Allowance Bill is from *Seventy Years. Being the Autobiography of Lady Gregory* (New York, 1976), ed. Colin Smythe.

H. Montgomery Hyde, *The Cleveland Street Scandal* (New York, 1976), furnishes extensive details on the male bordello affair. See also books by and about Reginald Brett, later Lord Esher, including his diaries, and quotations from his correspondence, especially James Lees-Milne, *The Enigmatic Edwardian. The Life of Reginald 2nd Viscount Esher* (London, 1986). In March 1975 the Public Records Office in London unsealed papers about the attempted cover-up. Home Secretary Henry Matthews, acting for Prime Minister Salisbury, had warned the Director of Public Prosecutions against any 'fishing enquiries about other charges and other persons' beyond Lord Arthur Somerset. The press in the United States, less circumspect about the case, published the rumour that to get Prince Eddy out of the way, he might meet with a fortunate accident on his tour of India (*New York Times*, 17 November 1889), or that Eddy might be recalled under circumstances 'peculiarly painful to himself and his family ...' (*New York Herald*, 22 December 1889).

The Prince's involvement with Lady Brooke, afterwards the Countess of Warwick, is covered in several books, notably Theo Lang's *My Darling Daisy* (London, 1966) and other sources noted in Chapter 14 where the affair develops further. Mrs Gerald Paget, the anonymous author of *Lady River,* is quoted from Margaret Blunden's *The Countess of Warwick* (London, 1967). HRH's amorous coded telegram to 'Darling Daisy' is reproduced by Sophie Dupré as item 91 in her catalogue 46.

The Tranby Croft affair was aired at length in the press and in the courts, complete (in newspapers) to full transcripts of testimony. The most definitive source is Michael Havers, Edward Grayson and Peter Shankland, *The Royal Baccarat Scandal* (London, 1977). Henry James's 'extraordinary stamp of vulgarity' characterization of the Prince's conduct is from his letter to R. L. Stevenson, 18 February 1891, in *Henry James Letters,* III. Since Daisy Warwick was at Tranby Croft, books about her extend the coverage.

The Prince's troubled relations with Bismarck, Willy, et al., are again documented from the *Holstein Papers,* and from Queen Victoria's *Letters.* The Prince's gift to the Kaiser of a machine-gun and limber, and its wartime outcome, are described in Lyn Macdonald, *1915. The Death of Innocence* (London, 1925). His racing endeavours are drawn from Sidney Lee and (re. Hirsch) *Edward VII and His Jewish Court.* Data about Mrs Mahlon Sands and Mrs Ogden Goulet are from the *Letters of Henry James,* Wendy Baron's *Miss Ethel Sands and Her Circle* (London, 1977), and stories about them and their husbands in the *New York Times* into 1929. The first royal journey by tube railway is described in Mike Horne and Bob Bayman in *The First Tube* (London, 1990).

Walter Annenberg's visit to the House of All Nations in Paris in 1926 is drawn from an interview with him in Christopher Ogden, *Legacy. A Biography of Moses and Walter Annenberg* (Boston, 1999). Henri Charpentier's story about the origin of *crêpes Suzette* is quoted in his obituary in the *New York Times,* 25 December 1961. Much the same story appears in James Trager, *The Food Chronology* (New York, 1995). The Prince's Parisian pleasure haunts are described in June Rose, *Suzanne Valadon* (see above) and in Charles Rearick, *Pleasures of the Belle Epoque. Entertainment and Festivity in Turn-of-the-Century France* (New Haven, 1985).

14 King-in-Waiting

For Eddy's death, see Rose, *George V,* and Weintraub, *Victoria,* above. Everett Emerson in *Mark Twain. A Literary Life* (Philadelphia, 1999), describes how the Prince of Wales was the inspiration for the novelist's *The Prince and the Pauper.* The African prince, Sebele, is quoted from Neil Parsons, *King Khama, Emperor Joe, and the Great White Queen. Victorian Britain through African Eyes* (Chicago, 1998). The Prince's misguided appreciation of Wilde's 'leper in purple' line is from Ellmann's *Oscar Wilde.* The subject of his access to Cabinet decisions is again taken from the diaries of Gladstone and Hamilton.

Marie Corelli's involvement in the Prince's life is described in Eileen Bigland,

Marie Corelli. The Woman and the Legend (London, 1953); her novel *The Sorrows of Satan* was published in 1895. The Prince's appeals to the Earl of Rosebery urging him to serve in the Cabinet are from Rhodes-James and Edward Hamilton. The Queen's and Prince's monarchist antipathy to changing the Legation in Washington to an embassy is noted in Hamilton's diary for 31 March 1893. W. T. Stead ('I asked her') is quoted from Lady Gregory's *Diaries*. Also employed for details on Lady Warwick are her own discreet *Life's Ebb and Flow* (London, 1920) and Theo Aronson, *The King in Love. King Edward's VII's Mistresses – Lillie Langtry, Daisy Warwick, Alice Keppel, and Others* (London, 1988). The Prince's appearances in public with both Alix and Lady Warwick are noted in gossip columns in *The World* in June 1893.

Henry Adams writes about the Prince's accented English in a letter to Charles Milnes Gaskell, 25 April 1895. The Prince's continued intervention on moral grounds with the theatre censor is described in John Johnston, *The Lord Chamberlain's Blue Pencil* (London, 1990). The report of the opening of the Imperial Institute (with Bernard Shaw's anonymous contribution identified here) is from *The Star*, 9 May 1893. Edgar Mackennal's bronze Salome is reproduced in Mark Evans, ed., *Princes as Patrons. The Art Collections of the Princes of Wales* ... (London, 1998). The Prince's response to 'my good man' is recalled in Consuelo Vanderbilt Balsan's *The Glitter and the Gold* (London, 1953). Yvette Gilbert writes about the machinations to get her to the Riviera to sing for the Prince in *The Song of My Life: My Memories*, trans. Béatrice de Holthoir (London, 1929).

Victoria's '*il faut payer pour être Prince*' was said to Marie Mallet, quoted in Victor Mallet, ed., *Life with Queen Victoria. Marie Mallet's Letters from Court, 1887–1901* (London, 1968). The Prince's overheard Jubilee comment about 'my eternal mother' is from Fadiman (above). Dr Reid's comments about the Munshi are from Michaela Reid, *As Sir James* (London, 1987).

15 Prince No More

HRH's rejected overture to bring his mistresses, with Alix, to Knole, is from Victoria Glendinning, *Vita. The Life of V. Sackville-West* (London, 1983). The footnoted comment by the Prince on the Duke of Sutherland's equally unacceptable behaviour is from K. D. Reynolds, *Aristocratic Women and Political Society in Victorian Britain* (Oxford, 1998). The Prince's jettisoning of Lady Warwick, then pregnant by her own husband, is from Theo Lang, *My Darling Daisy* (see above), Margaret Blunden's *Countess of Warwick* (see above), and Theo Aronson's *The King in Love* (see above). Aronson also suggests HRH's impotence since *c.* 1895, quoting Skittles and noting that HRH as King often seated the Archbishop of Canterbury next to Mrs Keppel at dinners, a gross solecism had the King's relationship not been platonic. My own judgement on his likely later-years impotence is based upon the fact that both his final companions had children by their own husbands during his relationship, in Lady Warwick's case near the close, in Mrs Keppel's case in the early years; on medical evaluations solicited from distinguished physicians at a medical college, based on the apparent physical evidence; and on Alice Keppel's impulsive comment at the end that there had been 'nothing wrong' between them (see Afterword). His meeting and subsequent relationship with Mrs Keppel is described in *Violet to Vita. The Letters of Violet Trefusis to Vita Sackville West, 1910–1921* (London, 1983) ed. Mitchell A. Leaska and John Phillips; Diana Souhami, *Mrs Keppel and Her Daughter* (New York, 1996); Philippe Jullian and John Phillips, *Violet Trefusis, Life and Letters* (London, 1976); Henrietta Sharpe, *A Solitary Woman. A Life of Violet Trefusis* (London, 1981); Allison Pearson, 'Love in a Cold Climate', *The New Yorker*, 25 August–1 Sept. 1997; in Anita Leslie, *The Marlborough Set* (see above); in Sonia Keppel, *Edwardian Daughter* (New York, 1959), the source of the Mafeking Night claim; in Raymont Lamont-Brown, *Edward VII's Last Loves* (Thrupp, 1998); and (for Mrs Keppel as a 'valuable institution' – hardly a sexual suggestion) Hamilton's diary entry for 21 October 1903.

His accident at Waddesdon, and recovery therefrom, are from a Marie Mallet letter in *Life with Queen Victoria*, in Blunden, *The Countess of Warwick*, and a Henry James letter to Paul Bourget, 23 December 1898, in *Letters*, IV. HRH's X-ray 'treatment' is mentioned in *The Times* on 29 July 1898. His involvement in Gladstone's funeral, to his mother's chagrin, is described in the Queen's *Letters*, in Lees-Milne's *The Enigmatic Edwardian*, and in Hamilton's diary. His relationship with young Winston Churchill is documented in Randolph Churchill, ed., *Winston S. Churchill. Companion*, 1 (see Chapter 11, above). His continuing relationship with George Cornwallis-West is told by his 'godson' in *Edwardian Hey-Days* (see above). Count Muraviev's Boer War anti-British proposal, revealed by the Kaiser to the Prince, is quoted by Sir Sidney Lee in *King Edward VII*, 1 (London, 1925).

His relationship with Agnes Keyser is in part the subject of Richard Hough's *Sister Agnes. The History of King Edward VII's Hospital for Officers, 1899–1999* (London, 1998); in Anita Leslie's *Marlborough House Set*; and referred to twice in Lady Gregory's *Diaries*, where his luncheon arranged by Lady Dorothy Nevill is described. The assassination attempt in Belgium is described in all the biographies of both the Prince and Alexandra, and in Victoria's *Letters*, as well as in a letter from the Prince, 12 April 1900, to his sister Louise, in Longford, ed., *Darling Loosy*. David Lindsay's slur about the Prince's friendships with Jews is quoted in Fergusson, *The World's Banker* (see above). HRH's dinner for *DNB* biographers is described in Beatrice Webb, *Diaries*, II (Cambridge, MA, 1983); and in a Leslie Stephen letter to Mary (Mrs Herbert) Fisher, 27 May 1900, quoted from at length in *The Life and Letters of Leslie Stephen* (London, 1906), ed. Frederic William Maitland.

The Queen's plea to her son in April 1900 *not* to go to Paris is quoted by Bolitho in *Victoria, the Widow....* The Prince's remark about her walking *behind* the angels is in Fadiman (see above). The fullest account of the Queen's death is in Michaela Reid, *Ask Sir James* (see above).

Afterword

Henry James's letters to Oliver Wendell Holmes and Clara and Clare Benedict are in Leon Edel, *Henry James. The Master: 1901–1916* (New York, 1972), and *Henry James. Letters*, IV (Cambridge, MA, 1984). Winston Churchill's is in Randolph S. Churchill, *Winston S. Churchill, I. Youth. 1874–1900* (Boston, 1966). Lady Gregory's is in her *Diaries* (above). Lord Esher's is in *Enigmatic Edwardian* (above). 'The King's loose box' was a contemporary comment quoted in Laura Beatty, *Lillie Langtry: Manners, Masks and Morals* (London, 1999). Mrs Keppel's appearance at the end is drawn from many biographies of Edward VII and of Alexandra, and Souhami's *Mrs Keppel* (see above).

Acknowledgements

I owe the concept for this book to Grant McIntyre. For research and editorial assistance without which this biography would have been impossible I am also indebted to Lucy R. Addington, Richard Atkins, Erica W. Austin, Philip Baldi, Michael Broyles, Harry P. Clark, Norma Condee, the late Fred D. Crawford, Frances Dimond, Robert Eckhardt, Beate Engel-Doyle, Oliver Everett, Bonny Farmer, the late Kim Fisher, Frederick N. Frank, Colleen Franklin, Victor Gray, Alan Hanley-Browne, Eileen Hanley-Browne, Mark Hanley-Browne, Paul Harvey, Bridget Henisch, Heinz Henisch, Elizabeth Longford, Nancy McCall, Bonnie MacEwan, Ben McLaren, the late Charles W. Mann, the late Colin Matthew, George Mauner, Bruce Nichols, Nigel Nicolson, Michel Pharand, William Pierce, Martin R. Quinn, Shirley Rader, Susan Reighard, Barbara Ryan, J. Bryce Rumbles, Willa Silverman, Sandra Stelts, Gerhard Strasser, John Sutherland, Elliot Vesell, Ian Walls, Herbert H. Weintraub, Rodelle Weintraub, M. G. Wiebe, Philip Winsor, Richard E. Winslow III. Douglas Matthews compiled the index.

Index

For convenience, as the Prince of Wales, while never 'Edward' until his accession, became Edward VII, all references to him below are to his ultimate name.